Philadelphia

Main Line Classics

Published by
THE SATURDAY CLUB
Wayne, Pennsylvania
1982

Additional copies of Philadelphia MAIN LINE CLASSICS may be obtained by
sending $18.95 each plus $3.50 each to cover postage and handling
(Pennsylvania residents add $1.14 sales tax) to the following address:

The Saturday Club
P.O. Box 521
Wayne, Pennyslvania 19087
(610) 688-3252

International Standard Book Number
0-9650818-1-8
Previously 0-939114-44-5

Manufactured by
Favorite Recipes® Press
an imprint of

FRP

P.O. Box 305142
Nashville, Tennessee 37230
1-800-358-0560

TABLE OF CONTENTS

HISTORY OF THE SATURDAY CLUB

On Saturday, February 16 1886, in Wayne, Pennsylvania, nine women met to discuss the creation of a women's club. Living a distance from Philadelphia, the women felt a need to stimulate "an intellectual and social life without detracting from the duties of wifehood and motherhood." Programs each week would usually take the form of papers given by members in established areas of Literature, Art, Science, Music and Household. Often there were guest speakers.

In 1900, these forward-reaching women raised the $5,000 needed to purchase the land and begin the building of their clubhouse, which has recently been placed in the National Register of Historic Places.

In 1907, the Junior Saturday Club was formed as part of the Saturday Club for girls seventeen to twenty-three. New mothers needed to share their experiences with others their age.

Volunteerism was becoming a predominant force in the Club. In 1908, the Club founded the first kindergarten in Wayne and ran the town's Coffee House. No saloon was permitted while the women ran the Coffee House.

During the influenza epidemic in 1918, the clubhouse became a hospital taking the overflow from crowded area hospitals. The Juniors also produced vaudeville shows to raise money for French children orphaned by the war.

World War II saw the clubhouse again as an emergency hospital. The Club received a citation from the Treasury Department for the amount of bonds and stamps sold by the members.

Dedicated outreaching into the community continues to be the major thrust of the Junior Saturday Club. Frequent requests for financial and personal support are received from area clinics, special schools and foundations. Members participate on a personal level in a chosen community service while the Club's Ways and Means projects provide financial assistance. It is because of these increasing requests that the Junior Saturday Club decided to publish this cookbook. We hope that its sale will support our philanthropies for many years.

Look for Our Sequel

PHILADELPHIA

MAIN LINE CLASSICS II

Cooking Up a Little History

Philadelphia MAIN LINE CLASSICS

EDITOR
Gwen Fields Gilmore

TESTING
Lois Rising Pogyor, Editor
Dolly Eastburn Somers
Liz Nelson Mayer

ART
Grace Burdett Nellis, Editor
Susan Coates Oliver
Cynthia Borden-Ritz, Graphic Designer
Jane Curtis, Illustrator
Meredith Herting Swift, Consultant

COPY
Lori Adams Del Rossi, Editor
Rosalie VanMetre Baker
Denise McCarthy Brown
Catherine Webber Curtis
Robin Truitt Hayman

PRODUCTION
Eve Pantellas Walker, Manager
Susan Johnson Mader

MARKETING
Ann Wheeler Sinatra, Manager

TREASURER
Sandra Johnson McConnell

Recipes without an individual's name were submitted by committees of JSC members from International Luncheons, Progressive Dinners and Gourmet Dinner functions.

ACKNOWLEDGEMENT

The Cookbook Committee is most grateful to our many friends who generously shared their recipes with us. These contributions to our book ultimately aid the organizations and charities supported by the Junior Saturday Club. Space limitations and duplications prevented us from using all the recipes submitted. We gratefully appreciate the generosity of Jane Curtis in permitting us to use her illustrations of the Main Line train stations.

BRIEF HISTORY OF THE MAIN LINE

William Penn had great plans for his Pennsylvania, or Penn's Woods. He mapped out the city of Philadelphia and convinced other groups seeking religious freedom to settle in the adjoining countryside. Welsh farmers arrived in the area immediately west of the city and prospered until after the Revolution.

With the opening of the Ohio Valley, Penn's Woods became a throughway for the Conestoga wagons travelling west. Farmers, tired of increased traffic damaging their market road, forced the opening of Lancaster Avenue (Route 30), the first turnpike or toll road. Fees collected were to pay for the road's upkeep. With the arrival of the railroad, the turnpike and its colorful taverns lost their predominant place. The Pennsylvania Railroad took over the state transportation system of canals and railroads called the Main Line of Public Works. Shortly thereafter, the railroad began its development of the area along the right of way between Philadelphia and Paoli.

Many "Main Line" towns were created by the railroad. At first, executives sought only to escape the city in the summer when Philadelphia's red brick radiated too much heat. Later, tuberculosis and other diseases breeding in crowded conditions drove those who could afford it out into the "salubrious air" of the countryside. With travel to the country increasing, enterprising railroad executives built hotels at various railroad stops to whet the appetites of people for rural living. Eventually, wives and families wanted to extend their summer vacations permanently. Homes were built within walking distance or a brief carriage drive to the railroad station. Haverford Station became known as the "kissing station" because Victorian wives made a social event out of greeting their husbands each evening.

Joining the new permanent Main Line residents were wealthy businessmen who built large estates along the line. New stops were added convenient to their homes.

Names of the newly built stations fit the tastes of the executives. In keeping with the original Welsh ties, names like Bala, Cynwyd and Narberth were lifted from a map of Wales. Some of the stations took their names from local estates such as Villa Nova. The area terminus for the line, Paoli received its name during the Revolution when local patriots named their tavern after the Corsican general who led a revolt against Genoese tyranny. The town grew up around the tavern and took its name.

Besides providing transportation and encouraging settlement, the railroad was responsible for much of the modernization of the towns. One railroad executive, hoping to keep out competing trolley companies and being an avid carriage racer, paved a major road from Bryn Mawr to Paoli.

The railroad has been intricately involved in the growth of the Main Line for over 100 years. The trains still take children to school, men and women to work and elderly residents to visit friends. The Main Line is a classic example of enterprising men influencing America to change from loosely connected farms to self-sufficient cities in a powerful nation.

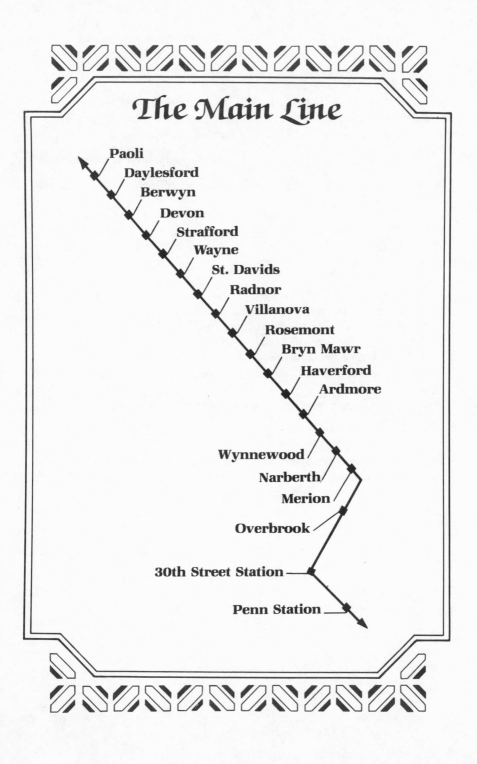

Philadelphia MAIN LINE CLASSICS represents several years of thought and effort on the part of the membership of the Junior Saturday Club. In order to make the recipes as foolproof as possible, each recipe has been tested and evaluated by individuals other than the donor. However, please remember (1) oven thermostats vary slightly and (2) different people may work at different speeds. Our time guides are to be used as a gauge in deciding how long the recipe may take to prepare. Most terms are self-explanatory; however several may need some clarification. *"Preparing"* has been used to define the time you actually work with the food or recipe. *"Cooking"* is the time during which food cooks on top of the range unattended. *"Baking"* is the time during which food cooks in the oven.

We have tried to present a balance of relatively easy recipes as well as more complicated gourmet fare. The editors hope you will enjoy using Philadelphia MAIN LINE CLASSICS and that it will be both a "friend" and a "classic" in your collection of kitchen references.

Some Tips in Using Our Recipes:
1) Read the recipe from beginning to end before starting it.
2) Follow our "Do Ahead" instructions where they apply.
3) Always use the size pan or dish specified.
4) Measure ingredients accurately.
5) Never alter key ingredients (you may vary spices, seasoning, etc., to your taste).
6) The yield when given in servings does not mean people but individual portions.

The recipes in this book have been collected from various sources, and neither the Junior Saturday Club, nor any contributor, publisher, printer, distributor or seller of this book is responsible for errors or omissions.

Beverages

Merion

Merion, named for an ancient Welsh hero, Meriawn, is just five miles from Philadelphia. Its fertile lands and convenience to the growing city attracted farmers in the early 1700's. Ever since, it has existed as a continuous settlement.

Because of Merion's proximity to the city of Philadelphia yet rural setting, it became the site of the first summer estates built by the Pennsylvania Railroad's wealthy executives. Most of these estates are still in use as private residences and schools, such as Lower Merion Academy, the first free public school in suburban Philadelphia.

A Summer Family Gathering

hors d'oeuvre

Spinach Dip with Crudités   Shrimp Mold

soup

Cold Cucumber Soup

entrée

Barbecued Leg of Lamb

vegetable

Potato Salad   Fresh Vegetable Marinade

bread

Old Fashioned Honey Whole Wheat Bread

dessert

Texas Sheet Cake

beverage

Iced Tea with Fresh Mint   Fruit Punch

AMARETTO MILK PUNCH

Preparing: 5 minutes   *Do Ahead*   *Yield: 1 serving*

4 ounces (½ cup) whole milk or
   half and half cream
1 heaping teaspoon powdered
   sugar

1 ounce bourbon
1 ounce Amaretto
Nutmeg (garnish)

Mix milk and sugar in container until sugar dissolves. Add bourbon, Amaretto and ice; stir. Strain into a wine glass. Garnish with freshly grated nutmeg. *When increasing to larger quantity, chill mixture rather than adding ice and straining.*

Frances Marincola Blair

PARTY PUNCH

Preparing: 5 minutes   *Do Ahead*   *Yield: 30 servings (4½ quarts)*

1 (12-ounce) can concentrated
   orange juice, thawed
1 (12-ounce) can concentrated
   lemonade, thawed

½ gallon white sauterne wine,
   chilled
2 quarts club soda, chilled

Combine juices and wine; add club soda before serving.

Dolly Eastburn Somers

SPICED COFFEE

Preparing: 5 minutes   *Yield: 8 servings*

1 cup regular grind coffee
6 sugar cubes
8 whole allspice or ⅛ teaspoon
   ground allspice

8 whole cloves or ⅛ teaspoon
   ground cloves
1 (8-inch) stick cinnamon or ⅛
   teaspoon ground cinnamon

Place coffee and spices in coffee percolator basket. Use 6 measuring cups water. Percolate as usual.

Elise Rice Payne

BRANDIED HOT CHOCOLATE

Preparing: 15 minutes   *Do Ahead*   *Yield: 4 to 6 servings*
Cooking: 5 minutes

1 (1-ounce) square unsweetened
   chocolate, cut up
3 tablespoons sugar
2 teaspoons instant coffee powder
Dash salt

½ cup water
2 cups light cream
1 cup milk
⅓ cup brandy
½ cup heavy cream

In saucepan, combine chocolate, sugar, coffee powder, salt and water. Cook and stir over low heat until chocolate melts. Bring to boil, stirring constantly; let simmer 2 minutes. Gradually stir in cream and milk. Heat just to boiling. Stir in brandy. Pour into hot cups, mugs or demitasse cups. Whip cream; spoon some atop each mug.

Frances Marincola Blair

LE PUNCH

Preparing: 15 minutes   *Do Ahead: Partially*   *Yield: 40 servings (5 quarts)*

1 (¾-quart) bottle Cointreau
1 fifth vodka
1 (6-ounce) can frozen orange juice
   concentrate
1 (6-ounce) can frozen pineapple
   juice concentrate

3 quarts club soda
Orange slices, fresh cranberry
   (garnish)

Place clear block of ice in punch bowl. Add first 4 ingredients. Stir to blend. Add club soda right before serving; garnish with orange slices. To prevent ice from diluting punch, ice blocks made of orange and/or pineapple juice may be used.

CHAMPAGNE PUNCH

Preparing: 10 minutes   *Yield: 3½ quarts*
Cooking: 5 minutes

½ cup sugar   3 bottles champagne
½ cup water   1 quart club soda
3 ounces Triple Sec or Curacao   Jar cherries, drained
3 ounces brandy

In a saucepan combine sugar and water. Cook, stirring occasionally until mixture boils; cool. Combine Triple Sec, brandy and cooled syrup. When ready to serve, combine champagne, club soda and syrup mixture in punch bowl. Garnish with cherries.

Barbara Fullerton Strong

CRANBERRY MULLED WINE

Preparing: 5 minutes   *Do Ahead*   *Yield: 1½ quarts (10 to 12 cups)*

1 pint cranberry juice cocktail   6 whole cloves
1 cup water   ⅘ quart burgundy wine
¾ cup sugar   1 lemon, thinly sliced
2 sticks cinnamon

Combine ingredients; heat 1-2 hours (crockpot works well). Serve warm. *May be doubled or tripled,* but do not increase lemon.

Elise Rice Payne

CRANBERRY SHRUB

Preparing: 5 minutes   *Do Ahead: Partially*   *Yield: 2½ quarts*

1 (46-ounce) bottle cranberry juice,   Lemon, orange or pineapple
  chilled   sherbet
1 (46-ounce) bottle pineapple juice,
  chilled

Mix juices well, pour into glasses and top with a scoop of sherbet. Serve immediately. May be used as punch by adding 1 quart 7-Up for every gallon shrub.

Pam Bartels Morris

POTENT EGG NOG

Preparing: 40 minutes   *Do Ahead*   *Yield: 30 servings*

12 eggs, separated
1 pound powdered sugar
1 quart whiskey
2-3 ounces rum
7 ounces brandy

1 quart milk
1½ quarts light cream
1 pint heavy cream
½ teaspoon salt

Beat egg yolks until light; beat in powdered sugar. Add whiskey, rum, brandy, milk and light cream slowly, beating constantly. Whip heavy cream until stiff. Beat egg whites until frothy; add salt and beat until stiff. Fold whipped cream and egg whites into other ingredients. *Put in refrigerator 3-4 days before serving, stirring occasionally.* Top with nutmeg when serving.

Nancy DiSabatino D'Angelo

EGGNOG

Preparing: 45 minutes   *Do Ahead*   *Yield: 8 or 30 servings*

8 servings:
6 eggs
½ cup sugar
1 cup bourbon
½ cup brandy

1 cup heavy cream
2 cups milk
1 cup vanilla ice cream

30 servings:
2 dozen eggs
2 cups sugar
1 quart bourbon
1 pint brandy

1 quart heavy cream
2 quarts milk
1 quart vanilla ice cream

Separate eggs. Mix egg yolks with sugar; beat until thoroughly mixed. Add bourbon and brandy; mix thoroughly. Add milk and heavy cream; mix well. Break ice cream into small pieces and add, while stirring. Beat egg whites to soft peaks with mixer; fold into yolk mixture. Chill and serve.

Note: Work with large bowls.

Christine Arnold Holly

EASY FRUIT PUNCH

Preparing: 5 minutes **Do Ahead** *Yield: 50 servings*

2 (46-ounce) cans unsweetened
  pineapple juice
2 (6-ounce) cans frozen orange
  juice, undiluted

10 (10-ounce) bottles Sprite
Thin orange slices (garnish)
Mint leaves (garnish)

Mix pineapple juice and *undiluted* orange juice. Add Sprite and mix when ready to serve. Garnish with thin orange slices and/or ice cubes, made from pineapple or orange juice, and mint leaves.

Lois Rising Pogyor

HAWAIIAN RUSSIAN

Preparing: 5 minutes *Yield: 1 serving*

½ ounce pineapple juice
½ ounce dark creme de cacao

¾ ounce vodka
1 ounce heavy cream

Pour ingredients into blender containing ¼ cup shaved ice; blend. Pour into 8-ounce glass over cubed ice. Garnish with open paper parasol stuck into an 8-inch striped straw.

KAHLUA

Preparing: 10 minutes **Do Ahead** *Yield: 2 quarts*
Cooking: 1 hour

3 cups sugar
3 cups water
10 teaspoons instant coffee

1 (fifth) bottle vodka
3 teaspoons vanilla

Bring sugar, water, and coffee to a boil. Simmer one hour uncovered for thick mixture; covered for thinner mixture. Cool. Add vanilla and vodka. This gets better with age.

Charity Power Folk

LIME COOLER

Preparing: 5 minutes   *Yield: 6 servings*

2 cups cracked ice
1 (6-ounce) can frozen limeade,
    partially frozen
¼ cup lemon juice
1¼ cups vodka

1 (10-ounce) bottle club soda,
    chilled
Fresh strawberries, pineapple and
    mint (garnish)

Combine ice, limeade, and lemon juice in blender; mix at medium speed
1 minute. Add vodka; mix well. Pour in soda; mix briefly on low speed. Serve
in stemmed glasses with garnishes.

Grace Burdett Nellis

ROSÉ PUNCH

Preparing: 5 minutes   *Do Ahead*   *Yield: 32 servings*
                                                  Makes one gallon

1 cup light corn syrup
1 (1-quart) bottle apple juice,
    chilled
3 (⅘ quart) bottles rosé wine,
    chilled

1 small red apple, thinly sliced
    (garnish)

Combine corn syrup and apple juice in large punch bowl; stir in wine. Garnish
with apple slices. Serve over ice cubes, if desired.

Note: To lessen sweetness, decrease corn syrup.

Carol Sutcliffe Kramer

RASPBERRY MINT CRUSH

Preparing: 10 minutes   *Do Ahead*   *Yield: 8 servings*

¼ cup sugar
½ cup lightly packed, fresh mint
  leaves
1 cup boiling water

1 (10-ounce) package frozen
  raspberries
1 (6-ounce) can frozen lemonade

Combine sugar, mint leaves and boiling water. Let stand for 5 minutes in large pitcher. Add raspberries and lemonade; stir until thawed. Add 2 cups cold water and stir. Strawberries may be substituted for raspberries. Rum may also be added (about 6 ounces).

Gretchen Dome Hagy

RESTORATION PUNCH

Preparing: 5 minutes   *Do Ahead*   *Yield: 8 to 12 servings*
Holding: 24 hours

2 cups lemon juice
2 cups sugar
1 quart rum

1 quart ginger ale, chilled
1 quart club soda, chilled

Mix lemon juice, sugar and rum; *age 24 hours.* Just before serving, add ginger ale and club soda.

Jeanne Kronmiller Honish

SANGRIA

Preparing: 15 minutes   *Do Ahead*   *Yield: 48 servings*
Chilling: 3 to 4 hours

3 cups sugar
2 gallons burgundy
5-6 oranges, sliced

2 lemons, sliced
2 limes, sliced
3 cups club soda, chilled

Mix wine and sugar; add fruit. Best if chilled 3-4 hours. Add club soda and ice before serving.

Elise Rice Payne

MOTHER'S RUM PUNCH

Preparing: 15 minutes   *Do Ahead*   *Yield: 7 quarts*
Chilling: 2 hours

2 (12-ounce) cans frozen orange   ½ large bottle chilled club soda or
  juice, diluted as directed   ginger ale
1 (20-ounce) can grapefruit juice   1½-2 cups light rum (to taste)
Dash fresh lemon juice

Mix all ingredients; best if all ingredients but club soda are mixed two hours
before serving and chilled. Add club soda, mix and serve.

HOT BUTTERED RUM

Preparing: 30 minutes   *Do Ahead*   *Yield: 50 servings*
                                 Freeze

2 cups butter, softened   1 teaspoon allspice
2 pounds light brown sugar   Cinnamon sticks
2 eggs   Rum
1 teaspoon cinnamon   Boiling water
1 teaspoon nutmeg

Combine butter, sugar, eggs and spices. Beat at medium speed 3-4 minutes.
Put in container and refrigerate or freeze. To serve, thaw slightly. Place 1 cinnamon stick, 1 tablespoon butter mixture and 1 jigger of rum in a mug. Fill with
boiling water and stir well. *Recipe can be halved.*

Elizabeth Taylor Young

STRAWBERRY DAIQUIRI

Preparing: 5 minutes   *Do Ahead*   *Yield: 12 servings*
                               Freeze

1 (10-ounce) package frozen sliced   1 (6-ounce) can pink lemonade
  strawberries, slightly thawed   concentrate
6 ounces light rum   3-5 cups crushed ice

Blend all ingredients until smooth.

Note: To make ahead of time, substitute water for ice and freeze in a plastic container. (Remains slushy.)

Linda Zajicek Moore

SUMMER PUNCH

Preparing: 10 minutes   *Do Ahead*   *Yield: 32 servings*
Chilling: 1 to 2 hours

1 quart lemonade   2 (28-ounce) bottles ginger ale
1 (46-ounce) can pineapple-   Strawberries or blueberries
  orange juice   (garnish)

Combine ingredients and chill. Pour into punch bowl; float strawberries and/ or blueberries.

Note: In place of ginger ale, you may use 1 fifth vodka or gin.

Kathy Horracks Merchant

HEALTH DRINK

Preparing: 5 minutes   *Yield: 2 servings*

2 cups milk (2% or skim)   1 tablespoon granular lecithin
1 large banana, very ripe   2 tablespoons protein powder
1 egg   2 teaspoons vanilla or honey

Place all ingredients in blender and whirl until smooth.

Ginny Moffitt Gehring

MULLED WINE

Preparing: 5 minutes   *Do Ahead: Partially*   *Yield: 6 to 8 servings*
Cooking: 10 minutes
Standing: 1 hour

1 lemon rind
2 orange rinds
2 cups sugar
12 allspice, whole
12 cloves, whole
6 pieces cinnamon

1 teaspoon ginger
⅘ quart water
2 cups orange juice
1 cup lemon juice
⅘ quart burgundy or claret

Mix all ingredients except wine and fruit juice; bring to boil. Reduce heat; simmer 10 minutes. Set aside for 1 hour. *(May be done ahead to this point.)* Drain spices from liquid. Add fruit juices and wine; heat through. Serve warm.

A. J. DelRossi

MAY WINE

Preparing: 10 minutes   *Do Ahead*   *Yield: 60 servings (7½ quarts)*
Marinating: 12 to 24 hours

Mix:
1 gallon white wine
3 cups Triple Sec

20 sprigs sweet woodruff (ground-
   cover herb)

Punch:
1 gallon Rhine wine
½ gallon wine mix
2 quarts club soda

Strawberries and sweet woodruff
   (garnish)

The day before serving, prepare mix from white wine, Triple Sec, and sweet woodruff. After marinating the mix overnight, remove woodruff from mixture. When ready to serve, combine Rhine wine, mix, and club soda in punch bowl. Float strawberries and sweet woodruff on surface.

Gretchen Dome Hagy

Appetizers

ARDMORE STATION
ARDMORE, PENNA.

Ardmore

Ardmore, meaning "high hill" in Gaelic, was renamed from Athensville. Since a large number of Irish farmers already lived in the surrounding area, the Pennsylvania Railroad hoped to entice more to settle in the community.

In 1873, the railroad built the station building, the largest on the line. A retail center soon developed around the station, including the first suburban drug store and ice cream "saloon."

In the 1920's, Suburban Square, the first planned shopping center in the United States, was built near the earlier business center. Ardmore has been the site of continuous business activity for over 100 years.

Holiday Feast

hors d'oeuvre

Stuffed Celery   Lemon-pepper Cucumbers

appetizer

Cranberry Shrub

entrée

Crown Roast of Pork with Sausage and Raisin Stuffing

vegetable

Sautéed Cherry Tomatoes   Fresh Steamed Green Beans

salad

Tossed Green Salad with Easy French Dressing

dessert

Strawberries Romanoff

beverage

Potent Egg Nog

ARTICHOKE-CHILI DIP

Preparing: 10 minutes   *Do Ahead*   *Yield: 2⅔ cups*
Baking: 20 minutes

1 (14-ounce) can artichoke hearts   **1 cup grated Parmesan cheese**
1 (4-ounce) can green chili peppers   **1 cup mayonnaise**

Preheat oven to 350° F. Drain and chop artichoke hearts. Rinse, seed and chop peppers. Combine ingredients; turn into 8-inch round baking dish. Bake 20 minutes or until heated through. Serve warm with tortilla chips and breadsticks.

Catherine More Keller

CHUTNEY CHEESE DIP

Preparing: 10 minutes   *Do Ahead*   *Yield: 1 cup*
Chilling: 4 hours

1 (8-ounce) package cream cheese   **1 teaspoon curry powder**
¼ cup chutney   **Toasted almonds**
¼ teaspoon dry mustard   **Pineapple half**

Blend cream cheese, chutney and seasonings well. Chill at least 4 hours. Scoop out pineapple half; fill with mixture. Top with toasted almonds.

Note: Try also in celery.

CAVIAR DIP

Preparing: 15 minutes   *Do Ahead*   *Yield: 2 cups*
Chilling: 3 hours

½ cup sour cream   **2 teaspoons lemon juice**
1 cup mayonnaise   **1 (2-ounce) jar black caviar**
2 scallions, chopped
1 tablespoon chopped parsley

Mix ingredients; chill. Serve with vegetables.

Mary Lou Kerigan Batchelder

BLEU CHEESE DIP

Preparing: 15 minutes   *Do Ahead*   *Yield: 2 cups*
Chilling: 4 to 6 hours

1 clove garlic (optional)
4 ounces bleu cheese, cut up
8 ounces cream cheese, cut up
½ cup sour cream

1 tablespoon brandy
½ teaspoon dry mustard
1 teaspoon chopped parsley

Place peeled garlic clove in processor with steel blade and mince finely. Add all other ingredients except parsley to processor; blend until creamy and smooth. *Cover and refrigerate 4-6 hours.* Sprinkle with chopped parsley before serving.

Note: Without a processor, press garlic and blend all ingredients with a hand mixer.

Liz Nelson Mayer

CRAB DIP

Preparing: 10 minutes   *Do Ahead*   *Yield: 2½ cups*
Chilling: 1 hour

1 (6-ounce) package frozen
   crabmeat
½ cup chili sauce
1 (3-ounce) package cream cheese
½ cup mayonnaise
½ teaspoon dry mustard

1 tablespoon horseradish
1 tablespoon Worcestershire sauce
Few drops Tabasco sauce
½ teaspoon salt
2 chopped hard-cooked eggs

Mix all ingredients together; chill. Serve with corn chips.

Sandra Schild Fletcher

CAVIAR DIP WITH ENDIVE

Preparing: 15 minutes   *Do Ahead*   *Yield: 3 cups*
Chilling: 2 hours

1 (3-ounce) package cream   1 (4-ounce) jar red caviar
  cheese, softened   6 whole Belgian endive (¾ pound)
1 pint sour cream   or dark bread
2 tablespoons lemon juice
3 tablespoons finely chopped green
  onions

Stir cream cheese in small bowl until softened. Beat in sour cream, lemon juice
and onions. Gently fold in caviar; chill until thickened, at least 2 hours. Garnish
with additional onions and caviar if desired. Use endive leaves and/or a dark
bread to dip.

Note: Soak whole endive in warm water 5 minutes to remove bitterness.

Alice Marks Preston

CUCUMBER DIP

Preparing: 30 minutes   *Yield: 2 cups*
Chilling: 4 hours

4 ounces cream cheese   ¼ cup minced onion
1 tablespoon mayonnaise   ½-¾ teaspoon cider vinegar
½ cup peeled, seeded and diced   Various raw vegetables
  cucumber

Beat cream cheese into mayonnaise until smooth. Stir in cucumber, onion and
vinegar; season with salt and pepper to taste. *Chill at least 4 hours.* Stir before
serving with raw vegetables.

Variation: In place of onions, ¼ cup chopped scallions and a pinch of dill weed
may be used.

Joan Stievater Lindstrom

HOLIDAY APPETIZER PIE

Preparing: 10 minutes   *Yield: 8 to 10 servings*
Baking: 20 minutes

1 (8-ounce) package cream
  cheese, softened
1 teaspoon instant minced onion
2 tablespoons finely chopped green
  pepper
2 tablespoons milk

1 (2½-ounce) jar sliced dried beef,
  or ¾ cup package beef, finely
  snipped
⅛ teaspoon pepper
½ cup sour cream
Almonds, sliced

Preheat oven to 350° F. Blend cream cheese and milk using electric mixer. Stir in dried beef, onion, green pepper and black pepper; mix well. Stir in sour cream. Put in small baking dish and sprinkle sliced almonds on top; bake 20 minutes. Serve with corn chips or crackers.

Variation: For "meatier" taste, use additional package of chipped beef and an extra ¼ cup sour cream instead of milk.

Barbara Aune Cahill

CURRY DIP FOR RAW VEGETABLES

Preparing: 10 minutes   *Do Ahead*   *Yield: 2 cups*
Chilling: 1 hour

2 cups mayonnaise
3 teaspoons curry powder
3 tablespoons chili sauce
1 tablespoon Worcestershire sauce

½ teaspoon salt
Pepper
½ teaspoon garlic salt
1 teaspoon instant onion

Combine all ingredients; blend well. Refrigerate. Serve with assorted raw vegetables like carrots, string beans, cauliflower, green pepper pieces, etc.

Ginny Thornburgh
Wife of the Governor of Pennsylvania

COUNTRY PATÉ

Preparing: 40 minutes *Do Ahead* *Yield: One 2-quart mold*
Baking: 1½ hours
Chilling: 4 to 5 hours

Pork and Veal Stuffing:

½ cup very finely minced onion
1 clove garlic (use 2 for stronger
  flavor), finely mashed
2 tablespoons butter
½ cup port, Madeira, or cognac
¾ pound *each* lean pork and veal,
  ground together

2 lightly beaten eggs
1½ teaspoons salt
⅛ teaspoon pepper
Big pinch allspice
½ teaspoon thyme

Cook onions slowly with butter in small skillet 8-10 minutes until tender. Scrape into mixing bowl. Pour wine into skillet; simmer until reduced by half; scrape into mixing bowl. Add remaining ingredients and beat vigorously with wooden spoon until mixture has lightened in texture and is thoroughly blended. If not to be used immediately, cover and refrigerate.

1 pound thick sliced bacon
4 cups Pork and Veal Stuffing
3 tablespoons cognac
Big pinch salt and pepper
Pinch thyme
Pinch allspice

1 tablespoon finely minced shallots
  or green onions
½ pound lean boiled ham, sliced
  ¼-inch thick
1 bay leaf

Cut ham slices into ¼-inch thick strips. Blanch bacon in boiling water 2 minutes. Line bottom and sides of 8-cup (rectangle or oval) baking terrine with bacon. Beat cognac, spices and shallots together; add to veal stuffing. Preheat oven to 350° F. Divide stuffing mixture into 3 parts. Dip hands into cold water; arrange first layer of stuffing in bottom of terrine. Cover with half the strips of ham. Cover with second third of stuffing and final layer of ham strips. Spread on last of meat stuffing. Lay bay leaf on top; cover with bacon strips. Enclose top of terrine with aluminum foil. Cover; set in pan of boiling water. Water should come about ½ way up the outside of terrine; add boiling water during cooking, as necessary. Set in lower third of oven; bake about 1½ hours. A long loaf pan will cook faster than a round or oval casserole. The paté is done when it has shrunk slightly from the sides of terrine and surrounding fat and juices are clear yellow with no traces of rosy color. When done take terrine from water, remove lid and place a pan or casserole, which will just fit into the terrine, on top of the foil covering the paté. On or in it, place 3-4 pounds of weights. This will pack paté, removing air spaces. *Allow paté to cool at room temperature for several hours or overnight.* Chill it, still weighted down. Serve from terrine or unmold onto a platter.

Judy Grenamyer Donohue

DEVILED HAM DIP

Preparing: 10 minutes   *Do Ahead*   *Yield: 1½ cups*
Chilling: 1 hour

1 cup sour cream
1 (4-ounce) can deviled ham
3 tablespoons chili sauce

1 teaspoon instant minced onion
¼ teaspoon horseradish

Combine ingredients and chill about 1 hour before serving. Serve with corn chips.

Dolly Eastburn Somers

DIPSY DEVIL DIP

Preparing: 10 minutes   *Do Ahead*   *Yield: 1 cup*
Chilling: 1 hour

1 (5-ounce) jar cream cheese with
   pimento
1 (2¼-ounce) can deviled ham
¼ cup mayonnaise

2 tablespoons minced parsley
1 tablespoon minced onion
4 drops Tabasco sauce
Dash monosodium glutamate

Combine ingredients until creamy. Chill. Serve with bugle chips.

Mary Lou Kerigan Batchelder

DILL WEED DIP

Preparing: 10 minutes   *Do Ahead*   *Yield: 2 cups*
Chilling: 4 hours

1 cup sour cream
1½-2 cups mayonnaise
2 tablespoons onion flakes
2 tablespoons parsley flakes

2 teaspoons dill weed
2 teaspoons Beau Monde
   seasoning

Mix all ingredients and refrigerate several hours before serving with raw vegetables.

Carol Houston Robinson

HOT CLAM DIP

Preparing: 10 minutes   *Do Ahead*   *Yield: 1½ to 2 cups*
Baking: 30 minutes

1 (8-ounce) package cream
  cheese, softened
1 (10½-ounce) canned clams,
  minced
1 teaspoon lemon juice
2 tablespoons clam broth

1 teaspoon prepared mustard
2 teaspoons Worcestershire sauce
¼ teaspoon garlic powder
Dash cayenne or Tabasco
2 teaspoons grated onion
  (optional)

Preheat oven to 350° F. Mix all ingredients except clams; then add clams. Bake 30 minutes.

Note: May be mixed one day ahead and baked the next day.

HEARTS OF PALM DIP

Preparing: 10 minutes   *Do Ahead*   *Yield: 4 cups*
Chilling: 12 hours

1 pint sour cream
1 pint mayonnaise
3 cloves garlic, crushed with 1
  tablespoon salt
1 tablespoon A-1 sauce
1 tablespoon Worcestershire sauce

2 drops Tabasco
1 tablespoon minced parsley
4 scallions, chopped
1 tablespoon lemon juice
1 can hearts of palm, thinly sliced

Mix all ingredients well, except hearts of palm. Add hearts of palm. Refrigerate. Serve with mild crackers.

Note: Better if made one day ahead.

MEXICAN DIP

Preparing: 20 minutes   *Yield: 12 servings*

1 avocado, chopped and coated   1 cup shredded sharp Cheddar
  with lemon juice, salt and pepper   cheese
1 pint sour cream   Chopped scallions to cover
1 jar Old El Paso hot taco sauce

In a clear glass bowl, layer ingredients in order given, ending with thin layer of
scallions; serve with corn chips or plain taco chips. Dip deep.

Jeanne Kronmiller Honish

MARINATED VEGETABLES WITH CURRY DIP

Preparing: 30 minutes   *Do Ahead*   *Yield: 8 to 12 servings*
Marinating: 12 hours

1 large bunch fresh broccoli   1 pint cherry tomatoes
1 head cauliflower

Cut flowerets from broccoli and cauliflower with stems no longer than 1-1½
inches (bite-sized). Place pieces in bowl; cover with marinade. Chill.

Marinade:
¼ cup cider or wine vinegar   1 teaspoon sugar
¾ cup vegetable oil   2 teaspoons dill
2 cloves garlic, split

Combine ingredients in a jar and shake well.

Dip:
2 cups mayonnaise   1 tablespoon catsup
1½ tablespoons curry powder   ¼ teaspoon Worcestershire sauce

Mix ingredients and refrigerate.

Frances Marincola Blair

SPINACH DIP

Preparing: 15 minutes　　　　*Do Ahead*　　　　*Yield: 2½ cups*

1 (8-ounce) package cream cheese
1 cup sour cream
½ cup mayonnaise
1 envelope onion soup mix
¼ teaspoon garlic powder

Pinch dried dill weed
1 (10-ounce) package frozen
　chopped spinach, thawed,
　drained, and squeezed dry

Combine cream cheese and sour cream; blend well. Stir in mayonnaise and soup mix; add seasonings. Gently stir in spinach. Serve with assorted vegetables.

Variation: Substitute ½ package leek soup mix for onion soup; increase mayonnaise to 1 cup. Omit cream cheese and garlic; add ½ cup fresh parsley.

Jeanne Kronmiller Honish

HOT SHRIMP DIP IN PUMPERNICKEL BREAD

Preparing: 30 minutes　　*Do Ahead: Partially*　　*Yield: 2 to 3 cups*
Baking: 20 minutes

2 (1-pound) round loaves
　pumpernickel bread
1 (6-ounce) can tiny shrimp

1 (10¾-ounce) can cream shrimp
　soup
1 (8-ounce) package cream cheese

Combine soup and cream cheese in pan; stir constantly over low heat until smooth. Hollow out loaves of bread, cutting "cap" off top. Cut hollowed out chunks in pieces for dipping. *(Can be done ahead to this point. Wrap bread in foil or plastic wrap.)* Preheat oven to 350° F. Heat soup mix; add shrimp and continue heating until hot. Pour in bread shell, wrap with foil; bake 20 minutes. Serve with bread cubes in basket.

Variation: ½-1 teaspoon of curry may be added to dip. Adjust curry to your taste.

Dee Anthony DuPont

ALMOND BACON CHEESE SPREAD

Preparing: 25 minutes   *Do Ahead*   *Yield: 1½ cups*
Chilling: 1 to 2 hours

¼ cup unblanched almonds
2 strips bacon, cooked crisp
1 cup shredded American cheese,
   packed

1 tablespoon chopped green onion
   or chives
½ cup mayonnaise
¼ teaspoon salt

Roast and finely chop almonds. Crumble bacon. Blend all ingredients thoroughly. Allow to chill 1-2 hours. Serve with mild crackers or melba toast rounds.

Note: May substitute 2 slices of minced hard salami for bacon.

Lois Rising Pogyor

ASPARAGUS ROLL-UPS

Preparing: 15 minutes   *Do Ahead*   *Yield: 160 pieces; 40 rolls*
Baking: 15 minutes   *Freeze*

1 pound butter
2 large loaves white bread
1 (8-ounce) jar grated Parmesan
   cheese

2 cans asparagus stalks (or
   broccoli)

Preheat oven to 350° F. Remove crust from bread and flatten with rolling pin. Dip both sides of bread in melted butter, then in cheese. Roll one asparagus stalk in each slice of bread. Cut into bite-sized pieces. Bake 15 minutes.

Note: Recipe can be halved.

Carol Myers Anderson

MARINATED ARTICHOKES

Preparing: 15 minutes   *Do Ahead*   *Yield: 8 servings*
Marinating: Overnight

2 (9-ounce) packages frozen   ¼ cup olive oil
   artichoke hearts, cooked and   4 teaspoons sugar
   drained or 1½ cans artichokes,   2 teaspoons finely cut fresh
   drained   tarragon or 1 teaspoon dried
½ cup tarragon vinegar   tarragon leaves

In small bowl combine vinegar, oil, sugar and tarragon; stir until sugar dissolves. Pour over artichoke hearts; *refrigerate, covered overnight.* Carefully turn artichoke hearts occasionally. To serve, arrange in shallow serving dish and garnish with sprigs of fresh tarragon.

ARTICHOKE NIBBLERS

Preparing: 15 minutes   *Do Ahead*   *Yield: 77 pieces*
Baking: 30 minutes

2 (6-ounce) jars marinated   ⅛ teaspoon pepper
   artichoke hearts   ⅛ teaspoon oregano
1 small onion, chopped fine   ⅛ teaspoon hot pepper sauce
1 clove garlic, minced   ½ pound sharp Cheddar, shredded
4 eggs, beaten   or Parmesan cheese, grated
¼ cup fine, dry bread crumbs   2 tablespoons minced parsley
¼ teaspoon salt

Preheat oven to 325° F. Drain marinade from one jar of artichokes into frying pan. Drain other jar; save marinade for another use. Chop both jars of artichokes and set aside. Add onion and garlic to frying pan, sauté until onion is limp, about 5 minutes. Add onion and garlic to eggs, crumbs, salt, pepper, oregano and hot pepper sauce. Stir in cheese, parsley and artichokes. Combine thoroughly. Turn into greased 7x11-inch baking pan. Bake 30 minutes, or until set. Cool; then cut into 1-inch squares. Serve cold or reheat 10-12 minutes at 350° F.

Note: This recipe can be cut in half.

Pat Sunner Horning

BACON ROLL-UPS

Preparing: 10 minutes   *Do Ahead*   *Yield: 3 dozen*
Chilling: 1 hour   *Freeze*
Baking: 35 minutes

¼ cup butter or margarine   1 egg, slightly beaten
½ cup water   ¼ pound hot or mild bulk pork
1½ cups packaged herb-seasoned   sausage
   stuffing   ½-⅔ pound sliced bacon

In saucepan, melt butter in water; add to stuffing, mix. Add egg and sausage; blend thoroughly. Chill 1 hour for easier handling. Shape into small oblongs, about size of pecans. Cut bacon slices into thirds. Wrap each piece of stuffing mixture with bacon and fasten with toothpick. Preheat oven to 375° F. Place on rack in shallow pan. Bake 35 minutes or until brown and crisp, turning at halfway point in cooking. Drain on paper towel and serve hot.

Note: These may be frozen before baking; just thaw and bake.

Joan Walling Gray

BACON AND CREAM CHEESE ROLL-UPS

Preparing: 30 minutes   *Do Ahead*   *Yield: 40 appetizers*
Cooking: 20 minutes   *Freeze*

20 slices white bread   1 pound bacon
1 (8-ounce) container whipped
   cream cheese

Remove crusts from bread, roll slices thin. Preheat oven to 400° F. Spread bread with cream cheese and roll up jelly-roll fashion. Cut each roll in half. Cut bacon strips in half; wrap around each bread roll. Place on baking sheet seam-side down; bake until bacon is crisp (about 20 minutes). *May be frozen before cooking. Allow to thaw before baking.* Drain on paper towel before serving.

Dolly Eastburn Somers

HAWAIIAN BEEF STICKS

Preparing: 40 minutes   *Do Ahead*   *Yield: 4 dozen*
Marinating: 2 hours

2-inch piece fresh ginger, sliced   2 tablespoons red wine vinegar
2 cloves garlic, mashed   4 teaspoons cornstarch
2 small onions, chopped   ½ cup water
1 cup soy sauce   2 pounds beef sirloin
4 tablespoons sugar

In small pan, combine ginger, garlic, onions, soy sauce, sugar and vinegar. Cook over medium heat until slightly thick, about 20 minutes. Combine cornstarch with water; gradually add sauce. Cook, stirring until clear and thickened. Pour mixture through wire strainer pressing out all juices; discard pulp and cool. Cut beef into thin slices; add to marinade. *Allow to stand, covered, 2 hours.* Thread 2 or 3 pieces of meat on each skewer; barbecue over hot coals or broil.

Note: Marinade may be made a day ahead.

Karen Klabau Meyers

BRAUNSCHWEIGER CANAPÉ

Preparing: 6 minutes   *Do Ahead*   *Yield: 20 to 30 servings*
Chilling: 2 hours

2 cans beef consommé   A bit of grated onion
2 envelopes unflavored gelatin   4 drops Worcestershire sauce
1 pound liverwurst   2-3 dashes garlic salt
1 (8-ounce) package cream cheese   Sliced olives

Heat consommé and dissolve gelatin in it. Grease a 1-quart mold or 2 ice cube trays. After slicing olives, arrange them on the bottom of mold. Pour a thin layer of heated consommé on olives and place in freezer 5 minutes, until consommé hardens. Mix liverwurst and cheese together; pour remainder of consommé into it. Add rest of seasonings; beat with mixer until smooth. Pour over hardened olive mixture. *This recipe will keep refrigerated for 3 weeks.* Before serving, unmold. Serve with crackers.

Note: Can be cut in half.

MY BOURSIN

Preparing: 10 minutes   *Freeze*   *Yield: 12 to 20 servings*

2 (8-ounce) packages cream
  cheese
½ cup butter
2 cloves garlic, mashed
½ teaspoon salt
1 teaspoon oregano

¼ teaspoon thyme
¼ teaspoon marjoram
¼ teaspoon dill weed
¼ teaspoon basil
¼ teaspoon white pepper

Soften cream cheese and butter to room temperature. Add spices and mix by hand. Chill.

Note: Cheese freezes well; after thawing, beat well.

Kathy Mohn Wilmot

RAW BROCCOLI AND CAULIFLOWER DIP

Preparing: 30 minutes   *Do Ahead*   *Yield: 8 servings*
Marinating: 6 to 12 hours

1 large bunch fresh broccoli   1 large head cauliflower

Marinade:
¼ cup cider or wine vinegar   1 teaspoon sugar
¾ cup vegetable oil   2 teaspoons dill
2 cloves garlic, split

Cut flowerets; split larger ones to make them bite-sized. Combine ingredients for marinade in jar; shake well. Put vegetables in plastic bag; pour in marinade. Tie bag; *refrigerate up to day before serving.* Drain vegetables; serve with dip. For more color, add cherry tomatoes at last minute.

Dip:
2 cups mayonnaise   1 tablespoon catsup
1½ tablespoons curry   ¼ teaspoon Worcestershire sauce

Mix ingredients and refrigerate.

Jeanne Kronmiller Honish

BEEF HORSERADISH SPREAD

Preparing: 10 minutes   *Do Ahead*   *Yield: 1½ cups*
Chilling: 1 hour

1 (8-ounce) package cream   **4 ounces chipped dried beef,**
   cheese, softened   **chopped**
¾ (5-ounce) jar horseradish

Combine ingredients in bowl and mix thoroughly; refrigerate. Serve with pumpernickle bread.

Gwen Fields Gilmore

STUFFED CELERY

Preparing: 20 minutes   *Do Ahead*   *Yield: 40 to 50 pieces*

2 bunches celery   **1 cup sour cream**
1 (8-ounce) package cream cheese   **Dash garlic salt**
4 ounces bleu cheese

Clean celery; set aside. Combine remaining ingredients. Fill celery with mixture and cut into 2 to 3-inch pieces.

CHILE CON QUESO

Preparing: 10 minutes   *Do Ahead*   *Yield: 12 servings*
Cooking: 20 minutes   *Freeze*

1 cup chopped onion   **1 can green chilies, chopped**
1 tablespoon shortening   **1 pound yellow processed cheese**
1½ cups stewed tomatoes, drained

Sauté onions in shortening until soft. Add *drained* tomatoes, chilies, and cheese. Simmer over low heat, stirring frequently until cheese melts (about 20 minutes). Serve warm with nacho cheese chips.

Joyce Kenny Cassetta

CHEESE BALLS IN CHIPPED BEEF

Preparing: 30 minutes   *Do Ahead*   *Yield: 24*
Chilling: 1½ hours

2 (8-ounce) packages cream   Few drops lemon juice
  cheese   Dash Tabasco sauce
½ teaspoon ground sage   5 ounces chipped beef, finely
½ teaspoon onion juice   chopped
½ teaspoon Worcestershire sauce

Blend all ingredients except chipped beef. Chill mixture 1 hour; shape cheese into about 24 marble-sized balls. Roll balls in finely chopped chipped beef. Chill.

Nancy Bowen Rainey

SENATE CHEESE STRAWS

Preparing: 30 minutes   *Do Ahead*   *Yield: 6 dozen*
Baking: 10 minutes   *Freeze*
Chilling: 15 minutes

1 pound sharp Cheddar cheese   1 teaspoon salt
¼ pound butter   ¼-½ teaspoon cayenne
1¾ cups flour

Preheat oven to 350° F. Finely shred cheese. Combine cheese with butter; beat until creamy. Add flour, salt, cayenne and blend well, adding a few drops of water if necessary to form a firm dough. Divide dough in half. Roll each half ¼-inch thick. Cut into 6x⅜-inch strips. Twist each strip and place on ungreased cookie sheet. Chill in freezer 15 minutes or longer to maintain shape. Bake 10-12 minutes.

Variation: You may form dough into oblong rolls one inch in diameter; chill at least one hour. Slice into ⅓-inch slices; place on baking sheet one-inch apart. Bake at 400° F. 10 minutes.

Liz Nelson Mayer

CHEESE NEAPOLITAN

Preparing: 30 minutes   *Do Ahead*   *Yield: 8 to 10 servings*
Chilling: Overnight

First Layer:
2 (3-ounce) packages cream   **½ cup shredded sharp cheese**
    cheese   **½ cup chopped parsley**

Blend; spread in bottom of lightly oiled 3-cup mold.

Second Layer:
2 (3-ounce) packages cream   **Dash onion salt**
    cheese   **½ cup shredded Cheddar cheese**
⅛ teaspoon garlic powder

Blend; spread evenly over first layer.

Third Layer:
2 (3-ounce) packages cream   **2 tablespoons tomato paste**
    cheese   **2 tablespoons shredded sharp**
¼ teaspoon basil   **   cheese**
½ teaspoon sugar

Blend; spread over second layer. Cover with foil; chill overnight. Unmold as would a gelatin mold; sprinkle top with parsley. Serve with crackers. *(Pretty at Christmas.)*

Jeanne Kronmiller Honish

CHEESE BISCUITS

Preparing: 20 minutes   *Do Ahead*   *Yield: 48 pieces*
Baking: 5 to 10 minutes   *Freeze*

1 cup chopped black olives   **½ teaspoon curry powder**
1½ cups shredded Cheddar cheese   **½ teaspoon salt**
½ cup mayonnaise   **6 English muffins**

Mix first 5 ingredients. Spread evenly on split muffins. Bake at 350° F. 5-10 minutes or until bubbly. Cut in quarters and serve.

Dolly Eastburn Somers

CHEESE NIBBLES

Preparing: 45 minutes **Do Ahead** *Yield: 32 pieces*
Baking: 10 minutes *Freeze*

1 large loaf Pepperidge Farm
  homestyle bread, sliced and
  frozen
1 (8-ounce) package cream cheese

8 ounces sharp cheese, shredded
1 stick margarine
1 egg white
1½ teaspoons dill weed

Preheat oven to 400° F. Blend cream cheese and margarine; stir in cheese. Add egg white and dill weed and mix well. Remove 3 slices of bread at a time from the freezer. Cut off crust. Spread cheese filling thinly between slices (as in triple-decker sandwich). Cut in half and each half into quarters (8 rectangles). Spread top and sides *(not bottom)* with cheese mixture (not too thickly) and place on lightly greased baking sheet. Repeat with remaining bread until cheese mixture is gone. Bake until lightly browned (about 10 minutes). *These can be frozen until ready to bake.*

Note: Be sure to keep bread frozen until ready to use to avoid cut edges of bread crumbling while being spread with cheese.

Lois Rising Pogyor

CHICKEN LIVER PATÉ

Preparing: 10 minutes **Do Ahead** *Yield: 3 cups*
Chilling: 3 to 4 hours *Freeze*

1 pound chicken livers
¼ cup minced shallots
¼ cup melted butter
¼ cup cognac or brandy
¼ cup heavy cream

½ teaspoon salt
⅛ teaspoon pepper
⅛ teaspoon tarragon leaves
⅛ teaspoon whole thyme leaves
½ cup melted butter

Sauté livers and shallots in ¼ cup butter over low heat until livers are lightly browned; remove from pan and set aside. Pour cognac into pan, simmer until reduced to 2 tablespoons. Combine livers, shallots, cognac, cream and seasonings; pour into food processor or blender and process 30 seconds or until smooth. With processor or blender running, slowly add ½ cup melted butter and process until smooth. Pour mixture into oiled 3-cup mold or individual 1-cup molds. Refrigerate several hours.

Barbara Sue Massengale Brodie

CHEESE PUFFS

Preparing: 30 minutes　　　　*Do Ahead*　　　　*Yield: 3 dozen*
Baking: 25 minutes　　　　*Freeze*

1 cup water	4 eggs
½ cup butter	1 teaspoon white pepper
1 cup sifted flour	1 cup shredded Cheddar cheese
1 teaspoon salt	(4 ounces)
1 teaspoon dry mustard	Grated Parmesan cheese

Preheat oven to 400° F. Heat water and butter to full rolling boil in large saucepan. Mix flour with salt and mustard all at once. Stir vigorously with wooden spoon until mixture forms a thick, smooth ball that leaves side of pan clean. Remove from heat; cool slightly. Add eggs, one at a time, beating well after each addition, until paste is shiny-smooth. Stir in pepper and Cheddar cheese. Drop rounded teaspoon for each puff ½-inch apart on lightly greased cookie sheet. Sprinkle tops with Parmesan cheese. Bake 25 minutes, or until puffed and golden brown. Remove to wire rack; cool completely. (For best results, cook one cookie sheet at a time in center of oven.)

Note: Freeze puffs in a single layer about 30 minutes. Place in plastic bags and keep frozen until ready to use. Reheat in 350° F. 8-10 minutes.

Lucetta Bahn Ebbert

ROSALYNN CARTER'S "PLAINS SPECIAL" CHEESE RING

Preparing: 15 minutes　　　　*Do Ahead*　　　　*Yield: 3 to 4 cups*
Chilling: 3 to 4 hours　　　　*Freeze*

1 pound sharp Cheddar cheese, shredded	⅛ teaspoon cayenne pepper
1 cup chopped pecans	Strawberry preserves, green grapes, or pecans for garnish
1 cup mayonnaise	(optional)
1 small onion, finely grated	

Combine cheese, nuts, onion, and pepper; add mayonnaise and blend well. Line a 3-4 cup mold with plastic wrap, allowing enough overlap to seal. Pat cheese mixture into mold firmly; seal and chill. Refrigerate until firm *(for several hours or overnight)*. To serve, unmold and fill center with strawberry preserves, green grapes, or pecans. Serve with plain crackers.

MANGO CHUTNEY AND CREAM CHEESE ON GINGER SNAPS

Preparing: 1 hour   *Do Ahead*   *Yield: 1 cup dip*
Chilling: 2 hours   *or 6 dozen snaps*

Gingersnap dough:
¼ **cup dark brown sugar**   ¼ **teaspoon allspice**
⅓ **cup molasses**   ½ **teaspoon cinnamon**
¼ **cup unsalted butter, softened**   ¼ **teaspoon ginger**
1 **egg**   ¼ **teaspoon ground cloves**
1 **teaspoon baking soda**   2¼ **cups flour**
¼ **teaspoon salt**

In a large mixing bowl, cream sugar, molasses and butter; add egg and beat until fluffy. Sift into another bowl, baking soda, salt, allspice, cinnamon, ginger, cloves and ¾ cup flour. Add this mixture all at once to molasses mixture and beat until ingredients are just mixed. Stir in remaining 1½ cups flour and beat to form a stiff dough. Divide dough into 1 cup amounts; flatten portions and wrap each in plastic wrap. *Refrigerate at least 2 hours or overnight.* To bake cookies, preheat oven to 350° F. Lightly butter two cookie sheets. On lightly floured surface, roll out dough to about ⅛-inch thickness. With a crimped pastry wheel, cut dough in 1x2-inch rectangles. Place them on cookie sheets and prick tops with a fork in an even pattern. Bake cookies until crisp, about 10 minutes. Transfer to wire racks to cool.

Topping:
1 (8-ounce) package cream   ¼ **cup mango chutney, finely**
   cheese, softened   chopped

Blend cream cheese and chutney well; transfer into a serving bowl surrounded with cookies. Allow guests to spread their own.

Note: In a pinch, the cream cheese chutney mixture can be served with purchased gingersnaps.

Liz Nelson Mayer

CHUTNEY CHEESE BALL

Preparing: 10 to 15 minutes   *Do Ahead*   *Yield: 1 ball*
Chilling: 3 to 4 hours   *Freeze*

2 (8-ounce) packages cream   3 teaspoons curry powder
  cheese, softened   ½ (12-ounce) can cocktail peanuts
3 tablespoons sour cream   ½ pound crisp bacon, crumbled
1 (1-ounce) package raisins,   ½ cup chopped onion
  chopped (do not use food
  processor)

Cream cheese; mix in sour cream. Add other ingredients; blend well. Put into a bowl lined with foil or plastic wrap and form a ball. *Refrigerate at least several hours or preferably overnight so flavors will meld.* Serve with a mild cracker.

Mary Isabel Meade Laroque

CRUNCHY PUMPKIN SEEDS

Preparing: 15 minutes   *Do Ahead*
Baking: 20 to 25 minutes

Preheat oven to 375°F. Wash seeds thoroughly. Drain; spread on dry cookie sheet. Roast 20-25 minutes to dry. Increase heat to 400°F; dot seeds with margarine and brown slightly. Sprinkle with salt, cool and serve.

Pam Bartels Morris

CHUTNEY CIRCLES

Preparing: 15 minutes   *Do Ahead*   *Yield: 40 servings*
Cooking: 3 minutes

½ pound hard salami, sliced thin   1 (8-ounce) jar chutney

Fill 2-inch circles of salami with a teaspoon of chutney, being careful not to include too much liquid. Fold each circle in half and secure with a toothpick. Broil for approximately 3 minutes and serve hot.

Note: These can also be made by placing chutney on a Ritz cracker and topping with a quarter slice of salami; broil.

Joyce Kenny Cassetta

CREAM CHEESE PUFFS

Preparing: 25 minutes   Do Ahead   Yield: 40
Baking: 5 minutes   Freeze

1 (8-ounce) package cream   3 drops Tabasco sauce
   cheese, room temperature   ½ cup freshly grated Parmesan
3 tablespoons mayonnaise   cheese
3 tablespoons chopped green   10 slices firm white bread
   onion

Combine all ingredients, except bread; chill. Cut 4 circles from each slice of bread (40 circles total). Place circles on cookie sheet. Broil until lightly brown; cool. Spread cheese mixture on circles, completely covering them. Broil puffs until heated through and lightly browned.

Note: *If preparing ahead, place on cookie sheet and put in freezer until puffs are frozen. Place puffs in plastic bag and return to freezer. To serve, broil puffs while still frozen, 4-5 minutes or until heated through and lightly browned. Or, bake at 400°F. 5-6 minutes or until lightly browned.*

Variation: Add 4-ounce can crabmeat to cheese mixture.

Sandra Pocius Mowry

SWEET AND SOUR CHICKEN WINGS

Preparing: 15 minutes   Do Ahead   Yield: 6 to 10 servings
Baking: 1 hour
Marinating: Overnight

3-5 pounds chicken wings   ¼ cup brown sugar
½ cup orange juice   ½ cup cranberry sauce (optional)
½ cup soy sauce

Cut chicken wings, separating drumsticks. Combine remaining ingredients; add chicken and marinate overnight. Preheat oven to 350° F.; bake 1 hour, basting frequently.

Sandra Johnson McConnell

LEMON-PEPPER CUCUMBERS

Preparing: 15 minutes   *Yield: 30 to 40 pieces*
Chilling: 1 hour

2 cucumbers
Lemon-pepper seasoning or Crazy
   Jane's Mixed Up Salt

Pepperidge Farm Party Rye or
   white bread, decrusted and
   quartered
Mayonnaise

Peel and slice cucumbers; soak in cold water 1 hour. Drain, placing slices on paper towel and rolling up for 10 minutes to remove all moisture. Spread bread slices with mayonnaise. Place cucumber on top and sprinkle with seasoning. *(Do not prepare too far ahead because bread will become soggy.)*

Harlene Galloway DeMarco

DILL MARINATED VEGETABLES

Preparing: 20 minutes   *Do Ahead*   *Yield: 6 to 8 servings*

1 (10-ounce) package frozen
   cauliflower
1 (9-ounce) package frozen sliced
   green beans
2 tablespoons olive oil
2 tablespoons red wine vinegar

1 teaspoon dill seed
½ teaspoon instant minced garlic
½ teaspoon salt
¹⁄₁₆ teaspoon ground black pepper
Crisp bacon bits (garnish)

Cook vegetables according to package directions; drain. Combine oil, vinegar, dill, garlic, salt and pepper. Pour over cauliflower and beans. Toss gently. Serve either hot or cold garnished with crisp bacon bits.

Note: Frozen peas, carrots, waxed or Italian beans, mixed vegetables or Brussel sprouts may be used in place of cauliflower and green beans.

Catherine More Keller

GUACAMOLE

Preparing: 25 minutes   *Do Ahead*   *Yield: 2 cups*
Chilling: 1 hour

2 avocados, peeled and pitted   **1 teaspoon salt**
1 medium onion, finely chopped   **½ teaspoon coarsely ground**
2 green chili peppers, finely   **pepper**
**   chopped (or 1 teaspoon chili**   **1 medium tomato, peeled and**
**   powder)**   **finely chopped**
1 tablespoon lemon juice   **Mayonnaise**

Mash avocados; add onion, peppers, lemon juice, salt and pepper. Beat until creamy. Fold in tomato. Spread top with thin layer of mayonnaise. Cover and chill. Just before serving, stir gently to mix.

ITALIAN SMASH CANAPÉ

Preparing: 15 minutes   *Do Ahead*   *Yield: 48*
Broiling: 5 minutes   *Freeze*

4 ounces sharp cheese, shredded   **¼ teaspoon dry mustard**
4 slices raw bacon, finely chopped   **¼ teaspoon Worcestershire sauce**
1 cup chopped onion   **6 English muffins, split and**
1 tablespoon mayonnaise   **quartered**

Mix all ingredients except muffins; roll into log, 1½ inches in diameter; wrap in waxed paper. Cover with foil; freeze. *(Will keep frozen for months.)* Slice frozen and place on muffins. Broil 5 minutes; serve.

Kathy Mohn Wilmot

HAWAIIAN MEATBALLS

Preparing: 1 hour   *Do Ahead: Partially*   *Yield: 7 dozen meatballs*
Cooking: 15 minutes   *Serves 6*

1½ pounds ground beef
⅔ cup cracker crumbs
½ cup minced onion
1 egg
1½ teaspoons salt
¼ teaspoon ginger
¼ cup milk
1 tablespoon shortening

2 tablespoons cornstarch
⅓ cup packed brown sugar
1 (13½-ounce) can pineapple
  chunks in heavy syrup (drained);
  reserve juice
⅓ cup vinegar
1 tablespoon soy sauce
⅓ cup chopped green pepper

Mix meat, crumbs, onion, egg, salt, ginger and milk. Shape (about a rounded tablespoon) into bite-sized balls. Melt shortening in skillet, brown meatballs and remove. Pour off fat. Mix cornstarch and sugar; stir in reserved pineapple syrup, vinegar and soy sauce until smooth. Pour into skillet. At medium heat, stir constantly until it thickens and boils. Boil one minute. Add meatballs, pineapple and green pepper. Heat through.

Note: To serve as a main course, make meatballs slightly larger.

Grace Burdett Nellis

JOSEFINAS

Preparing: 20 minutes   *Do Ahead*   *Yield: 2 dozen*
Baking: 5 minutes

2 long thin sour dough rolls
¾ cup butter
1 large clove garlic, finely minced
½ small can green chilies,
  chopped
1 cup mayonnaise

¼ pound Monterey Jack cheese,
  shredded
Sliced radishes and chopped
  parsley (garnish)

Cut rolls ¼-inch thick crosswise; toast on both sides. Mix butter, garlic and chopped chilies (use chilies to taste). Spread on one side of bread. Mix mayonnaise and cheese. Top buttered side with mayonnaise-cheese mixture. Place on tray and broil until light brown. Remove to a serving tray, place a thin slice of radish and a sprinkle of finely chopped parsley on each josefina. Serve at once.

Sandra Schild Fletcher

HA' PENNIES

Preparing: 10 minutes　　　*Do Ahead*　　　*Yield: 5 to 6 dozen*
Baking: 10 to 15 minutes　　*Freeze*

½ cup butter, softened　　　　½ package dry onion soup mix
½ pound sharp Cheddar cheese,　1 cup flour
　finely shredded

Preheat oven to 375° F. Combine softened butter, cheese, onion soup mix and flour. Roll into logs ½-inch in diameter; wrap in waxed paper and chill. Slice into rounds ¼-inch thick. Bake on greased cookie sheet for 10-15 minutes. Serve hot or cold.

Note: If desired, place almond, pecan half or piece of crystalized ginger on top of each appetizer "cookie" before baking.

Joyce Kenny Cassetta

HAM CHEESE CUBES

Preparing: 30 minutes　　　*Do Ahead*　　　*Yield: Approximately 100*
Chilling: 2 hours　　　　　*Freeze*

2 tablespoons horseradish　　　½ teaspoon seasoned salt
1 teaspoon Worcestershire sauce　1 (8-ounce) package cream cheese
⅛ teaspoon pepper　　　　　　12 thin slices boiled ham
2 tablespoons mayonnaise

Beat all ingredients together (except ham) until creamy and of spreading consistency. Place one ham slice on a piece of waxed paper. With spatula, spread on some of creamed mixture. Place another slice of ham on top; spread with more cheese. Repeat, using 6 slices, ending with ham slice on top. With slice number 7, start process again. Wrap securely in waxed paper; place in freezer 2 hours or more. *About 1 hour before serving, remove from refrigerator* and cut lengthwise and crosswise into ½-inch cubes. Pierce each cube with a toothpick.

Note: Recipe can be cut in half.

GLAZED MEATBALLS

Preparing: 30 minutes   *Do Ahead*   *Yield: About 50 meatballs*
Cooking: 25 minutes

1½ pounds ground chuck   **½ teaspoon ground cinnamon**
1½ slices white bread   **1 teaspoon salt**
1 egg   **½ teaspoon pepper**
2 tablespoons minced green onion   **1 (12-ounce) jar crabapple jelly**
2 tablespoons minced parsley   **½ cup catsup**

Soak bread in a little cold water until soft. Squeeze dry and mash well. Add to meat; mix together with eggs, onion, parsley, cinnamon, salt and pepper. Blend thoroughly; form into 1-inch balls. In large skillet combine jelly and catsup; slowly bring to boil. Stir to blend; add meatballs. Simmer 25 minutes or until cooked. Turn meatballs carefully after 10-15 minutes. Serve in a chafing dish.

OVEN ROASTED NUT MEATS

Preparing: 10 minutes   *Do Ahead*   *Yield: 2 cups*
Baking: 1½ hours

2 cups whole nut meats   **⅛ teaspoon celery salt**
3 tablespoons butter   **⅛ teaspoon garlic powder**
½ teaspoon salt

Preheat oven to 225° F. Melt butter in 9x13-inch pan. Add seasonings; mix well. Stir in nuts. Bake 1½ hours, stirring every 15 minutes. Drain on paper towels. Store in airtight container.

Note: Any combination of walnuts, almonds, brazil nuts or pecans may be used.

BAKED MUSHROOMS WITH SAUSAGE

Preparing: 30 minutes   *Do Ahead: Partially*   *Yield: 1½ dozen*
Baking: 30 minutes

18 mushrooms   **½ pound bulk sausage**

Remove stems from mushrooms; chop stems. Mix sausage and stems together. Fill mushroom caps with sausage mixture. (Pack caps high and wide as they will shrink while baking.) Preheat oven to 350° F.; bake 30 minutes.

Sauce:
1 cup tomato sauce   **½ clove garlic, minced**
1 cup white wine   **½ teaspoon oregano**

Heat ingredients together. Pour over baked mushrooms and serve in chafing dish.

Dolly Eastburn Somers

MARINATED MUSHROOMS AND ARTICHOKE HEARTS

Preparing: 20 minutes   *Do Ahead*   *Yield: 6 to 7 cups*
Marinating: 24 hours

1½ cups water   **1½ tablespoons salt**
1 cup cider vinegar   **½ teaspoon pepper**
2 pounds small fresh mushrooms   **½ teaspoon thyme**
2 (9-ounce) packages frozen   **½ teaspoon oregano**
  artichoke hearts or 2 cans   **½ teaspoon chervil**
  artichoke hearts, drained   **1 bay leaf**
½ cup vegetable oil   **Chopped parsley**

In large bowl combine water and vinegar. Clean and prepare mushrooms. Mix all ingredients except parsley in bowl and toss lightly. Refrigerate covered, stirring occasionally, *at least 24 hours.* When ready to serve, drain and sprinkle with chopped parsley.

Lynn Green

MUSHROOM STRUDEL

Preparing: 45 minutes   *Do Ahead*   *Yield: 2 strudels; 16 servings*
Cooking: 30 minutes

Filling:
1¼ pounds (6 cups) finely minced mushrooms
2 tablespoons finely chopped shallots
1 teaspoon salt
¼ teaspoon ground pepper

3-4 teaspoons curry powder
1 tablespoon sherry
4 tablespoons butter or margarine
1 cup sour cream
2 tablespoons bread crumbs

Sauté mushrooms, shallots, salt, pepper, curry powder and sherry in butter until liquid evaporates, about 15 minutes. Set aside to cool. Add sour cream and 2 tablespoons crumbs.

Dough:
1 (1-pound) package phyllo dough
½ cup butter, melted

¾ cup bread crumbs

Preheat oven to 375° F. Spread out a cool damp cloth to work on. Unwrap dough carefully. Keep dough covered with damp towel to keep moist. Lay out one layer of dough on towel. Brush with some melted butter and sprinkle with some crumbs. Repeat to make 4 layers total. Spoon half mushroom mixture about 2-3 inches wide at the short side of the dough. Turn long sides of dough in about 1-inch. Roll up jelly-roll fashion, starting at the short side. Repeat with remaining dough and filling to make two strudels. Place seam-side down on greased cookie sheets. Bake 25-30 minutes.

Note: If this is done ahead, it is very important to wrap strudels in damp cloth and wrap tightly with foil or plastic wrap.

Susan Coates Oliver

PICKLED MUSHROOMS AND ONIONS

Preparing: 15 minutes   *Do Ahead*   *Yield: 2 cups*
Chilling: 3 hours

⅓ cup red wine vinegar
⅛ cup vegetable oil
⅛ cup olive oil
1 medium onion, thinly sliced
1 teaspoon salt

2 teaspoons dried parsley flakes
1 teaspoon prepared mustard
2 (6-ounce) cans mushroom caps,
   drained
1 tablespoon sugar, white or brown

In small saucepan, combine all ingredients except mushrooms; bring to boiling.
Add mushrooms, simmer 5-6 minutes. Pour into bowl; cover. Chill several
hours (or overnight), stirring occasionally. Drain and serve with cocktail picks.

Sandy Sullivan Ryder

MEAT-STUFFED MUSHROOM CAPS

Preparing: 25 minutes   *Do Ahead*   *Yield: 2 dozen*
Marinating: 1 hour   *Freeze*
Broiling: 8 to 10 minutes
Baking: 8 to 10 minutes

2 dozen large mushrooms, stems
   removed and reserved

½ cup soy sauce

Marinate caps for 1 hour.

Stuffing:
Mushrooms stems
½ pound ground beef or sausage
2 tablespoons bread crumbs
1 tablespoon minced onion
½ clove garlic

¼ teaspoon salt
¼ teaspoon pepper
¼ teaspoon rosemary
1 tablespoon lemon juice
2 tablespoons white wine

Drain caps. Mix all stuffing ingredients. Stuff caps, mounding high. Brush tops
with soy sauce. Broil 8-10 minutes. Refrigerate or freeze. *Bring to room temperature.* Preheat oven to 350° F.; bake 8-10 minutes.

Lori Adams DelRossi

MUSHROOM ROLLS

Preparing: 1 to 1½ hours　　　*Do Ahead*　　　*Yield: 7 or 8 dozen*
Cooking: 20 minutes　　　*Freeze*

**1 pound mushrooms, finely
  chopped
½ cup butter
6 tablespoons flour
1½ teaspoons salt
½ teaspoon monosodium
  glutamate**

**2 cups light cream
2 teaspoons lemon juice
1 teaspoon onion salt or minced
  chives
1½ loaves bread
Melted butter**

Preheat oven to 375° F. Sauté mushrooms in butter 5 minutes; cool. Add flour; blend well. Add salt and MSG. Stir in cream and cook until thick, stirring constantly. Add lemon juice and onion salt; cool. Remove crust from bread and roll slices flat. Spread slices with mushroom mixture and roll up. Freeze slightly and cut into thirds *(or freeze at this point).* Dip in melted butter. Bake for 15-20 minutes.

Note: To serve rolls from freezer; defrost, cut each roll in half. Dip in melted butter. Bake at 375° F. for 15-20 minutes.

Pam Labor Weaver

MUSHROOM CROUSTADES

Preparing: 25 minutes　　　*Do Ahead*　　　*Yield: 24 servings*
Baking: 20 minutes　　　*Freeze*

**1 (10-ounce) package Pepperidge
  Farm frozen patty shells
3 tablespoons butter
1 large onion, finely chopped
½ pound mushrooms, chopped
¼ teaspoon thyme**

**½ teaspoon salt
Dash pepper
2 tablespoons flour
¼ cup sour cream
1 tablespoon sherry**

Defrost patty shells; cut each into quarters. Shape and mold into mini tart pans. Heat butter, sauté onion; add mushrooms and cook 3 minutes. Add seasonings; sprinkle in and mix to blend. Stir in sour cream. Cook until thick but not boiling. Remove from heat; add sherry. Preheat oven to 400° F. Fill pastry shells (about 1 teaspoon per tart); bake 20 minutes. Serve hot. *Tarts can be frozen before baking. If frozen, bake at 350° F. for 30 minutes.*

Gail White Dillon

STUFFED MUSHROOMS

Preparing: 30 minutes   Do Ahead   Yield: 30 to 36 pieces
Cooking: 5 minutes   Freeze

2 pounds medium size mushrooms   ½ teaspoon salt
2 (8-ounce) packages cream   ¼ teaspoon cayenne pepper
  cheese   1 cup bread crumbs
8 scallions, finely chopped   1 cup grated Parmesan cheese
4 tablespoons mayonnaise

Salt mushroom caps. Mix cream cheese, scallions, mayonnaise, salt and pepper together and fill mushrooms. Sprinkle with bread crumbs and Parmesan cheese. Broil 5 minutes and serve warm.

Lucetta Bahn Ebbert

MUSHROOM CHEESE BALL

Preparing: 20 minutes   Do Ahead   Yield: 1 ball
Chilling: 1 hour

1 (8-ounce) package cream   1 teaspoon grated onion
  cheese, softened   1 teaspoon Worcestershire sauce
1 (4½-ounce) jar sliced   ½ teaspoon salt
  mushrooms, diced

Mix ingredients together, chill slightly; shape into a ball. Serve with crackers.

MUSHROOMS ON TOAST POINTS

Preparing: 10 minutes   Yield: 6 to 8 servings
Cooking: 15 minutes

6 tablespoons butter   Buttered toast, cut in quarters (6 to
1½ pounds mushrooms, chopped   8 slices)
1 teaspoon salt   Chopped chives and parsley
½ teaspoon black pepper   Crisp bacon (6 to 8 slices
Dash Worcestershire sauce   quartered)

Melt butter in heavy skillet; add mushrooms and sauté over medium heat. Stir and shake pan from time to time; cook until mushrooms are lightly browned and still crisp. *Do not overcook.* Add salt, pepper and Worcestershire; serve on buttered toast with chopped herbs and crisp bacon.

SPICED PINEAPPLE

Preparing: 10 minutes   Do Ahead   *Yield: 2 to 3 cups*

1 (20 or 28-ounce) can pineapple
  chunks
½ cup vinegar
½ cup sugar

¼ teaspoon whole cloves
½ stick of cinnamon (broken in
  little pieces)

Drain syrup from pineapple chunks; mix with remaining ingredients. Place in refrigerator; gently shake now and then. Enhances flavor after standing a day or two. Excellent with ham and turkey dinners or as bite-sized hors d'oeuvres.

Charity Power Folk

PINEAPPLE CHEESE BALL

Preparing: 20 minutes   Do Ahead   *Yield: 2 small or 1 large ball*
Chilling: 3 hours

2 (8-ounce) packages cream
  cheese
¾ cup crushed sweetened
  pineapple, drained well
  (almost dry)

¾ cup chopped nuts
⅓ cup chopped green pepper
½ cup finely chopped onion

Mix all ingredients well. Shape into ball or balls and refrigerate 3 hours. Serve with buttery or wheat crackers.

Shirley Richert Walsh

SNACK TREAT MIX

Preparing: 5 minutes   Do Ahead   *Yield: 1 pound mix*

½ cup black raisins
½ cup pepita (hulled, unsalted
  pumpkin seeds)
½ cup unsalted, chopped cashews

½ cup carob dots
1 cup unsalted roasted soy nuts
½ cup raw unsalted sunflower
  seeds

Mix all ingredients together in bowl. Store in sealed container in refrigerator.

Note: Chopped dates or additional raisins may be substituted for the carob dots.

Gail Agerton Ebert

MINIATURE PIZZAS

Preparing: 15 minutes   *Do Ahead*   *Yield: 8 servings*
Cooking: 3 to 5 minutes

½ pound pepperoni, unsliced   1 (8-ounce) bag shredded
1 loaf party rye   mozzarella cheese
Catsup, hot or plain   Oregano

Slice pepperoni to desired thickness (about ⅛ inch). Spread slices of bread with catsup. Place 1-2 slices of pepperoni on top. Add 1 teaspoon cheese and dash of oregano. Broil 3-5 minutes until cheese melts.

Note: May substitute cooked Italian sausage for pepperoni and add chopped mushrooms.

Lori Adams DelRossi

HERB SAUSAGE BALLS

Preparing: 1 hour   *Do Ahead*   *Yield: 4 dozen*
Baking: 20 minutes   *Freeze*

1 (8-ounce) package Pepperidge   ½ cup finely chopped onion
   Farm Herb Stuffing   ½ cup finely chopped celery
1 pound hot pork sausage   1 cup warm water
1 egg, beaten

Preheat oven to 400° F. Mix all ingredients and form into small balls. Bake on a rack in shallow pan 20 minutes.

Note: These can be made and frozen; remove from freezer and bake 25-30 minutes.

Elizabeth Taylor Young

SAUERKRAUT BALLS

Preparing: 1 hour   *Do Ahead*   *Yield: 8 to 10 servings*
Chilling: 30 minutes   *Freeze*
Baking: 15 minutes

½ pound pork sausage, crumbled
¼ cup finely chopped onion
1 (14-ounce) can sauerkraut, well
   drained and snipped
2 tablespoons dry bread crumbs
1 (3-ounce) package cream
   cheese, softened
2 tablespoons parsley

1 tablespoon prepared mustard
¼ teaspoon garlic salt
¼ teaspoon pepper
¼ cup all-purpose flour
2 eggs, well beaten
¼ cup milk
1 cup bread crumbs
Vegetable oil

In skillet, cook sausage and onion until meat is brown; drain. Add sauerkraut and 2 tablespoons bread crumbs. Combine cream cheese, parsley, mustard, garlic salt and pepper; stir into sauerkraut mixture. Chill. Preheat oven to 375° F. Shape into small balls; coat with flour. Add milk to beaten eggs. Dip balls into egg-milk mixture and roll in 1 cup bread crumbs. Fry in deep fat until brown (about 2 minutes). *The balls may be frozen at this point.* Bake about 15-20 minutes.

Pam Labor Weaver

HOT SPINACH BALLS

Preparing: 45 minutes   *Do Ahead*   *Yield: 3 to 4 dozen*
Chilling: 2 hours   *Freeze*
Baking: 30 minutes

4 (10-ounce) packages frozen
   chopped spinach, thawed and
   drained
4 cups Pepperidge Farm herb
   stuffing mix
2 large onions, diced

8 eggs
1 cup Parmesan cheese
1½ cups butter, melted
1 tablespoon thyme
2 cloves garlic
Salt and pepper to taste

Mix ingredients; chill 2 hours. Roll into 1-inch balls. *(May freeze at this point.)* Preheat oven to 300° F.; bake on cookie sheet 30 minutes.

Joanne Feehery Duffy

BAMBINI

Preparing: 20 minutes   *Do Ahead*   *Yield: 40 appetizers*
Baking: 20 minutes

1 cup ricotta cheese   **2 (10-ounce) packages flaky**
½ cup shredded mozzarella cheese   **refrigerator biscuits**
¼ cup grated Parmesan cheese   **40 very thin slices pepperoni**

Combine ricotta, Parmesan and mozzarella. Halve each biscuit, making 40 thin pieces. Gently shape each biscuit into an oval about 2½ x 4 inches. Place slice of pepperoni on the dough, top with scant tablespoon of cheese mixture. Moisten edges, fold dough over to enclose filling, pinching edges to seal. Repeat with remaining dough and place on lightly greased cookie sheet. Preheat oven to 350° F.; bake 20 minutes and serve warm.

Robin Truitt Hayman

PARTY TURNOVERS

Preparing: 15 to 20 minutes   *Do Ahead*   *Yield: 48*
Cooking: 15 minutes   *Freeze*

1 envelope onion soup mix   **3 (8-ounce) packages refrigerator**
1 pound ground beef   **crescent rolls**
1 cup shredded Cheddar cheese

Preheat oven to 375° F. Brown meat; drain off fat. Pour onion soup mix over meat and mix. Blend in cheese. Separate crescent rolls according to package directions. Cut each roll in half. Place spoonful of meat mixture in center of each triangle. Fold over and seal edges. Place on ungreased cookie sheet. Bake 15 minutes or until golden brown.

Regina Shehadi Guza

SESAME PARTY STACKS

Preparing: 20 minutes   *Do Ahead*   *Yield: 16 stacks*
Baking: 10 minutes   *Freeze*

1 stick pie crust mix   **1 tablespoon sesame seeds**
1 tablespoon melted butter or
margarine

Prepare pie crust mix or make pastry from your favorite one-crust recipe. Roll out to an 8-inch square on lightly floured surface; brush with melted butter; sprinkle with sesame seeds. Preheat oven to 450° F. Cut square in half; place one half, sesame seed side up, on top of other half. Cut lengthwise into 4 even strips, then cut each strip crosswise into quarters. Place on cookie sheet. Bake 10 minutes or until golden.

WATERMELON TIDBITS

Preparing: 30 minutes   *Do Ahead*   *Yield: 24*
Cooking: 5 minutes

1 pound bacon   **1 jar preserved watermelon rind**

Cut bacon strips in half. Roll one half of a strip of bacon around a 1-inch piece of preserved watermelon rind. Broil, watching carefully until bacon is crisp. Serve hot with toothpicks.

Joyce Kenny Cassetta

ZUCCHINI APPETIZER

Preparing: 20 minutes   *Yield: 24 to 36 pieces*

6 hard-cooked eggs, finely   **⅓-½ cup mayonnaise**
chopped   **5 small raw zucchini**
½ pound small cooked shrimp,
chopped

Combine chopped eggs and shrimp with enough mayonnaise to hold ingredients together without making soupy. Slice zucchini into ½-inch rings. Place egg and shrimp mixture on top of each zucchini slice.

Pam Bartels Morris

CREAM CHEESE PASTRY

Preparing: 20 minutes   *Do Ahead*   *Yield: 4 dozen pieces*
Chilling: Overnight   *Freeze*

1 cup butter
1 (8-ounce) package cream cheese
½ teaspoon salt

2 cups flour
1 egg yolk
2 teaspoons cream or milk

Beat butter, cheese and salt in mixer until completely smooth. Work in flour to a smooth dough (mixer can be used but pastry blender is superior). *Chill overnight.* (Will keep several days.) Remove from refrigerator 10 minutes before using. Divide dough for ease in handling; keep unused portion in refrigerator. Shape as directed in recipes. Chill before baking. Brush tops of pastries (if directed) with egg yolk beaten with cream. Bake at 350° F. unless otherwise specified.

Note: This recipe is used in the following recipes: Miniature Quiches, Parmesan Twists, Pork Ginger Roll, Feta Cheese Tarts and Ham Crescents.

MINIATURE QUICHES

Preparing: 20 minutes   *Do Ahead*   *Yield: 24*
Baking: 30 minutes   *Freeze*

½ recipe Cream Cheese Pastry,
   chilled

Filling:
1 large egg, slightly beaten
½ cup milk

¼ teaspoon salt
1 cup shredded Swiss cheese

Preheat oven to 350° F. Divide dough into 24 balls and press each into miniature muffin pan cups. Combine egg, milk, and salt. Fill pastry shells with cheese. Dribble egg mixture over cheese. Bake 30 minutes; serve warm.

Variation: 3-4 slices cooked and crumbled bacon and 1 tablespoon minced onion may be added to cheese.

Beverly Brinsfield Wilson

HAM CRESCENTS

Preparing: 1 hour   *Do Ahead*   *Yield: 60*
Baking: 20 minutes   *Freeze*

1 recipe Cream Cheese Pastry, chilled

Filling:
1 cup heavy cream   **2 tablespoons minced parsley**
1 pound ham, ground or chopped   **2 teaspoons Dijon mustard**
  fine

In a skillet, reduce heavy cream over high heat by half. Remove the pan from heat. Stir in ham, parsley, and mustard; cool.

Glaze:
1 egg, beaten   **1 teaspoon water**

Mix well. Preheat oven to 375° F. Place ⅙ of dough on floured pastry cloth and roll out to a 9-inch circle. Spread with ⅙ of the ham filling; cut in 12 pie-shaped wedges. Roll each jelly-roll fashion (starting at outside toward point). Place each little roll, with point down, on ungreased cookie sheet. Brush with glaze. *(Can be frozen at this point.)* Bake 20 minutes. Serve warm.

PARMESAN TWISTS

Preparing: 30 minutes   *Do Ahead*   *Yield: 24 to 30*
Chilling: 1 hour   *Freeze*
Baking: 15 minutes

½ recipe Cream Cheese Pastry,   **½ cup grated Parmesan cheese**
  chilled   **Egg yolk mixed with cream**

Using one-half of pastry at a time, roll to ¼-inch thick. Sprinkle with cheese and press in with rolling pin. Fold pastry over in thirds; roll out again. Sprinkle with more cheese, pressing in cheese. Fold pastry in thirds again; roll out in rectangle, 4x18 inches (scant ¼-inch thick). Brush with egg yolk mixed with cream. Sprinkle with remaining cheese (use about ¼ cup for each half of pastry). Cut in ¾-inch strips; twist each strip and place on ungreased baking sheet. *Refrigerate one hour.* Bake at 350° F. for 15-20 minutes. Serve cold or warm.

Lois Rising Pogyor

FETA CHEESE TARTS

Preparing: 1 hour *Do Ahead* *Yield: 24*
Baking: 40 minutes *Freeze*

½ cup light cream
½ pound feta cheese
2 eggs
1 clove garlic, crushed
½ teaspoon dried thyme

1 teaspoon cornstarch
Pepper to taste
½ recipe Cream Cheese Pastry,
  chilled (omit salt)
Olives (garnish)

Blend cream, cheese and eggs in blender for 2 minutes. Add cornstarch and seasonings; blend 45 seconds. Preheat oven to 350° F. Evenly press about 2 teaspoons of pastry on bottom and sides of 1½-inch tart pans. Bake 7-8 minutes. Pour 1-2 tablespoons of cheese mixture in each prepared tart shell. Top each with olive slice. Place on cookie sheets and bake 30-35 minutes. Allow to set 5-10 minutes before removing from pans; serve immediately.

Note: Unfilled tart shells can be frozen. Cheese mixture will keep in refrigerator 1-2 weeks.

Carol Myers Anderson

PORK GINGER ROLL

Preparing: 30 minutes *Do Ahead* *Yield: 8 dozen*
Chilling: 1 hour *Freeze*
Baking: 30 minutes

1 recipe Cream Cheese Pastry,
  chilled
1 pound lean ground pork
½ cup crabmeat, flaked
1 teaspoon salt
½ cup minced water chestnuts

2 green onions, minced
½ teaspoon ground ginger
2 tablespoons soy sauce
1 small clove garlic, crushed
1 egg, unbeaten
¼ cup dry bread crumbs

Cook and stir pork in skillet until whitish-looking, not dry or crumbly. Add remaining ingredients; mix well and cool thoroughly. Divide pastry in 4 pieces. Roll each in rectangle about 12x9 inches. Cut in half lengthwise and spread each piece with filling. Press filling lightly into dough. From long side, roll up tightly like jelly-roll. Moisten edges to seal. Place seam down on ungreased baking sheet. Chill 1 hour. Brush with egg-cream mixture; bake at 375°F. 30-35 minutes until golden brown. Cool slightly; cut in 1-inch slices. Serve warm.

Lois Rising Pogyor

CLAMS CASINO

Preparing: 20 minutes   *Yield: 6 clams*
Cooking: 15 minutes
Broiling: 5 to 10 minutes

¼ cup butter
2 onions, minced
2 green peppers, minced
2 pimentos, minced

4 strips bacon, minced
6 cherrystone clams, washed
Rock salt

Put onions, peppers, pimentos, bacon and butter into saucepan; cook over medium heat 5 minutes. Wash and open clams. Place rock salt on sizzle dish (or cast iron skillet). Place approximately 2 tablespoons mixture on top of raw clam or enough to cover. Place clams on salt; broil or bake in hot oven until mixture is browned and heated through.

The Ship Inn
Exton, Pennsylvania

CRAB AND BACON ROLLS

Preparing: 30 minutes   *Do Ahead*   *Yield: 2 dozen*
Baking: 20 minutes

1 (6-ounce) package frozen
  crabmeat
1½ cups fine fresh bread crumbs
¼ cup freshly grated Parmesan
  cheese
1 egg, slightly beaten
¼ cup tomato juice

⅓ cup finely chopped celery leaves
2 tablespoons chopped fresh
  parsley
1 tablespoon finely chopped
  shallots
Salt and pepper
10-12 strips of bacon

Pick over crab to remove all trace of bone and cartilage; flake meat. Place in mixing bowl; add 1 cup bread crumbs, cheese, egg, tomato juice, celery, parsley, shallots and salt and pepper to taste; blend well. If necessary, add more bread crumbs. Mixture should be moist but not soupy. Preheat oven to 400° F. Cut bacon strips in half crosswise and place each half on a flat surface. Mound about 1 tablespoon of crab mixture on one end of each bacon piece and roll up to enclose crab. Fasten with toothpicks; arrange on rack in roasting pan. Bake 20 minutes or until bacon is crisp.

Barbara Alphin Chimicles

CRAB PUFFS

Preparing: 30 minutes   *Do Ahead*   *Yield: 40*
Cooking: 10 to 20 minutes   *Freeze*

10 slices whole wheat bread   Sea salt to taste
12 ounces frozen crab   Pinch of cayenne pepper
8 ounces Swiss cheese, shredded ½ teaspoon dill weed
⅓ cup mayonnaise   Grated Parmesan cheese
2 tablespoons sherry   Paprika
1 tablespoon lemon juice

Preheat oven to 350° F. Remove crusts from bread slices and divide slices into quarters. Bake on cookie sheet 4 minutes; cool. Mix all ingredients except Parmesan and paprika. Place mixture on toasted side of bread; sprinkle lightly with Parmesan and paprika. Place on cookie sheet. *(Can freeze at this point.)* To serve, bake 10 minutes, or until light brown. If frozen, bake 20-25 minutes.

Denise Horton Jackson

MOCK CRAB MOLD

Preparing: 20 minutes   *Do Ahead*   *Yield: 1 quart*
Chilling: 4 hours

1 (16-ounce) can sauerkraut or 2½   2 tablespoons chopped onion
  cups   2 tablespoons chopped pimento
1 pound American cheese,   1 hard-cooked egg, chopped
  shredded   1 tablespoon sugar
¼ cup mayonnaise   ½ teaspoon salt
3 tablespoons chopped green   1 (8-ounce) package cream cheese
  pepper   2-4 tablespoons milk

Drain sauerkraut well and chop with scissors. Combine sauerkraut, American cheese, green pepper, onion, pimento, egg, sugar and salt. Mix well and shape into log or ball. Gradually combine milk with cream cheese until spreading consistency is reached. Spread over log or ball. *Refrigerate at least 4 hours.* Serve with crackers.

Barbara Trimble Blake

BAKED CRABMEAT HORS D'OEUVRES

Preparing: 10 minutes   *Yield: 8 servings*
Baking: 15 minutes

2 (8-ounce) packages cream
  cheese, softened
8 ounces fresh crabmeat
3 tablespoons onion, finely
  chopped

2 tablespoons milk
1 teaspoon horseradish
½ teaspoon salt
Dash pepper
½ cup sliced almonds, toasted

Preheat oven to 375° F. Combine all ingredients except almonds, mixing until well blended. Spoon mixture into small oven-proof dish. Sprinkle with almonds. Bake 15 minutes. Serve with crackers.

Lori Adams DelRossi

CRAB PATÉ

Preparing: 20 minutes   *Do Ahead*   *Yield: 4-cup mold*
Chilling: 4 to 5 hours

1 (10¾-ounce) can cream of
  mushroom soup
1 envelope unflavored gelatin
3 tablespoons cold water
¾ cup mayonnaise
1 (8-ounce) package cream
  cheese, softened

1 (6½-ounce) can crabmeat,
  drained and flaked
1 small onion, grated
1 cup finely chopped celery
Parsley sprigs (garnish)

Heat soup in saucepan. Remove from heat. Dissolve gelatin in cold water. Add to soup, stirring well. Add rest of ingredients except parsley; mix well. Spoon into 4-cup mold. Chill until firm. Unmold and garnish with parsley. Serve with crackers.

Kathleen Harry Andrew

CRABMEAT HORS D'OEUVRES

Preparing: 30 minutes   *Do Ahead*   *Yield: 48*
Baking: 10 minutes   *Freeze*

1 (5-ounce) jar Old English Cheese   ½ teaspoon salt
   spread   ½ teaspoon garlic salt
1 (6½-ounce) can crabmeat   6 English muffins, split
¼ pound plus 1½ teaspoons butter

Preheat oven to 375° F. Mix ingredients and spread on each muffin. *Freeze at least 10 minutes.* Cut each muffin into quarters and bake 10 minutes or until bubbly.

Elizabeth Taylor Young

FRESH SHRIMP SPREAD

Preparing: 20 minutes   *Do Ahead*   *Yield: 1 cup*

15 large cooked shrimp (1-1½   3 teaspoons grated onion
   pounds medium shrimp)   Salt and pepper
½ cup mayonnaise   2 tablespoons dry sherry
5 drops Tabasco sauce   Light cream

Mince shrimp with sharp knife. Add all ingredients except cream. Adjust seasonings. Gradually add enough cream to make mixture easy to spread. Serve with bland crackers.

Mary Ann Parke Mattson

SHRIMP SPREAD

Preparing: 15 minutes   *Do Ahead*   *Yield: 1½ cups*
Chilling: 1 hour

1 (8-ounce) package cream   Dash Worcestershire sauce
   cheese, softened   2 tablespoons or more chili sauce
2 tablespoons lemon juice   1 (4-ounce) can small shrimp

Rinse and clean shrimp well. Mix with remaining ingredients and chill. Serve with crackers.

Kathy Mohn Wilmot

ORIENTAL SHRIMP TOASTS

Preparing: 20 to 25 minutes   *Do Ahead*   *Yield: 32 pieces*
Cooking: 10 minutes   *Freeze*

1 (4½-ounce) can tiny shrimp
⅓ cup finely chopped green onion
½ cup drained bamboo shoots,
  finely chopped
1 clove garlic, minced

½ teaspoon salt
1 egg, well beaten
2 tablespoons cornstarch
8 slices white bread, crust removed
Peanut oil for frying

In a medium bowl, combine shrimp, onions and bamboo shoots. Mash together until pasty. Add garlic, salt, egg and cornstarch; mix thoroughly. Cut bread into triangles. Spread one side of each slice thickly and evenly with shrimp mixture. Set aside.

Hot Dipping Sauce:
½ cup soy sauce
1 clove garlic, minced
2 tablespoons dry sherry

½ teaspoon ground ginger
2 tablespoons thinly sliced green
  onion

In a saucepan, combine all ingredients. Heat just to boiling point. Set aside and keep warm. Heat oil (¾ inch deep) to 375° F. Fry triangles, shrimp side down, until golden brown. Drain on absorbent paper. Serve piping hot with hot dipping sauce.

Note: These may be cooked ahead and frozen after frying. To reheat, place on baking sheet and bake at 325° F. for 10 minutes.

Pam Bartels Morris

PICKLED SHRIMP

Preparing: 20 minutes   *Do Ahead*   *Yield: 8 to 10 servings*
Marinating: 24 hours

1½ cups vegetable oil
¾ cup vinegar
1½ teaspoons salt
2½ teaspoons celery seed
2½ tablespoons capers and juice

Dash hot pepper sauce
2 pounds shrimp, cooked and
  cleaned
1 onion, thinly sliced, separated
  into rings
2-3 bay leaves

Combine all ingredients except shrimp and mix well. Pour sauce over shrimp. Cover with onion; add bay leaves. *Cover and store in refrigerator at least 24 hours.* Drain and serve.

SHRIMP DIVINE WITH FRESH VEGETABLES

Preparing: 15 minutes   *Do Ahead*   *Yield: 1½ to 2 cups*

1 cup sour cream
1 (8-ounce) package cream cheese
1 package mild Italian salad
   dressing mix
2 tablespoons finely chopped green
   pepper

1 (5 to 6-ounce) can small shrimp
Fresh cauliflower, carrot sticks,
   green pepper rings and zucchini
   sticks for dipping

Blend cheese and sour cream with dressing mix. Add remaining ingredients.
Serve with fresh vegetables.

SHRIMP PATÉ

Preparing: 5 minutes   *Do Ahead*   *Yield: 2 cups*
Chilling: 4 hours

2 (6-ounce) cans shrimp
8 ounces cream cheese
1 tablespoon dehydrated onion
1 tablespoon horseradish

1 tablespoon lemon juice
Paprika and chopped parsley
   (garnish)

Mix all ingredients in bowl with mixer. Line round smooth pan with plastic
wrap, sprinkle with paprika and small bits of parsley. Press mixture in pan and
refrigerate. Unmold, garnish and serve with crackers. An inexpensive shrimp
cocktail dish.

Ruth Henderson Campbell

SHRIMP MOLD

Preparing: 15 minutes   *Do Ahead*   *Yield: 15 to 20 servings*
Chilling: Overnight

3 envelopes unflavored gelatin
2 cups cold water
5 (3½-ounce) cans shrimp (drain
   and mash with fingers)

2 onions, finely grated
Juice of 2 lemons
4 cups mayonnaise
1 tablespoon horseradish

Dissolve gelatin in water in double boiler. Mix other ingredients with gelatin.
Place in 5½-cup mold. *Chill overnight.* Serve with party bread slices or
crackers.

Judy Lane Davies

SALMON MOUSSE

Preparing: 30 minutes   *Do Ahead*   *Yield: 4-cup mold*
Chilling: 4 to 6 hours

1 envelope unflavored gelatin   1 (16-ounce) can salmon, flaked
2 tablespoons lemon juice   and cleaned
1 small onion, diced   ½ teaspoon paprika
½ cup boiling water   1 cup heavy cream
½ cup mayonnaise

Empty gelatin into blender. Add lemon juice, onion, and water; cover and
blend. Add mayonnaise, salmon, and paprika; cover and blend. Blending on
low speed, slowly add heavy cream. Pour into greased 4-cup mold; chill well.
Unmold carefully by quickly dipping mold into warm water. Garnish with a few
greens. Serve with party rye, plain melba toast or plain wafers.

Catherine More Keller

SEAFOOD DIP ELEGANTE

Preparing: 10 minutes   *Do Ahead*   *Yield: 2 scant cups*
Cooking: 5 to 10 minutes

1 (8-ounce) package cream cheese   1 teaspoon sugar
¼ cup mayonnaise   Dash seasoned salt
1 clove garlic, minced (⅛ teaspoon   3 tablespoons sauterne (or other
   instant garlic)   dry white wine)
1 teaspoon grated onion   5-6 ounces frozen or canned,
1 teaspoon prepared mustard   lobster, shrimp or crab

Melt cream cheese in medium saucepan over low heat, stirring constantly.
Blend in mayonnaise, garlic, onion, mustard, sugar, and salt. Stir in seafood
and sauterne. Heat through. Pour into small soufflé or casserole and serve hot
with bland crackers.

Note: If doing ahead, heat through when ready to serve.

Lois Rising Pogyor

SHRIMP CANAPÉS

Preparing: 1 hour   *Yield: 36 pieces*

1 (8-ounce) package cream
  cheese, softened
¼ cup sherry
¼ cup sliced green onion
1 loaf party pumpernickel or rye
  bread

36 cucumber slices
1¼ pounds small cooked shrimp,
  shelled, deveined and split
36 radish slices
Crushed dill weed or lemon pepper

Blend cheese, sherry and green onion in bowl, with electric mixer. Spread bread with thin layer of cheese mixture; top each with a cucumber slice and additional cheese mixture. Arrange shrimp halves and radish slice on each; sprinkle with dill and/or lemon pepper.

Carol Madden Pappas

OYSTERS ROCKEFELLER

Preparing: 45 minutes   *Do Ahead: Partially*   *Yield: 9 servings*
Cooking: 5 minutes

6 tablespoons butter
6 tablespoons finely chopped raw
  spinach
3 tablespoons finely chopped
  parsley
3 tablespoons finely chopped
  celery
3 tablespoons finely chopped onion

5 tablespoons fine dry bread
  crumbs
Few drops Tabasco
½ teaspoon salt
36 oysters on half-shell
Rock salt
½ teaspoon Pernod or Anisette
  (optional)

Melt butter in saucepan and stir in all ingredients, except oysters and rock salt. Cook over low heat, stirring constantly for 15 minutes. Work through sieve or food mill and set aside. Line bottom of shallow baking pan with coarse rock salt and place oysters on the half-shell on top. Put one teaspoon of vegetable mixture on each oyster. Broil under preheated 400° F. broiler 3-5 minutes or until topping begins to brown.

Salads, Salad Dressings and Soups

BRYN MAWR STATION
BRYN MAWR, PENNA.

Bryn Mawr

In the 1860's, the Pennsylvania Railroad built the Bryn Mawr Hotel to attract summer visitors to the area. Summer guests soon wanted to become year-round residents. Homes built with railroad money were sold for "not less than $5,000." Stores, shops, livery stables and "buildings for an offensive occupation" were prohibited in the residential development.

Bryn Mawr College, the area's first college for women, opened its doors to students in 1885. It was founded by the Society of Friends in response to community encouragement.

Potpourri Buffet

hors d'oeuvre

Stuffed Mushrooms   Ham and Cheese Cubes

entrée

Eye of Round Roast   Easy Chicken Divan

vegetable

Potatoes Romanoff   Steamed Carrots with Parsley

salad

Cold Pea Salad

bread

Irish Sweet Bread

dessert

Chocolate Intemperance Cake

beverage

Champagne Punch

COLD AVOCADO SOUP

Preparing: 10 minutes   *Yield: 4 servings*
Chilling: 4 hours

1 large avocado   ½ cup light cream
1 clove garlic   Chopped chives, dill or parsley
1½ cups canned chicken broth   (garnish)
⅛ teaspoon liquid hot pepper
   seasoning

Place avocado, broth, garlic and hot pepper seasoning in blender and mix for 15 seconds. Add cream and mix for additional 10 seconds. Chill and serve cold with chopped greens.

Note: This can be doubled or tripled, but check taste before tripling garlic or hot pepper seasoning.

Alice Marks Preston

BLACK BEAN SOUP

Preparing: 20 minutes   *Do Ahead*   *Yield: 6 to 8 servings*
Soaking: 12 hours
Cooking: 1½ hours

1 cup black beans   4 sprigs parsley
1 onion, finely chopped   2 bay leaves
1 carrot, peeled and diced   2 tablespoons lemon juice
2 cloves garlic, minced   2 tablespoons Madeira or sherry
2 tablespoons butter   Salt and pepper
6 cups chicken or beef broth   1 cup sour cream (garnish)

Soak beans, if necessary (some black beans do not require presoaking). Sauté onion, carrot and garlic in butter. Bring broth to a boil; add sautéed vegetables. Add drained beans, parsley and bay leaves. Cover and simmer over low heat 1½ hours, until beans are soft. Remove parsley and bay leaves. Purée ¾ of soup in blender. Return blender portion to remaining soup; heat, adding lemon juice and sherry. Check seasoning, adding salt and pepper if necessary. Serve hot or cold with garnish of sour cream.

Frances Marincola Blair

BOOKY'S MANHATTAN STYLE CLAM CHOWDER

Preparing: 45 minutes   *Yield: 2 quarts*
Cooking: 1 hour

8 bullnose clams or 12 cherry stones
2 quarts cold water
2 small peeled potatoes, diced in about half-inch cubes
½ cup butter
1½ ounces vegetable oil
½ small onion, finely minced
2 stalks celery, chopped fine
½ medium-sized green pepper, finely minced
1 clove garlic, finely minced

2 teaspoons salt
1 teaspoon white pepper
1 teaspoon thyme
1 teaspoon marjoram leaf
1 teaspoon dry mustard
3 chicken bouillon cubes
½ cup of non-baking flour
3 teaspoons paprika
1 teaspoon Worcestershire sauce
1 pinch poultry seasoning
1 (28-ounce) can tomatoes
Parsley (garnish)

Wash clams thoroughly in cold water. Put clams in 4-quart saucepan with 2 quarts cold water; bring to a full boil. Strain juice through cheese cloth or fine strainer. Set clam juice on low heat until ready to use. At same time, boil potatoes in water until soft but *not mushy;* drain and set aside. In 4-quart saucepan, add butter and 1½ ounces vegetable oil. When butter is thoroughly melted, add onion, celery, green peppers, garlic, salt, pepper, thyme, marjoram, mustard and bouillon. Sauté over medium heat about 15 minutes or until vegetables are soft. Add flour, paprika, Worcestershire and poultry seasoning. Stir with a wire whisk. Cook about 5 minutes; add 1½ quarts of hot strained clam juice. Continue to stir until mixture thickens. Let cook about 15 minutes, stirring constantly. If mixture is still too thick, add more clam juice. Add tomatoes and minced clams. Stir to keep clams from settling. Let cook 15 minutes; add potatoes and cook about 10 minutes. Remove from heat and serve. Top with parsley.

Note: If fresh clams are not available, these may be substituted: 1 quart frozen minced clams, thawed or 1 quart can minced clams, strained (discard liquid) plus 2 quarts clam juice, heated.

Bookbinders—South 15th Street
Philadelphia, Pennsylvania

EASY CONNOISSEUR SOUP

Preparing: 5 minutes   *Yield: 4 servings*
Cooking: 10 minutes

1 (10¾-ounce) can cream of   1 (10¾-ounce) can consommé
   tomato or tomato soup   ½ (10¾-ounce) soup can of sherry
1 (10¾-ounce) can split pea soup

Stir undiluted soups together and heat through. Stir in sherry and serve.

Julie Nixon Eisenhower

CALIFORNIA CONSOMMÉ

Preparing: 10 minutes   *Yield: 8 servings*
Cooking: 10 minutes

8 cups chicken broth   2 lemons, thinly sliced
2 avocados, peeled and thinly   8 tablespoons sherry
   sliced   ½ cup chopped fresh parsley

Heat broth to near boiling in medium-sized saucepan. Place thin slices of avocado (about ¼ of an avocado per person) and 2-3 lemon slices in bottom of each soup bowl. Ladle hot chicken broth over fruit. Add 1 tablespoon sherry to each serving; sprinkle parsley on top.

CAULIFLOWER AND ONION SOUP

Preparing: 20 minutes   *Do Ahead*   *Yield: 4 servings*
Cooking: 30 minutes

1 cup chopped onion   ¾ cup milk
2 tablespoons butter   ½ cup heavy cream
2 tablespoons flour   Cayenne, salt, pepper
2½ cups chicken broth   Minced parsley (garnish)
2 cups cauliflower flowerets

Sauté onion until soft; stir in flour and cook 3 minutes. Add broth; whisk until smooth. Add cauliflower; simmer 30 minutes. Purée in blender. Add milk, cream and seasonings to purée. Heat thoroughly. Garnish with minced parsley.

CHICKEN SPINACH SOUP

Preparing: 2 hours   *Yield: 6 servings*

6 chicken legs
4 chicken breasts
Salt to taste
½ pound fresh or 1 (10-ounce)
** package frozen spinach**

Meatballs
1 package narrow noodles
4-5 eggs, beaten (optional)

Simmer chicken in 3-5 quarts boiling water for about 1¼ hours. Strain broth. Cool chicken, debone, and cut into 1-inch pieces. Partially cook spinach, drain and chop; add to broth. Prepare meatballs; add to broth and spinach. Cook noodles according to package directions; add with chicken to broth. Add more water if soup is too thick. If desired, add eggs to broth while hot.

Meatballs:
1½ pounds ground sirloin
4 tablespoons parsley
½ cup cheese (Romano or
** Picorino), grated**
Salt and pepper to taste

3 cloves garlic, chopped
4 eggs
4 slices bread, soaked in water and
** drained**

Mix ingredients until smooth. Shape into *tiny* meatballs, about size of quarter; fry and drain.

Mary Jane Palmieri Durkin

CHICKEN VELVET SOUP

Preparing: 45 minutes   *Yield: 6 servings*
Cooking: 20 minutes

2 whole cooked chicken breasts
¾ cup butter
¾ cup flour
1 cup milk, warmed

6 cups chicken stock, divided
1 cup heavy cream, warmed
½ teaspoon salt
Dash pepper

Bone and cube chicken. In a 3-quart saucepan, melt butter; blend in flour. Gradually add warm milk, 2 cups of chicken stock and warm cream, stirring constantly. When well-blended, simmer for at least 20 minutes. Add chicken, remaining chicken stock and seasonings. *Do not boil.* Serve hot.

Pam Bartels Morris

CHICKEN CORN SOUP

Preparing: 1 hour   *Do Ahead*   *Yield: 4 to 6 servings*
Cooking: 3 hours   *Freeze*

4-5 pound stewing chicken
1 onion, sliced
1 stalk celery, diced
1-2 dozen ears of fresh corn

2-3 diced hard-cooked eggs
1 (16-ounce) can cream-style corn
(optional)

Stew chicken in 3-4 quarts water, with onion and celery, until tender. Remove chicken, debone and put into broth. Cut corn off cobs and milk cobs by scraping with knife. Cook corn in broth 10 minutes. After it boils, add hard-cooked eggs and cream-style corn. Serve hot.

Nancy Bowen Rainey

CHEDDAR CHEESE SOUP

Preparing: 10 minutes   *Do Ahead*   *Yield: 12 to 16 servings*
Cooking: 2 hours

½ cup butter
4 large stalks celery, diced
2 carrots, diced
½ medium onion, diced
½ cup flour
¾ teaspoon paprika
8 cups chicken stock

½ pound sharp Cheddar cheese,
shredded
1 quart half and half, heated or 2
cups milk plus 2 cups light
cream, heated
1½ teaspoons Worcestershire
sauce

In large kettle melt butter. Add celery, carrots and onion; cook until vegetables are soft. Add flour and paprika; cook, stirring until mixture is bubbly. Add chicken stock, stirring until mixture is smooth. Simmer covered, 1 hour. Add cheese, heated half and half and Worcestershire. Continue cooking, stirring constantly just until cheese is melted and mixture is heated through.

Ann Keenan Seidel

CORN CHOWDER

Preparing: 30 minutes   *Do Ahead*   *Yield: 6 to 8 servings*
Cooking: 15 to 20 minutes

2 medium onions   1 bay leaf
2 tablespoons butter   ¼ teaspoon celery salt
1½ cups chicken broth   1 (16-ounce) can creamed corn
2 cups diced potatoes   2 cups milk
Salt and pepper to taste

Sauté onions in butter. In saucepan, combine onions, broth, potatoes, and seasonings. Cook, covered, about 15-20 minutes or until potatoes cook through. Add corn and milk; heat through. For richer soup, use 1 cup half and half in place of milk.

Charity Power Folk

COLD CUCUMBER SOUP

Preparing: 30 minutes   *Do Ahead*   *Yield: 6 servings*
Chilling: 3 hours

1 tablespoon butter   ¼ cup cold water
1 small onion, chopped   1 cup sour cream
2½ large cucumbers, peeled,   Salt and pepper to taste
   seeded and sliced   6 cucumber slices
1 quart boiling chicken broth   6 dill sprigs
3 tablespoons snipped fresh dill
½ envelope unflavored gelatin
   (omit if using broth with high
   gelatin content)

Melt butter over medium heat. Cook onion until soft, not brown; add sliced cucumbers and stir 1 minute. Add broth and snipped dill; simmer 10-15 minutes or until cucumber is tender. Soften gelatin in cold water, add to soup; stir until dissolved. Remove from heat and stir in sour cream. Whirl in blender to purée. Strain into bowl and add salt and pepper to taste. Chill at least 3 hours. Garnish with cucumber slices and dill.

Note: Best if made a day ahead.

Catherine More Keller

GAZPACHO

Preparing: 25 minutes   *Do Ahead*   *Yield: 8 servings*
Chilling: 2 hours

5 large tomatoes, peeled and cored   5 beef bouillon cubes
1 cucumber, peeled   3 cups boiling water
1 large onion   1 tablespoon Worcestershire sauce
1 green pepper   ¼ cup vegetable oil
2 cloves garlic   ¼ cup vinegar

Blend vegetables in blender (do about ½ at a time). Dissolve bouillon cubes in boiling water. Add vegetables, Worcestershire, oil and vinegar. *Chill and serve very cold.* May be necessary to stir well before serving.

Robin Truitt Hayman

SUNDAY SOUP

Preparing: 40 minutes   *Do Ahead*   *Yield: 6 servings*
Cooking: 50 minutes

1½ pounds ground beef   2 (16-ounce) cans tomatoes,
1 egg, slightly beaten   undrained
3 tablespoons water   1 envelope dry onion soup mix
½ cup soft bread crumbs   3 cups carrots, pared and sliced
¼ teaspoon salt   ½ cup chopped celery tops
1 tablespoon chopped parsley   ¼ cup fresh chopped parsley
2 tablespoons margarine   ½ teaspoon pepper
4 cups water   ½ teaspoon oregano
2 (10½-ounce) cans beef broth,   ½ teaspoon dried basil
   undiluted   1 bay leaf

To make meatballs, in medium bowl combine beef, egg, water, bread crumbs, salt and parsley. Mix lightly; shape into 24 balls. Melt margarine in 5-quart Dutch oven; sauté meatballs, single layer at a time, until browned on all sides. Drain off fat; set aside. In same Dutch oven, combine remaining ingredients; bring to a boil. Reduce heat; simmer 30 minutes, covered. Stir occasionally to break up tomatoes. Add meatballs and simmer 20 minutes longer. Serve in tureen or individual bowls. Garnish with chopped parsley.

Grace Burdett Nellis

MINESTRONE SOUP

Preparing: 1¼ hours   *Do Ahead*   *Yield: 4 servings*
Cooking: 2 hours

1 cup dried white Navy beans
2 (10¾-ounce) cans condensed
  chicken broth
1 small head cabbage (1½ pounds)
4 carrots (½ pound)
2 medium potatoes (¾ pound)
1 (1-pound) can Italian style
  tomatoes
Salt

2 medium onions (½ pound)
¼ cup olive or vegetable oil
1 stalk celery
2 zucchini (½ pound)
1 large fresh tomato
1 clove garlic
¼ teaspoon pepper
¼ cup chopped parsley
1 cup broken-up thin spaghetti

Day before: In bowl, cover beans with cold water. Refrigerate, covered, overnight. *Next day,* drain. Pour chicken broth into a 1-quart measure, add water to make 1 quart. Pour into 8-quart kettle with 2 more quarts water, 2 teaspoons salt and beans. Bring to a boil. Reduce heat; simmer, covered, 1 hour. Meanwhile, wash cabbage and quarter; remove core and slice each quarter thinly. Pare carrots; slice diagonally, ¼-inch thick. Pare potatoes; cut into ½-inch cubes. Add to soup with canned tomatoes. Cover; cook ½ hour longer. Peel onions and slice thinly. In ¼ cup hot oil in medium skillet, sauté onion, stirring about 5 minutes. Remove from heat. Slice celery diagonally, ⅛-inch thick. Wash zucchini; slice into rounds ¼-inch thick. Peel tomato; cut into ½-inch cubes. Press garlic. Add celery, zucchini, tomato and garlic to onion with ½ teaspoon salt and the pepper. Cook slowly, uncovered, stirring occasionally 20 minutes. Add to bean mixture with ¼ cup parsley and spaghetti. Cover and cook slowly 30 minutes, stirring occasionally.

Elise Rice Payne

CRAB SOUP

Preparing: 20 minutes   *Do Ahead*   *Yield: 4 to 8 servings*
Cooking: 10 minutes

1 (10¾-ounce) can pepper pot   1 (13-ounce) can evaporated milk
   soup, undiluted   1 (7-ounce) can crabmeat
1 (10¾-ounce) can chicken rice   ¼-½ cup sherry
   soup, undiluted

Drain crab and rinse well with tap water; drain again. Examine crab for shell
and membranes. Combine soups and milk. Add crab; heat to a simmer *(do not
boil)*. Add sherry and serve.

Carol Nelson DeVol

CREAM OF LEEK AND MUSHROOM SOUP

Preparing: 15 minutes   *Freeze*   *Yield: 1 gallon*
Cooking: 35 minutes

6 tablespoons butter   2 (46-ounce) cans chicken broth
½ cup chopped onions   4 cups cubed potatoes
2 cloves garlic, chopped   ½ teaspoon salt
4 cups chopped leeks   ½ teaspoon pepper
¼ cup chopped parsley   ½ teaspoon dried tarragon
1 pound mushrooms, sliced   2 cups heavy cream

In very large saucepot, melt butter; add onion and garlic; cooking until soft.
Add leeks; cook until soft. Add parsley and mushrooms; cook 5 minutes. Add
potatoes and enough chicken broth to cover; simmer until potatoes are cooked
(approximately 15 minutes). Run mixture through a food mill. Return to saucepot; add remaining chicken stock, salt, pepper and tarragon. Simmer 10 minutes. Add heavy cream; heat through and adjust seasoning. Serve hot.

Note: If frozen, soup should be defrosted and whisked to blend. Recipe may
be halved.

"Breads and Soups" by Susan Norcini
"The Cooking School" at Waterloo Gardens, Inc., Devon, Pennsylvania

HUNGARIAN MUSHROOM SOUP

Preparing: 40 minutes   Yield: 6 to 8 servings
Cooking: 40 minutes

½ cup butter, divided
2 onions, chopped
2 green peppers, chopped
2 carrots, grated
2 cloves garlic, minced
1 tablespoon sweet Hungarian
   paprika
1½ pounds mushrooms, sliced
½ pound mushrooms, unsliced

½ teaspoon basil
5 cups chicken broth
Salt and pepper, to taste
1 cup sour cream
2 tablespoons chopped fresh dill
1 tablespoon butter, melted
2 tablespoons flour
Fresh parsley and dill (garnish)

Sauté onions in butter 5 minutes. Add peppers, carrots and garlic; sauté 5 minutes. Add paprika and sauté 3 minutes more. Add more butter as needed. Put mixture into pot. Sauté mushrooms in butter in small batches 3-5 minutes; add to vegetables. Add basil and chicken broth; salt and pepper to taste. Simmer slowly ½ hour. Dip out 1 cup of broth; mix with sour cream, stirring until smooth. Stir into pot; add chopped dill. Blend butter and flour; thicken soup with blended mixture. Simmer 10 minutes. Garnish with fresh dill and parsley.

Columbia Hotel
Phoenixville, Pennsylvania

SPRIG O' SPRING SOUP

Preparing: 10 minutes   Do Ahead   Yield: 4 (1-cup) servings
Cooking: 10 to 15 minutes

2 (10-ounce) cans condensed
   cream of asparagus soup
2¾ cups milk or half and half
   cream

½ bunch watercress (about ¼ cup)
¼ teaspoon basil
Dash black pepper

Blend all ingredients for 2 minutes in blender. Pour into saucepan and heat. Stir occasionally; do not let boil. Garnish with sprig of watercress.

Pam White Brotschul

MUSHROOM BISQUE

Preparing: 30 minutes   *Do Ahead*   *Yield: 2 quarts*
Cooking: 30 minutes

1 pound fresh mushrooms	1 cup heavy cream
1 quart chicken broth	1 teaspoon salt
1 medium onion, chopped	White pepper
7 tablespoons butter	Tabasco sauce
6 tablespoons flour	2 tablespoons sherry (optional)
3 cups milk	

Wash mushrooms; cut off stems. Slice 6 caps and reserve. Discard any dried ends from stems. Grind or chop remaining caps and stems very fine. Simmer, covered, in broth with onion for 30 minutes. Sauté reserved caps in 1 tablespoon butter and reserve for garnish. Melt remaining butter in saucepan; add flour and stir with wire whisk until blended. Bring milk to boil and add all at once to flour mixture, stirring vigorously with whisk until sauce is thickened and smooth. Add cream. Combine mushroom-broth mixture with sauce and season to taste with salt, pepper, and Tabasco. Reheat and add sherry before serving. Garnish with sautéed sliced mushrooms.

Jeanne Kronmiller Honish

MUSHROOM AND DILL SOUP

Preparing: 25 minutes   *Yield: 6 to 8 servings*

2-3 tablespoons clarified butter	1 cup heavy cream
1 pound mushrooms, sliced	3 cups chicken stock
1 medium onion, chopped	¼ teaspoon salt, to taste
1 bunch fresh dill	⅛ teaspoon pepper, to taste
1 clove garlic, minced	
2 medium potatoes, boiled and chopped	

Sauté mushrooms, onions, dill and garlic in butter. Purée ½ of sautéed mixture with potatoes. Combine purée plus remaining sautéed mixture with cream and stock. Season to taste. Reheat to warm through.

Carolanne Flagg
Illusions Restaurant, Bryn Mawr, Pennsylvania

MUSHROOM AND BARLEY SOUP

Preparing: 30 minutes   *Do Ahead*   *Yield: 10 to 12 servings*
Cooking: 15 minutes

1 Spanish onion
1 bunch parsley
2 carrots
2 stalks celery
2 cloves garlic, finely chopped
3 tablespoons butter
3 tablespoons flour
3 quarts chicken stock

¾ pound mushrooms,
  finely chopped
1 teaspoon salt
1 teaspoon pepper
¼ teaspoon nutmeg
½ teaspoon thyme
½ pound barley

Soak barley in water at least 1 hour. Finely chop onion, parsley, carrots and celery; blend well. In saucepan, sauté blended vegetables and garlic in butter. When translucent, add flour and stir. Add chicken stock, mushrooms, salt, pepper, nutmeg and thyme. Bring to a simmer; add barley and simmer 15 minutes. Correct seasoning.

Note: Soup is best if made in advance and then reheated. If soup is too thick when reheated, add more chicken stock.

Frog Restaurant
Philadelphia, Pennsylvania

ONION WINE SOUP

Preparing: 20 minutes   *Do Ahead*   *Yield: 6 to 8 servings*
Cooking: 30 minutes

¼ cup butter
5 large onions, chopped
5 cups beef broth
½ cup celery leaves
1 large potato, sliced
1 cup dry white wine

1 tablespoon vinegar
2 teaspoons sugar
1 cup light cream
1 tablespoon minced parsley
Salt and pepper

Melt butter in large saucepan. Add chopped onion; mix well. Add beef broth, celery and potato. Bring to boiling. Cover; simmer 30 minutes. Purée mixture in blender. Return to saucepan; blend in wine, vinegar and sugar. Bring to boiling; simmer 5 minutes. Stir in cream, parsley and salt and pepper to taste. Heat thoroughly but do not boil.

Nancy Reagan
First Lady

MUSHROOM-SHRIMP CHOWDER

Preparing: 50 minutes   *Do Ahead*   *Yield: 6 servings*

1 pound fresh mushrooms, sliced
1½ cups water
1 teaspoon salt
¼ cup chopped onion
3 tablespoons butter
¼ cup flour

½ teaspoon salt
⅛ teaspoon pepper
½ cup heavy cream
2 cups chopped cooked shrimp
2 tablespoons dry sherry
(optional)

Combine mushrooms, water and salt in saucepan; bring to boil. Reduce heat and cover; simmer 10 minutes. Drain mushrooms, reserving liquid. Sauté onion in butter. Add flour, salt and pepper. Mix well. Stir in reserved liquid gradually and cook, stirring constantly until mixture boils and thickens. Remove from heat; add cream, shrimp and mushrooms. Serve at once if hot soup is desired. Chill if cold soup is desired. *This is a thick chowder. If you prefer more liquid, increase water, flour and cream proportionately.*

Variation: Add to sauce 2 tablespoons dry sherry mixed with 1 teaspoon cornstarch; stir bringing to a boil for 2 minutes. Serve over toast or rice.

Bonnie Kennedy Beverly

SAUSAGE SOUP

Preparing: 1 hour
Cooking: 3 hours

Do Ahead
Freeze

Yield: 8 servings

1 pound ground beef
1 pound Polish sausage
½ teaspoon seasoned salt
¼ teaspoon oregano
¼ teaspoon basil
1 tablespoon soy sauce
1 cup sliced celery

1 cup sliced carrots
⅓ cup dried split peas
1 envelope dry onion soup
1 (28-ounce) can tomatoes
6 cups hot water
1 cup elbow macaroni, uncooked
Parmesan cheese, grated

Brown meats and drain. Add everything except macaroni; simmer 1-2 hours. One hour before serving, stir in macaroni and simmer until done. Serve with Parmesan cheese.

Elizabeth Taylor Young

HEARTY PEA SOUP

Preparing: 20 minutes
Cooking: 1 hour 20 minutes

Do Ahead
Freeze

Yield: 6 to 8 servings

1 pound dry green split peas
7 cups water
Ham bone or ham hocks
1 cup coarsely chopped carrots
½ cup chopped onions

1 (16-ounce) can tomatoes, cut up
½ cup green pepper, chopped
½ cup chopped celery
Salt to taste

Soak peas in water 1 hour; drain and rinse. In Dutch oven combine peas, water, ham, carrots and onion. Bring to boil; reduce heat; cover and simmer 1 hour or until peas are tender. Remove ham bone; cut off meat. Set aside; discard bone. Press half pea mixture through a food mill (or blender or food processor) until smooth. Return to Dutch oven. Stir in meat. Add undrained tomatoes, green pepper and celery; simmer 20 minutes. Season to taste with salt and pepper.

Note: Good served with whole wheat muffins.

Elizabeth Vanden Heuvel von dem Hagen

SPINACH HERB SOUP

Preparing: 30 minutes   *Do Ahead: Partially*   *Yield: 8 servings*

2 tablespoons butter
⅓ cup chopped green onions and
  tops
2 tablespoons finely chopped
  parsley
2 tablespoons finely chopped
  chives
1 cup watercress, chopped

1 cup chopped lettuce
1 cup chopped fresh spinach
½ teaspoon salt
⅛ teaspoon pepper
½ teaspoon dried tarragon,
  crushed
4 (10½-ounce) cans consommé
½ cup light cream

Melt butter in large saucepan; add all ingredients except consommé and cream. Cook over low heat 15 minutes. Pour in consommé and continue cooking 15 minutes. Before serving, stir in cream and bring just to a boil. Whirl the vegetables in a blender if you prefer smooth-textured soup.

Jeanne Kronmiller Honish

CREAM OF SPINACH SOUP

Preparing: 10 minutes   *Do Ahead: Partially*   *Yield: 6 servings*
Cooking: 25 minutes

⅓ cup minced green onions
1 tablespoon butter
3-4 packed cups of fresh spinach
½ teaspoon salt
3 tablespoons flour

5½ cups boiling chicken broth
2 egg yolks
½ cup heavy cream
1-2 tablespoons softened butter
Parsley (garnish)

Wash, dry and finely chop spinach. In a covered saucepan, cook onions slowly in butter 5-10 minutes, until tender and translucent but not browned. Stir in spinach and salt. Cover; cook slowly 5 minutes or until leaves are tender and wilted. Sprinkle in flour; stir over moderate heat 3 minutes. Remove from heat; beat in boiling stock. Simmer 5 minutes; purée through food mill. Return to saucepan; season if necessary. (If not serving immediately, set aside uncovered. Reheat to simmer before proceeding.) Blend yolks and cream in mixing bowl; beat in 1 cup hot soup by driblets. Gradually beat in rest of soup in thin stream. Return to saucepan; stir over moderate heat 1-2 minutes to poach yolks. *Do not bring soup to a simmer.* Remove from heat; stir in butter 1 tablespoon at a time. Pour into tureen or soup cups; garnish with a sprig of parsley.

Note: If spinach is finely chopped, do not puree.

SPINACH SOUP

Preparing: 15 minutes   *Yield: 6 servings*
Cooking: 20 minutes

1 pound spinach
2 tablespoons butter
6-8 thin scallions, finely chopped
1 clove garlic, crushed
1 tablespoon flour

6 cups chicken broth
Salt and pepper
½ cup freshly grated Parmesan
  cheese

Remove heavy stems from spinach and wash carefully. Shred spinach into small pieces. In saucepan, sauté scallions in melted butter; add garlic, then spinach. Cover and steam spinach for 8 minutes until it has wilted but remains bright green in color. Stir in flour. Add chicken broth and simmer 5 minutes. Season with salt and pepper, if necessary. Serve with Parmesan cheese.

Sydney Davis Regan

WINTER TOMATO SOUP

Preparing: 15 minutes   *Yield: 6 servings*
Cooking: 20 minutes

½ cup celery
2 tablespoons butter or bacon
  drippings
1 (1-pound) can stewed tomatoes
1 (10½-ounce) can consommé or
  chicken broth
½ cup dry wine or ½ cup additional
  stock

1 tablespoon instant minced onion
  or 3 tablespoons chopped green
  onion
1 tablespoon lemon juice
1 tablespoon cornstarch blended
  with ½ cup water
Dash curry powder
Cheese croutons (optional)

Sauté celery in butter until tender (about 5 minutes). Add remaining ingredients, except croutons; blend well. Simmer 15-20 minutes stirring occasionally. Garnish with croutons.

Jeanne Kronmiller Honish

CREAM OF WATERCRESS SOUP

Preparing: 20 minutes   *Do Ahead: Partially*   *Yield: 8 servings*

3 bunches watercress
3 tablespoons butter
¼ cup minced onion
1½ cups water
1 teaspoon salt
½ teaspoon white pepper

2 tablespoons flour
2 (13-ounce) cans chicken broth
2 cups milk
2 egg yolks
1 cup heavy cream

Rinse and drain watercress; remove coarse stems. Melt 1 tablespoon butter in saucepan; add onion and cook until golden. Add watercress, water, salt and pepper. Cook over high heat 5 minutes; cool slightly. Put in blender for a few seconds on high speed. Melt remaining 2 tablespoons butter in saucepan; stir in flour. Add chicken broth and milk; bring to a boil. Stir in watercress mixture. *(Can be done ahead to this point).* Beat yolks and heavy cream together; stir 1 cup of the hot soup into egg cream mixture. Add this mixture to hot soup, stirring constantly. Heat thoroughly, but *do not boil.*

Sandra Schild Fletcher

POTAGE CRESSONAIRE
(Watercress Soup)

Preparing: 30 minutes   *Do Ahead: Partially*   *Yield: 5 to 6 servings*
Cooking: 35 minutes

2 tablespoons butter
2 leeks, cleaned and chopped
3 medium-sized potatoes, peeled
    and sliced
2 (10¾-ounce) cans chicken broth

2 cans water
1 bunch fresh watercress, chopped
Salt and pepper to taste
1 cup heavy cream
Watercress leaves (garnish)

Heat butter in saucepan without letting it brown; add leeks and sauté without browning. Add potatoes, chicken broth and water; bring to a boil and simmer 30 minutes. Add watercress, salt and pepper to taste; simmer for 2 minutes. Cool soup and put through blender. Add cream and reheat gently, *but do not boil.* Garnish with watercress leaves. *Can be served cold.*

Pam Bartels Morris

VEGETABLE CHOWDER

Preparing: 35 minutes   *Yield: 6 servings*
Cooking: 20 minutes

2 tablespoons butter
1 medium onion, chopped
1 green pepper, chopped
1 tablespoon flour
2 medium potatoes, diced
1 (8-ounce) package frozen corn
2 carrots, cooked and sliced

8 ounces chicken stock
10 ounces milk
4 ounces sliced mushrooms,
    drained
2 teaspoons salt
½ teaspoon pepper
8 ounces heavy cream

Melt butter. Add onion and green pepper; cook until soft. Stir in flour to make paste; set aside. Place potatoes, corn and carrots in a large pot; add milk and broth; bring to boil. Pour small amount of liquid into onion paste. Add to potato mixture. Add mushrooms, cover and reduce heat. Simmer 20 minutes, stirring occasionally. Season with salt and pepper. Add cream and blend. Serve at once.

Bonnie Kennedy Beverly

HEARTY TURKEY SOUP

Preparing: 20 minutes   *Do Ahead*   *Yield: 4 to 6 servings*
Cooking: 30 minutes

1 tablespoon butter
2 tablespoons chopped onion
1 teaspoon curry powder
1 cup diced potatoes
½ cup diced carrots
½ cup diagonally sliced celery
3 cups turkey broth
Salt and pepper to taste

½ (10-ounce) package frozen
    French-style green beans
1 cup diced cooked turkey
½ teaspoon dried oregano
1 tablespoon minced parsley
13 ounces evaporated milk
2 tablespoons flour

Melt butter; cook onion until transparent. Stir in curry powder; cook 1-2 minutes. Add potatoes, carrots, celery, broth, salt and pepper. Bring to a boil. Lower heat; cook 10-15 minutes. Stir in green beans, turkey, oregano and parsley. Continue cooking until vegetables are barely tender, but crisp. Combine milk and flour; stir in gently until well-blended. Soup should be slightly thick.

Gwen Fields Gilmore

VICHYSSOISE

Preparing: 1 hour   *Do Ahead*   *Yield: 3 quarts*
Chilling: 3 hours or overnight

¼ cup butter
1½ cups chopped onions or leeks
3½ cups chicken broth
4 cups diced potatoes
½ teaspoon salt

½ teaspoon garlic salt
½ teaspoon celery salt
2 cups half and half cream
White pepper
Finely chopped chives

In soup kettle, sauté onions in butter until soft, but not brown. Add 1 cup of broth; simmer, covered, for 10 minutes. Add remaining broth, potatoes, salt, garlic salt, and celery salt. Cover and cook over low heat until potatoes are soft, 15-20 minutes; cool. Pour mixture into blender in small batches; blend until smooth. Stir in cream. Season with pepper and additional salt, to taste. Mix well. *Refrigerate several hours or overnight.* Serve cold garnished with chives.

Pam Bartels Morris

VICHYSSOISE AND AVOCADO SOUP

Preparing: 15 minutes   *Do Ahead*   *Yield: 6 to 8 servings*
Chilling: 1 to 2 hours

1 quart vichyssoise (divided in half)
2-3 ripe avocados, peeled and
   diced
1 cup half and half cream
1 cup sour cream

1-2 tablespoons lemon juice
Salt
⅛ teaspoon white pepper
Dash Tabasco sauce
Lemon wedges

In blender, combine half the vichyssoise with the avocados; blend until smooth. In a mixing bowl, add blended mixture to remaining vichyssoise. Stir in sour cream, half and half, lemon juice and seasonings. Serve cold with lemon wedges.

Note: For additional zip, add ¼ teaspoon Tabasco and/or ½ teaspoon Worcestershire sauce.

Pam Bartels Morris

SHRIMP BISQUE

Preparing: 45 minutes   *Do Ahead*   *Yield: 12 servings*

2½-3 pounds shrimp
¾ cup butter
¾ cup flour
7½ cups milk
3 cans shrimp soup (undiluted)

3 cups heavy cream
Salt and pepper to taste
Worcestershire sauce to taste
¾-1 cup sherry

Cook shrimp; shell, devein and chop slightly. Melt butter; stir in flour. Add milk, stir until thickened. Add soup, cream, shrimp, salt and pepper, Worcestershire and sherry. *May be made ahead and kept on low.*

Note: Recipe can be cut in half easily without losing quality. Serves 8-12 as a first course when cut in half.

Pam Bartels Morris

COLD ZUCCHINI SOUP

Preparing: 25 minutes   *Do Ahead*   *Yield: 8 servings*
Cooking: 15 minutes   *Freeze*

2 tablespoons olive oil
2 tablespoons butter
2 onions, thinly sliced
1 clove garlic, minced
6 small or 3 medium zucchini,
   washed and sliced

5 cups chicken broth
2 tablespoons mixed fresh herbs,
   finely chopped (parsley, chives,
   oregano, basil, dill)
2 or 3 teaspoons lemon juice
Salt and pepper to taste

Heat oil and butter in large pot. Add onion and garlic; cook over low heat about 10 minutes. (Do not allow to brown.) Add zucchini; continue cooking 5 minutes longer, stirring occasionally. Add chicken broth; simmer, covered, 15 minutes or until zucchini is just tender. Purée in blender or processor. Add herbs, lemon juice, salt and pepper. *Chill or freeze as desired.* Serve cold.

Kessler's Cutlery & Cookware
Spread Eagle Village, Strafford, Pennsylvania

BRAN SPINACH SALAD

Preparing: 30 minutes   *Do Ahead: Partially*   *Yield: 8 servings*

¼ cup butter
1½ teaspoons chopped chives
1 teaspoon dried basil
¾ teaspoon paprika
½ teaspoon dried dill weed
1 cup wheat bran cereal, flakes, or
  buds

4 cups torn spinach leaves
4 cups torn lettuce leaves
4 hard-cooked eggs, sliced
1 cup halved cherry tomatoes
¼ pound fresh mushrooms, sliced

Preheat oven to 350° F. In shallow baking pan, combine butter, chives, basil, paprika and dill weed. Place in oven 3 minutes or until butter is melted; stir to mix. Add bran; mix and return to oven for 5 minutes or until bran is slightly toasted. Remove and cool. In large bowl combine remaining ingredients; sprinkle in bran mixture and add mustard dressing. Toss lightly; serve immediately.

Mustard Dressing:
1 tablespoon Dijon mustard
½ teaspoon salt
¼ teaspoon pepper
1½ tablespoons lemon juice

¼ cup red wine vinegar
½ cup vegetable oil
1 tablespoon parsley, chopped

Mix ingredients with a whisk or shake in a jar.

Ann Keenan Seidel

MAJESTIC SPINACH SALAD

Preparing: 35 minutes   *Do Ahead*   *Yield: 8 servings*
Chilling: 12 hours

1 quart washed torn spinach
2 cups sliced mushrooms
1 cup red onion rings
1 (10-ounce) package frozen peas,
  uncooked

1 cup mayonnaise
½ teaspoon sugar
1 teaspoon curry powder
8 slices bacon, cooked crisp and
  crumbled

Remove stems from spinach. Layer first 4 ingredients in large bowl. Mix mayonnaise, sugar and curry powder. Top salad with this mixture. Cover with foil and *refrigerate overnight*. Mix and top with bacon before serving.

Jan Carmst Rhein

WILTED SPINACH SALAD

Preparing: 20 minutes   *Do Ahead: Partially*   *Yield: 4 servings*

½ pound spinach (1 pound for
   larger salad)
4 slices bacon
1 small white onion, finely minced

2 teaspoons salt
1 teaspoon pepper
6 tablespoons white wine vinegar

Cut stems off spinach, wash leaves well, drain in colander. Chop spinach. Cook bacon until browned and crisp; remove, drain on paper towels, and crumble. Add bacon, minced onion, salt and pepper to spinach. Add vinegar to bacon fat, bring to a boil, stir and pour over the spinach. Serve immediately, while spinach is still crisp.

Jeanne Kronmiller Honish

GREEN AND WHITE SALAD BOWL

Preparing: 1 hour   *Do Ahead*   *Yield: 25 servings*
Chilling: 12 hours

1 head iceberg lettuce, washed
   and torn
¾ pound fresh spinach, washed
   and torn
1 small onion, chopped
1 large cucumber, peeled and
   thinly sliced

1 head cauliflower
1 (10-ounce) package frozen peas,
   cooked one minute
Bleu cheese dressing
Chopped nuts

In a large glass bowl, layer all vegetable ingredients. Cover salad with dressing, sealing to edges; *refrigerate at least 12 hours.* Sprinkle with chopped nuts just before serving.

Bleu Cheese Dressing:
1 pint sour cream
1 (8-ounce) package cream cheese
2 tablespoons mayonnaise

4-6 ounces bleu cheese
Salt and pepper to taste

Mix all ingredients well; chill.

Note: This can be cut in half.

Eloise Taylor Ewing

GREEK SALAD

Preparing: 20 minutes   *Do Ahead*   *Yield: 6 to 8 servings*

1 large head iceberg lettuce
6 scallions, bulb only
1 large cucumber, peeled and
    thinly sliced
2 tablespoons finely chopped fresh
    parsley or watercress
6 radishes, sliced
½ green bell pepper, slivered
¼ cup olive oil
¼ cup corn oil

¼ cup tarragon or wine vinegar
⅛ teaspoon salt
¼ teaspoon black pepper
10 capers
½ teaspoon Worcestershire sauce
6-8 wedges feta cheese
2 large ripe tomatoes, quartered
2 large Greek olives (or black)
6-8 anchovy filets

Cut lettuce in half from top to base. Lay flat; with sharp knife slice thinly, then shred. Place in a large salad bowl; add scallions, cucumbers, parsley or watercress, radishes and green pepper. *Cover and refrigerate until serving.* Place oils, vinegar, salt, pepper, capers and Worcestershire in a jar; seal and refrigerate. Just before serving, shake dressing well and pour over salad and toss thoroughly. Garnish with feta cheese, tomatoes, olives and anchovies.

BOSTON LETTUCE SALAD
WITH L'AUBÉRGE HOUSE DRESSING

Preparing: 20 minutes   *Do Ahead: Partially*   *Yield: 8 servings*
Chilling: 24 hours

2 heads Boston lettuce
1 red onion, sliced in rings

½ pound fresh mushrooms, sliced

Combine ingredients; toss in L'Aubérge House Dressing.

Dressing:
1 cup olive oil
1 cup peanut oil
2 cloves garlic, crushed
¼ cup white wine vinegar

3 tablespoons Worcestershire
    sauce
1 teaspoon salt

In a small bowl combine oils and garlic; let stand 24 hours. Strain oil into another small bowl, discarding garlic; whisk in vinegar, Worcestershire, and salt. Store dressing in covered container at room temperature; shake before using. Makes about 2½ cups.

LETTUCE-CAULIFLOWER SALAD

Preparing: 20 minutes   *Do Ahead*   *Yield: 8 to 10 servings*
Chilling: 12 hours

1 head lettuce, torn into bite-sized
  pieces
1 onion, chopped
1 head cauliflower, broken into
  bite-sized pieces
1 pound bacon, fried crisp,
  crumbled

2 cups mayonnaise
⅓ cup sugar
¼ cup grated Parmesan cheese
Salt and pepper to taste

In a large bowl, layer lettuce, onion, cauliflower and bacon. In a separate bowl, mix mayonnaise, sugar, and cheese; season to taste with salt and pepper. Spread dressing over salad to seal. Cover tightly. *Refrigerate overnight.* Toss before serving.

Dede Dubois Shimrak

OVERNIGHT SALAD

Preparing: 1 hour   *Do Ahead*   *Yield: 12 servings*
Chilling: Overnight

½ head lettuce
½ pound fresh spinach
6 hard-cooked eggs, chopped
½ pound ham, cut in julienne strips
½ pound Swiss cheese, cut in
  julienne strips
1 red onion, sliced

1 (6-ounce) package frozen crab or
  shrimp (optional)
1 cup sour cream
1 cup mayonnaise
½ pound grated Parmesan cheese
Sour cream and chive croutons
  (garnish)

Wash and dry lettuce and spinach; tear into pieces. In a large salad bowl, layer lettuce and spinach, then eggs, ham and cheese. Top with onion and seafood. Mix sour cream, mayonnaise and cheese; spread over top of salad to seal. *Cover and refrigerate overnight.* Toss before serving, adding croutons.

Denise Horton Jackson

MANDARIN ORANGE-LETTUCE SALAD

Preparing: 25 minutes   *Do Ahead*   *Yield: 8 servings*
Chilling: 1 hour

1½ heads lettuce
2 cups chopped celery
3 tablespoons minced parsley
6 whole green onions, chopped

3 small cans mandarin oranges,
  drained
¾ cup slivered almonds, toasted

Wash lettuce; break into bite-sized pieces. Combine all ingredients and chill.

Dressing:
1½ teaspoons salt
¾ teaspoon Tabasco sauce
¾ cup oil

6 tablespoons sugar
6 tablespoons tarragon vinegar

Mix all dressing ingredients except oil; whisk in oil. Toss dressing with salad just before serving.

MARINATED VEGETABLE SALAD

Preparing: 30 minutes   *Do Ahead*   *Yield: 8 to 10 servings*
Chilling: 4 to 12 hours

1 head cauliflower
1 onion, sliced
4-6 small zucchini, diced
1 green pepper, diced

½ cup diced celery
1 cup olives, sliced
1 tablespoon chopped parsley
½-¾ cup sugar

Clean cauliflower; break into flowerets. Combine all ingredients; mix well.

Dressing:
¾ cup oil
½ cup red wine vinegar
½ cup cider vinegar
1 teaspoon dry mustard

1 tablespoon salt
1 teaspoon celery seed (optional)
2 tablespoons sugar

Combine all ingredients in small saucepan. Bring to a boil and pour over vegetables. Cover and refrigerate at least 4 hours, *preferably overnight*, before serving.

SALAD BY COMMITTEE

Preparing: 1 hour   *Yield: 24 to 30 servings*
Marinating: 3 to 4 hours

2 pounds cooked chicken or turkey
   breast, diced
2 pounds cooked ham, diced
2 pounds Cheddar cheese,
   shredded
2 pounds bacon, fried and
   crumbled
1 dozen eggs, hard-cooked, grated
3-4 ripe avocados, diced
1 pound fresh mushrooms, thinly
   sliced

1 (7¾-ounce) can pitted ripe olives,
   thinly sliced
2 bunches radishes, thinly sliced
2 bunches green onions, thinly
   sliced
2 (6-ounce) jars marinated
   artichoke hearts, diced (reserve
   juice)
1½ pints cherry tomatoes, halved
5-6 heads of lettuce, preferably
   mixed greens

Dressing:
1 cup salad oil
⅓ cup wine vinegar
Reserved artichoke juice
½ teaspoon dry mustard

½ teaspoon garlic powder
1 teaspoon sugar
½ teaspoon salad herbs
Salt and pepper to taste

Mix oil, vinegar, artichoke juice and seasonings to make dressing. Marinate mushrooms and artichoke hearts in dressing 3 to 4 hours. When ready to serve, mix all remaining ingredients together in very large wooden bowl. Toss with dressing, mushrooms, and artichoke hearts.

Note: This is a favorite of a group who picnic together. Each person brings one ingredient. They like it with Sangria, warm muffins and brownies. To serve 8-10, use ¼ to ⅓ of ingredients.

Kathleen Gilligan English

SPINACH SALAD

Preparing: 30 minutes   *Do Ahead: Partially*   *Yield: 6 to 8 servings*

1 package fresh spinach
½ pound fresh mushrooms, sliced
1 (12-ounce) can sliced water
  chestnuts
1 (14-ounce) can bean sprouts,
  drained

7 strips bacon, cooked crisp and
  crumbled
3 hard-cooked eggs, crumbled

Clean and trim spinach; drain and break into bite-sized pieces. Add remaining ingredients to spinach. Toss lightly with dressing and serve chilled.

Dressing:
1 cup vegetable oil
½ cup sugar
⅓ cup catsup

1 tablespoon Worcestershire sauce
1 teaspoon salt
1 medium onion, diced

Mix dressing ingredients together, blending well.

Denise McCarthy Brown

MIXED GREEN SALAD WITH BLEU CHEESE DRESSING

Preparing: 30 minutes   *Do Ahead: Partially*   *Yield: 12 to 16 servings*
Chilling: 1 hour

1 cup sour cream
3 ounces bleu cheese, crumbled
¼ cup thinly sliced green onions
  with tops
1 tablespoon lemon juice
1 teaspoon sugar

½ teaspoon salt
½ teaspoon celery seed (optional)
¼ teaspoon pepper
1 pound fresh spinach
2 small heads Boston lettuce or 1
  head iceberg lettuce

Combine sour cream, half the cheese, onion, lemon juice, sugar, salt, celery seed and pepper in blender. Blend until almost smooth; add remaining cheese, so consistency will be lumpy. Chill. Wash greens; pat dry. Tear into pieces. Toss with dressing in salad bowl. If making dressing for daily use, it will keep for 1 week.

Ann Bateman Capers

SUNSHINE SALAD

Preparing: 15 minutes   *Yield: 6 to 8 servings*

1 head lettuce
2 cups orange sections
½ mild white onion, sliced and
    separated into rings

⅓ cup mild Italian salad dressing
½ cup walnut croutons

Lightly toss lettuce, orange sections and onion with salad dressing. Top with walnut croutons.

Walnut Croutons:
1 tablespoon butter
¼ teaspoon salt

½ cup chopped walnuts

Melt butter; add salt and walnuts. Stir over medium high heat until crisp.

Sandra Pocius Mowry

ARTICHOKE RICE SALAD

Preparing: 15 minutes   *Do Ahead*   *Yield: 8 servings*
Marinating: 3 hours
Chilling: 1 hour

1 package chicken flavored Rice-
    A-Roni
4 scallions, chopped
½ cup chopped green peppers
12 pimento olives, sliced

1 (14-ounce) can artichoke hearts
⅔ cup Italian dressing
¾ teaspoon curry
½ cup mayonnaise

Cook rice according to package directions; chill. Add onions, peppers and olives to chilled rice. Marinate artichokes in ⅔ cup Italian dressing, 3 hours. Drain artichokes; reserve marinade. Cut artichokes in quarters; add to rice. Mix curry with mayonnaise and add marinade. Pour over rice mixture. Chill.

Lin Bricker Kilburn

ARTICHOKE SALAD

Preparing: 10 minutes   *Do Ahead*   *Yield: 6 servings*
Marinating: Overnight

1 (9-ounce) can artichoke hearts,   ½ cup vegetable oil
    drained and quartered   ¼ cup cider vinegar
1 (10-ounce) package frozen baby   1 teaspoon salt
    peas, uncooked   ½ teaspoon sugar
1 cup celery, sliced diagonally   ¼ teaspoon pepper
½ cup pitted green olives

Put vegetables, except celery, in a bowl; combine dressing ingredients and pour over vegetables. *Let marinate overnight in refrigerator.* Add celery several hours prior to serving. Drain and serve on a bed of bibb or romaine lettuce.

Linda Zajicek Moore

BEAN AND ARTICHOKE SALAD

Preparing: 30 minutes   *Do Ahead*   *Yield: 6 servings*
Chilling: 2 hours

2 (9-ounce) packages frozen Italian   Lettuce
    style green beans, cooked
1 (9-ounce) package frozen
    artichoke hearts, cooked

Dressing:
¼ cup red wine vinegar   ½ teaspoon salt
1 teaspoon onion juice   ½ teaspoon oregano
¼ cup diced pimento   ¼ teaspoon rosemary
½ cup vegetable or olive oil   ¼ teaspoon pepper

Cook beans and artichoke hearts separately according to package directions. Drain, cool and pat dry; cover and chill. Combine all dressing ingredients except pimento. Lightly toss beans, artichoke hearts and pimento with dressing; chill well. To serve, drain salad from dressing and place on bed of lettuce. Serve dressing on side if desired.

Regina Shehadi Guza

AVOCADO AND GRAPEFRUIT SALAD
WITH CELERY SEED DRESSING

Preparing: 20 minutes   *Do Ahead*   *Yield: 8 servings*

2 (16-ounce) cans grapefruit   Watercress (garnish)
   sections   1 cup pomegranate seeds or
1 ripe avocado, peeled and sliced   cranberries (garnish)

Drain grapefruit; reserve juice. Brush avocado slices with juice. Arrange grapefruit sections and avocado slices on small plates. Add watercress trim; sprinkle with pomegranate seeds or sweetened halved cranberries. Pass celery seed dressing.

Dressing:
⅔ cup sugar   ⅓ cup honey
1 teaspoon dry mustard   ⅓ cup vinegar
1 teaspoon paprika   1 tablespoon lemon juice
1 teaspoon celery seed   1 teaspoon grated onion
¼ teaspoon salt   1 cup vegetable oil

Mix dry ingredients; blend in honey, vinegar, lemon juice and onion. Add oil in slow stream beating constantly with electric or rotary beater.

COUNTRY PEA SALAD

Preparing: 15 minutes   *Do Ahead*   *Yield: 8 servings*
Chilling: 1 hour

1 (1-pound) can English peas or 1   ¼ cup chopped pimento
   (10-ounce) package frozen tiny   2 hard-cooked eggs, chopped
   peas, cooked   ⅛ teaspoon pepper
2 tablespoons minced onion   ½ cup mayonnaise
¼ cup minced celery   ¼ teaspoon salt
½ cup Cheddar cheese, cut in ½-
   inch cubes

Mix all ingredients and chill.

Note: Can be made several hours before serving.

Elizabeth Taylor Young

COLD PEA SALAD

Preparing: 10 minutes   *Do Ahead*   *Yield: 6 to 8 servings*
Chilling: Overnight

1 cup sour cream
1 teaspoon seasoned salt
¼ teaspoon lemon pepper
¼ teaspoon garlic salt
1 (20-ounce) bag frozen peas,
   thawed

1 (6½-ounce) jar artichoke hearts,
   drained
½ pound bacon, cooked and
   crumbled
2 medium tomatoes, diced or 1 cup
   cherry tomatoes
1 small red onion, thinly sliced

Combine sour cream, seasoned salt, lemon pepper and garlic salt in a bowl. Add peas, artichoke hearts, bacon, tomatoes and onion; mix well. *Chill overnight.* Great with grilled meat and French bread.

Susan Collins Stevens

HEARTS OF PALM SALAD

Preparing: 30 minutes   *Do Ahead: Partially*   *Yield: 6 to 8 servings*
Chilling: 1 hour

2 cans hearts of palm
1 head bibb lettuce

Stuffed olives slices (garnish)
Regency dressing

Cut hearts of palm into lengthwise strips. Serve on bibb lettuce. Garnish with stuffed olive slices. Serve with Regency dressing.

Regency Dressing:
1 tablespoon flour
2 cups chicken bouillon
1 tablespoon finely chopped onion
1 clove garlic
½ cup vegetable oil

2 tablespoons French-style
   mustard
Salt and pepper to taste
½ cup vinegar
1 egg yolk, lightly beaten

Mix flour thoroughly with ½ cup chicken bouillon. Bring remaining 1½ cups bouillon to a boil; stir in flour mixture. Cook 5 minutes over medium heat, stirring constantly; remove from heat. Purée onion and garlic in ¼ cup vegetable oil in a blender; transfer to mixing bowl. Add mustard, seasonings, vinegar and egg yolk; mix. Add remaining oil very slowly, beating constantly. Add hot stock while continuing to beat. *Cool to room temperature before refrigerating.*

POTATO SALAD

Preparing: 1½ hours   *Do Ahead*   *Yield: 10 to 12 servings*
Marinating: 3 hours or overnight

3 pounds unpared medium   1½ teaspoons salt
    potatoes (about 10), well
    scrubbed

In a 5-quart Dutch oven, pour just enough boiling water over unpeeled potatoes to cover; add salt. Simmer covered, until potatoes are fork-tender, not
mushy (30-35 minutes). Drain; cool 20 minutes.

Marinade:
1 teaspoon salt   ¼ cup cider vinegar
1 teaspoon dry mustard   ½ cup salad oil
⅛ teaspoon pepper   ¼ cup chopped green onion
Dash of cayenne

Combine all ingredients. Peel warm potatoes; slice, ¼-inch thick, into large
bowl. Cover with marinade; toss gently to coat well. *Refrigerate covered, 3
hours or overnight, tossing potatoes several times.* Potatoes will absorb
marinade.

Dressing:
1¼ cups mayonnaise   3 hard-cooked eggs, peeled and
1 cup coarsely chopped celery   coarsely chopped

Add celery, hard-cooked eggs and mayonnaise to potatoes. Toss gently.

Mary Murtagh Krull

MARINATED BEAN SALAD

Preparing: 15 minutes   *Do Ahead*   *Yield: 10 to 12 servings*
Marinating: Overnight

1 (28-ounce) can green beans,
   drained
1 (28-ounce) can yellow beans,
   drained
1 (28-ounce) can red kidney beans,
   drained, rinsed with water
1 onion, thinly sliced
½-¾ cup sugar
⅓ cup oil

3 tablespoons prepared mustard
⅔ cup red wine vinegar
1 teaspoon salt
1 small green pepper, chopped
   (optional)
Pimento (optional)
Chick peas (optional)
2 cups chopped celery (optional)

Toss beans and onion in salad bowl; add any optional vegetables. Mix sugar, oil, mustard, vinegar and salt; heat to a boil. Pour over beans and chill. Let marinate overnight for best flavor.

Donna Nelson Brown

TABBOULEH SALAD

Preparing: 30 minutes   *Do Ahead*   *Yield: 6 to 8 servings*
Chilling: 8 hours or overnight

1 cup fine bulgar (cracked wheat)
1 pound fresh tomatoes, peeled,
   seeded and chopped
2 cups chopped green onions
3 cups chopped parsley
¼ cup chopped fresh mint

½ cup olive oil
⅓ cup fresh lemon juice
1¼ teaspoons salt
½ teaspoon ground pepper
Pine nuts (optional)

Rinse wheat, cover with boiling water and let stand 30 minutes. Drain and squeeze dry in cheesecloth. Combine tomatoes, onions, parsley and mint. Beat oil, lemon juice, salt and pepper; fold into tomato mixture. Mix in wheat. *Chill 8 hours or overnight.* Serve on lettuce leaves.

Note: This salad is a nice accompaniment to lamb. Can also be served in pita bread.

Eve Pantellas Walker

SALADE NICOISE

Preparing: 1 hour   *Do Ahead*   *Yield: 12 servings*
Marinating: 3 hours or overnight

3 cups cold blanched green beans
3 or 4 tomatoes, quartered
1½ cups vinaigrette with herbs
    (see below)
1 head Boston lettuce, separated,
    washed and drained
3 cups cooked potatoes, peeled
    and sliced

1 cup canned tuna chunks, drained
½ cup pitted black olives
2 or 3 cold, hard-cooked eggs
6-12 (1 can) canned anchovy filets,
    drained
Minced fresh parsley

Marinate potatoes in ½ cup vinaigrette. Before serving, season beans and to-matoes with few spoonfuls of vinaigrette. Toss lettuce with vinaigrette and place in bottom of bowl. Arrange potatoes, beans, tomatoes, tuna, olives, quartered eggs and anchovies in a design on top of greens (stripes or concentric circles). Pour rest of dressing over salad. Sprinkle with minced parsley.

Vinaigrette:
¼ cup wine vinegar
¼ cup lemon juice
1 tablespoon dry mustard
1 teaspoon salt
1½ cups vegetable oil (or ½ olive
    oil and ½ vegetable oil)

Pepper to taste
¼ cup minced green onion
    (optional)
¼ teaspoon tarragon (optional)

Shake vinegar, lemon juice, mustard and salt in a jar. Add oil slowly and shake. If desired, stir in green onion and tarragon.

Judy Grenamyer Donohue

SAUSAGE, RICE AND VEGETABLE SALAD

Preparing: 30 minutes   *Do Ahead*   *Yield: 6 servings*
Chilling: 1 hour

2 cups chicken stock
1 cup rice
1 pound sweet Italian sausage
2 tablespoons vegetable oil
1 cup thinly sliced zucchini
¾ cup chopped green pepper
¾ cup chopped red pepper

¼ cup chopped onion
1 (15-ounce) jar artichoke hearts,
    quartered
16 pitted ripe olives, halved
Lettuce
Sliced tomatoes (garnish)

Bring chicken stock to a boil; add rice. Simmer covered until liquid is absorbed. Cool in large bowl. Sauté sausage in oil until browned; cool. Cut into thin slices; add to rice. Mix in remaining ingredients. Toss with dressing; chill. Arrange on lettuce; garnish.

Dressing:
½ cup olive oil
2 tablespoons wine vinegar
1 garlic clove, minced

½ teaspoon dry mustard
¼ teaspoon salt
⅛ teaspoon pepper

Whisk ingredients in small bowl.

Mary Ann Davidson Berry

CHILLED NOODLE SALAD

Preparing: 30 minutes   *Do Ahead*   *Yield: 8 to 10 servings*
Chilling: 2 to 3 hours

1 (16-ounce) package green
    spinach noodles
½ cup chopped scallions
½ cup Italian dressing

½-¾ cup sour cream
½-¾ cup mayonnaise
Sunflower seeds
Pimentos, chopped

Cook and drain noodles according to package directions; toss in serving bowl with Italian dressing. Add scallions. Mix sour cream and mayonnaise together and mix with noodles. Sprinkle sunflower seeds and pimento over mixture and toss. Chill 2-3 hours.

Emilie Pontius Christensen

STUFFED LETTUCE WITH SAUCE

Preparing: 20 minutes   *Do Ahead*   *Yield: 4 to 8 servings*
Chilling: 12 hours

1 (8-ounce) package cream   2 tablespoons minced green onion
  cheese, softened   1 medium head of iceberg lettuce
¼ cup mayonnaise
½ cup chopped olives with
  pimento

Beat cream cheese until fluffy. Stir in mayonnaise, olives and onion. Core lettuce. (Pound bottom of lettuce head on counter and remove core.) Cut in half. Remove center leaving a 1-inch shell, fill with cheese mixture. Put halves back together and wrap in aluminum foil.

Sauce:
½ cup mayonnaise   ¾ teaspoon chili powder
¼ cup catsup   Dash Tabasco sauce
2 teaspoons vinegar

Mix mayonnaise with catsup, chili powder and Tabasco; cover. Chill lettuce and dressing overnight. To serve, cut into wedges and serve with dressing.

Pam White Brotschul

EGG SALAD FOR DIETERS

Preparing: 10 minutes   *Do Ahead*   *Yield: ¾ cup*

2 hard-cooked eggs, chopped   1 tablespoon Dijon mustard
¼ cup plain yogurt   1 tablespoon sweet pickle relish
2 tablespoons finely chopped onion   (optional)
¼ cup diced celery   1 teaspoon curry powder (optional)

Combine all ingredients; blend gently. Chill.

Frances Marincola Blair

SEAFOOD SALAD

Preparing: 15 minutes   *Do Ahead*   *Yield: 12 servings*
Chilling: 30 minutes

1 (16-ounce) package fine egg   2 cups crabmeat
   noodles   1 onion, finely chopped
2 (13-ounce) cans tuna fish

Cook noodles according to package directions; drain and cool. Add tuna, crab and onion to noodles. Add dressing and toss. Chill.

Dressing:
½ cup mayonnaise   ½ cup sour cream
2 tablespoons vinegar   2 tablespoons sugar
2 tablespoons cream

Combine ingredients and blend well.

Note: Recipe may be halved.

Nancy Lynch Rivenburgh

WILD RICE SEAFOOD SALAD

Preparing: 35 minutes   *Do Ahead*   *Yield: 6 servings*
Chilling: 1 to 2 hours

½ cup wild rice   Dash pepper
½ cup brown rice   1 (6½-ounce) can minced clams,
1 tablespoon instant chicken   drained
   bouillon granules   1 (7-ounce) can shrimp, drained
⅓ cup vegetable or olive oil   2 tablespoons snipped parsley
3 tablespoons white wine vinegar   6 lettuce cups
1 teaspoon sugar   Tomato wedges (garnish)
1 teaspoon dried tarragon, crushed   Pitted ripe olives (garnish)

In saucepan, bring 3 cups water, rices, and bouillon to a boil. Reduce heat, cover and simmer 45 minutes or until rice is tender; cool. Combine oil, vinegar, sugar, tarragon and pepper; stir into rice mixture. Carefully fold in clams, shrimp and parsley. Cover and chill. Serve in lettuce cups. Garnish with tomato wedges and ripe olives.

Frances Marincola Blair

AVOCADO AND SHRIMP SALAD

Preparing: 30 minutes   *Do Ahead*   *Yield: 4 servings*
Marinating: 2 hours

3 tablespoons olive oil
2 tablespoons white wine vinegar
  (preferably French)
1 teaspoon Dijon mustard
1 pound fresh shrimp, cooked,
  deveined and cubed
1 cup mayonnaise
2 tablespoons chili sauce
1 large clove garlic, crushed
Hot pepper sauce

Salt and freshly ground pepper
1 large ripe avocado
Juice of ½ lemon
2 tablespoons finely minced fresh
  dill
2 tablespoons finely minced fresh
  chives
Dill sprigs, lemon wedges and
  avocado slices (garnish)

Whisk together oil, vinegar and mustard until well blended. Add to shrimp; toss thoroughly, cover and marinate 2 hours. Whisk mayonnaise, chili sauce, garlic, hot pepper sauce, salt and pepper until smooth; set aside. Drain shrimp. Cube avocado and toss with lemon juice. Add cubed avocado, dill and chives to shrimp and toss slightly. Fold in enough mayonnaise mixture to coat lightly. Taste and adjust seasoning. Cover and chill until serving time. Divide salad on chilled plates; garnish with dill sprigs, lemon wedges and avocado slices. Serve immediately.

Catherine More Keller

EXOTIC LUNCHEON SALAD

Preparing: 1 hour   *Do Ahead*   *Yield: 12 servings*
Chilling: 3 hours

2 quarts (3 pounds) coarsely cut
  cooked turkey
1 (20-ounce) can water chestnuts
2 pounds seedless grapes
2 cups sliced celery
2-3 cups toasted slivered almonds
3 cups mayonnaise

1 tablespoon curry powder
2 tablespoons soy sauce
Boston or Bibb lettuce
1 (1-pound 13-ounce) can
  pineapple chunks or 1 (20-
  ounce) can litchi nuts (garnish)

Slice or dice water chestnuts, mix with turkey. Wash grapes, add with celery and 1½-2 cups toasted almonds. Mix mayonnaise with curry powder and soy sauce. (Few tablespoons lemon juice may be added.) Combine with turkey mixture. Chill for several hours; spoon into nests of lettuce. Sprinkle with remaining almonds and garnish with litchi nuts or pineapple chunks on each serving. (Easy recipe to multiply.)

Jeanne Kronmiller Honish

SPINACH AND SHRIMP SALAD

Preparing: 10 minutes   *Do Ahead: Partially*   *Yield: 10 servings*

¼ cup mayonnaise
2 tablespoons vegetable oil
2 tablespoons olive oil
2 tablespoons tarragon vinegar
2 tablespoons Dijon mustard
Salt and pepper
2 pounds fresh spinach, washed,
  stems removed

8 slices cooked bacon, drained and
  crumbled
10 fresh mushrooms, thinly sliced
½ pound tiny cooked shrimp
  (about 1½ cups)
2 cups croutons

In a small bowl, mix mayonnaise, oils, vinegar and mustard. Season with salt and pepper to taste; cover and refrigerate until ready to use. Place spinach, bacon, mushrooms, shrimp and croutons in a large salad bowl; add dressing and toss thoroughly.

Ann Keenan Seidel

BEEFEATER SALAD

Preparing: 30 minutes   *Do Ahead*   *Yield: 6 servings*

¼ pound mushrooms, sliced
2 tablespoons butter
1 pound cooked beef, cut into
   julienne strips
2 potatoes, peeled, boiled and
   diced

1 green pepper, chopped
1 onion, chopped
1 stalk celery, chopped
1 dill pickle, chopped
Parsley and hard-cooked eggs,
   sliced (garnish)

Dressing:
1 cup vegetable oil
¼ cup red wine tarragon vinegar
1 teaspoon lemon juice
1 teaspoon salt
1 teaspoon dry mustard
1 teaspoon minced fresh chives

1 teaspoon chopped parsley
1 teaspoon tarragon
½ teaspoon Worcestershire sauce
¼ teaspoon pepper
¼ teaspoon thyme

Sauté sliced mushrooms in butter until golden; set aside. In large bowl, combine mushrooms, beef, potatoes, green pepper, onion, celery and dill pickle. To prepare dressing, combine all ingredients and shake well. Pour over salad. *Chill at least 24 hours.* Serve on a bed of lettuce and garnish with parsley and egg slices.

Jeanne Kronmiller Honish

CURRIED CHICKEN SALAD

Preparing: 15 minutes   *Do Ahead*   *Yield: 8 to 10 servings*
Chilling: 1 to 2 hours

1 (4-pound) chicken, cooked
½ cup diced celery
1 tart apple, peeled and diced
3 teaspoons grated onion
1 cup seedless grapes, halved

½ cup toasted slivered almonds
3 teaspoons curry powder
1½ cups mayonnaise
1 teaspoon salt
Dash pepper

Remove chicken from bones; dice. Mix remaining ingredients and combine with chicken. Chill.

Suzanne O'Neil Goodman

CHICKEN SALAD WITH LIME CURRY DRESSING

Preparing: 30 minutes   *Do Ahead*   *Yield: 4 to 6 servings*
Chilling: 1½ hours

2 cups cooked chicken
2 cups cooked rice, chilled
2 green onions, chopped

2 cups cubed melon (cantaloupe or
    honeydew)
2 tablespoons sliced almonds

Combine all ingredients; set aside.

Dressing:
¾ cup mayonnaise
Juice of 3 limes
1 tablespoon grated lime peel

1 teaspoon curry
1 teaspoon salt
¼ teaspoon pepper

Combine ingredients; pour over salad when served.

Sheila Widmer Connors

CHICKEN SALAD ELEGANT

Preparing: 1 hour   *Do Ahead: Overnight*   *Yield: 8 servings*
Chilling: 1 hour

4 cups cubed, cooked chicken
1½ cups chopped celery
3 green onions, sliced
1 (5-ounce) can water chestnuts
2 medium pieces candied ginger

1 teaspoon salt
1 cup mayonnaise
½ cup heavy cream, whipped
½ cup toasted almonds, slivered

Drain and slice water chestnuts. Finely cut up ginger. Mix chicken, celery, onion, water chestnuts, ginger and salt. Fold mayonnaise into whipped cream, mix with chicken. *Chill 1 hour before serving.* Garnish with slivered almonds.

Note: Cook chicken in stock of water just to cover with a little white wine, 1 piece of celery, 1 carrot, 1 onion quartered, and a piece of ginger. Cook until tender. *Let chicken cool in liquid overnight before cubing.*

Ann Bateman Capers

CHICKEN AND LOBSTER SALAD

Preparing: 20 minutes   *Do Ahead*   *Yield: 4 to 6 servings*
Marinating: 1 hour

1 whole cooked chicken breast
½ pound lobster meat
3 hard-cooked eggs
1 cup finely chopped celery
1 cup mayonnaise
2 tablespoons chili sauce

1 tablespoon chopped chives
⅛ teaspoon salt
½ cup whipped cream
2 cups shredded lettuce or cabbage
French dressing

Cut chicken meat into julienne strips; dice lobster. Prepare French dressing. Add chopped egg whites and celery; marinate in refrigerator 1 hour. Mash or sieve egg yolks and blend with mayonnaise, chili, chives and salt. Fold in whipped cream; chill. *To serve:* Make a bed of lettuce in salad bowl. Mix chicken, lobster and dressing; place on lettuce.

French Dressing:
1 teaspoon salt
½ teaspoon black pepper
¼ teaspoon dry mustard
¼ teaspoon Dijon mustard
Few drops lemon juice

2 tablespoons tarragon vinegar
6 tablespoons vegetable oil
2 tablespoons olive oil
Chopped garlic to taste

Mix ingredients in jar and shake.

Jeanne Kronmiller Honish

CRUNCHY TUNA SALAD

Preparing: 10 minutes   *Do Ahead*   *Yield: 6 servings*
Chilling: 1 hour

1 (9-ounce) can tuna, drained
    and flaked
2 cups cooked peas
2 cups diced raw carrots
2 cups diced celery
2 tablespoons finely chopped
    onion

¼ cup chopped pimento
¼ cup Italian dressing (Good
    Seasons preferred)
1 tablespoon lemon juice
1 teaspoon salt
1 (5-ounce) can Chinese chow
    mein noodles

Combine all ingredients except noodles; chill thoroughly. Add noodles just before serving. Serve on bed of lettuce, if desired.

Sandra Perski Berg

TUNA MACARONI SALAD

Preparing: 20 minutes   *Do Ahead*   *Yield: 8 to 10 servings*
Chilling: 4 hours

3 cups macaroni
1 cup mayonnaise
4 tablespoons sweet and sour salad
    dressing
⅛ teaspoon pepper
4 tablespoons thinly sliced
    scallions

½ cup finely diced green pepper
¾ teaspoon salt
2 (12½-ounce) cans tuna, drained
2 hard-cooked eggs
1 cup diced tomatoes
3 tablespoons chopped parsley

Cook macaroni; drain and set aside. Blend mayonnaise, dressing, salt and pepper in large bowl. Add scallions, green pepper, tuna, eggs and macaroni; toss together and mix well. Fold in tomatoes and parsley; chill at least 4 hours.

Note: If you want macaroni to be predominant, use only one can (12½-ounce) tuna.

Nancy Evans Breitling

CRANBERRY TUNA MOLD

Preparing: 40 minutes   *Do Ahead*   *Yield: 8 to 10 servings*
Chilling: 4 to 6 hours

1 envelope unflavored gelatin
¼ cup cold water
¼ cup boiling water
2 (6½-ounce) cans tuna

1 cup mayonnaise
1 cup chopped celery
1 onion, chopped

Soften gelatin in cold water and dissolve in boiling water. Add remaining ingredients; mix and spoon into 8x8-inch pan. Chill to firm; add topping. Chill several hours.

Topping:
1 (3¼-ounce) package lemon
   gelatin
¾ cup boiling water

1 cup (8-ounce can) jellied
   cranberry sauce, melted and
   cooled
¼ cup orange juice

Mix gelatin in boiling water. Add cranberry sauce and orange juice; spoon over tuna.

Note: This can be made in a bundt pan; tuna is on top when unmolded. Chicken or turkey can be substituted for tuna.

Joan Stievater Lindstrom

TUNA SALAD FOR DIETERS

Preparing: 10 minutes   *Do Ahead*   *Yield: ¾ cup*
Chilling: 20 minutes

3 ounces water-packed tuna
¼ cup diced celery

¼ cup diced onion
2 tablespoons plain yogurt

Combine ingredients; chill 20 minutes before serving.

Frances Marincola Blair

CUCUMBER RING MOLD

Preparing: 20 minutes   *Do Ahead*   *Yield: 8 servings*
Chilling: 4 hours

2 (3-ounce) packages lime gelatin
2 cups boiling water
2 teaspoons cider vinegar
2 tablespoons hot horseradish
2 teaspoons grated onion
1 large cucumber, peeled and
   grated

1 cup mayonnaise (do not use
   imitation)
Salad greens and cucumber slices
   to garnish

In a bowl, mix gelatin, water and vinegar; cool. Add horseradish, onion and cucumber. Put mixture into a blender. Add mayonnaise and blend thoroughly. Pour into a 6-cup ring mold. Chill until firm. Unmold onto serving dish and garnish with salad greens and cucumber slices.

Pam Bartels Morris

CRANBERRY MOLD

Preparing: 20 minutes   *Do Ahead*   *Yield: 6 servings*
Chilling: 3 to 4 hours

1 (3-ounce) package strawberry or
   raspberry gelatin
1 cup boiling water
¾ cup canned pineapple juice

1 (8-ounce) can whole berry
   cranberry sauce
1 cup diced apples and/or celery
⅓ cup coarsely chopped nuts

Dissolve gelatin in boiling water. Add pineapple juice and cranberry sauce. Chill until slightly thickened; stir in remaining ingredients. Pour into lightly oiled 4-cup mold. *Chill until firm.*

Variation: ½ cup grape halves may be added. May also be made in individual molds and served on a pineapple slice placed on lettuce-lined plate.

Dru Huber Hammond

FRUIT AND NUT LIME JELLO SALAD

Preparing: 20 minutes   *Do Ahead*   *Yield: 10 servings*
Chilling: 4 hours

1 (20-ounce) can crushed
   pineapple
1 (3-ounce) package lime gelatin
1 (8-ounce) package cream
   cheese, softened

1 cup chopped celery
1 cup chopped walnuts
¼ cup diced pimento, drained
½ pint sour cream

In saucepan heat pineapple; stir in lime gelatin. Set aside to cool. With a fork stir in cream cheese until smooth. Add celery, walnuts and pimento. Stir in sour cream until smooth. Pour into 9-inch square pan or 1½-quart mold; refrigerate until firm. Cover to keep from drying out.

Variation: For a simple salad use first 3 ingredients. Another version uses first 5 ingredients.

Susan Johnson Mader

PEAR-ROSÉ GELATIN MOLD

Preparing: 20 minutes   *Do Ahead*   *Yield: 6 servings*
Chilling: 3 to 4 hours

1 (3-ounce) package raspberry
   gelatin
1 cup boiling water
1 cup rosé wine
1 tablespoon lemon juice

Pinch of salt
6 canned pear halves, drained
1 (3-ounce) package cream cheese
½ cup chopped walnuts
   (approximately)

Dissolve gelatin in boiling water; add wine and blend. Add lemon juice and salt; chill until mixture begins to thicken. Place drained pear halves, cut side up, with pointed ends toward the center, in oiled 8-inch round cake pan. Cut cream cheese into 6 equal pieces; roll in chopped walnuts, forming a ball. Set ball in center of each pear half. When gelatin begins to thicken, pour around pears. (Pears will not be entirely covered by gelatin.) Chill until firm. Cut into pie-shaped wedges; place on lettuce-lined salad plates. Serve with any desired dressing.

Jan Carmst Rhein

SUNSET SALAD

Preparing: 15 minutes   *Do Ahead*   *Yield: 4 to 6 servings*
Chilling: 3 to 4 hours

1 (3-ounce) package orange gelatin	1 tablespoon lemon juice
½ teaspoon salt	1 cup coarsely grated carrots
1½ cups boiling water	⅓ cup chopped pecans (optional)
1 (8¾-ounce) can crushed pineapple, undrained	

Dissolve gelatin and salt in boiling water. Add undrained pineapple and lemon juice. Chill until very thick. Fold in carrots and pecans. Pour into a 1-quart mold; chill.

Dolly Eastburn Somers

VEGETABLE GELATIN SALAD

Preparing: 10 minutes   *Do Ahead*   *Yield: 8 servings*
Chilling: 3 to 4 hours

1 (6-ounce) package lemon gelatin	2 large carrots, shredded
1 (20-ounce) can crushed pineapple, drained	1 large celery stalk, finely chopped

Prepare gelatin according to package directions; chill to consistency of egg whites. Mix in remaining ingredients. Pour into 5-cup mold. Chill until firm.

Linda Stilwell Teets

CELERY SEED FRENCH DRESSING

Preparing: 10 minutes   *Do Ahead*   *Yield: 1¼ cups*

¼ cup sugar
1 teaspoon dry mustard
1 teaspoon paprika
1 teaspoon celery seed
1 teaspoon salt

5 tablespoons tarragon vinegar
3 tablespoons lemon juice
1 tablespoon grated onion
⅔ cup olive oil

Mix dry ingredients. Add vinegar and lemon juice, mixing thoroughly. Add onion, then olive oil gradually, stirring constantly. Shake well before using.

Alice Marks Preston

CITRUS DRESSING

Preparing: 10 minutes   *Do Ahead*   *Yield: 1 cup*

1 small lemon
½ cup mayonnaise
¼ cup light corn syrup

1 tablespoon grated orange peel
Dash salt

Into small bowl, grate peel from lemon. Squeeze and strain juice from lemon; add to peel. Stir in mayonnaise, corn syrup, orange peel and salt. Cover and refrigerate up to 1 week. Serve on fruit salads.

Frances Marincola Blair

DILL SALAD DRESSING

Preparing: 5 minutes   *Do Ahead*   *Yield: 1 cup*
Cooking: 5 minutes
Chilling: 30 minutes

⅔ cup oil
¼ cup red wine vinegar
1 tablespoon sugar
1 teaspoon salt

½ teaspoon dill
⅛ teaspoon curry powder
⅛ teaspoon pepper

Combine all ingredients in a saucepan. Heat for several minutes until blended. Chill.

Grace Burdett Nellis

DRESSING FOR COLE SLAW

Preparing: 10 minutes   *Do Ahead*   *Yield: 1 cup*

1 cup mayonnaise
4 scallions, chopped
1 tablespoon catsup
2 teaspoons vinegar

⅛ teaspoon Worcestershire sauce
¼ teaspoon salt
⅛ teaspoon pepper
¼ teaspoon sugar

Mix all ingredients and pour over shredded cabbage and carrots.

Sandra Schild Fletcher

EASY FRENCH DRESSING

Preparing: 5 minutes   *Do Ahead*   *Yield: ⅔ cup*

3 tablespoons lemon juice
½ teaspoon salt
⅛ teaspoon pepper

¼ teaspoon sugar
¼ teaspoon dry mustard
½ cup olive oil

Mix lemon juice with dry ingredients. Slowly add olive oil. Great over Bibb lettuce.

Dolly Eastburn Somers

HONEY CURRY DRESSING

Preparing: 15 minutes   *Do Ahead*   *Yield: 2 cups*

1¼ cups mayonnaise
½ cup vegetable oil
¼ cup honey
¼ cup prepared mustard
3 tablespoons lemon juice

1 small onion, chopped
1 tablespoon chopped fresh
   parsley
1 teaspoon celery seed
¼ teaspoon curry powder

Put all ingredients in jar; shake vigorously. Serve with any mixture of salad greens.

Ardyth Beidleman Sobyak

PINK YOGURT DRESSING

Preparing: 15 minutes   *Do Ahead*   *Yield: 1¾ cups*

½ cup vegetable oil
2 tablespoons white vinegar
3 tablespoons chili sauce
1 cup plain yogurt
¼ teaspoon salt

2 teaspoons minced onion
2 teaspoons chopped parsley
½ teaspoon dry mustard
¼ teaspoon fresh ground pepper

Beat all ingredients with wire whisk or in blender (¼ cup water may be added for thinner dressing). Store in refrigerator. *Keeps approximately 2 weeks. Shake well before serving. Serve on greens.*

Gretchen Dome Hagy

POPPY SEED DRESSING

Preparing: 15 minutes   *Do Ahead*   *Yield: 1 cup*

⅓ cup vinegar
½ onion, finely chopped
1 teaspoon dry mustard
1 teaspoon salt

¼-½ cup sugar (to taste)
½ cup vegetable oil
1-3 teaspoons poppy seeds (to
   taste)

Blend vinegar with onions, dry mustard and salt. Add sugar to taste. Slowly add oil, blending constantly. Add poppy seeds; mix well. Serve on favorite salad; great on spinach. *This recipe may be doubled.*

Westways on Kezar Lake
Lovell, Maine

ZIPPY DRESSING

Preparing: 5 minutes   *Do Ahead*   *Yield: 2 cups*

½ cup vinegar
6 tablespoons sugar
1 teaspoon dry mustard
1 teaspoon paprika
1 tablespoon Worcestershire sauce

1 teaspoon salt
¼ teaspoon pepper
1 teaspoon celery seed
⅛ teaspoon garlic powder
1 cup vegetable oil

Put vinegar in a jar with lid or use blender. Add remaining ingredients except oil. Mix until dissolved, add oil; mix again. Very good served on fruit or greens.

Grace Burdett Nellis

Breads

Rosemont

In 1863, Joshua Ashbridge gave a portion of his land to the Pennsylvania Railroad providing that the name of his home, Rosemont, would become the station's name. At first, the station was a flagstop since few people except Ashbridge used it.

As train ridership increased and the surrounding community grew, people complained because the tracks were at grade level crossing the thoroughfare. The railroad moved the station to a higher part of the track, but patrons refused to drive or walk up the steep incline. They moved it again and carved a road beneath the tracks. Whenever it rained, carriages would splash mud on those walking to the station. The railroad offered its employees a prize for the best suggestions on improving the situation. The station remained on the site but the roadway was drained and paved.

A Candlelight and Roses Dinner

hors d'oeuvre
Crab Puffs

soup
Vichyssoise and Avocado Soup

entrée
Veal Bertrand

vegetable
Pilaf de Champignons   Lemon Artichokes

dessert
Brennan's Banana Foster

beverage
Hawaiian Russians

ANNA'S DANISH PASTRY RING

Preparing: 40 minutes   *Do Ahead*   *Yield: Two 9-inch rings*
Chilling: Overnight   *Freeze*
Rising: 13 hours
Baking: 45 minutes

Dough:
½ pound butter   3 egg yolks
1 tablespoon sugar   2 cups flour
1 package yeast, dissolved in Pinch salt
   ¼ cup warm milk

Cream butter with sugar; add yeast dissolved in milk, egg yolks and salt. Gradually add flour. Cover and place in refrigerator overnight.

Filling:
3 egg whites   ½ cup shredded coconut
¾ cup sugar   ½ cup chopped pecans
Cinnamon to taste   ¼ cup raisins

Beat egg whites and sugar until frothy. Divide dough in half; roll on floured surface into 6x12-inch rectangle. Spread half of egg white mixture on dough; sprinkle with cinnamon and half the raisins, coconut and nuts. Roll up dough, beginning with 12-inch side; form into open ring and place seam-side down, in well-greased 9-inch round pan. Repeat procedure with remaining dough and filling ingredients. Cover with towel; let rise in warm place 1 hour. *(Do not be alarmed if some filling leaks out.)* Preheat oven to 425°F. Bake rings 10 minutes; lower oven to 350°F. and bake until light brown, about 25-30 minutes. Remove from pans immediately. When cool, ice with glaze.

Glaze:
1 cup powdered sugar   2 tablespoons milk
½ teaspoon vanilla

Combine all ingredients, adding milk 1 tablespoon at a time.

Joanne Stanek Murphy

FRENCH HERB SWIRL BREAD

Preparing: 1½ hours   *Do Ahead*   *Yield: 2 small loaves or*
Rising: 45 minutes, 20 minutes   *Freeze*   *1 large loaf*
Baking: 20 to 30 minutes

1½ cups flour	1 cup buttermilk
2 packages dry yeast	¼ cup water
2 tablespoons sugar	¼ cup butter or margarine
1 teaspoon salt	2-2½ cups flour

Combine all dry ingredients in large mixing bowl. Heat buttermilk, water and butter in saucepan over low heat until very warm (120°-130°F.); butter does not need to melt. Add warm liquid to flour mixture. Blend at low speed until moistened; beat 3 minutes at medium speed. By hand, stir in 1-1½ cups additional flour to make a sticky dough. Knead (about 5 minutes) on floured surface, adding ½-1 cup additional flour until dough is smooth and pliable and no longer sticky. Place dough in greased bowl; cover. Let rise in warm place until doubled in size, about 45 minutes.

Filling:

2 tablespoons butter or margarine	1 clove garlic, minced
½ cup minced onion	½ teaspoon salt
1 tablespoon minced parsley	

Combine filling ingredients in a small saucepan over low heat, stirring constantly until butter is melted. Set aside. Punch down dough. Knead several times to remove air bubbles. For one large loaf, roll or pat dough into a 16x3-inch rectangle. Spread filling evenly over dough, leaving 1-inch edge on all sides. Roll up tightly at long edge, jelly-roll style; pinch edges and sides of dough to seal. For two small loaves, cut in half; seal. Place loaves seam-side down on greased cookie sheets; cover. Let rise until doubled, about 20 minutes. Preheat oven to 400°F. Bake for 20-30 minutes until golden; remove immediately from sheets to cooling rack. If desired, brush loaves with melted butter after baking; sprinkle with chopped parsley. Serve warm.

Note: As a substitute for buttermilk use 1 tablespoon vinegar plus milk to make 1 cup.

Liz Nelson Mayer

CINNAMON APPLE SWIRL

Preparing: 1 hour   *Do Ahead*   *Yield: Two 9x5-inch loaves*
Rising: 3 hours   *Freeze*
Baking: 40 to 50 minutes

4-4½ cups flour
½ cup milk
2 teaspoons salt
¼ cup butter

2 packets yeast
½ cup warm water
2 eggs
⅓ cup sugar

Scald milk, stir in ⅓ cup sugar, salt and ¼ cup butter. Cool to lukewarm. Dissolve yeast in warm water in large mixing bowl. Stir in milk mixture and eggs. Gradually add flour to form stiff dough. Knead on a well-floured surface until smooth and satiny (5-10 minutes). Place in a greased bowl, turning dough to grease all sides. Cover and let rise in a warm place until light and doubled in size (1½-2 hours). Combine filling ingredients. Roll out dough on floured surface to a 15x11-inch rectangle. Spread with soft butter; top with filling mixture. Starting with 15-inch side, roll up dough; seal edges. Cut in half. Place each half in greased 9x5x3-inch pan. Cut with scissors into 10 slices. Cover and let rise in a warm place until light and doubled in size (1-1½ hours). Preheat oven to 350°F. Bake 40-50 minutes or until a deep golden brown. Remove from pans. Combine glaze ingredients; frost warm loaves. Best when served warm.

Filling:
1½ cups finely diced apples
⅔ cup sugar
1 tablespoon flour

½ cup chopped walnuts
2 teaspoons cinnamon

Glaze:
2 tablespoons butter
1 cup sifted powdered sugar

1-2 tablespoons orange or
   apple juice

Grace Burdett Nellis

GRANDMOTHER'S DINNER ROLLS

Preparing: 1 hour   *Do Ahead*   *Yield: 1 to 2 dozen*
Rising: 1 to 2 hours
Chilling: 12 hours
Baking: 12 minutes

½ cup scalded milk
1 yeast cake
¼ cup sugar
¼ teaspoon salt

2 cups plus 6 tablespoons flour
⅓ cup butter, softened
1 egg plus 2 egg yolks
½ teaspoon lemon extract

Cool scalded milk to lukewarm; add yeast and stir until dissolved. Beat sugar, salt and 1 cup flour until smooth. Beat in butter; add egg and yolks one at a time. Add remaining flour and lemon extract; beat until smooth. Brush dough with butter, cover with towel and plate. Let rise in a warm place until doubled. Chill, covered, in refrigerator 12 hours. Preheat oven to 375°F. Using one half dough at a time, roll on floured board to about ½ inch thickness. Cut in strips ½ inch wide; cut each strip in thirds crosswise. Braid strips, pinching ends together. Cover and let rise until doubled. Bake 12 minutes. Cool; glaze rolls.

Glaze:
1 cup powdered sugar
2 tablespoons water

½ teaspoon vanilla

Blend all ingredients well. Glaze rolls.

Ann Keenan Seidel

MOCK BLINTZ

Preparing: 30 minutes   *Do Ahead*   *Yield: 3 to 4 dozen*
Baking: 10 minutes   *Freeze*

8 ounces whipped cream cheese
1 loaf thin white bread (not melba
   thin)

½ cup melted butter
1 cup sugar
2 tablespoons cinnamon

Trim crusts off bread, roll bread flat with rolling pin, and spread with cream cheese. Tightly shape bread like a jelly-roll. Roll in melted butter, then in combined sugar and cinnamon. Cut in half. Bake at 350°F. 10 minutes to heat. *Baking optional.* (May serve cold with coffee or hot as a dessert.)

Betsy Gillespie Miller

HERB SWIRLED OATMEAL BREAD

Preparing: 1 hour   *Do Ahead*   *Yield: 2 loaves*
Rising: 2 hours   *Freeze*
Baking: 30 minutes

5 cups flour
1½ cups old fashioned oatmeal,
  uncooked
2 envelopes dry yeast
1 tablespoon salt
2½ cups milk
½ cup butter
3 tablespoons brown sugar

3 tablespoons parsley flakes
2 teaspoons onion powder
2 teaspoons dried onion flakes
1 teaspoon marjoram
1 teaspoon rosemary
1 teaspoon pepper
1 egg, beaten
Sesame seeds

In large mixing bowl, combine 2 cups flour with oats, yeast and salt. In saucepan, combine milk, 3 tablespoons butter and brown sugar; heat to lukewarm. Pour into bowl with flour. Beat at low speed until blended; beat at high speed about 3 minutes. Stir in 2 cups flour to make a soft dough. Knead in remaining flour. Place in greased and floured bowl. Cover; let rise until doubled in size, about 1 hour. Melt remaining 5 tablespoons butter in saucepan; stir in herbs and cool. Punch dough down; divide in half. Roll each half into 8x12-inch rectangles. Brush liberally with herb butter. Roll up jelly-roll fashion; place seam-side down in 2 greased 9x5-inch loaf pans. Cover and let rise until doubled, about 1 hour. Preheat oven to 400°F. Brush with beaten egg; sprinkle with sesame seeds. Bake about 30 minutes or until golden.

Elizabeth Vanden Heuvel von dem Hagen

BREAD STICKS

Preparing: 20 minutes   *Do Ahead*   *Yield: 2 dozen*
Rising: 30 minutes
Baking: 20 minutes

1 loaf frozen bread dough,
  defrosted
2 egg yolks, beaten

Sesame seeds
Parmesan cheese
Coarse salt

Roll out dough to ¼-inch thick. Cut dough into ½-inch sticks (about 24 sticks). Place sticks on greased cookie sheets; brush with egg yolks. Top 1 sheet with sesame seeds and salt; generously sprinkle other with Parmesan cheese. Cover; allow to rise at least 30 minutes. Preheat oven to 350°F.; bake 20 minutes.

BAGELS

Preparing: 45 minutes	*Do Ahead*	*Yield: 12 to 15*
Rising: 3 hours	*Freeze*	
Baking: 30 minutes		

1 package yeast	4 tablespoons sugar
⅔ cup warm potato water	3 tablespoons salad oil
3 cups flour	2 eggs
1 teaspoon salt	2 tablespoons sugar

Dissolve yeast in ⅓ cup potato water. Add yeast to flour, salt, sugar and oil. Add eggs. Knead until *very* smooth. Let rise in buttered bowl. Punch down. Rise again. Punch down; knead again. Divide into 12-15 portions. Form into 6x¾-inch strips. Fold ends together into rings. Add sugar to 4 quarts boiling water; drop in bagels. Simmer 5-6 minutes after they rise to surface. Drain; cool 5 minutes on cookie sheets. Preheat oven to 375°F. Brush with water and egg yolk. Bake 25-30 minutes.

Note: Each rising should take about 1½ hours. May need extra flour depending on the weather.

Kessler's Cutlery & Cookware
Spread Eagle Village, Strafford, Pennsylvania

CHEESE BREAD

Preparing: 10 minutes	*Do Ahead*	*Yield: 8 to 10 servings*
Baking: 10 minutes		

1 loaf French or Italian bread	6 scallions, chopped
¾ pound Cheddar cheese, shredded	Fresh parsley, chopped
	Dash Worcestershire sauce
¼-½ pound soft butter or margarine	Paprika

Preheat oven to 400°F. Mix cheese and butter; add scallions, parsley and Worcestershire. Cut loaf of bread in half horizontally; spread with cheese mixture. Sprinkle with paprika. Wrap each half loaf loosely in aluminum foil. Bake 10-15 minutes or until melted and heated through.

Barbara Alphin Chimicles

HERB FRENCH BREAD

Preparing: 1½ hours   *Do Ahead*   *Yield: 2 loaves*
Baking: 25 to 30 minutes   *Freeze*

5½-7½ cups flour
2 packages instant dry yeast
4 teaspoons dry ranch-style
    buttermilk salad dressing mix
1½ cups water

¼ cup shortening
1 egg
1 tablespoon melted butter or
    margarine
1½ cups buttermilk

In large bowl, combine 2 cups flour, yeast, 3 teaspoons dressing; mix well. Heat buttermilk, water, shortening until warm (120°-130°F.; *shortening need not melt).* Add to flour mixture. Add egg; blend until moistened. Beat 3 minutes at medium speed. Gradually stir in enough remaining flour to make a firm dough. Knead on well-floured surface until smooth and elastic (5-10 minutes). Place in greased bowl, turning dough to grease top. Cover; let rise 20 minutes in warm oven. (Turn oven to lowest setting for 1 minute; turn off.) Punch down dough; divide into 2 parts. On lightly floured surface, roll or pat each half into a 12x7-inch rectangle. Starting with longer side, roll up tightly, sealing edges and ends. Place seam-side down on greased cookie sheet. Make diagonal slashes about 2 inches apart in top of loaves. Cover; let rise in warm oven until light and doubled (about 30 minutes). Preheat oven to 375°F. Bake 25-30 minutes. While warm, brush with melted butter and sprinkle with 1 teaspoon reserved salad dressing mix. Cool on wire rack.

Ann Keenan Seidel

OLD-FASHIONED HONEY WHOLE WHEAT BREAD

Preparing: 3½ hours   *Yield: Two 9x5-inch loaves*
Rising: 2 hours
Baking: 40 to 50 minutes

1½ cups water   1 cup whole wheat flour
1 cup cottage cheese   2 tablespoons sugar
½ cup honey   3 teaspoons salt
¼ cup butter   2 packages dry yeast
5½-6 cups all-purpose flour   1 egg

Preheat oven to 350°F. Heat water, cottage cheese, honey and butter until very warm. Combine with 2 cups white flour, sugar, salt, yeast, and egg. Beat 2 minutes at medium speed. Add remaining flour; knead 2 minutes. Let rise in greased bowl 1 hour or until doubled. Punch down; shape into 2 loaves and let rise in 2 greased 9x5-inch loaf pans 1 hour. Bake 40-50 minutes or until sounds hollow when tapped.

Elise Rice Payne

EASY STICKY BUNS

Preparing: 15 minutes   *Do Ahead*   *Yield: 2 loaves*
Rising: 1 hour
Baking: 40 minutes

1 (3¾-ounce) package   4 tablespoons soft butter or
  butterscotch pudding mix   margarine
  (not instant)   1 teaspoon ground cinnamon
1 cup chopped walnuts or raisins   2 (16-ounce) loaves frozen bread
½ cup packed brown sugar   dough, thawed

In bowl, combine all ingredients except bread dough; stir until crumbly. Cut bread in half lengthwise, then in 8 pieces crosswise. (Each loaf should have 16 pieces.) Sprinkle ¼ of topping into each of two greased 9x5x3-inch loaf pans. Arrange 16 dough pieces in each. Sprinkle each with half the remaining topping; cover and let rise in a warm place until almost doubled, about 1 hour. Preheat oven to 350°F.; bake 35-40 minutes. Turn out of pans *immediately*. Serve warm.

Ginny Moffitt Gehring

SOUR DOUGH FRENCH BREAD

Preparing: 1 hour   *Do Ahead*   *Yield: 2 loaves*
Rising: 2 hours   *Freeze*
Baking: 40 minutes

Starter:
¼ cup milk   ¼ cup warm water
½ cup water   2 teaspoons sugar
2 teaspoons vegetable oil   1¼ teaspoons salt
1 package dry yeast   2⅓ cups flour

Starter must be made at least 18 hours before bread. Bring to boiling point milk, water and oil; cool to lukewarm. Dissolve yeast in warm water. Add sugar and salt to cooled milk mixture. Stir both liquids into flour, mixing just enough to blend well. Cover; let stand in warm place 12-18 hours to sour. Stir dough enough to release air; divide into two portions. Wrap individually in foil; freeze until ready to use. Allow starter to come to room temperature before using.

Bread:
½ cup milk   1½ tablespoons sugar
1½ tablespoons vegetable oil   2½ teaspoons salt
1 cup water   4¾ cups flour
1 package dry yeast   2 portions starter dough
¼ cup warm water   1 egg white

Heat to boiling point milk, oil and water; cool to lukewarm. Dissolve yeast in warm water. Add sugar and salt to cooled milk mixture. Place flour in large bowl; make a well in center; add 2 portions starter dough (room temperature) and milk mixture. Stir until well-blended, but do not knead. Cover; let rise until doubled in volume (about 1 hour). Turn dough onto lightly floured board; divide in half (or fourths if you want more crust). Flatten dough with hands and fold in half to form long rectangle. Flatten dough again and fold in thirds (as if folding a letter) to form long cylinder. Place seam-side down on lightly greased baking sheet. Repeat with other portion(s) of dough. Slash tops of loaves with sharp knife; let rise until doubled in size. Preheat oven to 425°F.; bake 15 minutes. Reduce heat to 350°F.; bake 15-20 minutes longer. Brush crust with 1 egg white which has been beaten with 1 tablespoon water; bake 5 minutes longer.

Chris Sopko

THREE-FLOUR BRAIDED BREAD

Preparing: ½ hour   *Do Ahead*   *Yield: 2 loaves*
Rising: 2 hours   *Freeze*
Baking: 40 minutes

2½ cups white flour   ¼ cup softened margarine
2 tablespoons sugar   2¼ cups *very* warm water
1 tablespoon salt   (115°-120°F.)
2 packages dry yeast   1 cup white flour

Combine 2½ cups flour, sugar, salt and yeast; add margarine. Add water; beat 2 minutes at medium speed. Add 1 cup white flour. Beat at high speed 2 minutes. Divide into 3 bowls. Mix the following 3 doughs by hand.

Whole Wheat Dough:
2 tablespoons molasses   1¼ cups whole wheat flour

Add to ⅓ of batter; blend.

Rye Dough:
2 tablespoons molasses   1 tablespoon cocoa
1 teaspoon caraway seed   1¼ cups rye flour

Add to ⅓ of batter; blend.

White Dough:
1¼ cups white flour

Add to ⅓ of batter; blend.

Knead each dough on board dusted with white flour until smooth and elastic, about 5 minutes. Grease each bowl lightly. Turn each dough in its bowl until lightly greased; cover. Let rise in warm place until doubled, about 1 hour. Punch down. Divide each dough in half. Roll each half into 15-inch rope on a floured board. Dampen outside of each strand just before braiding. Braid three kinds together on greased cookie sheets. Lightly grease tops. Sprinkle with caraway seeds, lightly pressing down. Cover; let rise until doubled, about 1 hour. Preheat oven to 350°F. Bake 30-40 minutes. Cool.

Elise Rice Payne

TOMATO HERB BREAD

Preparing: 45 minutes   *Do Ahead*   *Yield: 2 loaves*
Rising: 2½ hours   *Freeze*
Baking: 20   30 minutes

2 tablespoons brown sugar	**Butter or margarine**
2 teaspoons salt	**2 medium tomatoes**
2 packages dry yeast	**2 eggs**
5½ cups flour (approximately)	**¾ teaspoon thyme leaves**
1 cup milk	**½ teaspoon basil**

Peel, seed and mince tomatoes to make one cup. In large bowl combine sugar, salt, yeast and 1 cup flour. In 1-quart saucepan over low heat, heat milk and 3 tablespoons butter until very warm (120°-130°F.). Butter need not melt. Mix with mixer at low speed; beat liquid gradually into dry ingredients until just blended. Increase speed to medium; beat 2 minutes, scraping bowl. Beat in tomatoes, eggs, thyme, basil and 1½ cups flour to make a thick batter; beat 2 more minutes, scraping often. Stir in enough additional flour (about 2½ cups) to make soft dough. Turn dough onto floured surface and knead until smooth and elastic, about 10 minutes, adding more flour if necessary. Shape into ball and place in greased large bowl, turning over to grease top. Cover; let rise in warm place, away from draft, until doubled, about 1½ hours. Punch down dough; put on lightly floured surface. Cover with bowl; let rest 15 minutes. Grease two 9x5-inch loaf pans. Cut dough in half. Lightly flour surface and rolling pin; roll one half into 12x8-inch rectangle. Starting at 8-inch end, tightly roll jelly-roll fashion. Pinch seam to seal; press ends to seal and tuck under. Place seam-side down in loaf pan. Repeat with remaining dough. Cover with towel; let rise in warm place until doubled, about 1 hour. Preheat oven to 400°F. In small saucepan over low heat, melt 2 tablespoons butter; brush on loaves. Bake 20-30 minutes until golden and sound hollow when lightly tapped with fingers. Remove from pans immediately; cool on wire racks.

Ann Keenan Seidel

TRICKY CHEESE BREAD

Preparing: 30 minutes   *Do Ahead*   *Yield: 2 loaves*
Rising: 1¼ hours   *Freeze*
Baking: 30 to 40 minutes

2 packages dry yeast   **½ package dry garlic salad**
½ cup warm water   **dressing mix**
1 (10¾-ounce) can condensed   **3½-4½ cups flour**
  cheddar cheese soup

Soften yeast in warm water in large bowl. Add undiluted soup and salad dressing. Gradually add flour to form stiff dough. Beat well after each addition. Knead on floured surface until smooth and elastic (5 minutes). Knead in additional flour if necessary. Place in greased bowl; cover with towel; let rise in warm place until light and doubled in size (45 minutes). Punch dough down. Divide in half, shape into loaves and place in two 9x5-inch loaf pans. Cover; let rise again (30 minutes). Preheat oven to 400°F. Bake 30-40 minutes. Remove immediately; cool on racks.

Judy Lane Davies

APRICOT NUT BREAD

Preparing: 50 minutes   *Do Ahead*   *Yield: One 9x5-inch loaf*
Baking: 1½ hours   *Freeze*

½ cup diced dried apricots   **¼ teaspoon baking soda**
1 egg   **¾ teaspoon salt**
1 cup sugar   **½ cup strained orange juice**
2 tablespoons melted butter   **¼ cup water**
2 cups sifted flour   **1 cup sliced almonds**
3 teaspoons baking powder

Soak apricots ½ hour; drain and grind (in blender). Preheat oven to 350°F. Beat egg until light; stir in sugar and mix well. Stir in butter. Sift flour with baking powder, baking soda and salt; add alternately with orange juice and water. Add almonds and apricots; mix well. Bake in greased 9x5-inch loaf pan (or 3 or 4 smaller loaf pans) for 1½ hours (45 minutes to 1 hour for small pans).

Note: This bread is delightful when spread with softened cream cheese flavored with a small amount of apricot brandy.

Lois Rising Pogyor

APPLE BREAD

Preparing: 30 minutes   *Do Ahead*   *Yield: One 9x5-inch loaf*
Baking: 1 to 1¼ hours   *Freeze*

½ cup butter or margarine
1 cup sugar
2 eggs
2 cups sifted flour
½ teaspoon salt

2 tablespoons sour milk* or
   buttermilk
1 teaspoon baking soda
2 cups peeled and chopped apples
½ cup nuts, chopped

Preheat oven to 350°F. Cream butter and sugar; add eggs. Blend in flour and salt. Dissolve baking soda in sour milk; add to batter. Fold in apples and nuts; pour into greased 9x5-inch loaf pan. Spread topping over batter. Bake 1-1¼ hours. Test center carefully; cool 10 minutes in pan; turn on rack to cool completely.

*To sour fresh milk, blend ½ teaspoon vinegar with 2 tablespoons milk. Let stand; remeasure to use.

Topping:
2 tablespoons sugar
2 tablespoons flour

2 tablespoons melted butter

Mix ingredients well.

Dolly Eastburn Somers

BANANA NUT BREAD

Preparing: 15 minutes   *Do Ahead*   *Yield: One 9x5-inch loaf*
Baking: 1 hour   *Freeze*

1 cup sugar
1 (8-ounce) package cream
   cheese, softened
1 cup mashed ripe banana
   (2-3 bananas)

2 eggs
2 cups Bisquick biscuit mix
½ cup chopped pecans

Preheat oven to 350°F. With electric mixer, cream sugar and cream cheese until light and fluffy. Beat in mashed bananas and eggs. Add biscuit mix and pecans. Stir until dry ingredients are moistened. Pour into greased 9x5x3-inch loaf pan. Bake 1 hour or until done. Cover with foil last 15 minutes if bread browns too quickly. Cool partially, remove from pan and cool thoroughly before slicing.

Mary Murtagh Krull

APPLE BUTTER BREAD

Preparing: 20 minutes   *Do Ahead*   *Yield: 1 large loaf*
Baking: *Freeze*

⅓ **cup sugar**   2 **cups Bisquick baking mix**
1 **egg**   ¼ **cup flour**
1 **cup apple butter**   ½ **cup chopped nuts**

Preheat oven to 350°F. Blend sugar, egg and apple butter in large mixer bowl on low speed. Gradually beat in remaining ingredients on low speed; beat 2 minutes medium speed. Pour batter into greased and floured 9x5x3-inch loaf pan. Bake about 50 minutes or until it tests done. Cool thoroughly before slicing.

Frances Marincola Blair

BANANA SOUR CREAM WALNUT LOAF

Preparing: 30 minutes   *Do Ahead*   *Yield: 1 loaf*
Baking: 1¼ hours   *Freeze*

⅔ **cup margarine**   1 **teaspoon baking powder**
1⅓ **cups sugar**   1 **teaspoon baking soda**
2 **eggs**   ½ **teaspoon salt**
1½ **cups mashed banana**   ½ **cup sour cream**
2¾ **cups sifted flour**   1 **cup walnuts, coarsely chopped**

Preheat oven to 350°F. Grease and flour bottom of 9x5-inch loaf pan. Cream butter and sugar until light and fluffy. Add eggs and bananas; beat until well-blended. Sift dry ingredients. Add alternately with sour cream, stirring just to blend. Stir in walnuts. Spoon batter into pan; bake 1¼ hours. Cool 20 minutes on a rack; remove from pan and cool thoroughly. *May freeze up to 2 months.*

Banana Glaze:
1 **cup mashed banana**   2 **tablespoons lemon juice**
1 **cup sugar**

Combine banana and sugar in small saucepan and bring to a boil. Cook over low heat, stirring 5 minutes. Remove from heat and add lemon juice. While warm, push through strainer. Cool and pour over bread.

Arlene Allman Seeger

BEER BREAD

Preparing: 10 minutes   *Do Ahead*   *Yield: Two 9x5-inch loaves*
Baking: 70 minutes

6 cups flour	6 tablespoons sugar
6 teaspoons baking powder	2 (12-ounce) cans beer
3 teaspoons salt	

Start in a cold oven. Mix all ingredients together. Place in two greased 9x5-inch loaf pans. Place in oven and turn on to 375°. Keep in oven 60-70 minutes. Butter top of loaf 15-20 minutes before done.

Note: 6 cups self-rising flour may be substituted for flour, baking powder and salt.

Westways on Kezar Lake
Lovell, Maine

BLUEBERRY-ORANGE BREAD

Preparing: 20 minutes   *Do Ahead*   *Yield: One loaf*
Baking: 1 hour and 10 minutes   *Freeze*

2 tablespoons butter	2 cups flour
¼ cup boiling water	1 teaspoon baking powder
½ cup orange juice	¼ teaspoon baking soda
3 teaspoons grated orange rind	½ teaspoon salt
1 egg	1 cup blueberries
1 cup sugar	

Preheat oven to 325°F. Melt butter in boiling water. Add orange juice and rind. Beat egg with sugar until light and fluffy. Sift dry ingredients; add alternately with orange liquid into bowl. Add egg mixture; beat until smooth. Fold in berries. Bake in 1½-quart loaf pan 70 minutes. Remove from pan; add topping.

Topping:

2 tablespoons orange juice	2 tablespoons honey
1 teaspoon grated orange rind	

Combine ingredients. Spoon over hot loaf.

Jeanne Kronmiller Honish

CRANBERRY BANANA BREAD

Preparing: 25 minutes   *Do Ahead*   *Yield: One 9x5-inch loaf*
Baking: 1 hour   *Freeze*

2 cups sugar
1 cup water
4 cups fresh cranberries
1¾ cups sifted flour
½ teaspoon salt
2 teaspoons baking powder

¼ teaspoon baking soda
⅔ cup sugar
⅓ cup butter, melted
2 eggs, beaten
½ cup chopped walnuts
1 cup mashed banana

In large saucepan, bring 2 cups sugar and water to a boil, stirring to dissolve sugar. Add berries; simmer over low heat 10 minutes or until berries pop open. Cool. Drain berries, reserving juice and measuring 1 cup of berries for use in bread. Grease and lightly flour 9x5-inch loaf pan. Preheat oven to 350°F. Sift flour, salt, baking powder and soda. In a large bowl combine ⅔ cup sugar, butter, eggs, walnuts, banana and berries. Add flour mixture to berry mixture, stirring until blended. Pour mixture into loaf pan; bake 1 hour or until a toothpick inserted in the center comes out clean.

Glaze (optional):
¼ cup cranberry juice, reserved
    from cooked berries

2 tablespoons sugar
2 tablespoons Grand Marnier

Combine reserved cranberry juice, sugar and Grand Marnier in a small saucepan and stir over low heat until heated through. Poke a few holes in baked loaf; pour topping over loaf. Cool 10 minutes in pan. Turn loaf out on a rack; cool completely. *Wrap in foil and store 1 day before slicing.*

Note: *Must be prepared 24 hours in advance.* The bread keeps refrigerated for 3 weeks or frozen for 3 months. The recipe may be doubled for 2 loaves.

ORANGE BUTTER

Preparing: 10 minutes   *Do Ahead*   *Yield: 1 cup*

½ cup butter, softened
2 tablespoons powdered sugar

½ cup light corn syrup
2 teaspoons orange peel

Beat butter and sugar in small bowl until fluffy. Beat in syrup gradually; stir in peel. This is a nice addition to a brunch to spread on bread and rolls.

Ginny Moffitt Gehring

BRETHREN'S CHEESE BREAD

Preparing: 25 minutes   *Yield: One 9x5-inch loaf*
Baking: 40 to 45 minutes

2 cups sifted flour
2 teaspoons baking powder
1 tablespoon sugar
½ teaspoon salt
4 tablespoons butter
1 cup (¼ pound) natural sharp
   Cheddar cheese, shredded

1 tablespoon onion, grated
1½ teaspoons dried dill weed
¾ cup milk
1 egg, slightly beaten

Preheat oven to 350°F. Lightly grease 9x5x3-inch loaf pan. Sift flour, baking powder, sugar and salt into large bowl. With 2 knives, cut in butter until mixture resembles coarse crumbs. Stir in cheese, onion and dill weed; mix well. In small bowl, combine milk and egg; pour into flour mixture all at once. Stir quickly with fork to moisten; turn into pan. Bake 40-45 minutes. Let cool in pan 10 minutes before turning out.

Roberta West Cowley

CRANBERRY-ORANGE NUT BREAD

Preparing: 20 minutes   *Do Ahead*   *Yield: 1 loaf*
Baking: 1 hour   *Freeze*

2 cups sifted flour
½ cup sugar
4 teaspoons baking powder
1 teaspoon salt
½ cup chopped walnuts (optional)
1 tablespoon grated orange rind

1 egg
¼ cup water
¾ cup orange juice
2 tablespoons melted butter
½ (16-ounce) can whole cranberry
   sauce

Preheat oven to 350°F. Sift flour with sugar, baking powder and salt. Beat egg well; add water, orange juice, melted butter, and cranberry sauce and mix. Add all at once to flour mixture and blend lightly (about 25 strokes). Put batter into lightly greased 9x3-inch loaf pan. Bake 1 hour. Cool 5 minutes; remove loaf from pan.

Patricia Jacobs Mendicino

PEAR BREAD

Preparing: 15 minutes
Baking: 60 to 70 minutes

Yield: One 9x5-inch loaf

2 cups flour
½ cup wheat germ
½ cup brown sugar
1 tablespoon baking powder
1 teaspoon salt
¼ teaspoon ground coriander

1 cup lemon yogurt
2 eggs
⅓ cup milk
¼ cup vegetable oil
1½ cups pears, chopped (canned
    or very ripe)

Preheat oven to 350°F. Mix yogurt, eggs, milk and oil. Mix flour, wheat germ, sugar, baking powder, salt and coriander. Combine. Fold in pears by hand. Pour into greased 9x5-inch loaf pan. Bake 60-70 minutes.

Note: If bread is brown before done, cover loosely with foil.

Ann Keenan Seidel

PECAN BREAKFAST BREAD

Preparing: 10 minutes
Baking: 40 minutes

Do Ahead

Yield: 12 to 16 servings

2 (8-ounce) cans crescent dinner
    rolls
2 tablespoons butter, softened

½ cup sugar
1-2 teaspoons cinnamon
¼ cup chopped pecans

Preheat oven to 375°F. Separate rolls into 16 triangles. Spread each with softened butter. Combine sugar, cinnamon and pecans; sprinkle on triangles. Roll each triangle at wide-end to opposite point. Place rolls point side down in greased 9x5-inch loaf pan, forming 2 layers of 8 rolls each. Bake 35-40 minutes. Remove from pan at once. Place right side up and drizzle topping over. Decorate top with pecan halves.

Topping:
2 tablespoons light corn syrup
¼ cup powdered sugar
2 tablespoons butter

1 teaspoon vanilla
¼ cup pecan halves

In medium saucepan, combine all ingredients except pecans. Bring to a boil, stirring constantly. Stir in pecans; cool slightly.

Liz Nelson Mayer

HOT BUTTERED RUM CRESCENTS

Preparing: 20 minutes   *Yield: 16*
Baking: 15 minutes

2 (8 each) cans crescent rolls

Topping:
¼ cup margarine   **1 tablespoon milk**
½ cup brown sugar, firmly packed   **½ teaspoon rum flavoring**
2 teaspoons flour

Mix topping ingredients; spoon about 2 teaspoons of topping into 16 greased muffin cups.

Stuffing:
½ cup brown sugar, firmly packed   **¼ cup chopped nuts**
½ teaspoon rum flavoring   **¼ cup margarine, melted**

Combine brown sugar, rum flavoring and nuts for stuffing; set aside. Separate crescent dough into 16 triangles. Use ½ of melted butter to brush each triangle. Sprinkle each with 1 tablespoon brown sugar mixture. Starting at shortest side of triangle, roll to opposite point. Cut rolls in half crosswise; place both halves, cut-side down in each prepared muffin cup. Brush tops with remaining melted butter. Preheat oven to 375°F.; bake 15-20 minutes or until golden brown. Immediately invert pan to remove rolls. If desired, drizzle with glaze.

Glaze:
½ cup sifted powdered sugar   **¼ teaspoon rum flavoring**
2-3 teaspoons milk

In small saucepan, combine ingredients. Cook over medium heat until mixture comes to a rolling boil.

Variation: You may substitute 1 tablespoon rum for rum flavoring in stuffing; omit rum flavoring in glaze.

Note: Soak pan right after inverting or use teflon coated pans.

Grace Burdett Nellis

POPPY SEED BREAD

Preparing: 1¼ hours   *Do Ahead*   *Yield: 10 servings*
Baking: 1 hour   *Freeze*

2¼ ounces poppy seeds   ¼ teaspoon salt
1 cup milk   ½ cup butter or margarine
2 cups flour   2 eggs, slightly beaten
1½ cups sugar   ½ teaspoon vanilla
2½ teaspoons baking powder

Soak seeds in milk for one hour. Preheat oven to 350°F. Sift flour, sugar, baking powder, and salt together. Cut in butter until mixture is crumbly. Add seeds and milk; mix 2 minutes until smooth. Add vanilla and eggs; mix 2 minutes. Pour into a greased and floured 9x5-inch loaf pan. Bake 1 hour. Cool in pan 10 minutes before removing.

Carol Sutcliffe Kramer

ORANGE GLAZED BROWN 'N SERVE ROLLS

Preparing: 45 minutes   *Do Ahead*   *Yield: 2 to 3 dozen*
Rising: 2¼ hours   *Freeze*
Baking: 20 minutes

Rolls:
1 package dry yeast   ¼ cup sugar
¾ cup warm water (105°-115°)   1¼ teaspoons salt
¾ cup lukewarm milk (scalded, ¼ cup shortening
   then cooled)   4½ cups flour

Dissolve yeast in warm water. Stir in milk, sugar, salt, shortening and 2½ cups flour. Beat until smooth. Mix in remaining flour to form soft dough. Turn dough onto lightly floured board; knead until smooth and elastic, about 5 minutes. Place in greased bowl; turn greased side up. Cover; let rise in warm place until doubled, about 1½ hours. Punch down dough; turn onto floured surface; divide into 24 equal pieces (36 if you wish smaller rolls). Shape each into smooth balls; place about 3 inches apart on greased baking sheet. Cover; let rise until doubled, about 45 minutes. Preheat oven to 275°F. Bake 20-30 minutes *(do not allow to brown)*. Remove from pans; cool. *Store in refrigerator or freeze until ready to use. At serving time:* Preheat oven to 400°F. Cover with glaze or bake plain on ungreased baking sheet for 7-10 minutes.

Glaze:
4 tablespoons margarine, melted   1 cup sugar
2 tablespoons grated orange peel   Orange juice

Combine sugar and orange peel; add just enough orange juice to make a dry paste. Dip Brown 'N Serve roll into melted butter (cover top and half of side), then into sugar mixture (may be necessary to pat sugar mixture on top of roll). Place on well-greased baking sheet and bake as directed above.

Lois Rising Pogyor

IRISH SWEET BREAD

Preparing: 15 minutes   *Do Ahead*   *Yield: 1 loaf*
Baking: 1 hour

2¼ cups sifted flour
2¼ teaspoons baking powder
¼ teaspoon baking soda
¾ teaspoon salt
¾-1 cup sugar
2 tablespoons oil

1 egg
¾ cup milk
½ cup raisins, tossed in flour
1 tablespoon caraway seeds
   (optional)

Preheat oven to 350°F. Sift dry ingredients. Stir in oil, egg and milk. Fold in raisins and caraway seeds. Pour into greased 9x5-inch loaf pan. Bake 55-60 minutes or until done.

Dolores Prodoehl Adams

RAISIN BRAN MUFFINS

Preparing: 10 minutes   *Do Ahead*   *Yield: 3 dozen*
Baking: 15 minutes   *Freeze*

½ box (2¼ cups) raisin bran
2½ cups flour
1½ cups sugar
2½ teaspoons baking soda

1 teaspoon salt
½ cup oil
1 pint buttermilk
2 eggs

Preheat oven to 400°F. Mix all ingredients. Bake in greased muffin tins 15 minutes. *This batter will keep in a sealed jar in the refrigerator up to 6 weeks.*

Note: Kids love these!

Elizabeth Taylor Young

BREAK AWAY COFFEE CAKE

Preparing: 30 minutes   *Yield: 8 to 12 servings*
Rising: 1 hour
Baking: 35 to 40 minutes

2 loaves, 1 pound each, frozen   **1½ cups sugar**
  bread dough   **2 teaspoons cinnamon**
½ cup plus 3 tablespoons butter,   **1 cup chopped walnuts**
  melted

Defrost dough to room temperature. Shape dough into balls the size of cherry tomatoes. Roll balls in butter, then mixture of sugar and cinnamon, then nuts. Put in a greased tube pan, leaving space to rise. Sprinkle remaining butter, nuts, and cinnamon sugar mixture over cake. Preheat oven to 200°F. and turn off. Cover dough and place pan in oven for 1 hour or until dough is at top of pan. Remove pan from oven. Preheat oven to 375°F. Bake cake for 35-40 minutes. Cover top loosely with foil if browning too much. Remove cake from pan immediately after removal from oven.

Note: Two 9x5-inch bread pans may be substituted for tube pan.

Sandra Johnson McConnell

BLUEBERRY COFFEE CAKE

Preparing: 45 minutes   *Do Ahead*   *Yield: One 9-inch cake*
Baking: 45 minutes   *Freeze*

¾ cup sugar   **2 cups flour**
¼ cup butter, softened   **2 teaspoons baking powder**
1 egg   **½ teaspoon salt**
½ cup milk   **2 cups blueberries**

Preheat oven to 375°F. Sift dry ingredients. Cream butter and sugar; add egg, then milk. Combine dry ingredients with wet. Fold in blueberries; pour into greased 9-inch square pan. Sprinkle topping over batter; bake 45-50 minutes.

Topping:
½ cup sugar   **½ teaspoon cinnamon**
⅓ cup flour   **¼ cup butter**

Mix ingredients; top batter.

Linda Stillwell Teets

STRAWBERRY BREAD

Preparing: 15 minutes   *Do Ahead*   *Yield: 2 large loaves*
Baking: 1 hour   *Freeze*

2 (10-ounce) packages frozen   3 teaspoons cinnamon
   strawberries, thawed   1 teaspoon baking soda
4 eggs   1 teaspoon salt
1¼ cups vegetable oil   2 cups sugar
3 cups flour   1¼ cups pecans, chopped

Preheat oven to 350°F. Grease and flour two 9x5-inch loaf pans. Mix together berries, eggs, and oil. Sift dry ingredients into berry mixture. Stir to blend thoroughly; mix in the nuts. Pour into loaf pans. Bake 1 hour or until toothpick comes out dry. Remove from oven; when partially cool, remove bread from pans to finish cooling.

Karen Klabau Meyers

ZUCCHINI BREAD

Preparing: 30 minutes   *Do Ahead*   *Yield: Two 9x5-inch loaves*
Baking: 1 hour   *Freeze*   *or four 3x5-inch loaves*

3 eggs   3 cups flour
1 cup granulated sugar   1 teaspoon salt
1 cup brown sugar   1 teaspoon baking soda
1 cup vegetable oil   ¼ teaspoon baking powder
2 cups grated, raw, peeled   3 teaspoons ground cinnamon
   zucchini   1 cup coarsely chopped walnuts
3 teaspoons vanilla extract   (optional)

Preheat oven to 350°F. Beat eggs until light and foamy. Add sugar, oil, zucchini and vanilla; mix lightly but well. Combine dry ingredients. Add to egg-zucchini mixture; stir until well-blended. Add nuts. Pour into two 9x5-inch loaf pans; bake 1 hour; cool on rack.

Variation: For darker bread, use 2 cups dark brown sugar in place of granulated and brown sugar and add 1 teaspoon pumpkin pie spice.

Lynne Stevens d'Entremont

BUTTER CREAM COFFEE CAKE

Preparing: 40 minutes   *Yield: 12 servings*
Baking: 45 minutes

⅓ cup butter	¾ teaspoon baking soda
¾ cup flour	½ teaspoon salt
1 cup firmly packed brown sugar	½ cup butter
1 teaspoon cinnamon	⅔ cup sugar
½ cup chopped walnuts	2 eggs
1½ cups sifted flour	1 teaspoon vanilla
½ teaspoon baking powder	1 cup sour cream

Preheat oven to 325°F. Grease and flour bottom of 9x9-inch square pan. Cut ⅓ cup butter in ¾ cup flour, brown sugar, and cinnamon until particles are fine. Stir in nuts. Set aside for topping. Sift 1½ cups flour with baking powder, soda, and salt. Cream ½ cup butter in large bowl; gradually add sugar and cream until light and fluffy. At medium speed, add eggs, one at a time, beating well after each. Blend in vanilla. At low speed, add dry ingredients alternately with sour cream; begin and end with dry ingredients. Spread in pan; Sprinkle with walnut mixture. Bake 45-55 minutes. Cool 10 minutes then remove from pan. Allow to finish cooling completely. Cut in half horizontally. Fill with butter cream filling and refrigerate.

Butter Cream Filling:

¼ cup flour	⅔ cup butter
½ teaspoon salt	1 cup sugar
1 cup milk	1 teaspoon vanilla

Combine flour, salt, and milk in a small saucepan. Cook over low heat, stirring constantly until *very thick;* cool. Cream butter; gradually add sugar and cream well. Add flour mixture. Beat until light and fluffy. Blend in vanilla.

Grace Burdett Nellis

POPPY SEED BREAD STICKS

Preparing: 20 minutes   *Do Ahead*   *Yield: 4 to 5 dozen*
Baking: 10 minutes   *Freeze*

8 hot dog buns, split in half	⅓ cup poppy seeds
½ cup grated Parmesan cheese	Butter or margarine, softened

Preheat oven to 350°F. Cut each bun half into 3 or 4 lengthwise pieces; butter each piece. Press cheese and poppy seeds onto buns. Bake 10-12 minutes.

Gretchen Dome Hagy

SOUR CREAM COFFEE CAKE

Preparing: 30 minutes   *Do Ahead*   *Yield: 12 servings*
Baking: 50 minutes   *Freeze*

1 cup butter
1¼ cups sugar
3 eggs
2½ cups flour
3 teaspoons baking powder

½ teaspoon salt
1 teaspoon baking soda
1 cup sour cream
1 teaspoon lemon juice
1 teaspoon vanilla

Topping:
½ cup sugar
1 teaspoon cinnamon

½-1 cup chopped pecans

Preheat oven to 350°F. Cream butter; beat in 1¼ cups sugar until light and fluffy. Beat in eggs one at a time. Sift flour; add baking powder, salt and soda and sift again. Add flour mixture to beaten mixture alternately with sour cream. Blend in lemon juice and vanilla. Pour half batter into greased tube pan or 13x9x2-inch pan. Sprinkle half sugar-cinnamon mixture and half nuts over batter. Cover with rest of batter and top with remaining topping mixture. Bake 45-60 minutes; cool on rack.

Lucetta Bahn Ebbert

FRENCH BREAKFAST PUFFS

Preparing: 25 minutes   *Do Ahead*   *Yield: 12*
Baking: 25 minutes   *Freeze*

⅓ cup soft shortening
½ cup sugar
1 egg
1½ cups sifted flour
1½ teaspoons baking powder
½ teaspoon salt

¼ teaspoon nutmeg
½ cup milk
6 tablespoons melted unsalted
   butter
½ cup sugar
1 teaspoon cinnamon

Preheat oven to 350°F. Mix shortening, sugar and egg thoroughly in medium bowl. Sift flour, baking powder, salt and nutmeg. Stir in sifted ingredients alternating with milk, beginning and ending with dry ingredients. Fill greased muffin cups ⅔ full. Bake 20-25 minutes or until golden brown. Immediately roll in melted butter and then in cinnamon-sugar mixture. Serve hot. *Tastes like a sugar donut.*

Liz Nelson Mayer

BLUEBERRY MUFFINS

Preparing: 20 minutes   *Do Ahead*   *Yield: 12 muffins*
Baking: 20 minutes   *Freeze*

2 cups sifted flour
⅓ cup sugar
3 teaspoons baking powder
1 teaspoon salt
1 egg, well beaten

1 cup milk
¼ cup butter or margarine, melted
  and cooled
1 cup fresh or slightly thawed
  dry-pack frozen blueberries

Preheat oven to 425°F. Sift flour, sugar, baking powder and salt into a large bowl. Mix egg, milk and melted, cooled butter in small bowl; add all at once to flour mixture. Stir lightly with a fork just until liquid is absorbed. (Batter will be lumpy.) Fold in blueberries. Spoon into greased medium-sized muffin tins, filling each ⅔ full. Bake 20 minutes, or until golden. Remove from pans. Serve hot.

Lucetta Bahn Ebbert

WHOLE WHEAT MUFFINS

Preparing: 15 minutes   *Do Ahead*   *Yield: 1½ dozen*
Baking: 15 minutes   *Freeze*

1 cup all-purpose flour
1 cup whole wheat or graham flour
4 teaspoons baking powder
½ teaspoon salt
½ cup brown sugar

1 cup milk
2 beaten eggs
⅓ cup melted butter or margarine
½ cup chopped walnuts

Preheat oven to 450°F. Add and mix all dry ingredients. In separate bowl add and mix all wet ingredients. Stir mixtures together just enough to moisten. Fill greased muffin cups ¾ full. Bake about 15 minutes or until golden. *Do not overbake.*

Elise Rice Payne

Cheese, Eggs and Pasta

Radnor Station
Radnor, Pa.

Jane Curtis
© 1978

Radnor

Radnor, both a town and township, has been continuously settled since 1683 when William Penn first plotted its boundaries. The last parcel of free land in Radnor was claimed in 1762. Families directly descending from original Welsh settlers still own many portions of the land.

The township, which includes Villanova, Radnor, St. David's, Wayne and Ithan, developed into an area of large estates as more prosperous Philadelphians made the suburbs their permanent homes. Some of these estates are still privately maintained, while others have become colleges or schools such as Villanova University and Cabrini College.

Radnor Hunt Tailgate

hors d'oeuvre

Beef Horseradish Spread   Seafood Dip Elegante

entrée

Salad By Committee

bread

Apple Butter Bread

dessert

Cranberry Tarts   Black Bottom Cakes

beverage

Sangria

ARTICHOKE PIE

Preparing: 30 minutes   *Yield: One 9-inch pie*
Baking: 45 minutes

1 9-inch pie crust, unbaked
2 (9-ounce) packages frozen
  artichoke hearts, cooked *or* 1-
  1½ cans artichoke hearts,
  drained
4 tablespoons butter or margarine
½ cup chopped onion
1 tablespoon flour
½ cup half and half

½ cup sour cream
4 eggs, beaten
Salt and pepper to taste
¼ teaspoon ground nutmeg
2 teaspoons minced fresh parsley
½ cup shredded Cheddar cheese
½ cup shredded Swiss cheese
¼ cup freshly grated Parmesan
  cheese

Bake crust in preheated 425°F. oven 4 minutes. Cut artichoke hearts into bite-sized pieces. Melt butter in skillet. Add onion; cook over medium heat until tender but not browned, about 5 minutes. Stir in flour until well-blended; add half and half. Cook stirring until thickened, 3-5 minutes. In a small bowl combine sour cream, eggs, salt, pepper, nutmeg and parsley. Add to sautéed onions. Place a layer of artichoke hearts on the bottom of pie crust. Sprinkle Cheddar over top. Add another layer of artichokes; top with Swiss cheese. Pour egg mixture over layers and top with Parmesan. Preheat oven to 350°F.; bake 45 minutes. Cut in wedges and serve at once. Pie can be made ahead by preparing egg mixture and layering pie separately and combining at baking time.

Alice Marks Preston

NO CRUST QUICHE

Preparing: 25 minutes   *Yield: 4 to 6 servings*
Baking: 55 minutes

12 slices bacon, cooked and
   crumbled
1-2 cups shredded Swiss cheese
¾ cup onions

4 eggs
½ cup Bisquick
2 cups milk
Nutmeg

Preheat oven to 350°F. Combine bacon, cheese and onions in well-greased 9-inch pie pan. In medium bowl, blend eggs, Bisquick and milk. Pour over cheese in pie pan. Sprinkle with nutmeg. Bake 55 minutes or until knife inserted in center of quiche comes out clean.

Joy Fleishman Sherry

ASPARAGUS QUICHE

Preparing: 20 minutes   *Yield: 8 to 12 servings*
Baking: 1 hour

1 10-inch pastry shell	4 eggs
1½ pounds fresh asparagus	1½ cups half and half
8 strips bacon	1 teaspoon salt
1 (6-ounce) package processed	⅛ teaspoon pepper
Gruyere cheese, shredded	⅛ teaspoon nutmeg

Preheat oven to 375°F. Make pastry and fit into pie plate. Line shell with foil and 1 cup raw rice; bake 5 minutes at 375°F.; remove foil and rice. Clean asparagus; snap off ends and discard. Set aside 12 spears of about 5-inch length. Slice remaining asparagus into ½-inch pieces. Dice bacon; cook until crisp; drain. Sprinkle bacon in pie shell. Add cheese, then cut asparagus. Mix eggs, half and half and seasonings. Pour into shell. Arrange asparagus spears in wheel-spoke fashion over ingredients. Bake 1 hour or until filling is set.

Ginny Moffitt Gehring

CRUSTLESS VEGETABLE QUICHE

Preparing: 20 minutes   *Yield: 6 servings*
Cooking: 20 to 25 minutes
Baking: 40 to 45 minutes

3 medium zucchini, cubed	1 tablespoon minced parsley
1 large onion, chopped	½ teaspoon basil
½ cup olive oil	½ teaspoon oregano
4 medium tomatoes, peeled	Salt and pepper to taste
and sliced	¼ pound thinly sliced mozzarella
3 eggs	cheese
¾ cup grated Parmesan cheese	

Sauté zucchini and onion in oil until softened. Add tomatoes, cover and simmer 20-25 minutes or until tender. Transfer to mixing bowl; cool. Preheat oven to 350°F. Beat eggs with ¼ cup Parmesan, parsley, basil and oregano; add to vegetables. Season with salt and pepper. Pour half of mixture into greased 9-inch pie pan and top with ½ cup more Parmesan. Layer remaining vegetables and Parmesan. Top with mozzarella; bake 40-45 minutes or until pie is set and cheese is golden brown.

Ardyth Beidleman Sobyak

VEGETABLE CHEESE PIE

Preparing: 30 minutes *Do Ahead* *Yield: 15 to 20 servings*
Chilling: 24 hours

1 (10-ounce) package Nips cheese
 crackers
1 small onion, cut up
2 tablespoons lemon juice
1 teaspoon salt
1 teaspoon Worcestershire sauce
¼ teaspoon paprika
Dash Tabasco

2 cups sour cream
10-12 stuffed green olives
1 medium green pepper, cut up
1 large stalk celery, cut up
Ripe olive rings and pimento strips
 (garnish)
Party rye bread

Grease 9-inch springform pan. Blend cheese crackers to fine crumbs. Line pan with half the crumbs; reserve others. Mix remaining ingredients in blender until liquified. Pour into pan; cover with remaining cheese crumbs. Cover with waxed paper; *refrigerate at least 24 hours.* Garnish with ripe olive rings and pimento strips. Serve on party rye.

Alice Marks Preston

QUICHE LORRAINE

Preparing: 25 minutes *Do Ahead* *Yield: 4 to 8 servings entrée,*
Baking: 35 to 40 minutes *Freeze* *25 servings appetizer*

1 (9-inch) pastry shell
1 cup thinly sliced onions
2 tablespoons butter
1½ cups Gruyère or Swiss cheese,
 cubed
4 slices of ham, cubed or 8 bacon
 slices, fried and crumbled

4 eggs, lightly beaten
1 cup light cream
1 cup heavy cream
½ teaspoon salt
¼ teaspoon white pepper
¼ teaspoon nutmeg

Preheat oven to 425°F. Bake pastry shell 5 minutes. Remove partially baked shell; turn oven to 450°F. Sauté onions in butter until transparent. Cover bottom of pastry with cheese, onions, ham or bacon. Combine remaining ingredients and pour over onion and cheese. Bake 10 minutes; reduce oven to 325°F. and bake for 20-25 minutes or until a knife inserted in center comes out clean.

Mary Campanelle Downey

ITALIAN SPINACH QUICHE

Preparing: 45 minutes   *Do Ahead*   *Yield: 6 to 8 servings*
Baking: 25 to 30 minutes   *Freeze*

1 unbaked 10-inch pastry shell
¼ pound Italian sausage (removed
  from casing)
1 package frozen spinach, thawed
  and drained
¼ pound mushrooms, sliced
2 cups ricotta cheese

½ cup shredded Gruyere cheese
¼ cup Parmesan cheese
¼ cup chopped onions
1-2 tablespoons Dijon mustard
½ teaspoon oregano
1 egg, slightly beaten
Salt and pepper to taste

Preheat oven to 375°F. Brown and crumble sausage; spread evenly in pie shell. Combine spinach, mushrooms, cheeses, onions, mustard, oregano and egg. Add salt and pepper. Spread evenly over sausage. Bake 25-30 minutes or until set. *(May freeze pie, thaw and bake.)*

Note: Serve with ½ cup favorite tomato sauce.

Alice Marks Preston

SPINACH PIE

Preparing: 15 minutes   *Do Ahead*   *Yield: 12 to 15 servings*
Baking: 1 hour   *Freeze*

5 (10-ounce) packages chopped
  frozen spinach
¼ cup melted butter
½ pound finely shredded sharp
  cheese

2 sticks pie crust, or any recipe for
  2 pie crusts

Preheat oven to 350°F. Cook spinach until just thawed; drain well and pour into two 8x8-inch pans or one 10x13-inch pan. Brush with most of melted butter; cover with cheese. Make pie crust and place over spinach mixture; brush with remaining butter. (Can be frozen before baking.) Bake for 1 hour or until lightly browned.

Note: If you like very cheesy dishes, you can use ¾ pound cheese.

Elise Rice Payne

SPANAKOPITA
(Spinach-Cheese Pie)

Preparing: 1 hour　　　　　*Do Ahead*　　　　　*Yield: 8 to 10 servings*
Cooking: 15 minutes
Baking: 1 hour

¼ cup olive oil
½ cup finely chopped onions
¼ cup finely chopped scallions,
　include 2 inches of tops
2 pounds fresh spinach or
　2 (10-ounce) packages frozen
　chopped spinach
2 tablespoons dried dill weed

¼ cup finely chopped parsley
½ teaspoon salt
Freshly ground pepper
⅓ cup milk
½ pound feta cheese, crumbled
4 eggs, lightly beaten
1 cup butter, melted
16 sheets (½ pound) phyllo pastry

In heavy skillet, heat oil over moderate heat until a light haze forms. Add onions and scallions; cook 5 minutes, stirring frequently or until onions are soft and transparent. Wash, thoroughly drain and finely chop spinach. Stir into vegetables; cover tightly and cook 5 minutes. Add dill, parsley, salt and a few grindings of pepper, stirring and shaking pan almost constantly. Cook uncovered 10 minutes or until most of liquid in skillet has evaporated and spinach has begun to stick lightly to pan. In deep bowl, mix spinach mixture and milk. Cool to room temperature; add cheese and slowly beat in eggs. Taste for seasonings. Preheat oven to 300°F. Coat bottom and sides of 12x7x2-inch baking dish with melted butter. Line dish with a sheet of phyllo, pressing into corners and against sides of dish. Brush entire surface of pastry with 2-3 teaspoons melted butter, spreading to outside edges; lay another sheet of phyllo on top. Spread with another 2-3 teaspoons butter; continue constructing pie in this manner until 8 sheets of phyllo have been used. Spread spinach mixture evenly over last layer of phyllo, smoothing into corners. Layer remaining 8 sheets of phyllo pastry on top, coating each with butter as before. Trim excess pastry from around rim of dish. Brush top of pie with remaining butter; bake 1 hour in middle of oven until pastry is crisp and delicately browned. Cut into small squares; serve hot or at room temperature.

TOMATO-CHEESE TART

Preparing: 25 minutes   Do Ahead   Yield: 6 servings
Baking: 15 minutes; 20 minutes

½ package pie crust mix
4 ounces Cheddar cheese,
    shredded (1 cup)
2 (6-ounce) packages shredded
    Gruyère or Muenster cheese (or
    any other favorite cheese)
3 ripe medium-sized tomatoes or
    basket of cherry tomatoes, cut
    in halves

1 teaspoon salt
1 teaspoon basil, crushed
1 teaspoon oregano, crushed
⅛ teaspoon pepper
½ cup chopped green onions or
    scallions or spring onions
2 tablespoons butter or margarine
2 tablespoons soft bread crumbs

Preheat oven to 425°F. Prepare pie crust mix according to directions, adding
½ cup Cheddar cheese. Roll out to fit into a 9-inch pie plate. Prick well with a
fork; flute edges of crust. Bake 10-15 minutes; cool. Turn oven down to 325°F.
Spoon remaining Cheddar and Gruyère (or other cheese) into crust. Slice tomatoes in half lengthwise, then into thin wedges. Arrange, overlapping in a
circular pattern, over cheese. Sprinkle with seasonings. Sauté green onions in
butter or margarine until tender; sprinkle in center of pie. Top with bread
crumbs. Bake 20 minutes or until tomatoes are tender. *The Tomato-Cheese
Tart is excellent with a roast or as a meatless main dish at a luncheon.*

Gail White Dillon

CHEESY BREAKFAST CASSEROLE

Preparing: 20 minutes   Do Ahead   Yield: 8 to 10 servings
Chilling: 12 hours
Baking: 45 minutes

1½ pounds bulk sausage, browned
    and drained
1 dozen eggs, beaten
12 pieces bread, cubed, no crust

1½ teaspoons dry mustard
1 pound sharp Cheddar cheese,
    cubed

Mix all ingredients; put in ungreased 9x13 inch glass baking dish. *Let sit in
refrigerator overnight.* Take out of refrigerator ½ hour before baking. Preheat
oven to 350°F.; bake 45 minutes. Cool 10 minutes before serving.

Nancy Woodland Phillips

BREAKFAST CASSEROLE

Preparing: 20 minutes　　　　*Do Ahead*　　　　*Yield: 4 to 6 servings*
Baking: 45 minutes

1 pound pork sausage, cooked,
　drained, crumbled
6 eggs, whipped
2 slices bread, cubed

2 cups milk
1 cup shredded Cheddar cheese
1 teaspoon dry mustard
1 teaspoon salt

Preheat oven to 350°F. Combine ingredients and place in greased casserole. Bake 45 minutes.

Note: Ingredients may be assembled in greased casserole, covered and refrigerated overnight. In morning remove from refrigerator and bake as directed.

Variation: 6-10 slices crisp cooked bacon may be substituted for sausage. For cheesier flavor, increase cheese by 1 cup and bread by 2 slices.

John Goodchild

EGGS PRESNOV
(Baked Eggs)

Preparing: 20 minutes　　　*Do Ahead: Partially*　　　*Yield: 8 servings*
Baking: 40 minutes

6 eggs, beaten
1 cup milk
2 teaspoons sugar
1 teaspoon salt
½ pound Monterey Jack cheese,
　cubed
1 (3-ounce) package cream
　cheese, cubed

1 (8-ounce) container cottage
　cheese
3 tablespoons butter, cubed
1 teaspoon baking powder
½ cup flour
Chives or parsley (garnish)

Preheat oven to 325°F. Mix eggs, milk, sugar and salt together in greased 9x12-inch casserole. Add 3 cheeses and butter to egg mixture; blend. Add baking powder and flour *just before baking. This dish may be prepared a day ahead and refrigerated;* add baking powder and flour just prior to baking. Bake 40 minutes or until set. Garnish with chives or parsley.

Gail White Dillon

LUTIE'S EGG CASSEROLE

Preparing: 20 minutes   Do Ahead: Partially   Yield: 12 to 16 servings
Baking: 30 to 35 minutes

¼ cup butter or margarine, melted
1½ dozen eggs
1 cup sour cream
1 cup milk
2 teaspoons salt

¼ cup chopped onion
¼-½ cup canned sliced
   mushrooms (optional)
¼-½ cup chopped green pepper

Preheat oven to 325°F. Grease 9x13-inch glass baking dish. Combine butter, eggs, sour cream, milk and salt; whip until well-blended. Fold in onion, mushrooms and green pepper. *Can be done this far 6-8 hours ahead of time.* To do ahead a full day, add combined vegetables immediately before baking. Bake 30-35 minutes or until set.

Lois Rising Pogyor

EGGS A LA BUCKINGHAM

Preparing: 30 minutes   *Yield: 4 servings*
Baking: 9 minutes

2 tablespoons butter
5 teaspoons flour
Dash salt and pepper
¾ cup milk
1 (3-ounce) package smoked beef
4 eggs

1 tablespoon milk
Salt and pepper
1 tablespoon butter
2 English muffins, split (toasting
   optional)
½ cup shredded American cheese

Melt 2 tablespoons butter; blend in flour and dash of salt and pepper. Add ¾ cup milk; cook and stir until bubbly. Cook 1 minute. Add beef and keep warm. Preheat oven to 350°F. Beat eggs with 1 tablespoon milk, salt and pepper. In pan, melt 1 tablespoon butter; add egg mixture. Cook over low heat just until set, lift and fold. Place muffins on baking sheet; spoon beef mixture over. Top with eggs. Bake 8 minutes and sprinkle with cheese. Bake 1 minute more or until cheese is melted.

Cynthia Harris Helsel

SHERRIED EGGS AND MUSHROOMS

Preparing: 30 minutes *Do Ahead* *Yield: 4 servings*
Cooking: 20 minutes

¼ pound mushrooms
6 tablespoons butter
1 tablespoon finely chopped onion
3 tablespoons flour
¾ teaspoon salt
¼ teaspoon ground red pepper

1½ cups light cream
6 hard-cooked eggs
4 teaspoons dry sherry
1 package frozen patty shells,
  baked

Rinse, pat dry and slice mushrooms. In small skillet heat 2 tablespoons butter, add mushrooms and onions. Sauté 4-5 minutes; set aside. In medium saucepan, heat 4 tablespoons butter; remove from heat, stir in flour, salt and pepper until smooth. Gradually stir in cream. Bring to boil, stirring constantly until sauce is thickened and smooth. Dice 5 of the 6 eggs; stir with mushrooms and sherry into sauce. Pour mixture into baked shells. Slice remaining egg into wedges and use to garnish.

Note: This is also good served over spinach instead of patty shells.

Ida Marie Jannetta Higgins

CONTINENTAL EGG CASSEROLE

Preparing: 30 minutes *Do Ahead* *Yield: 8 to 10 servings*
Baking: 45 minutes

3 cups unseasoned croutons
8 ounces shredded sharp cheese
6 eggs, slightly beaten
3 cups milk
1 teaspoon salt

¾ teaspoon dry mustard
¼ teaspoon onion powder
Dash pepper
6 slices bacon, cooked crisp and
  crumbled

Preheat oven to 325°F. In bottom of greased 2-quart casserole, place croutons. Sprinkle cheese on top. Combine eggs, milk, salt, mustard, onion powder and pepper. Pour over croutons and cheese. Sprinkle crumbled bacon on top. Bake uncovered 45 minutes or until eggs are set.

Judilee Cronrath Traynor

ELEANOR'S CHEESE AND MUSHROOM BAKE

Preparing: 20 minutes   *Do Ahead*   *Yield: 6 servings*
Baking: 45 minutes

½ cup chopped celery
¼ cup chopped onion
3 tablespoons butter or margarine
½ pound fresh mushrooms, sliced
4 cups day old bread or rolls, cubed
2 cups (8 ounces) sharp Cheddar
    cheese

2 eggs
2 cups milk
2 teaspoons dry mustard
1 teaspoon salt
½ teaspoon pepper

Preheat oven to 325°F. Sauté onions and celery in butter. Add mushrooms and cook until tender. In greased 2-quart casserole, layer half of the bread, then mushroom mixture and cheese. Repeat layers. Beat eggs, milk and seasonings. Pour evenly over bread mixture. Bake 45 minutes.

Barbara Trimble Blake

HAM AND CHEESE CUSTARD PUFF

Preparing: 15 minutes   *Yield: 6 to 8 servings*
Baking: 45 minutes

6 eggs
½ cup flour
1 teaspoon baking powder
1 cup milk
8 ounces cottage cheese
1 (3-ounce) package cream
    cheese, cut in small cubes
3 tablespoons firm butter, cut in
    small pieces

1 pound Monterey Jack cheese,
    shredded
¾ cup cooked ham, cut in small
    pieces
¼ cup chopped green pepper
    (optional)
¼ cup chopped onion (optional)

Preheat oven to 350°F. In large bowl beat eggs, flour, baking powder and milk until smooth. Stir in other ingredients; turn into greased 2-quart shallow casserole. Bake 45 minutes or until set. Serve hot.

Note: A good way to use odds and ends of cheese and bits and pieces of ham. *Can be reheated; may be halved.*

Doris Coady Devine

NOODLE CASSEROLE

Preparing: 20 minutes   *Do Ahead*   *Yield: 8 to 10 servings*
Baking: 45 to 60 minutes   *Freeze*

½ pound wide noodles   1 pint sour cream
8 eggs   2 teaspoons vanilla
1 cup melted butter   1 cup sugar
1 (8-ounce) package cream
  cheese, softened

Preheat oven to 350°F. Cook and drain noodles. Mix all ingredients, except noodles, in mixer for 10 minutes. Add noodles; mix gently. Pour into a 9x13-inch baking dish, arranging noodles in layered fashion. Bake 45-60 minutes. Use this as a side dish for a brunch; serve with honey or fresh fruit.

Lynn Green

RIGATONI AL CAPRICCIOSA

Preparing: 30 minutes   *Do Ahead: Partially*   *Yield: 8 to 10 servings*
Cooking: 10 minutes

¼ pound proscuitto ham, thinly   ½ pint heavy cream
  sliced   Parmesan cheese, freshly grated
¾ cup sweet butter   Black pepper
½ small onion   Salt
¾-1 cup fresh or frozen peas   Tomato sauce (optional)
¼ pound fresh mushrooms
1 pound rigatoni or penne rigate
  (smaller)

Cut proscuitto into small pieces; sauté in a little butter. Sauté chopped onion in butter until soft. Cook peas, drain and set aside. Thinly slice mushrooms; sauté or steam with a little butter until tender. Drain; set aside. This can be done early in the day. Boil noodles; cook to *al dente* stage. Drain; set aside. Melt butter in a large pan; add noodles. Toss; add a little cream. Add vegetables, one at a time; toss well. Add remainder of cream, some Parmesan cheese and black pepper; mix over low heat until cream begins to thicken. To make sauce red, you may add a few tablespoons tomato sauce. Serve with additional cheese.

ZUCCHINI LASAGNE

Preparing: 20 minutes   *Do Ahead*   *Yield: 6 servings*

¾ pound ground beef
½ cup finely chopped onion
1 (15-ounce) can tomato sauce
½ teaspoon oregano
½ teaspoon basil
Salt and freshly ground pepper
4 medium zucchini (about 8 inches
 long)

1 (8-ounce) container ricotta
 cheese or large curd cottage
 cheese
1 egg
½ pound mozzarella cheese
Grated Parmesan cheese

Preheat oven to 350°F. Cook beef and onion in large skillet; drain fat. Add tomato sauce and seasonings; simmer uncovered 10 minutes, stirring occasionally. Slice zucchini lengthwise about ¼-inch thick. Arrange half the slices in 8x12-inch shallow baking pan; salt lightly. Beat ricotta with egg; spread on zucchini. Top with ½ mozzarella and half of meat sauce. Layer with remaining zucchini, mozzarella and sauce. Sprinkle generously with Parmesan and bake uncovered 40 minutes. Let stand 10 minutes before serving.

Jeanne Kronmiller Honish

ARDYTH'S ZUCCHINI FETTUCINE

Preparing: 20 minutes   *Yield: 4 servings*

1 medium zucchini
2 cloves garlic
1 medium onion
¼ cup vegetable oil
¼ cup freshly grated Parmesan
 cheese
¼ cup chicken bouillon

2 tablespoons butter
1 teaspoon fresh basil leaves
2 teaspoons fresh parsley
Salt and pepper to taste
½ pound fettucine
Croutons

Slice zucchini crosswise into thin slices. Sauté zucchini, garlic and onions in oil until transparent. Mix in cheese, bouillon, butter and spices. Keep warm over low heat. Cook and drain fettucine; put in serving bowl. Stir in zucchini mixture and put croutons on top before serving. Serve with additional grated Parmesan cheese.

Ardyth Beidleman Sobyak

BAKED SAFFRON RICE

Preparing: 15 minutes   *Do Ahead: Partially*   *Yield: 6 to 8 servings*
Soaking: 2 hours
Cooking: 40 minutes

½ teaspoon saffron
1 cup cold water
½ cup butter
1 onion, chopped

1 clove garlic, minced
2 cups rice, uncooked
2 cups boiling water

Soak saffron in cold water 2 hours. Preheat oven to 400°F. Melt butter; add onion and garlic. Cook 3 minutes or until onion is soft. Add raw rice; stir until well coated with butter. Add saffron and water; bring to a boil. Place mixture in casserole, cover tightly and bake 10 minutes. Remove cover; stir to mix thoroughly. Add boiling water; cover. Continue to bake until done (about 30 minutes). If rice becomes dry before tender, add additional water. Fluff rice and serve warm.

Grace Burdett Nellis

STRAW AND HAY

Preparing: 45 minutes   *Yield: 8 to 10 servings*

1 (8-ounce) package green egg
  noodles
1 (8-ounce) package medium egg
  noodles
½ cup butter or margarine
½ cup chopped onion
1 cup (¼ pound) fresh mushrooms,
  sliced

1 (10-ounce) package frozen baby
  peas, thawed
6 ounces cooked ham, cut into
  1-inch cubes
2 cups heavy cream
1 cup grated Parmesan cheese
1½ teaspoons salt
½ teaspoon pepper

In large saucepan, cook both packages of noodles in boiling water until tender; drain and keep warm. Meanwhile, in Dutch oven or extra large skillet, melt ¼ cup butter or margarine over low heat. Add onion; cook until soft. Increase heat to medium. Add mushrooms; sauté until tender. Add peas and ham; sauté 2 minutes. Remove from heat; add noodles and toss well. Cover. In medium saucepan heat cream and remaining butter or margarine until hot *(butter need not be melted)*. Pour over noodles; sprinkle with cheese, salt and pepper. Toss well to combine.

Frances Marincola Blair

LINGUINE AND CLAM SAUCE

Preparing: 15 minutes   *Yield: 4 servings*

1 pound linguine, cooked
4 tablespoons butter
1 large clove garlic, chopped
1 tablespoon flour
2 (7-ounce) cans minced clams

4 tablespoons chopped parsley
¾ teaspoon dried thyme
¾ teaspoon dried basil
Salt and pepper to taste

Heat butter and cook garlic about 1 minute. Stir in flour and juice from clams. Bring to full boil stirring constantly. Add clams, parsley, thyme and basil. Simmer 5 minutes, stirring. Season to taste with salt and pepper. Serve over hot, cooked linguine.

Variation:
2-3 cloves garlic
2 tablespoons chopped parsley

1 tablespoon basil
½ cup olive oil

Cook garlic and herbs in oil until soft. Add clams and heat just enough to warm them. Serve over linguine.

Sandra Schild Fletcher

PILAF DE CHAMPIGNONS

Preparing: 15 minutes   *Do Ahead: Partially*   *Yield: 6 servings*
Cooking: 20 minutes

¾ pound fresh mushrooms
¼ cup butter
1 small onion, chopped
1 clove garlic
½ teaspoon turmeric

1 cup rice, uncooked
1 bay leaf
1½ cups chicken broth
Salt and pepper

Break stems off mushrooms; slice caps; set aside. Heat 2 tablespoons butter in a heavy skillet; add onion and garlic and cook until golden. Add mushrooms; cook about 5 minutes stirring constantly. Sprinkle with turmeric; add rice and bay leaf. Stir until rice is well coated. Add broth, salt and pepper. Cover and simmer until broth is absorbed. Toss with remaining butter.

PASTA PRIMAVERA

Preparing: 45 minutes   *Do Ahead: Partially*   *Yield: 6 servings*

1 cup zucchini, sliced
1½ cups broccoli, broken into
   flowerets
1½ cups snow peas
1 cup baby peas
6 stalks asparagus, sliced
1 pound spaghetti
12 cherry tomatoes, cut in half
3 tablespoons olive oil
2 teaspoons minced garlic
Salt and freshly ground pepper

¼ cup chopped Italian parsley
⅓ cup pine nuts
10 large mushrooms, sliced
⅓ cup butter
½ cup freshly grated Parmesan
   cheese
1 cup heavy cream
½ cup chopped fresh basil
½ cup chicken consommé
   (optional)

Blanch vegetables in boiling salted water 1-2 minutes each until just crisp-tender. Drain and refresh under cold water; set aside. *This can be done ahead of time.* Cook pasta in 4-6 quarts boiling salted water until *al dente*, about 8-11 minutes; drain. While pasta cooks, sauté tomatoes in 1 tablespoon oil with 1 teaspoon garlic, salt, pepper and parsley; set aside. In another large pan with 2 tablespoons oil, sauté pine nuts until brown. Add remaining garlic and all vegetables. Simmer a few minutes until hot. In pan large enough to hold pasta and vegetables, melt butter. Add cheese, cream and basil. Stir to blend; and melt cheese. Add pasta; toss to coat with sauce. (If sauce gets too thick, thin with a little chicken consommé.) Add about ⅓ of vegetables; toss again. Divide pasta among 6 broad soup plates; add remaining vegetables. Top with cherry tomatoes. Season to taste with salt, pepper and more grated Parmesan.

Frances Marincola Blair

PILAF WITH ALMONDS

Preparing: 15 minutes   *Yield: 8 servings*
Baking: 30 minutes

1 large onion, finely chopped
2 cups uncooked rice
4 tablespoons butter

3 cups chicken stock or broth
¾ cup blanched shredded almonds

Preheat oven to 375°F. Brown onion and rice in butter. Put in 2-quart baking dish; cover with stock. Add almonds and stir. Cover and bake 30 minutes or until rice is tender and liquid is absorbed.

WILD RICE SUPREME

Preparing: 35 minutes   *Yield: 4 to 6 servings*
Baking: 30 minutes

⅓ cup wild rice, uncooked   ¼ cup flour
2 cups water   1 teaspoon salt
½ teaspoon salt   2 cups milk
½ cup white rice, uncooked   2-3 tablespoons sherry
8 ounces fresh mushrooms, sliced   ¼ cup fine bread crumbs,
¼ cup butter   buttered

Wash and drain wild rice. Heat wild rice, water and salt to boiling. Reduce heat, cover and simmer until rice is tender, about 35 minutes; drain. Cook white rice according to package directions and mix. While rice is cooking, cook and stir mushrooms in butter in large skillet over low heat until tender, about 5 minutes. Mix flour and 1 teaspoon salt; sprinkle on mushrooms. Cook and stir until coated. Preheat oven to 375°F. Stir milk into mushroom mixture. Heat to boiling; reduce heat. Stir constantly over medium heat until thickened. Remove from heat; stir in sherry. Stir white and wild rice into mushroom sauce. Turn into greased 1½-quart casserole. Sprinkle with bread crumbs. Bake uncovered 30 minutes. If crumbs are not browned, run under broiler to crisp.

Grace Burdett Nellis

ELENA'S RICE

Preparing: 20 minutes   *Do Ahead*   *Yield: 6 to 8 servings*
Baking: 30 minutes

1 cup raw rice   1 (4-ounce) can peeled green chili
Salt to taste   peppers
2 cups sour cream   2 tablespoons butter
½ pound Monterey Jack cheese   ½ cup grated cheese (optional)

Cook rice according to package directions. (You may use quick cooking rice.) Combine cooked rice with salt and sour cream. Preheat oven to 350°F. Arrange half rice mixture in bottom of 1½-2 quart casserole; place cubes of cheese wrapped in strips of pepper on top. Add remaining rice mixture; dot with butter. Additional cheese can be grated over top. Bake 30 minutes.

Mary Jane Wright Knight

GREEN NOODLES WITH RICOTTA

Preparing: 15 minutes   *Do Ahead: Partially*   *Yield: 8 to 10 servings*
Cooking: 12 minutes

Ricotta Topping:
½ cup butter, melted   1 teaspoon freshly ground pepper
15 ounces skim milk ricotta cheese   1 teaspoon salt
½ cup freshly grated Parmesan
   cheese

In medium bowl, combine all ingredients. *(May be prepared in advance to this point. Cover and refrigerate up to 24 hours. Let sauce come to room temperature before tossing with hot noodles.)*

Noodles:
1 (16-ounce) package spinach   1 tablespoon salt
   noodles   1 tablespoon oil
6 quarts water

Heat water to boiling; add salt and oil. Gradually add noodles stirring to prevent sticking. Cook according to package directions; drain immediately. Transfer to large serving dish and toss well with ricotta mixture.

Karen Klabau Meyers

FETTUCINI CARBONARA

Preparing: 10 minutes   *Do Ahead*   *Yield: 4 servings as main dish;*
Cooking: 10 minutes   *more if side dish*

1 pound bacon, cooked and   ½ cup butter, cut into small pieces
   crumbled   1 cup heavy cream
1 pound fettucini, cooked to *al*   1 cup frozen peas, cooked
   dente (firm) and drained well   1 cup grated Parmesan cheese

Immediately after cooking fettucini, toss with bacon, butter, cream, peas and cheese. Stir over low heat just to warm through. Serve immediately.

Meredith Herting Swift

FETTUCINI WITH ZUCCHINI AND MUSHROOMS

Preparing: 25 minutes   *Yield: 6 servings*
Cooking: 15 minutes

½ pound mushrooms, thinly sliced   ½ cup butter
¼ cup butter   12 ounces fettucini
1¼ pounds zucchini, cut into   ¾ cup freshly grated Parmesan
   julienne strips   cheese
¾ cup heavy cream   ½ cup chopped fresh parsley

In large skillet, sauté mushrooms in ¼ cup butter for 2 minutes. Add zucchini, cream and ½ cup butter. Bring to boil; simmer 3 minutes. In large saucepan, cook fettucini in rapidly boiling water 7 minutes, or until done; drain in colander. Add pasta to large skillet with zucchini; with fork, toss gently with Parmesan cheese and parsley. Transfer to heated platter; serve with additional Parmesan cheese. *Quality of this dish demands using real butter, heavy cream and fresh Parmesan.*

Pam Bartels Morris

FETTUCINI ALFREDO

Preparing: 5 minutes   *Do Ahead: Partially*   *Yield: 10 servings*
Cooking: 12 minutes

1 cup butter or margarine   ½ cup grated Romano cheese
1 cup heavy cream   24 ounces fettucini
½ cup freshly grated Parmesan
   cheese

In small mixer bowl, cream butter; beat in cream a little at a time. Beat in Parmesan and Romano. *(If prepared in advance, chill mixture, then bring to room temperature again to serve.)* Cook fettucini in boiling salted water until tender, about 12 minutes. Drain well. Transfer to warm serving bowl. Add creamed mixture; toss noodles until coated.

Peggy Biglin Owen

RICE WITH RAISINS AND NUTS

Preparing: 15 minutes   *Yield: 4 servings*
Baking: 17 minutes

1 cup rice	2-3 tablespoons raisins
3 tablespoons butter	1½ cups chicken broth
⅓ cup finely minced onion	Freshly ground pepper to taste
¼ cup slivered almonds	

Preheat oven to 400°F. Melt 2 tablespoons butter in saucepan; add onion and sauté until wilted. Add rice; stir to coat with butter. Add raisins, nuts, pepper and broth. Bring to boil on top of stove; bake for 17 minutes *exactly*. Stir in remaining tablespoon butter with fork.

Jeffrey Preston

PESTO SAUCE

Preparing: 10 minutes   *Do Ahead*   *Yield: 1 cup*
Cooking: 10 minutes   *Freeze*

2 cups fresh basil leaves, torn in pieces	3 tablespoons freshly grated Romano cheese
2 cloves garlic, peeled, cut in half	6 tablespoons freshly grated Parmesan cheese
3 tablespoons walnuts or pignolias (pine nuts)	3 tablespoons soft butter
½ cup olive oil	1 pound pasta (spaghetti, fettuccini or any homemade noodles)
½ teaspoon salt	

Put basil, garlic, nuts, oil and salt into bowl of food processor or blender. Blend until just minced. Add cheeses and butter; blend briefly. Season to taste and let stand. Cook pasta *al dente*. Drain, reserving 2 tablespoons water. Place pasta in heated bowl, add pesto and reserved water. Toss lightly. Serve at once.

Kessler's Cutlery & Cookware
Spread Eagle Village, Strafford, Pennsylvania

NOODLES ANTIN

Preparing: 30 minutes   *Do Ahead*   *Yield: 8 to 10 servings*
Baking: 45 minutes   *Freeze*

10 ounces fine noodles   2 tablespoons Worcestershire
2 cups cottage cheese   sauce
2 cups sour cream   2 dashes Tabasco sauce
2 cloves garlic, minced   Salt
2 onions, finely chopped

Preheat oven to 350°F. Cook noodles and drain. Mix all other ingredients; add noodles. Pour mixture into buttered casserole dish. Bake 45 minutes or until brown and crusty on top.

Note: Can be frozen before baking.

Alice Marks Preston

NICE NOODLES

Preparing: 30 minutes   *Yield: 4 servings*

¼ cup sliced onion   3 tablespoons lemon juice
2 tablespoons butter   1 teaspoon salt
1 pound ground beef   ¼ teaspoon pepper
3 tablespoons dry sherry   Dash garlic salt
1 (10½-ounce) can beef consommé ¼ pound medium noodles
1 (6-ounce) can sliced mushrooms 1 cup sour cream
   and liquid   Chopped parsley (garnish)

Sauté onions in butter; add meat and brown, chopping to keep in small bits. Drain fat from pan. Stir in sherry, consommé, mushrooms and liquid, lemon juice, salt, pepper and garlic salt. Simmer, uncovered for 15 minutes. Stir in uncooked noodles. Cover and cook, stirring occasionally, for 10 minutes until noodles are tender. Stir in sour cream; remove from heat. Garnish with parsley.

Frances Marincola Blair

Entrées

Wayne

Originally named Louella, Wayne received its name to honor General Anthony Wayne, whose birthplace is nearby. Along with Bryn Mawr, it was one of the country's first planned suburban communities. In the 1870's, George W. Childs and A. J. Drexel built 80 "spacious homes" with "pure water in abundance," advertising them for sale in the newspapers in Philadelphia. This was the first time a family could choose from several new homes in an established neighborhood. As a result, Wayne became the center of the towns along the upper line of the train. It sported the first man-made outdoor swimming pool, an opera house and several hotels. Numerous clubs, such as the Saturday Club, were established to meet the intellectual needs of the former city dwellers who were accustomed to having literary, art and discussion societies nearby.

Welcome to Wayne Luncheon

hors d'oeuvre
Pickled Shrimp

entrée
Tomato Cheese Tart

salad
Spinach Salad

bread
Raisin Bran Muffins

dessert
Tortoni   Macaroons

beverage
Mother's Rum Punch

CRAB LOUIS

Preparing: 20 minutes   *Do Ahead*   *Yield: 6 servings*

½ cup mayonnaise
½ cup sour cream
2 tablespoons chili sauce
2 tablespoons vegetable oil
1 tablespoon vinegar
1 tablespoon prepared horseradish
1 tablespoon fresh lemon juice
1 tablespoon chopped fresh
  parsley

2 teaspoons grated onion
½ teaspoon salt
4 drops Tabasco
1 pound frozen crabmeat
1 medium head iceberg lettuce
Watercress sprigs (garnish)
Lemon wedges (garnish)

In small bowl, mix together all ingredients except crabmeat and lettuce. *Cover and refrigerate.* Thaw crabmeat and pat dry with paper towel; break lumps into bite-sized pieces. *Keep refrigerated until ready to use.* Shred lettuce thinly; arrange a portion on individual plates. Mound crabmeat over it; add sauce. Top with garnish. May use shrimp in place of crabmeat.

Jeanne Kronmiller Honish

CRABMEAT QUICHE

Preparing: 15 minutes   *Do Ahead: Partially*   *Yield: 6 to 8 servings*
Chilling: 1 hour   *Freeze*
Baking: 30 minutes

1½ cups crabmeat, fresh or frozen
1 tablespoon chopped celery
1 tablespoon chopped onion
2 tablespoons finely chopped
  parsley
2 tablespoons sherry

Pastry for one 9-inch pie crust
4 eggs, lightly beaten
2 cups cream
¼ teaspoon nutmeg
½ teaspoon salt
¼ teaspoon white pepper

Pick crabmeat to remove bits of shell and cartilage. Combine crabmeat, celery, onion, parsley and sherry; refrigerate one hour. Preheat oven to 450°F. Line 9-inch pie plate with pastry; bake 5 minutes. Cover bottom of crust with crabmeat mixture. Combine eggs, cream, nutmeg, salt and pepper; pour over mixture in pie shell. Bake 15 minutes. Reduce temperature to 350°F.; bake 10 minutes longer, or until a knife inserted 1-inch from pastry edge comes out clean. Serve immediately.

Regina Shehadi Guza

FRESH BACKFIN CRABMEAT
ON AVOCADO RINGS WITH REMOULADE SAUCE

Preparing: 20 minutes   *Do Ahead: Partially*   *Yield: 8 servings*
Cooking: 1 hour

2 avocados   **Lettuce**
Lemon juice   **1 pound fresh crabmeat**

Slice each avocado into 4 thick rings and sprinkle with lemon juice. Place one leaf of lettuce in dish and top with one slice of avocado. Place generous spoonful of crabmeat in center of avocado ring and top with Remoulade sauce.

Remoulade Sauce:
1¼ cups mayonnaise   **1 clove garlic, finely chopped**
1 rounded tablespoon finely   **1 teaspoon dry mustard**
chopped fresh tarragon   **1 teaspoons capers**
1 round tablespoon finely chopped **2 small pickles, finely chopped**
basil or chervil
1 rounded tablespoon finely
chopped fresh parsley

Combine all ingredients and chill.

CRABMEAT SOUFFLÉ

Preparing: 30 minutes   *Do Ahead*   *Yield: 8 servings*
Cooking: 1 hour

6 slices buttered bread (cut in   **2 cups milk**
fourths with crust removed)   **1 teaspoon salt**
1 small package Velveeta cheese, **1 teaspoon dry mustard**
cubed or sliced   **1 teaspoon Aćcent**
2 (7-ounce) cans crabmeat   **2 tablespoons sherry or**
(pick out membranes)   **Worcestershire sauce**
3 eggs, beaten slightly   **to taste**

Preheat oven to 350°F. Arrange bread, cheese and crab in layers in oblong baking dish. Mix eggs, milk and seasoning together. Pour liquid over layers and bake 1 hour, placing dish in a pan of water.

Note: May be completely put together the night before.

Ann Keenan Seidel

CRABMEAT CASSEROLE

Preparing: 15 minutes   *Do Ahead: Partially*   *Yield: 6 to 8 servings*
Baking: 20 minutes

1 (20-ounce) can artichoke hearts
1 pound crabmeat
½ pound fresh mushrooms,
  sautéed
4 tablespoons butter
2½ tablespoons flour
1 cup light cream

½ teaspoon salt
1 teaspoon Worcestershire sauce
¼ cup medium dry sherry
Paprika to taste
Cayenne to taste
Pepper to taste
½ cup grated Parmesan cheese

Preheat oven to 375°F. Place artichokes in bottom of baking dish; add layer of crabmeat. Top with mushrooms. Melt butter in saucepan; add remaining ingredients except cheese, stirring well after each addition to form a smooth sauce. Pour sauce over artichoke-crab layers; sprinkle cheese on top. Bake 20 minutes.

Nancy Reagan
First Lady

HOT CRABMEAT SANDWICH

Preparing: 15 minutes   *Do Ahead*   *Yield: 6 servings*
Chilling: 12 hours minimum
Baking: 1 hour

1 pound backfin crabmeat
⅛ teaspoon salt
⅛ teaspoon cayenne pepper
Juice of ½ lemon
12 slices bread

12 slices sharp Cheddar cheese
4 eggs
2 cups half and half
4-6 tablespoons sherry
  (not cooking)

Add salt, lemon juice and pepper to crabmeat; set aside. Remove crusts of bread; butter one side. Place 6 slices, buttered side down, in baking dish. On each slice of bread place a slice of cheese, a portion of crabmeat and another slice of cheese. Top with slice of bread, buttered side up. Pour mixture of beaten eggs, cream and sherry over bread. Place in refrigerator overnight. *Remove from refrigerator 1 hour before baking.* Preheat oven to 325°F.; bake 1 hour.

Joanne Behm Weyant

QUICK CRAB LUNCHEON

Preparing: 10 minutes   *Yield: 4 servings*
Broiling: 5 to 10 minutes

1 pound crabmeat
½ cup mayonnaise
1 level teaspoon prepared
  mustard
¼ teaspoon salt
Dash pepper
Pimento (optional)
1 teaspoon parsley

⅛ teaspoon powdered garlic
  (optional)
Sufficient milk or cream to thin to
  desired consistency
4 slices of buttered bread or
  English muffins
Paprika (garnish)

Mix all ingredients except crab and bread; blend in crabmeat. Pile mixture on bread slices; sprinkle lightly with paprika. Place on cookie sheet and broil 8-10 inches from heat until heated through. Serve with green salad.

Quality Seafood Market
Devon, Pennsylvania

IMPERIAL CRAB

Preparing: 20 minutes   *Do Ahead: Partially*   *Yield: 8 servings*
Cooking: 5 minutes

¼ cup butter
¼ cup flour
1 cup milk
Salt and pepper
¼ cup diced green pepper
2 pimentos, diced

½ teaspoon Worcestershire
  sauce
Drop of Tabasco sauce
2 tablespoons minced parsley
2 pounds cooked crabmeat
2 egg yolks, well beaten

Melt butter; add flour, and stir until smooth. Add milk and continue cooking over medium heat, stirring constantly, until thickened. Add rest of ingredients and mix well. Continue cooking until heated through, but do not boil. Put into 8 individual casseroles or shells and brown under broiler.

Variation: Lobster Imperial—Substitute lobster meat for crabmeat.

The Old Original Bookbinder's Restaurant
Philadelphia, Pennsylvania

SEAFOOD CASSEROLE

Preparing: 30 minutes   *Do Ahead*   *Yield: 8 servings*
Baking: 40 minutes to 1 hour

**2 (10¾-ounce) cans cream of
mushroom soup
1 cup mayonnaise
¼ cup sherry
½ cup milk
1½ pounds boneless lobster, crab,
or shrimp (if frozen, drain and
rinse well)**

**3 cups (1 box) packaged seasoned
croutons
2 (5-ounce) cans water chestnuts,
drained and sliced
½ cup minced green onion
1 cup shredded Cheddar cheese**

Preheat oven to 350°F. Mix soup, mayonnaise and sherry; stir in milk. Combine with all remaining ingredients except cheese. Turn into 3-quart baking dish; top with cheese. Bake 1 hour if has been refrigerated, 40 minutes if not.

Judy Lane Davies

LOBSTER NEWBURG

Preparing: 25 minutes   *Yield: 4 to 6 servings*

**6 tablespoons butter
2 tablespoons flour
1½ cups light cream
3 egg yolks, beaten
1 (12-ounce) package of Chilean
lobster meat (Langostino)**

**3 tablespoons dry white wine
2 teaspoons lemon juice
¼ teaspoon salt
Paprika
Frozen pastry shells**

Melt butter in medium saucepan; whisk in flour. Stir in cream; cook, stirring constantly until sauce thickens and bubbles. Stir 2 tablespoons of hot mixture into egg yolks. Add all yolk mixture at once back into saucepan. Cook, stirring constantly until thickened. Add lobster; heat through. Add wine, lemon juice and salt. (If too thick add more wine to thin.) Sprinkle with paprika. Bake pastry shells as directed on package. Serve Newburg in pastry shells.

Variation: Any combination of frozen crabmeat (thawed), cooked lobster and/ or cooked and cut up tile fish can be substituted for lobster (i.e., 1 (6-ounce) package frozen crab and 2 frozen lobster tails, cooked or 8 ounces tile fish, cooked.)

Dru Huber Hammond

SEAFOOD BAKE

Preparing: 35 minutes   *Do Ahead*   *Yield: 4 to 6 servings*
Baking: 15 minutes

1 (6½-ounce) can crabmeat   1-1½ cups finely cut celery
1 (4½-ounce) can shrimp, drained   ½ teaspoon salt
1 cup mayonnaise   1 teaspoon Worcestershire sauce
½ cup chopped green pepper   2 cups potato chips, crushed
¼ cup minced onion   Paprika

Drain crabmeat; remove cartilage and flake. Combine all ingredients except potato chips and paprika. Preheat oven to 400°F. Place in individual baking dishes or in ovenproof platter. Top with crushed potato chips; sprinkle with paprika. Bake 15 minutes.

Dru Huber Hammond

SEAFOOD QUICHE

Preparing: 20 to 25 minutes   *Yield: 6 servings*
Baking: 25 to 30 minutes

2 tablespoons minced shallots   2 tablespoons Madeira wine or
3 tablespoons butter   dry white vermouth
½ cup (¼ pound) diced scallops   3 eggs
½ cup (¼ pound) diced lobster   1 cup heavy cream
½ cup (¼ pound) diced shrimp   1 tablespoon tomato paste
¼ teaspoon salt   1 10-inch pastry shell
Pinch pepper   ¼ cup shredded Swiss cheese

Preheat oven to 375°F. Cook shallots in butter. Add seafood; stir gently for 2 minutes. Sprinkle with salt and pepper. Add wine, simmer for 1 minute; cool. Beat eggs, cream and tomato paste. Blend seafood gradually into egg mixture. Pour into pastry shell. Sprinkle cheese over top, bake 25-30 minutes until puffed and brown.

Note: Some cooks like to prebake pie shell 5 minutes to avoid sogginess. If air pockets form, gently lift pastry from side of pan to allow steam to escape and pocket to disappear.

Lori Adams DelRossi

LINGUINE WITH BROCCOLI AND BAY SCALLOPS

Preparing: 30 minutes   *Yield: 4 to 5 servings*

1 pound fresh broccoli
1 pound linguine
1 teaspoon salt
¼ teaspoon pepper
½ cup butter
2 teaspoons minced fresh garlic

1 pound bay scallops
1 teaspoon salt
¼ teaspoon pepper
⅓ cup freshly grated Parmesan
  cheese

Cut broccoli into flowerets and ¼-inch slices. Blanch in boiling salted water 2 minutes. Drain well; refresh under cold running water; set aside. Cook linguine to *al dente* according to package directions; drain well. Toss with salt, pepper and ¼ cup butter. Cover and keep warm while preparing scallops and broccoli. Heat remaining ¼ cup butter until very hot; add garlic and sauté a bit, being careful not to burn. Add broccoli and heat through. Add scallops, salt and pepper; sauté 3 minutes or until just done; immediately spoon seafood mixture over pasta and sprinkle with Parmesan cheese. Serve at once.

The Commissary
Philadelphia, Pennsylvania

MOCK NEWBURG SEAFOOD DISH

Preparing: 20 minutes   *Do Ahead*   *Yield: 6 to 8 servings*

1 (10¾-ounce) can cream of
  shrimp soup
1 (10¾-ounce) can cream of
  celery soup
¼ cup milk (more if thinner sauce
  is desired)
4 tablespoons of sherry (*not
  cooking sherry*)

½ pound sea scallops
1 pound fresh crabmeat
½ pound shrimp, cooked and
  cleaned (may be cut into pieces
  if desired)

If scallops are large, cut into quarters. Cook and clean shrimp; cut into small pieces if desired. Mix soups, milk and sherry together; heat, stirring constantly. Bring scallops to boil, starting in cold water; drain immediately. Add scallops, crabmeat and shrimp to hot soup and cook until seafood is heated thoroughly. Serve on hot rice with asparagus or green salad. *This dish may be prepared a day ahead and re-heated in double boiler or casserole in oven.*

Quality Seafood Market
Devon, Pennsylvania

CREVETTES AU VIN BLANC

Preparing: 20 minutes   *Do Ahead*   *Yield: 10 to 12 servings, appetizer,*
4 to 6 servings, entrée

2 small scallions, minced
2 sprigs parsley, chopped
1 cup sliced mushrooms
2 tablespoons butter
1 cup white wine
1½ pounds raw shrimp, cleaned
(crabmeat may be used)
½ teaspoon salt

Dash white pepper
2 tablespoons flour
2 tablespoons butter
3 tablespoons Crème Fraiche
(see below)
1 egg yolk
2 tablespoons Madeira wine
Parsley (garnish)

The day before serving, make Crème Fraiche. Day of serving sauté scallions, parsley and mushrooms in butter for 2 minutes; add wine and bring to boil. Reduce heat and simmer for 5 minutes; add shrimp. Gradually heat, breaking apart frozen shrimp. Bring to a boil, reduce heat and simmer for 2 minutes; season with salt and pepper. Mash flour into butter and blend well. Add enough of this paste to thicken sauce. Combine Crème Fraiche and egg yolk; stir a bit of hot sauce into it. Stir egg mixture into shrimp; heat but do not boil. Add Madeira; sprinkle with parsley. Serve in individual sea shells or on a bed of rice.

Crème Fraiche:
1 cup heavy cream

2 tablespoons buttermilk or whole
milk

Stir together in jar. *Let stand at room temperature for 24 hours.* Keeps 4 to 6 weeks in refrigerator.

Dede Dubois Shimrak

QUICK SHRIMP CURRY

Preparing: 20 minutes   *Yield: 4 servings*

½ cup chopped onion
1 tablespoon butter or margarine
1 (10¾-ounce) can cream of
shrimp soup

1 cup sour cream
½ teaspoon curry powder
1 cup cooked or canned shrimp
3 cups cooked rice

Cook onion in butter in medium saucepan until tender but not brown. Add soup; heat and stir until smooth. Stir in sour cream and curry powder; add shrimp. Serve over hot rice.

Liz Nelson Mayer

SHRIMP IN MUSTARD SAUCE

Preparing: 30 minutes   *Do Ahead*   *Yield: 8 servings*
Chilling: 2 to 3 hours

2½ pounds shrimp	½ cup olive oil
¼ cup finely chopped parsley	4 tablespoons Dijon mustard
¼ cup finely chopped shallots	2 teaspoons crushed red peppers
¼ cup tarragon vinegar	2 teaspoons salt
¼ cup wine vinegar	Freshly ground black pepper

Cook shrimp in boiling salted water to cover, just until they turn pink; shell and devein. Transfer to a large bowl. Mix remaining ingredients together; pour over warm shrimp. Mix well so every shrimp will be coated. *Cover and refrigerate.* Serve shrimp from a bowl with toothpicks or on individual plates with Bibb lettuce liner.

SCAMPI ALLA GRIGLIA
(Broiled Shrimp with Garlic Butter)

Preparing: 25 minutes   *Do Ahead: Partially*   *Yield:*
Cooking: 15 minutes   *8 to 10 servings (appetizer)*
                                                        6 servings (entrée)

4 pounds large fresh shrimp in shells	1 tablespoon finely minced garlic
¾ cup butter	1 teaspoon salt
¾ cup olive oil	Freshly ground black pepper
2 tablespoons lemon juice	4 tablespoons finely chopped fresh parsley
¼ cup finely chopped shallots or scallions	Lemon quarters (garnish)

Shell shrimp; do not remove last small segment of shell or tail. With a small sharp knife, partially split each shrimp down the back and lift out intestinal vein. Wash shrimp quickly under cold running water; pat thoroughly dry with paper towels. Preheat broiler to its highest temperature. In a shallow flame-proof baking dish, large enough to hold shrimp in one layer, melt butter over low heat (do not let it brown). Stir olive oil, lemon juice, shallots, garlic, salt and a few grindings of pepper; add shrimp and turn until they glisten on all sides. Broil 6 inches from heat 15 minutes, until lightly browned and firm to the touch. *Do not overcook.* With tongs, transfer shrimp to heated serving platter. Pour on sauce from pan; sprinkle with chopped parsley. Garnish with lemon quarters, and serve.

Susan Husband Goodchild

SHRIMP MOSCA

Preparing: 15 minutes   *Do Ahead: Partially*   *Yield: 6 to 8 servings, entrée;*
Baking: 10 minutes   *8 to 10 servings, appetizer*
Broiling: 5 minutes

3 pounds shrimp, heads removed
   and peeled
1 cup butter
½ cup olive oil
½ teaspoon oregano
1 tablespoon black pepper

¾ teaspoon salt
½ teaspoon paprika
1 tablespoon parsley
¾ teaspoon basil
¾ teaspoon garlic powder
1 teaspoon lemon juice

Preheat oven to 450°F. Put shrimp in single layer in large (7x11-inch) pan. Melt butter and add remaining ingredients; pour over shrimp. Bake 10 minutes. Broil 5 minutes. Serve with French bread and white wine.

Barbara Sue Massengale Brodie

SHRIMP MONT SERRAT

Preparing: 10 minutes   *Yield: 1 serving*

4 jumbo shrimp, shelled and
   deveined
Flour
Clarified butter
1 tablespoon amaretto
1 tablespoon brandy

Splash wine
Splash fresh orange juice
Dash of orange peel
1 tablespoon heavy cream
Parsley (garnish)

Dip shrimp in flour. Heat butter but do not let it brown. Sauté shrimp in butter about 1 minute; turn and continue to sauté until shrimp are almost done; remove from pan. Raise heat; add brandy, amaretto, wine, orange and orange peel to pan; mix well. Remove pan from heat. Add cream (make sure that cream is at room temperature) to pan and blend. Add shrimp; return pan to stove. Raise heat to high for about 1 minute. Garnish with parsley; serve immediately.

Mont Serrat
Philadelphia, Pennsylvania

RISOTTE WITH SHRIMP

Preparing: 30 minutes   *Yield: 4 servings*
Cooking: 20 minutes

1 tablespoon olive oil
1 tablespoon butter
1 small onion, minced
1 clove garlic, minced
1 cup raw rice
½ pound medium shrimp,
   shelled and deveined

1 tablespoon tomato paste
6 medium mushrooms, sliced
Juice of 1 lemon
Pinch oregano
Pinch cayenne pepper
2 cups well-seasoned chicken
   broth

In heavy saucepan with lid, sauté onion, garlic and mushrooms in oil and butter; add rice and sauté 2 or 3 minutes. Add remaining ingredients. Bring to boil; cover and simmer 20 minutes or until rice is cooked. Let rice rest 5 minutes before serving; add salt and pepper if necessary.

Variation: Substitute pinch of saffron for tomato paste.

Lori Adams DelRossi

SHRIMP CREOLE

Preparing: 30 minutes   *Yield: 4 servings*

2 cups raw shrimp, shelled and
   deveined
2 tablespoons butter
2 tablespoons oil
4 mushrooms, finely sliced
2 tablespoons Marsala wine
1 tablespoon mixed red and green
   pepper, finely chopped
¼ teaspoon tomato paste

¼ teaspoon meat glaze (Kitchen
   Bouquet)
1 cup light cream
2 tablespoons sour cream
Salt, cayenne pepper to taste
½ teaspoon dried red chili pepper
2 onions, diced, cooked brown and
   crisp

Toss shrimp in 1 tablespoon foaming butter and 2 tablespoons oil for 1-2 minutes. Remove shrimp and set aside. Add 1 tablespoon butter and mushrooms to mixture. Cook briskly for few minutes; add Marsala and chopped peppers. Cook until liquid is reduced. (Add little more butter, if necessary.) Stir in tomato paste and meat glaze. Mix in very slowly, cream, sour cream and seasonings. Add shrimp and onions; simmer slowly until sauce is heated through and shrimp are pink. Serve on rice pilaf.

Jeanne Kronmiller Honish

SHRIMP TOURKOLIMINO

Preparing: 20 minutes   *Yield: 4 servings*
Cooking: 20 minutes
Baking: 20 minutes

3 shallots
3 scallions (white and bottom
  half green)
2 tablespoons butter
2 tablespoons vegetable oil
1/4 cup dry vermouth
20 ounces Italian plum tomatoes,
  crushed
1/2 bunch parsley

3 garlic cloves, minced
2 tablespoons dry sherry wine
1/8 teaspoon basil
1/8 teaspoon Greek oregano
18 raw little neck clams
24 jumbo shrimp, cleaned
  and deveined
1/4 pound feta cheese

Strain clams reserving liquor; mince. Sauté shallots and scallions lightly in butter and oil; add vermouth. Simmer 3-5 minutes; add crushed tomatoes. Bring to boil and simmer. Add parsley, garlic, dry sherry, basil and oregano; simmer 20 minutes. Add reserved clam juice. Preheat oven to 375°F. Place shrimp in baking pan or casserole large enough so shrimp do not overlap. Add clams and enough sauce to come halfway up around shrimp. *(Do not use too much sauce as shrimp will release liquid when baking.)* Top with crumbled feta cheese. Bake 20 minutes or until cheese browns lightly. Excellent served over fettucini.

Stephen George, Chef
Upper Crust Cafe, Radnor, Pennsylvania

SHRIMP WITH DILL SAUCE

Preparing: 20 minutes   *Yield: 4 servings*
Cooking: 20 minutes

2 tablespoons butter
2 tablespoons finely chopped
  shallots
1/4 cup dry white wine
1 cup heavy cream

1 pound cooked shrimp
1 generous tablespoon chopped
  fresh dill leaves
Salt and pepper

Heat butter in skillet, add shallots; cook gently for 1 minute. Add wine and cook over high heat stirring 1 minute. Stir in cream and continue to cook and stir 2 minutes; add shrimp and almost all the dill. Season to taste. Cook gently until shrimp are heated through. Sprinkle with remaining dill. Serve over rice.

Grace Burdett Nellis

INDIA FISH

Preparing: 30 minutes *Do Ahead* *Yield: 4 servings*
Marinating: 1 hour

1½ pounds flounder, cod
  or haddock fillet
2 medium onions

¼ cup margarine or oil
1(16-ounce) can tomato sauce
  (plain, not Italian style)

Marinade:
¾ tablespoon sugar
¼ teaspoon ground red pepper
1 teaspoon garlic powder
½ teaspoon paprika

¼ teaspoon fenugreek
¼ teaspoon turmeric
3 tablespoons white vinegar

Cube fish into 2x2 inch pieces. *Marinate one hour.* Chop onions and fry in oil until brown. Add tomato sauce; simmer 10 minutes. Add fish and marinade; cook 15 minutes. Serve over rice.

Note: Best made one day ahead to let flavor develop.

Joanne Stanek Murphy

BROILED BLUEFISH

Preparing: 5 minutes *Yield: 4 to 6 servings*
Cooking: 8 to 10 minutes

1½-2 pounds bluefish fillets
⅓ cup mayonnaise
⅓ cup horseradish

1 lemon
Paprika

Clean and drain fish. Mix mayonnaise and horseradish together. Squeeze juice from lemon over fish fillets. Cover fillets completely with mayonnaise mixture and sprinkle with paprika. Place under broiler 8-10 minutes or until surface turns bubbly golden brown. Test with fork for doneness.

Variation: Thyme or dill may be added to lemon juice.

Patricia Lawler Wiedinmyer

STRIPED BASS WITH CARROTS AND LEEKS

Preparing: 45 minutes　　　　　　　　　　*Yield: 4 to 6 servings*
Baking: 10 minutes

2 **striped bass fillets, skin left on** (about 1¾ **pounds**)	1 **tablespoon finely chopped shallots**
1 **cup coarsely shredded leeks** (1-2 **leeks**)	**Salt and freshly ground pepper to taste**
1 **cup coarsely shredded carrots** (1-2 **carrots**)	½ **cup dry white wine**
	1 **cup Mustard Mayonnaise**

Make certain there are no scales left on skin of fish. Trim leeks; pull off and discard any tough outer leaves. Use only inner tender green and white leaves. Trim and clean carrots. Cut leeks and carrots crosswise into 1½-inch lengths. Cut pieces in half and shred or cut them as fine as toothpicks. Place in saucepan; set aside. Preheat oven to 400°F. Select dish (that can go on top of stove and in oven) large enough to hold fillets in one layer close together. Sprinkle bottom of dish with shallots, salt and pepper; arrange fillets skin side down. Sprinkle with salt and pepper. Pour wine over fish. Cover tightly with aluminum foil. Bring wine and fish to a boil on top of stove. Put in oven; bake 10 minutes or until fish is done. Carefully pour cooking liquid from fish into saucepan containing carrots and leeks. Cover and bring to a boil; cook about 4-5 minutes. Scatter equal portions of vegetables over each fillet. Spoon Mustard Mayonnaise over hot fish or serve separately. (If any liquid accumulates around fish before it is served, spoon it into the mayonnaise.)

Mustard Mayonnaise:

1 **egg yolk**	**Salt and freshly ground pepper to taste**
2 **teaspoons Dijon mustard**	¾ **cup peanut oil**
2 **teaspoons lemon juice**	

Put yolk in mixing bowl; add mustard, lemon juice, salt and pepper. Start beating with a wire whisk adding oil very gradually. Beat vigorously until thickened. (Yields 1 cup.)

William Keller

FLOUNDER AND BROCCOLI ROLL-UPS

Preparing: 30 minutes   *Yield: 4 to 6 servings*
Baking: 20 to 25 minutes

2-2½ pounds fresh thin flounder   **Juice of 1 lemon (3 tablespoons)**
   fillets (or sole)   **Salt and pepper**
2 (10-ounce) packages frozen   **Slivered almonds**
   broccoli spears   **Lemon wedges (garnish)**

Frozen fillets may be used thawed. Preheat oven to 350°F. Cook and drain broccoli. Wrap one fillet around each cooked broccoli spear. In greased 12x8x2-inch glass baking dish, arrange roll-ups, seam-side down. Sprinkle with lemon juice, salt and pepper. Pour cream sauce over fillets. Top with slivered almonds. Bake 20-25 minutes. Garnish with lemon wedges. Serve with rice.

Cream Sauce:
3 tablespoons butter   **Peel of 1 lemon, grated**
3 tablespoons flour   **⅛ teaspoon dry mustard**
½ teaspoon salt   **2 tablespoons sherry**
2 cups half and half cream

In medium saucepan, melt butter. Gradually stir in flour and salt until smooth. Remove from heat; gradually add cream. Cook and stir over medium heat until sauce boils. Stir in lemon peel, dry mustard and sherry. Pour over fillets.

Pam Bartels Morris

FILET OF SOLE CASSEROLE

Preparing: 10 minutes   *Yield: 6 servings*
Baking: 40 to 45 minutes

4 pounds filet of sole   **½ cup bordeaux red wine**
2 tablespoons butter   **1-2 cups shredded Cheddar cheese**
1 (10¾-ounce) can cream
   of mushroom soup

Preheat oven to 325°F. Grease shallow casserole with butter. Roll each filet; place in casserole. Mix soup and wine together; pour over filets. Sprinkle shredded cheese over top. Bake 40-45 minutes. Good served with wild rice

Lynne Stevens d'Entremont

RED SNAPPER IN PAPILLOTE

Preparing: 30 minutes   Do Ahead   Yield: 8 to 10 servings
Baking:10 minutes

10 red snapper fillets
4½ cups boiling salted water
1½ lemons, sliced
½ teaspoon crumbled dried thyme
2 bay leaves
4½ tablespoons butter
4½ tablespoons flour
3 tablespoons minced onion

2¼ cups fish stock
1½ cups cooked, coarsely
   chopped, shrimp
¾ cup flaked crabmeat
20-24 mushrooms, sliced
½ teaspoon salt
3 egg yolks

Lay fish flat in large shallow pan. To boiling water, add lemon, thyme, and bay leaf; pour over fish fillets. Simmer until fish flakes. Carefully remove fillets and place on large enough piece of foil to enclose fillets completely; set aside. Reserve 2¼ cups stock; strain. Melt butter; stir in flour. Add onion; slowly stir in fish stock. Cook over low heat, stirring constantly until smooth and thickened. Add shrimp, crab, mushrooms and salt. Stir sauce slowly into beaten egg yolks; blend. Spoon sauce over fillets; fold foil over fish to enclose completely. Preheat oven to 400°F. Place foil packet on cookie sheet; bake 10 minutes.

BAKED STUFFED FLOUNDER

Preparing: 30 minutes   Do Ahead   Yield: 8 servings
Baking: 35 minutes

2 pounds flounder fillets
   (or 12 pieces)

Stuffing:
¼ cup chopped onion
¼ cup margarine
1 (3-ounce) can mushroom stems
   and pieces

7½ ounces Alaskan king crabmeat
¼ cup saltine cracker crumbs
2 tablespoons snipped parsley
½ teaspoon salt

In skillet, cook onion in margarine until translucent. Drain mushrooms, reserving liquid. Add mushrooms, crab, crumbs, parsley and salt to skillet; mix. Lay flounder skin side down; divide stuffing among fillets; roll up. Put in baking dish, seam side down. Preheat oven to 350°F. Prepare sauce.

Sauce:

3 tablespoons butter
3 tablespoons flour
¼ teaspoon salt
1½ cups milk
⅓ cup dry white wine

1 cup (about 4 ounces) Swiss
  cheese, shredded
½ teaspoon paprika
Reserved mushroom liquid

Melt butter in saucepan over low heat. Blend flour and salt. Add enough milk to mushroom liquid to equal 1½ cups; add with wine to sauce. Cook, stirring constantly, until thick and bubbly. Pour over fillets; bake 25 minutes. Sprinkle with cheese and paprika. Return to oven 10 minutes. *Do not overcook.*

FILLET OF SOLE WITH ASPARAGUS MALTAISE

Preparing: 30 minutes   *Do Ahead*   *Yield: 8 servings*
Baking: 20 minutes

16-24 fresh asparagus spears,
  trimmed
8 fillets of sole
⅓ cup melted butter

Maltaise Sauce
2 tablespoons grated orange
  peel (garnish)

Bring 4-quart kettle of water to a boil. Drop trimmed asparagus spears into water, a few at a time; boil 6-7 minutes or until barely tender. Remove from water with slotted spoon; drain on paper. Place 2-3 asparagus spears on each fillet of sole, lengthwise. Roll fillet around asparagus; place in shallow 2-quart casserole, seam-side down. Pour ⅓ cup melted butter over fillets. Preheat oven to 350°F. Cover casserole with foil; bake 20 minutes. Remove from oven; drain all juices from fish. *Set aside to keep warm.* When ready to serve, pour Maltaise Sauce over fillets; broil 3-5 minutes or until golden brown and bubbly. Garnish fillets with grated orange peel.

Maltaise Sauce:

3 egg yolks
2 tablespoons fresh orange juice
2 tablespoons grated orange peel

¼ teaspoon salt
Pinch white pepper
½ cup melted butter

Place all ingredients except butter in blender. With lid on, blend at high speed for 1 second; turn blender off. Remove center portion of blender lid, turn to high speed; slowly pour hot, melted butter into blender. If blender does not have removable center in lid, make a foil lid with 2-inch hole in center, as mixture will splatter. *Sauce may be held until serving in top of a double boiler over hot, not boiling, water.* Stir occasionally.

FISH WITH FRESH MUSHROOMS

Preparing: 20 minutes
Cooking: 15 minutes

Yield: 4 servings

1 tablespoon vegetable oil
1 medium onion, thinly sliced
¾ pound fresh mushrooms,
   thinly sliced
1 pound fresh white fish,
   cut in 1-inch strips

Salt and pepper
1 tablespoon soy sauce
1 tablespoon dry sherry
1 large stalk celery, thinly sliced

Sauté onion 1 minute in oil. Add mushrooms; stir constantly until wilted. Spread layer of fish on mushrooms; sprinkle with salt and pepper. Add rest of fish; sprinkle with salt and pepper. Add soy sauce, sherry and celery. Cover and simmer 10 minutes.

Charity Power Folk

FISH STEW HAWAII

Preparing: 35 minutes
Cooking: 10 minutes

Yield: 3 to 4 servings

¼ pound bacon, cut into small
   pieces
1 large onion, chopped
1 green pepper, chopped
1¼ pound fish fillets (flounder
   or cod)
½ cup flour

1 tablespoon dry sherry
1 (15-ounce) can tomatoes
1 bay leaf
2 teaspoons sugar
½ teaspoon salt
Chopped parsley (garnish)

Fry cup-up bacon over moderate heat in large pan. After 4 minutes, add onion and green pepper; fry 4 minutes more. Cut fish into 1-inch cubes and gently toss in bag with flour. Add fish to vegetables and fry 3-4 minutes. Add sherry, tomatoes, bay leaf, salt and sugar. Simmer 10 minutes. Sprinkle with parsley before serving. Serve with rice.

Joanne Stanek Murphy

SMOKED SALMON WITH HORSERADISH CREAM

Preparing: 30 minutes　　　　*Do Ahead*　　　　*Yield: 8 servings*
Chilling: 1 hour

1½ teaspoons unflavored gelatin
6 tablespoons cold water
1 pound thinly sliced Nova Scotia
　smoked salmon
½ cup heavy cream
2 tablespoons prepared
　horseradish, drained

1 teaspoon lemon juice
¼ teaspoon sugar
Thin slices pumpernickle bread,
　buttered
Lemon wedges (garnish)
Watercress sprigs (garnish)
Freshly ground black pepper

Sprinkle gelatin over cold water in a small saucepan. Place pan over low heat; stir until gelatin is completely dissolved. Let cool slightly; then chill 10 minutes. Whip cream until stiff. Stir in horseradish, lemon juice, sugar and gelatin mixture. Continue to beat until cream mixture is quite thick. Chill for a few minutes. Place a generous spoonful of mixture down center of each salmon piece. Gently fold the two sides over so they overlap just slightly. Place each cream-filled salmon roll seam-side down on a baking sheet lined with waxed paper. Cover with plastic wrap; chill. Serve with triangles of buttered pumpernickle; garnish with lemon wedges and watercress. Pass a pepper mill.

SALMON SOUFFLÉ

Preparing: 20 minutes　　　　　　　　*Yield: 4 to 6 servings*
Baking: 45 to 60 minutes

1 cup soft bread crumbs
1 cup scalded milk
1 teaspoon salt
¼ teaspoon dry mustard
¼ pound sharp Cheddar,
　cut in pieces

3 eggs, separated
2 cups (16 ounces) salmon,
　cleaned and broken up

Preheat oven to 325°F. In saucepan, soak bread in milk; add salt, mustard and cheese. Heat until cheese melts; cool. Add egg yolks and salmon. Beat egg whites until stiff; fold into salmon mixture. Pour into 2-quart buttered casserole. Bake 45-60 minutes or until knife inserted in center comes out clean.

Charity Power Folk

CREAMY SEAFOOD IN SHELLS

Preparing: 25 minutes   *Do Ahead*   *Yield: 6 servings*
Cooking: 20 minutes

2 tablespoons butter
2 green onions, minced
¼ pound whitefish, boned and cut
  into ½-inch pieces
¼ pound sea scallops, halved or
  quartered
¼ pound small shrimp, shelled and
  deveined
2 tablespoons chopped fresh
  parsley

Salt and freshly ground white
  pepper
¾ cup White Sauce
2 hard-cooked eggs, coarsely
  chopped
6 (4-inch) scallop shells
2 tablespoons fine dry bread
  crumbs
2 tablespoons freshly grated
  Parmesan cheese

Preheat oven to 375°F. Melt butter in large skillet over medium heat. Add green onions and cook until just soft. Add fish, scallops and shrimp; simmer gently until scallops and shrimp are opaque and fish flakes when tested with fork. Stir in parsley; salt and pepper to taste. Remove from heat. Fold in white sauce and chopped egg. Divide mixture among shells. Sprinkle with bread crumbs and cheese and place on baking sheet. Bake until lightly browned and bubbly, 15-20 minutes.

White Sauce:
3 tablespoons butter
2½ tablespoons flour
1½ cups hot milk

Salt
Freshly ground white pepper

Melt butter in saucepan over low heat; gradually stir in flour, blending well. Slowly add milk, stirring constantly until sauce thickens. Season to taste with salt and pepper. Remove from heat and cover until ready to use. (Yields 1½ cups.)

Note: This can be served as a first course or a luncheon dish.

Barbara Alphin Chimicles

BAKED WHOLE CHICKEN ROSEMARY

Preparing: 10 minutes   *Yield: 4 servings*
Baking: 1 hour

1 (2½-3 pound) whole chicken   1 clove garlic, halved
Salt and pepper to taste   1 teaspoon chicken stock base
1 teaspoon rosemary   ¼ cup hot water
1 large stalk celery, halved   ¼ cup dry vermouth
½ medium onion, halved

Preheat oven to 450°F. Remove visible fat from cavity of chicken. Sprinkle cavity with salt, pepper and some of the rosemary; stuff with celery, onion and garlic. Twist wing tips and fold onto back so wings lie flat. Place chicken breast side up, in baking dish with tight-fitting lid. Dissolve chicken stock base in water; add vermouth and spoon over chicken. Sprinkle with salt, pepper and remaining rosemary. Cover; bake 1 hour. Remove chicken to platter. Pour juices into bowl; remove all possible fat. Reheat juices in a small saucepan; serve with chicken and/or rice.

Liz Nelson Mayer

CHINESE WALNUT CHICKEN

Preparing: 30 minutes   *Yield: 4 to 6 servings*
Cooking: 20 minutes

1 cup coarsely broken walnuts   1 teaspoon sugar
¼ cup vegetable oil   1 tablespoon cornstarch
2 chicken breasts, boned and cut   ¼ cup soy sauce
   lengthwise in very thin strips   2 tablespoons dry sherry
½ teaspoon salt   1 (5-ounce) can bamboo shoots,
1 cup sliced onion   drained (⅔ cup)
1½ cups bias-cut celery slices   1 (5-ounce) can water chestnuts,
1¼ cups chicken broth   drained and sliced

In skillet, toast walnuts in hot oil, stirring constantly. Remove nuts to paper towels. Put chicken into skillet; sprinkle with salt. Cook 5-10 minutes stirring frequently, until tender. Remove chicken. Put onion, celery and ½ cup of chicken broth in skillet. Cook uncovered 5 minutes or until slightly tender. Combine sugar, cornstarch, soy sauce and sherry; add remaining chicken broth. Pour over vegetables in skillet. Cook and stir until sauce thickens. Add chicken, bamboo shoots, water chestnuts and walnuts. Heat through. Serve with rice.

CHICKEN A LA ORANGE

Preparing: 25 minutes   *Yield: 8 servings*
Baking: 1 hour

8 boneless chicken breasts
   (10 ounces each)
⅓ cup flour
1½ teaspoons salt
½ teaspoon paprika
1 teaspoon garlic powder
5 tablespoons butter or margarine
⅓ cup sliced almonds

1 (6-ounce) can frozen
   concentrated orange juice
1½ cups water
1 teaspoon leaf rosemary,
   crumbled
1 teaspoon leaf thyme, crumbled
2 tablespoons cornstarch

Coat chicken with mixture of flour, 1 teaspoon salt, garlic powder and paprika. Sauté almonds until golden in butter or margarine in a large frying pan; remove from pan and drain on plate or paper towel. Brown chicken in drippings in same pan; place in a single layer in 13x9x2-inch baking pan. Discard drippings. Stir in orange juice concentrate, water, rosemary, thyme and ½ teaspoon salt into pan. Heat to boiling; pour over chicken; cover. Preheat oven to 350°F; bake 1 hour or until chicken is tender. Remove to another pan and keep warm. Reheat liquid in baking pan to boiling; thicken with cornstarch mixed in a little cold water. Arrange chicken on platter and pour some sauce on top. Sprinkle with almonds. Pass rest of sauce. Serve with rice.

Ginny Moffitt Gehring

CHICKEN WITH GOLDEN GLAZE

Preparing: 10 minutes   *Yield: 4 to 6 servings*
Baking: 1 hour

4-6 chicken legs, cut in half
1 tablespoon margarine, melted
1 (10¾-ounce) golden mushroom
   soup, undiluted

¼ cup sweet vermouth
⅛ teaspoon nutmeg

Preheat oven to 400°F. In 9x13-inch shallow baking dish, arrange chicken skin side up. Brush with margarine. Bake uncovered 45 minutes. Combine soup, vermouth and nutmeg; spoon over chicken. Bake 15 minutes more or until chicken is done. Serve with rice.

Lois Rising Pogyor

TERIYAKI CHICKEN

Preparing: 30 minutes
Baking: 1½ hours

Yield: 4 to 6 servings

¾ cup soy sauce (only use
  Kikkoman)
¼ cup sugar
2 tablespoons rice wine
1 large clove garlic, pressed

1 inch piece ginger root, skinned
  and mashed
1½ pounds chicken wings, cut
  in half

Preheat oven to 350°F. Combine all ingredients except chicken; bring to boil slowly. Strain out ginger root. Place chicken in baking pan. Stir sauce and pour over chicken. Bake 1½ hours.

Note: May use 3 chicken breasts, split, or legs, split. Sauce may be doubled easily.

Pat Schultz Weyant

CHICKEN KIEV

Preparing: 30 minutes
Baking: 35 to 40 minutes

Yield: 8 servings

4 whole chicken breasts
1 cup softened butter
1 clove garlic, minced
1 tablespoon chopped chives
1 tablespoon chopped parsley
1 teaspoon salt

½ teaspoon rosemary, crumbled
¼ teaspoon pepper
¼ cup milk
1 egg
1 cup dry bread crumbs

Preheat oven to 400°F. Skin and bone breasts; cut in half. Combine butter, garlic, chives, parsley, salt, rosemary and pepper; mix thoroughly. Place on waxed paper; pat into an 8-inch long roll. *Freeze until firm.* Place each chicken piece between 2 sheets of waxed paper; pound with mallet until ¼-inch thick. Divide butter mixture into 8 sections. Place 1 section on each chicken piece. Tuck in ends; roll up chicken tightly, securing with toothpicks. Combine milk and egg. Dip pieces of chicken in milk mixture. Place bread crumbs in bag. Shake chicken pieces individually in bread crumbs. Place chicken in single layer in shallow baking pan. Bake 35-40 minutes.

Jan Carmst Rhein

CHEESE CHICKEN STRATA

Preparing: 1 hour   *Do Ahead*   *Yield: 8 to 10 servings*
Baking: 1 hour
Chilling: Overnight

14 slices bread
8 ounces sharp American cheese,
   shredded
3 cups diced cooked chicken
2 (10½-ounce) cans cream of
   chicken soup
4 eggs, beaten

2 cups milk
4 tablespoons finely chopped onion
½ cup fine dry bread crumbs
   (Italian style)
4 tablespoons butter or margarine,
   melted
½ teaspoon paprika

Advance preparation: Trim crusts from bread. Arrange half the bread in bottom of buttered 13x9x2-inch baking dish, cutting one slice in half to fit. Sprinkle with cheese; top with chicken and remaining bread. Combine soup and eggs; stir in milk and onion. Pour soup mixture over casserole, cover; *chill overnight.*

Before serving: Preheat oven to 325°F. Melt margarine; add bread crumbs and brown slightly. Add paprika and sprinkle over casserole. Bake 1 hour or until set. Let stand 10 minutes before cutting and serving.

Note: For lighter version, use only 4 slices bread in top layer. A sharper cheese (Cheddar or Swiss) may be substituted for American cheese. For a "meatier" version, chicken may be increased by a cup.

Susan Childs Carr

EASY CHICKEN DIVAN

Preparing: 15 minutes   *Do Ahead*   *Yield: 6 to 8 servings*
Baking: 1 hour

3-4 whole chicken breasts, split
1-2 (10-ounce) packages frozen
   broccoli or string beans

1 (10-ounce) can cream of chicken
   soup
Shredded Cheddar cheese

Cook chicken breasts, then bone and skin. Preheat oven to 350°F. Put partially frozen vegetable in bottom of casserole. Lay chicken over the vegetable. Pour soup over chicken and then sprinkle shredded cheese on top. Bake 1 hour or until bubbly. For added flavor, add a little white wine and your favorite herb to soup.

Alice Marks Preston

BAKED CHICKEN PARMESEAN

Preparing: 15 minutes   *Do Ahead*   *Yield: 6 to 8 servings*
Baking: 1 hour; 15 minutes

1 (2½-3 pound) chicken or 6 boned
   and split chicken breasts
½ cup melted butter
⅓ clove garlic, crushed
1 teaspoon Dijon mustard

1 teaspoon Worcestershire sauce
1½ cups fresh bread crumbs
½ cup grated Parmesan cheese
1 teaspoon salt
1 tablespoon chopped parsley

Preheat oven to 350°F. Mix butter, garlic, mustard and Worcestershire in small bowl. In second bowl, mix bread crumbs, cheese, salt and parsley. Dip chicken in butter mixture, then in crumb mixture, coating well. Place chicken in shallow pan and bake uncovered 1¼ hours or until golden brown and tender. Baste once or twice with drippings.

Dolly Eastburn Somers

PAULETEN PERSILLADE
(Chicken with Parsley Sauce)

Preparing: 10 minutes
Cooking: 30 minutes   *Yield: 4 servings*

1 (2½-pound) chicken, cut into
   serving pieces
Salt and pepper to taste
4 tablespoons butter
¼ cup bread crumbs

2 tablespoons finely chopped
   shallots
1 small clove garlic, finely minced
2 tablespoons finely chopped
   parsley

Preheat broiler. Sprinkle chicken with salt and pepper. Heat butter in heatproof baking dish large enough to hold chicken pieces in one layer. Turn pieces in butter. Arrange skin side down; place under the broiler about 6 inches from heat source. Broil 5 minutes, remove from oven and turn skin side up. Return to oven and broil 5 minutes longer. Blend bread crumbs, shallots, garlic and parsley well. Sprinkle over chicken and baste to coat well with butter. Turn oven to 400°F; bake 10 minutes. Just before serving, reheat broiler; run briefly under broiler to brown quickly.

Note: If you prefer not to broil chicken, preheat oven to 400°F. Dip chicken in butter, then in crumb mixture and bake skin side up 45 minutes.

Ann Bateman Capers

COQ AU VIN

Preparing: 40 minutes
Baking: 1 hour

Yield: 4 servings

1 (5-pound) chicken, quartered	2 bay leaves
Salt and pepper	2 cloves garlic, crushed
Flour	1½ cups good red burgundy wine
Butter and oil	2 cups chicken stock or broth
½ teaspoon thyme leaves	

Salt and pepper chicken to taste; dredge lightly in flour. Pan fry in equal parts butter and oil until golden brown on all sides. Preheat oven to 400°F. Place chicken in casserole with remaining ingredients. Cover and bake for 1 hour. Remove chicken to platter; strain liquid. Place liquid in saucepan; reduce 15-20 minutes over medium heat. Thicken sauce with 2 tablespoons of roux (equal proportion butter to flour); stir until smooth. Adjust seasoning if necessary.

Garnish:
2 ounces lean fresh bacon, cubed   ½ cup whole fresh button
½ cup pearl onions   mushrooms

Sauté bacon and onions 5-10 minutes, add mushrooms and cook 2-3 minutes longer. Strain and add garnish to sauce. Pour sauce over chicken and serve.

Mauricette and Jacques Vitre, La Delicatesse,
Lancaster County Farmers Market, Wayne, Pennsylvania

PETTO DI POLLO ALLA CAVOUR

Preparing: 20 minutes   *Do Ahead: Partially*   *Yield: 8 to 10 servings*
Cooking: 30 minutes

8-10 boned chicken cutlets, skinless	½ cup sweet butter
8-10 mozzarella cheese slices	⅓ cup grated Parmesan cheese
8-10 proscuitto ham slices	½-1 cup dry white wine
	1 tablespoon flour

Pound cutlets; dredge in flour lightly. Fry in butter very slowly until cooked thoroughly; do not brown too much. Remove to shallow dish, cover with Parmesan cheese, a slice of proscuitto and a slice of mozzarella cheese. *Do ahead.* Broil only until cheese melts. Mix flour with 3 tablespoons wine; blend to remove all lumps. Add remaining wine, stir quickly until juices form sauce. Thicken with flour mixture if necessary. Pour over chicken and serve hot.

CHICKEN FOR ALL SEASONS

Preparing: 10 minutes
Cooking: 45 minutes

Yield: 4 servings

1 (3-pound) chicken, quartered
½ cup butter
Salt and pepper
1 cup dry white wine

1 cup chicken broth
2 egg yolks, beaten
2 ounces port wine
1 cup heavy cream

Sauté chicken in butter, salt and pepper. Add wine and broth; simmer 45 minutes or until done; remove chicken. Add egg yolks, port and cream to sauce; stir until smooth. Pour over chicken and serve with rice.

Ann Bateman Capers

COTILLION CHICKEN

Preparing: 1 hour
Baking: 45 minutes

Do Ahead
Freeze

Yield: 8 to 10 servings

1 (8-ounce) package herb-
  seasoned stuffing

5 cups diced cooked chicken
  (4 whole breasts)

Preheat oven to 325°F. Mix stuffing according to package directions. Place in bottom of 10x14-inch pan. Place chicken pieces on top. Pour sauce over chicken. Bake 45 minutes. Let stand 10 minutes; cut into squares. Serve with gravy; garnish with pimento if desired.

Sauce:
½ cup butter or margarine
½ cup flour sifted

4 cups chicken broth
6 eggs, lightly beaten

Melt butter, stir in flour and broth. Cook until thickened. Slowly pour in eggs, stirring constantly.

Gravy:
1 (10¾-ounce) can cream of
  mushroom soup
¼ cup milk

1 cup sour cream
Chopped pimento (optional)

Combine soup, milk and sour cream in double boiler and heat thoroughly.

Note: Be careful chicken does not dry out. Add more sauce if necessary.

Gail White Dillon

SHERRIED CHICKEN WITH DUMPLINGS

Preparing: 45 minutes   *Do Ahead: Partially*   *Yield: 8 servings*
Cooking: 1 hour

**4 boned chicken breasts,
  halved (8 pieces)
½ cup flour
1 teaspoon paprika
1 teaspoon salt
½ teaspoon pepper
¼ cup vegetable oil
1 small jar cooked onions
  (or 1 small onion, sliced
  and sautéed)**

**1 (4-ounce) can sliced mushrooms,
  drained
1(10¾-ounce) can cream of
  chicken soup
½ soup can water
½ soup can dry sherry**

Preheat oven to 350°F. Mix flour, paprika, salt and pepper; dredge chicken in flour mixture. In skillet, brown chicken in hot oil. Place invididually in 9x13-inch casserole dish. Distribute onions and mushrooms around chicken. Add soup to browned mixture in skillet; add water and sherry. Bring to a boil and pour over chicken. Bake 45 minutes. Serve with poppy seed dumplings or wild rice with gravy.

Poppy Seed Dumplings:
**2 cups Bisquick
1 teaspoon poultry seasoning
1 teaspoon celery seed**

**1 teaspoon poppy seeds
¼ cup vegetable oil
1 cup milk**

Mix all ingredients well. Drop by spoonfuls onto meat 20-25 minutes before done, cooking in 425°F. until golden brown.

Gravy:
1 cup sour cream

1 cup cream of chicken soup

Mix well. Heat slowly and thoroughly. (Do not allow to boil.) Serve separately.

Judy Lane Davies

CHICKEN CASSEROLE

Preparing: 15 minutes   *Yield: 4 to 6 servings*
Baking: 40 minutes

1 (3-4 pound) chicken, cooked,   1¼ cups milk
   deboned   1 package herb stuffing or
1 (10¾-ounce) can cream of celery   corn bread stuffing
   soup   ⅔ cup butter, melted
1(10¾- ounce) can cream of   1½ cups chicken broth
   chicken soup

Preheat oven to 350°F. Cut chicken into bite-sized pieces and place in casserole. Dilute soups with milk; pour over chicken. Mix stuffing with butter and chicken broth. Pour over chicken and soup mixture. Bake 40 minutes.

Mary Murtagh Krull

SHERRIED MUSHROOM AND CHICKEN FILLED CREPES

Preparing: 30 minutes   *Do Ahead: Partially*   *Yield: 6 servings*
Cooking: 15 minutes

½ pound fresh mushrooms   ½ cup sour cream
4 tablespoons butter, melted   3 tablespoons dry sherry
⅓ cup finely chopped onion   2 cups cooked chicken, cut
4 tablespoons flour   into chunks
2 cups milk   3 tablespoons finely chopped
2 chicken bouillon cubes   parsley
¾ teaspoon salt   12 crepes
⅛ teaspoon white pepper

Wash and dry mushrooms; slice. Sauté onions and mushrooms in butter 5 minutes, blend in flour. Cook and stir over low heat 2 minutes. Add milk, bouillon cubes, salt and pepper. Cook and stir until thickened. Stir in sour cream and sherry. Remove 1 cup sauce and keep warm. To remaining sauce, add chicken and 2 tablespoons parsley. Heat through. Place about ¼ cup mushroom-chicken mixture into each crepe; roll up. Arrange 2 crepes on each plate. Spoon about 2 tablespoons sauce over both. Sprinkle with parsley.

Note: To ease last minute preparation, crepes may be filled ahead of time and heated through in a 300°F. oven for 20 minutes.

Lori Adams DelRossi

CHICKEN SALTIMBOCCA CREPES

Preparing: 20 minutes   *Do Ahead*   *Yield: 10 crepes*
Baking: 20 to 25 minutes

10 cooked crepes
10 thin slices cooked ham
5 slices mozzarella cheese, halved
   (about 6 ounces)
1 cup chopped cooked chicken

1 small tomato, finely chopped
Seasoned salt
2 tablespoons Parmesan cheese
½ cup fine dry bread crumbs
¼ cup melted butter

Preheat oven to 350°F. Place one slice of ham and half slice cheese on each crepe. Top with chicken and tomato; sprinkle with seasoned salt. Fold over right and left sides of crepe to roll up. Combine Parmesan cheese and bread crumbs. Dip rolled crepe in butter, then into bread crumb mixture. Heat in shallow baking pan 20-25 minutes.

Optional: Serve with cheese sauce.

Nancy Fadler Brabson

CHICKEN LANCASTER

Preparing: 20 minutes   *Do Ahead*   *Yield: 6 to 8 servings*
Cooking: 20 minutes

4 cups water
2 whole chicken breasts
2 tablespoons butter
2 tablespoons flour
¾ cup milk
1 teaspoon dry parsley
1 teaspoon instant minced onion
½ teaspoon salt

¼ teaspoon pepper
1 tablespoon chopped pimento
   (optional)
¼ cup chicken broth
½ cup sharp cheese, shredded
2 teaspoons sherry
½ cup canned sliced mushrooms

Boil water in a large saucepan; add chicken and cook 20 minutes or until fork tender. Cool, cut into bite-sized pieces, and place in greased casserole. In medium saucepan, melt butter over low heat; remove from heat and stir in flour until smooth. Return to heat, cooking until mixture bubbles. Remove and slowly stir in milk. Heat, stirring constantly until thick; add seasonings. Stir in broth and add cheese. If too thick, add little more broth. Sprinkle chicken with sherry, add mushrooms, and stir in the sauce. Serve, or keep covered in a warm oven (275°F.), until serving time.

Gretchen Dome Hagy

CHICKEN MARSALA

Preparing: 1 hour　　　　*Do Ahead: Partially*　　　　*Yield: 6 servings*
Chilling: 2 hours

3 large whole chicken breasts,　　　**3 tablespoons butter**
　　split, skinned, and boned　　　**1 small onion, chopped**
1 egg, beaten　　　**½ pound small mushrooms, sliced**
¼ cup milk　　　**1 clove garlic, mashed**
½ cup flour　　　**1 cup Marsala wine**
1½ teaspoons salt　　　**1 envelope instant chicken broth**
¼ teaspoon pepper　　　**1 lemon, cut into thin slices**
3 tablespoons olive oil

Flatten chicken pieces between sheets of waxed paper with rolling pin or mallet
(pieces should be ¼-inch thick). Combine egg and milk in shallow dish. Combine flour, salt and pepper on waxed paper. Dip chicken into egg mixture, then
flour mixture to coat all sides. Refrigerate 2 hours. Heat oil and butter in large
skillet; brown chicken on both sides. Remove to platter. Sauté onion, mushrooms and garlic until barely tender. Remove to platter. Add wine and chicken
broth to pan; boil, uncovered 10 minutes to reduce liquid. Return chicken and
vegetables to pan; heat thoroughly. Arrange on platter. Top chicken pieces with
lemon slices.

Note: If chicken is not pounded thin enough (¼-inch), it may require baking in
a 350°F. oven for about 30 minutes. Place chicken in baking dish; cover with
sauce. Baste with sauce occasionally during baking.

John Goodchild

CHICKEN PIZZAZZ

Preparing: 10 minutes　　　　*Do Ahead*　　　　*Yield: 4 to 6 servings*
Baking: 1 hour

2-3 pounds cut-up chicken parts　　　**1 envelope Knorr's onion soup mix**
½ (8-ounce) bottle Italian salad　　　**½ cup water**
　　dressing

Preheat oven to 350°F. Mix dressing, soup mix and water. Place cut-up chicken
in casserole; pour over dressing mixture. Bake 1 hour. Also good over pork
chops.

Judilee Cronrath Traynor

CHICKEN SUPREME ROULADES

Preparing: 20 minutes   *Do Ahead*   *Yield: 4 servings*
Baking: 45 to 60 minutes

¼ cup margarine
¼ cup flour
1 teaspoon salt
1 teaspoon instant chicken
  bouillon
1 (4-ounce) can button mushrooms

Milk
4 whole chicken breasts, boned
  and skinned
8 slices processed Swiss cheese
½ pound boiled ham, shaved

Preheat oven to 350°F. In medium saucepan, melt margarine over low heat; blend in flour, salt, bouillon. Remove from heat. Drain mushroom liquid in measuring cup; add milk to make 2 cups. Gradually, stir milk liquid into margarine mixture. Over medium heat, stir constantly until sauce thickens and boils. Add mushrooms and remove from heat. On underside of each breast, place 2 slices of cheese and ¼ of ham. Spoon 1 tablespoon prepared sauce over ham. Roll tightly. Place rolled breasts, seam-side down on greased 13x2x9 inch baking pan. Pour half of sauce over chicken. Bake 45-60 minutes until chicken is tender. Heat remaining sauce and serve with chicken pieces.

Note: May be prepared ahead and refrigerated until ready to bake. May be doubled.

Ginny Moffitt Gehring

ITALIAN BAKED CHICKEN

Preparing: 15 minutes   *Yield: 6 to 8 servings*
Baking: 60 minutes

2-3 pounds whole chicken legs,
  separated
2 cups corn flake crumbs
⅔ cup grated Parmesan cheese

4 teaspoons dried oregano leaves
1 (10-ounce) can tomato soup
⅓ can water
¼ cup melted butter or margarine

Preheat oven to 400°F. Mix crumbs, cheese and oregano. Mix tomato soup and water. Dip pieces of chicken in tomato soup mixture; thoroughly coat with crumbs. Pour melted butter into shallow baking dish. Place chicken in dish, skin side up. Bake 55-60 minutes or until chicken is fork tender. *Children like its pizza flavor.*

Microwave: Cover glass baking dish with wax paper and microwave on high (full power) for 8 minutes per pound, turning or rotating at least once.

Lois Rising Pogyor

LEMON CHICKEN

Preparing: 45 minutes   *Yield: 4 servings*
Chilling: 30 minutes

4 chicken breasts, boned and   Cornstarch
** flattened to ½ inch**

Marinade:
1 tablespoon vegetable oil   2 teaspoons soy sauce
½ teaspoon sherry   Dash fresh ground pepper

Combine ingredients in a small bowl. Rub over chicken, allowing excess to drain. Coat lightly with cornstarch and refrigerate 30 minutes.

Lemon Sauce:
¾ cup water   Dash salt
3 heaping tablespoons sugar   1 teaspoon cornstarch, dissolved in
2 tablespoons catsup   small amount of water
Juice of one large lemon

Combine ingredients in small saucepan. Bring to a boil over medium heat, stirring occasionally, until slightly thickened. Keep warm.

Vegetables:
Vegetable oil   ⅔ cup water chestnuts, thinly
⅔ cup bean sprouts   sliced
⅔ cup snow peas, thinly sliced   Tomato wedges, lemon slices,
⅔ cup bamboo shoots, thinly   green onion and almonds
** sliced   (garnish)**

Heat ½ inch vegetable oil in large skillet over medium high heat until haze forms. Fry chicken until golden brown on each side. Drain, cut into strips ¾ inch wide. Set aside and keep warm. Wipe out skillet, add small amount of vegetable oil and heat as before. Add vegetables; stir-fry until crisp tender. Transfer to heated platter. Top with chicken and spoon over lemon sauce; add garnish.

Grace Burdett Nellis

COMPANY CHICKEN

Preparing: 30 minutes 　　　*Do Ahead* 　　　*Yield: 8 servings*
Baking: 45 minutes

2 cups diced chicken
1 (10¾-ounce) can cream of
　mushroom soup
1 (10¾-ounce) can cream of
　chicken soup
½ scant cup mayonnaise
1 (4-ounce) can mushroom pieces
　and juice

1 (8-ounce) package fine noodles
1 small can asparagus
½ cup grated Parmesan cheese
1 small green pepper, sliced
¼ cup chopped almonds

Preheat oven to 350°F. Cook noodles and drain. Heat chicken, soups, mayonnaise and mushrooms. Put one-half noodles on bottom of ungreased 2-quart casserole; cover with layer of asparagus. Top asparagus with one-half cheese; then half the chicken mixture. Repeat layering process; top with green pepper and almonds. Bake 45 minutes.

Sandra Schild Fletcher

HUNTER STYLE VEAL OR CHICKEN CUTLETS

Preparing: 30 minutes 　　　*Do Ahead* 　　　*Yield: 4 to 6 servings*
Cooking: 35 to 45 minutes

1 pound veal or chicken cutlets
5 tablespoons olive oil
½-1 cup chopped celery
½-1 cup chopped carrots
1 large onion
¼ cup chopped fresh parsley

1 clove garlic, chopped
2 tablespoons butter
½-1 cup chopped mushrooms
1 (6-ounce) can tomato paste
1 cup dry white wine
Salt, pepper and basil to taste

Melt butter and oil in heavy skillet. Brown cutlet well on both sides. Add chopped vegetables and spices; cover. Simmer 15 minutes or until vegetables are soft. Gradually add wine which has been well mixed with tomato paste. Stir occasionally adding more liquid (water or wine) if necessary. Cover; simmer over low heat 20 minutes or until meat is tender and vegetables are cooked. Serve over hot rice.

Regina Shehadi Guza

CRAB-STUFFED CHICKEN BREASTS

Preparing: 60 minutes   *Yield: 8 servings*
Cooking: 45 to 60 minutes

1 egg
¾ cup Pepperidge Farm stuffing
   mix
2 (10-ounce) cans cream of
   mushroom soup
1 (6-ounce) package frozen
   Alaskan king crab, thawed
   and drained
1 tablespoon lemon juice
2 teaspoons Worcestershire sauce

1 teaspoon prepared mustard
½ teaspoon salt
8 whole chicken breasts, boned
   with skin on
⅓ cup vegetable oil
¼ cup milk
2 teaspoons Gravy Master or
   A-1 sauce
2 tablespoons minced onion
⅛ teaspoon pepper

Beat egg lightly; add stuffing mix, ½ cup undiluted mushroom soup, crab, lemon juice, Worcestershire, mustard and salt; mix well. Sprinkle insides of breasts with salt; spoon ⅛ of stuffing mixture in center of each. Fold sides together and fasten with metal skewer or toothpick. In saucepan over medium heat, combine rest of soup with oil, milk, Gravy Master, onions and pepper until bubbly. Preheat broiler for 10 minutes. Broil stuffed breasts 6 inches from heat for 15 minutes; turn. Brush with some of sauce; broil 15 minutes longer. Turn and baste again; broil 15 minutes more. (Cook approximately 45 minutes to 1 hour; watch carefully to keep from burning.) Remove skewers and serve, passing sauce separately.

OVEN BAKED CHICKEN SALAD

Preparing: 30 minutes   *Do Ahead*   *Yield: 6 servings*
Baking: 30 minutes   *Freeze*

2 cups diced cooked chicken
½ cup slivered almonds
1 (8-ounce) can water chestnuts,
   drained and sliced
1 (2-ounce) jar pimento, chopped
¼ teaspoon salt
⅛ teaspoon pepper

2 tablespoons lemon juice
½ cup crumbled french fried
   onions
¾ cup shredded Cheddar cheese
2 tablespoons sherry
1 cup mayonnaise
1 teaspoon curry powder (optional)

Preheat oven to 350°F. Mix all ingredients except onions and cheese. Turn into casserole; top with onions and cheese. Bake 30 minutes.

Jean Hartsough Flanagan

SUPREMES DE VOLAITES AUX EPINARDS

Preparing: 30 minutes   Do Ahead: Partially   Yield: 2 to 4 servings
Cooking: 30 minutes

2 (14-ounce) chicken breasts,   3 tablespoons oil
   boneless with skin attached   3 cups strong chicken stock
4 pounds fresh spinach   1 cup vermouth
2 pounds mushrooms, sliced   1¾ cups Crème Fraiche
5 teaspoons minced shallots   Salt and pepper
½ pound butter

Preheat oven to 400°F. Wash and destem spinach. Blanch 1 minute in hot water; cool and refresh. Squeeze dry and chop finely. Over medium-low heat, stir 12 tablespoons butter into spinach, 1 tablespoon at a time along with 2 teaspoons shallots. Cook until butter is absorbed. Put mushrooms in pot without water; salt and cook in their own juices until tender. Cut breasts into halves, trim excess fat and membrane, flour lightly. Mix oil and 1 tablespoon butter. Sauté breasts until brown on all sides. Season; bake 9 minutes. Set breasts aside. Pour off oil. Deglaze with 2 teaspoons shallots, stock and vermouth. Reduce liquid to ½ cup. Strain; whisk in Crème Fraiche. Simmer gently until thickened; season. Whisk in 1 tablespoon butter. Heat mushrooms in 2 tablespoons butter with 1 teaspoon shallots. Slice chicken breasts into ¼-inch strips, lengthwise. Mound spinach on each plate and arrange chicken over it, as in spokes. Scatter mushrooms around rim and mask chicken with sauce

Crème Fraiche:
2 cups heavy cream (unwhipped)   ¼ cup buttermilk

Stir together in a jar. *Let stand at room temperature for about 24 hours.*

The Garden
Philadelphia, Pennsylvania

ORANGE-AVOCADO CHICKEN

Preparing: 30 minutes   *Yield: 8 to 12 servings*
Cooking: About 1 hour

4 whole chicken breasts, split	1 teaspoon paprika
4 whole leg quarters	½ teaspoon ground ginger
¼ cup melted butter	½ teaspoon tarragon leaves
1 teaspoon grated orange rind	2 tablespoons cornstarch
1 cup orange juice, divided	2 oranges, peeled and sliced
½ cup chopped onion	1 avocado, peeled and sliced
1 teaspoon salt	Fresh parsley sprigs (garnish)

Rinse chicken and pat dry. Brown on both sides in butter over medium heat. Add orange rind, ½ cup orange juice, onion and seasonings. Reduce heat to low; cover and cook 30 minutes or until chicken is tender. Remove chicken to serving dish; keep warm. Combine remaining ½ cup orange juice and cornstarch, stirring until smooth; add to pan drippings. Cook over low heat, stirring constantly until thickened. Arrange orange and avocado slices around chicken; pour orange sauce over top. Garnish with parsley.

Winnie deWitt Preston

CHICKEN BAKE

Preparing: 30 minutes   *Do Ahead*   *Yield: 6 to 8 servings*
Baking: 1½ to 2 hours   *Freeze*

2 cups herb seasoned stuffing	1 (10¾-ounce) can cream of celery
1 (4-ounce) package or	soup
(2 ½-ounce) jar dried beef	1 pint sour cream
5 whole chicken breasts, split	Dash of paprika on top
and boned	
10 strips bacon, partially cooked	
(optional)	

Prepare stuffing with ⅔ cup water and ⅓ cup butter. Roll each breast around a tablespoon of prepared stuffing. Wrap each one in bacon. Line shallow baking pan with dried beef. *(Can freeze at this point.)* Preheat oven to 300°F. Put 1 tablespoon of sour cream on top of each chicken roll-up. Dilute soup with ½ can of water and spoon over all. Sprinkle with paprika. Bake 1½-2 hours uncovered.

Nancy Kuper Crowell

TARRAGON CHICKEN IN WINE SAUCE

Preparing: 45 minutes   *Yield: 4 servings*
Cooking: 20 minutes

2 whole chicken breasts, boned   2 (10-ounce) packages frozen
  and skinned (about 2 pounds)   spinach
½ teaspoon salt   6 tablespoons butter or margarine
½ teaspoon pepper   2 cups sliced mushrooms
1½ tablespoons cornstarch   ⅔ cup Rioja white wine
1½ tablespoons vegetable oil   1 cup heavy cream
1 egg white, unbeaten   1 tablespoon dried tarragon

Slice chicken into ¼-inch strips. In medium bowl combine chicken with salt, pepper, cornstarch, oil and egg white; let stand 10 minutes. Cook spinach according to package directions; drain, keep covered. Melt butter in large skillet over medium heat. Add chicken and cook until golden, 8-10 minutes; remove. Add mushrooms to pan and cook until tender. Add wine, cream and tarragon to pan along with chicken. Simmer uncovered over medium heat, stirring occasionally until sauce is consistency of heavy cream. Arrange cooked spinach on platter. Spoon chicken and sauce over spinach.

Susan Coates Oliver

CHICKEN CORDON BLEU

Preparing: 30 minutes   *Do Ahead: Partially*   *Yield: 6 servings*
Cooking: 20 minutes

3 boned chicken breasts, split,   1 medium onion, sliced
  skinned and pounded   3 tablespoons flour
6 slices Swiss cheese (4x4 inches)   2 cups milk
6 slices cooked ham (4x4 inches)   ⅓ cup brandy
6 tablespoons butter   ½ to 1 pound medium egg noodles
½ pound fresh mushrooms, sliced

Top each half chicken breast with a piece of cheese, then ham. Roll up and secure with skewers or toothpicks. In large skillet, melt butter and brown chicken; remove. In same pan, cook mushrooms and onion until tender; blend in flour. Gradually add milk and brandy, stirring constantly until thickened. Return chicken to pan and simmer covered, stirring occasionally, 20 minutes or until tender. Cook noodles and drain; serve with chicken.

Mary Murtagh Krull

HOT CHICKEN SALAD

Preparing: 45 minutes　　　　　*Do Ahead*　　　　　*Yield: 6 servings*
Baking: 30 minutes

2 cups cooked chicken, diced　　　½ cup slivered almonds, toasted
1½ cups chopped celery　　　　　2 tablespoons lemon juice
3 tablespoons chopped onion　　　1 cup mayonnaise
½ teaspoon salt　　　　　　　　1 cup Chinese fried noodles
½ teaspoon tarragon　　　　　　⅓ cup freshly grated Parmesan
1 teaspoon Worcestershire sauce　　cheese

Combine all ingredients except fried noodles and Parmesan cheese; place in 2-quart casserole. Top with fried noodles; sprinkle with Parmesan cheese. Preheat oven to 350°F; bake 30 minutes.

Susie Curtiss Linvill

CHICKEN STIR FRY

Preparing: 45 minutes　　　　*Do Ahead: Partially*　　　*Yield: 4 servings*
Chilling: 20 minutes to 12 hours

2 whole chicken breasts, boned,　　2 teaspoons oil
　　skinned, cut into ½-inch pieces　¼ teaspoon ground ginger
3 tablespoons dry sherry　　　　1 cup diagonally sliced celery
¼ cup soy sauce　　　　　　　½ cup sliced green onion or
1 teaspoon cornstarch　　　　　　scallions
1 cup sliced mushrooms　　　　　1 teaspoon minced garlic
1 (6-ounce) package Chinese pea　　½ cup water
　　pods, thawed
1 (6-ounce) package bamboo
　　shoots, drained

In large bowl combine soy sauce, sherry, cornstarch and ginger. Stir until smooth; add chicken and stir to coat. Cover and refrigerate at least 20 minutes or up to 12 hours. Just before cooking, drain reserve liquid. To cook, heat large skillet over high heat, until drop of water sizzles. Add oil and tilt pan to coat. When oil is hot (not smoking) add vegetables and garlic. Stir fry 3 minutes until hot, remove. Add chicken and stir fry 4 minutes until cooked, remove. Add soy sauce mixture and water; stir over medium heat 3-5 minutes until boiling and thickened. Add vegetables and chicken to skillet and cook 2 minutes stirring constantly until hot.

Sandra Johnson McConnell

CHICKEN ARTICHOKE MUSHROOM CASSEROLE

Preparing: 25 minutes   *Yield: 6 servings*
Baking: 40 minutes

3 pounds chicken breasts   1 (9-ounce) can artichoke hearts
1½ teaspoons salt   2 tablespoons flour
Pepper to taste   ⅔ cup chicken broth
¼ teaspoon paprika   3 tablespoons sherry
6 tablespoons butter   ¼ teaspoon rosemary
¼ pound mushrooms, sliced   Dash of sugar

Preheat oven to 350°F. Sprinkle chicken with salt, pepper and paprika. Brown in 4 tablespoons butter; remove to casserole. Add remaining 2 tablespoons butter to drippings; sauté mushrooms. Drain artichoke hearts; turn into serving dish; arrange hearts between chicken pieces. Sprinkle flour over mushrooms; stir in chicken broth, sherry, rosemary and sugar. Cook a few minutes; pour over chicken. Cover; bake 40 minutes.

Nancy Lynch Rivenburgh

STUFFED CHICKEN ATHENIAN WITH KIMA SAUCE

Preparing: 1 hour   *Do Ahead: Partially*   *Yield: 6 to 7 servings*
Cooking: 20 minutes

6-7 split chicken breasts, skinned   ½ teaspoon salt
  and boned   ¼ teaspoon pepper
2 tablespoons crumbled feta   1 egg
  cheese   2 tablespoons milk
1 tablespoon chopped walnuts   2 tablespoons olive oil
1 tablespoon chopped parsley   2 tablespoons butter
¾ cup flour   Kima Sauce (optional)

Cut a pocket in each piece of chicken, being sure not to slit all the way through. Mix cheese, walnuts and parsley. Stuff 1 tablespoon cheese mixture into pocket; seal by pressing edges together. Mix flour, salt and pepper; dredge chicken in flour. Mix egg and milk. Dip in egg mixture; then in flour mixture again. Heat oil and butter in large skillet over medium heat until foam subsides. Cook chicken over medium-high heat until brown; turn. Reduce heat; cook uncovered until brown, turning occasionally. Serve over Rice Pilaf with Kima Sauce.

Kima Sauce:

3 tablespoons olive oil
¼ cup chopped onion
¼ cup chopped carrots
¼ cup chopped celery
1 clove chopped garlic
8-ounce can tomatoes, drained
   and chopped

2 tablespoons chopped parsley
¼ cup white wine
¼ teaspoon sugar
¼ teaspoon oregano

Heat oil in skillet. Cook onions, carrots, celery and garlic until limp. Add tomatoes, parsley, wine, sugar and oregano. Simmer uncovered 20 minutes or until thick.

Denise Horton Jackson

SHERRIED CHICKEN

Preparing: 20 minutes   *Do Ahead*   *Yield: 4 to 6 servings*
Baking: 1 hour   *Freeze*

2-2½ pounds split legs
   and/or breasts
½ teaspoon salt
¼ teaspoon pepper
¼ teaspoon garlic salt
½ cup butter
1 medium onion, thinly sliced

½ cup tomato sauce
½ cup sherry
½ cup water
½ pound fresh mushrooms,
   sliced and sautéed (optional)
½ cup toasted almonds
   (optional)

Preheat oven to 350°F. Clean and drain chicken; season with salt, pepper and garlic salt. Sauté chicken in butter until golden brown; remove and arrange in single layer in shallow baking pan, skin side down. Add onion to butter in skillet; cook until transparent but not brown. Add tomato sauce, sherry and water. Pour one-half of sauce over chicken. Bake 30 minutes. Turn chicken and add remaining sauce. Bake another 30 minutes, basting occasionally. Serve with rice. For added touch, add sliced mushrooms or toasted almonds when cooking time is almost up.

Microwave: Place chicken in glass baking dish and cover with half of sauce. Cover; microwave on full power 20 minutes. Turn chicken, cover with remaining sauce and microwave on high for 5-6 minutes or until fork tender. Let stand 5 minutes before serving.

Nancy Evans Breitling

CHICKEN ALMOND CASSEROLE

Preparing: 20 minutes   *Do Ahead*   *Yield: 6 to 8 servings*
Baking: 30 to 40 minutes

2 cups cooked chicken
1 cup rice, cooked in chicken broth
½ teaspoon salt
½ cup mayonnaise
1 cup milk
1 (10¾-ounce) can cream of
   mushroom soup

¼ cup chopped celery
¼ cup slivered almonds (toasting
   optional)
1 tablespoon finely chopped onion
½ cup bread crumbs
2 tablespoons butter

Preheat oven to 350°F. Mix all ingredients in casserole dish. *(Can cover at this point and keep overnight in refrigerator.)* Before baking, cover with bread crumbs and dot with butter. Bake uncovered 30-40 minutes.

Note: Can be cooked in microwave for 18 minutes on 80% power.

Grace Burdett Nellis

CHICKEN BROCCOLI

Preparing: 30 minutes   *Do Ahead*   *Yield: 4 servings*
Baking: 30 minutes   *Freeze*

4-6 split chicken breasts
1 stalk celery
1 carrot, chopped

2 (10-ounce) packages frozen
   broccoli

Sauce:
½ cup flour
1 cup milk
2 cups chicken broth
1 cup mayonnaise

1 teaspoon lemon juice
½ teaspoon curry powder
Bread crumbs

Cook chicken with celery and carrot in enough water to cover. When chicken is tender, remove and save broth. Bone chicken; cut into bite-sized pieces. Cook broccoli according to package directions. Blend flour and milk; add remaining ingredients; cook in double boiler until blended and thickened, stirring frequently. In a casserole, alternate layers of chicken, broccoli and sauce. Sprinkle with bread crumbs; bake at 350°F. 30 minutes or until bubbly.

Cynthia Harris Helsel

CHICKEN ROULADE

Preparing: 30 minutes   *Do Ahead: Partially*   *Yield: 4 servings*
Cooking: 45 to 60 minutes

¼ pound lobster meat, chopped
2 tablespoons butter
3 shallots, finely chopped
⅛ teaspoon cayenne pepper
1 ounce cognac
1½ cups heavy cream
4 large boneless chicken breasts, butterflied

1 (10¾-ounce) can cream of shrimp soup
¼ pound cooked shrimp, chopped
3 cups fine bread crumbs
2 cups flour
2 eggs, beaten
3-4 tablespoons margarine

Melt butter; add lobster and sauté 2-3 minutes. Add shallots, pepper and cognac. Stir carefully. Add 1 cup cream; lower heat. Simmer and reduce to medium sauce thickness (10 minutes); set aside to cool. Place portion of lobster mixture in each breast and roll. Secure with toothpicks or skewers. Dip rolled chicken breasts in flour, then in beaten eggs, then in bread crumbs. Melt 3-4 tablespoons margarine. Brown chicken lightly on all sides. In saucepan, heat shrimp soup, shrimp and remaining ½ cup heavy cream. Add liquid mixture from lobster to shrimp soup; stir to mix well. Preheat oven to 350°F. Pour ½ of sauce into baking dish. Arrange chicken breasts in sauce. Bake 45-60 minutes. Heat reserved mixture. Serve over individual breasts.

Lori Adams DelRossi

CHICKEN ENCHILADA CASSEROLE

Preparing: 20 minutes   *Do Ahead*   *Yield: 6 to 8 servings*
Cooking: 45 minutes   *Freeze*

3-4 cups cooked and cubed chicken breasts
2 (10¾-ounce) cans cream of chicken soup
1 (5⅓-ounce) can evaporated milk
½ cup chopped onion

1 (4-ounce) can green chilies, chopped
1 dozen corn tortillas, cut in small pieces
8 ounces Cheddar cheese, shredded

Preheat oven to 350°F. Mix chicken, soup, milk, onion and chili peppers. In greased 2-quart casserole, place a layer of tortillas, layer of chicken mixture and layer of cheese. Repeat layers ending with cheese on top. Bake 45 minutes or until hot and bubbly.

Gwen Fields Gilmore

PINEAPPLE CHICKEN

Preparing: 25 minutes   *Yield: 4 servings*
Cooking: 15 minutes

2 whole chicken breasts, skinned,   2 medium carrots, thinly sliced
  boned, cut into strips   1 (20-ounce) can unsweetened
½ teaspoon salt   pineapple chunks with liquid
1 tablespoon vegetable oil   1 tablespoon cornstarch
1 cup diagonally sliced celery   2 tablespoons soy sauce

Place chicken strips in medium bowl; season with salt. Heat oil in fry pan or
wok; add chicken and stir-fry 5 minutes. Push chicken to one side. Add celery
and carrots; cook 3-4 minutes. Add pineapple chunks with liquid and heat. In
small bowl, mix cornstarch with soy sauce. Stir into chicken mixture. Cook,
stirring constantly until thickened.

Sandra Johnson McConnell

BAKED HERB CHICKEN

Preparing: 10 minutes   *Do Ahead*   *Yield: 6 to 8 servings*
Baking: 1 hour

12-16 chicken pieces   2 teaspoons dried basil
1 teaspoon salt   2 teaspoons rosemary, crushed
½ teaspoon pepper   1 tablespoon grated lemon peel
2 teaspoons poultry seasoning   Lemon wedges (garnish)

Preheat oven to 350°F. Arrange chicken pieces in baking pan. Place pats of
butter on and under each chicken piece. Mix seasonings; sprinkle ½ over
chicken. Cover; bake 30 minutes. Remove cover; turn chicken. Sprinkle with
remaining seasonings; bake 30 minutes. Serve chicken with lemon wedges.

Microwave: Melt 2-3 tablespoons margarine in glass baking dish. Place
chicken in dish, coating with margarine. Sprinkle with ½ herb mixture. Cover
with waxed paper; microwave on full power for 12 minutes. Remove paper,
turn chicken; sprinkle with remaining seasoning. Recover with waxed paper;
microwave for 12 minutes on full power. Allow to set 5 minutes before serving.

Note: These times are for 8 pieces of chicken.

Grace Burdett Nellis

CHICKEN FLORENTINE

Preparing: 20 minutes   *Do Ahead*   *Yield: 8 servings*
Baking: 20 minutes

1 (5-pound) stewing chicken,   1 clove garlic, mashed
   cooked, cut into bite-sized pieces   Dash basil and marjoram
2 (10-ounce) packages frozen   1 tablespoon flour
   chopped spinach   ⅓ cup heavy or light cream
1 tablespoon butter

Preheat oven to 400°F. Cook spinach and drain very well. Melt butter; stir in garlic, basil and marjoram. Blend in flour; add cream, stirring constantly until mixture thickens and bubbles. Remove from heat; stir in spinach. Place mixture in 2-quart baking dish. Cover spinach mixture with chicken.

Sauce:
3 tablespoons butter   ¼-½ teaspoon salt
3 tablespoons flour   ⅛ teaspoon pepper
¾ cup light cream   1 cup Parmesan cheese
¾ cup chicken stock

Melt butter; blend in flour. Add cream, chicken stock, salt and pepper, stirring constantly over medium heat until thickened. Pour sauce over chicken. Top with Parmesan cheese. Bake 20 minutes.

Note: Recipe can be doubled easily; can be baked and served in individual ramekins.

CHICKEN BREASTS WITH CHIPPED BEEF

Preparing: 20 minutes   *Do Ahead*   *Yield: 6 to 8 servings*
Baking: 4 hours

½ chicken breast per person   1 cup sour cream
1 piece chipped beef per person   ½ cup sherry
1 (10¾-ounce) can cream of   Pepper to taste
   mushroom soup

Preheat oven to 200°F. Wrap each breast in thin slice of chipped beef. Place in baking dish. Heat soup with sour cream, sherry and pepper; mix thoroughly and pour over chicken. Bake 4 hours.

Note: This recipe can be increased to larger quantities, using amounts given for soup, sour cream and sherry for every 8 servings prepared.

Gail White Dillon

CHICKEN-WILD RICE CASSEROLE

Preparing: 40 minutes   *Do Ahead*   *Yield: 12 servings*
Cooking: 1½ hours
Baking: 30 minutes

1 (1⅜-ounce) package dehydrated onion soup	Dash pepper
1 pint sour cream	½ teaspoon dried basil
3 (2½ pounds) frying chickens, cut up	Pinch thyme
	1 teaspoon curry powder
2 cups dry sherry	6 tablespoons minced parsley
1 cup water	1 (10¾-ounce) can cream of mushroom soup
1 teaspoon salt	1½ cups uncooked wild rice

Blend dry onion soup into sour cream and allow to stand 2 hours. Preheat oven to 300°F. Place chicken in roasting pan, pour sherry and water over it; sprinkle with seasonings and parsley. Cover tightly; bake 1½ hours or until meat falls off bones. Remove chicken from pan, cover loosely; set aside to cool. Strain juices into pan; skim off fat. Simmer until reduced to 1½ cups. Blend mushroom soup until smooth; heat with juices a few minutes. Slowly combine with sour cream. Cook rice as directed on package. Skin and bone chicken; cut into bite-sized pieces. Combine with rice; turn into buttered casserole. Pour sauce over and toss lightly. When ready to serve, heat uncovered in preheated 250°F. oven 30 minutes.

Sandra Johnson McConnell

ROAST CHICKEN WITH SAUCE SUPREME

Preparing: 15 minutes   *Yield: 4 to 6 servings*
Baking: 1 hour

1 (3-4 pound) roasting chicken	1 teaspoon dried savory or marjoram
3 tablespoons butter, softened	Freshly ground black pepper to taste
1 teaspoon dried tarragon	
1 teaspoon dried parsley	

Preheat oven to 425°F. Combine butter, herbs and pepper. Rub butter-herb mixture on breast, legs and wings of chicken; place on side in roasting pan. Roast 15 minutes; turn bird on other side and roast 15 minutes more. Turn breast side up, reduce heat to 375°F. and roast 20-30 minutes. Remove to warm platter, pour off fat; reserve remaining liquid and solids for sauce.

Sauce:

2 tablespoons butter
2 teaspoons minced shallots
2 teaspoons flour

1¾ cups chicken broth
½ cup heavy cream (approximate)

In saucepan, melt butter and sauté shallots until soft. Add flour; stir well. Cook 1-2 minutes; add 1 cup broth and simmer, stirring until thickened. Remove from heat and cover. Deglaze roasting pan with remaining broth and reduce by one half. Strain shallot mixture into roasting pan; stir until combined. Add cream and reduce to desired consistency.

Jeffrey Preston

ORANGE LEMON CHICKEN

Preparing: 40 minutes
Baking: 30 minutes

Yield: 8 servings

2 (3-pound) frying chickens, cut up
¼ pound butter
2 tablespoons olive oil
1 teaspoon freshly grated lemon
  rind
1 teaspoon freshly grated orange
  rind
¾ cup *fresh* orange juice
¼ cup *fresh* lemon juice
½ teaspoon dried tarragon

1 cup heavy cream
½ cup Madeira wine
¼ cup dry white wine
Salt and freshly ground pepper
  to taste
2 tablespoons cornstarch
¼ cup freshly grated Parmesan
  cheese
¼ teaspoon paprika

Preheat oven to 350°F. Sauté chicken pieces in butter and oil until golden brown and almost cooked through. Transfer to shallow baking dish to be used for serving; set aside. To butter in skillet, add orange and lemon rind, ½ cup orange juice, lemon juice and tarragon. Cook and stir over low heat; gradually whisk in cream. Beat in both wines with salt and pepper. Dissolve cornstarch in remaining ¼ cup orange juice in separate bowl; gradually stir into sauce. Cook and stir just until thickened. Pour over chicken; sprinkle with cheese and paprika. Bake 30 minutes. Just before serving brown under the broiler.

Note: Split chicken breasts with skin may be substituted for fryer parts.

Susan Johnson Mader

WILD RICE CHICKEN SUPREME

Preparing: 30 minutes
Baking: 30 minutes

Do Ahead
Freeze

Yield: 6 to 8 servings

1 package wild rice
⅓ cup chopped onion
¼ cup butter
⅓ cup flour
1 teaspoon salt
Dash black pepper
1 cup light cream or evaporated
  milk

1 cup chicken broth
2 cups chicken, cooked and cubed
⅓ cup chopped pimento
⅓ cup fresh minced parsley
3 tablespoons blanched almonds,
  chopped

Preheat oven to 425°F. Cook wild rice according to package directions; set aside. Sauté onions in butter; blend in flour, salt and pepper. Gradually stir in cream and chicken broth; cook, stirring until thickened. Remove from heat; fold in chicken, pimento, parsley, almonds and cooked rice. Put in 2-quart casserole; bake 30 minutes.

Gwen Fields Gilmore

OVEN FRIED CHICKEN MONTEREY

Preparing: 25 minutes
Baking: 50 minutes

Yield: 6 to 8 servings

¼ cup flour
1 (1¼-ounce) package taco
  seasoning mix
5-6 whole chicken legs, divided
4-6 tablespoons margarine

1½ cups crushed tortilla chips
  (4-5 cups uncrushed)
Cheese sauce
Shredded lettuce

Preheat oven to 375°F. Combine flour and seasoning mix in bag. Add 2-3 pieces of chicken at a time and shake to coat. Melt margarine in shallow oblong baking dish. Dip flour-coated chicken in margarine and roll in crushed chips. Arrange in pan; bake in preheated oven 45-50 minutes. To serve, line serving dish with lettuce; top with shredded lettuce and chicken. Spoon some sauce over chicken; pass remaining sauce.

Cheese Sauce:

1 tablespoon finely chopped onion
1 tablespoon oil
1 tablespoon flour
⅛ teaspoon salt
¾ cup evaporated milk

⅛ teaspoon Tabasco Sauce
½ cup shredded Monterey Jack
    cheese (2 ounces)
½ teaspoon lemon juice

Cook onion in oil until tender; blend in flour and salt; add milk and Tabasco all at once, stirring constantly. Cook until thickened and bubbly. Add cheese and lemon juice, stirring until cheese melts. DO NOT BOIL. Serve with chicken.

Lois Rising Pogyor

ROAST DUCKLING WITH CHERRY BERNE

Preparing: 25 minutes
Roasting: 3 ½ hours
Chilling: 1 hour
Baking: 20 minutes

Yield: 6 servings

3 whole ducklings, 3 pounds each
2 stalks celery
2 oranges, peeled

Salt and pepper
Cherry Berne Sauce

Thaw and wash ducks. Preheat oven to 350°F. Cut off wing tips and excess fat and skin. Chop celery and oranges, coarsely; stuff ducks with this mixture for flavor. Place ducks on baking rack in shallow roasting pan, breast side up. Salt and pepper. Roast 3½ hours. Drain ducks of all excess grease and chill 1 hour. Cut in half and remove rib bones. Preheat oven to 400°F. Heat ducks 20 minutes, when ready to serve. Discard celery and orange mixture. Serve with Cherry Berne Sauce.

Cherry Berne Sauce:

1 (16-ounce) can bing cherries
2 ounces blackberry brandy

2 ounces Cherry Herring liquor
Arrowroot

Drain cherries, reserving juice. Place cherry juice and both liquors in small saucepan; bring to boil. When boiling, thicken with arrowroot (start with 1 teaspoon) and water to desired thickness. Add drained cherries and blend.

David A. Robinson, Jonarthur's Restaurant
Belmont Hills, Pennsylvania

ORANGE-TURKEY STEW

Preparing: 20 minutes   *Yield: 4 servings*
Cooking: 2 hours

3 pounds turkey parts   1 bay leaf
1 cup water   1 tablespoon salt
2 cups orange juice   ½ teaspoon pepper
2 cups diagonally sliced celery   ½ teaspoon thyme
¼ cup chopped celery leaves   2 cups pared, sliced carrots
1 cup chopped onion   ⅓ cup medium barley
4 parsley sprigs

Place all ingredients except carrots and barley in a large covered kettle. Bring to a boil. Reduce heat; simmer 1 hour. Add carrots and barley. Cover; simmer 1 hour longer. Remove turkey. Cut meat away from bones; dice to make 2 cups. Return meat to kettle; heat.

Sandra Johnson McConnell

CALVES LIVER A L'ANGLAISE

Preparing: 25 minutes   *Yield: 2 servings*
Cooking: 10 minutes

3 ounces thinly sliced onion   8 ounces calves liver (4 slices)
   (about ⅓ cup)   1½ tablespoons sour cream
1 ounce butter (2 tablespoons)   2 tablespoons Bordelaise sauce
2 ounces flour   Salt and pepper to taste

Sauté onions in butter lightly; add calves liver which has been floured. Cook to desired degree of doneness. Combine sour cream and Bordelaise sauce in sauté pan; blend with liver and onions; serve.

Bordelaise Sauce:
1 cup oil   1 cup burgundy wine
1 onion, diced coarsely   2 tablespoons tomato purée
1 cup flour   Salt and pepper
3 cups beef stock

Sauté onion in oil until brown. Add flour to make a roux; cook over low heat 2 minutes. Add purée, stock and wine. Bring to a boil; let simmer ½ hour. Season and strain.

The Greenhouse
Radnor, Pennsylvania

FILET DE BOEUF EN VERMOUTH

Preparing: 10 minutes
Cooking: 10 minutes

Yield: 4 servings

2 tablespoons butter	**1 tablespoon flour**
4 filets of beef, 1-inch thick	**¼ cup dry vermouth**
¾ teaspoon salt	**½ cup heavy cream**
¼ teaspoon pepper	**2 tablespoons parsley**

Melt butter in skillet. Brown filets over high heat 3 minutes on each side. Sprinkle meat with salt and pepper; stir flour into pan juice. Add vermouth and cream. Cook over medium heat 4-6 minutes longer or until done as desired, turning filets once. Arrange filets on serving dish; cover with sauce; sprinkle with parsley. Use sauce as gravy for rice.

Dede Dubois Shimrak

LOBSTER STUFFED FILET WITH WINE SAUCE

Preparing: 30 minutes
Roasting: 45 to 50 minutes

Yield: 8 servings

4-5 pounds whole filet of beef	**½ cup sliced green onion**
4 frozen lobster tails or 1 pound of lobster meat	**½ cup butter or margarine**
1 tablespoon butter or margarine, melted	**½ cup dry white wine**
1½ teaspoons lemon juice	**⅛ teaspoon garlic salt**
6 slices bacon, partially cooked	**Fluted whole mushrooms (garnish)**
	Watercress (garnish)

Cut filet lengthwise to within ½-inch of bottom to butterfly. Place frozen lobster tails in boiling salted water to cover. Return to boiling; reduce heat and simmer 5-6 minutes. Carefully remove lobster from shells. Cut in half lengthwise. Place lobster, end to end, inside beef. (If using lobster meat already out of shells, follow directions on package. It may have been cooked before.) Combine melted butter and lemon juice; drizzle on lobster. Close meat around lobster; tie roast together securely with string at intervals of 1-inch. Preheat oven to 425°F. Place on rack in shallow roasting pan. Roast 45-50 minutes for rare doneness. Lay bacon slices atop; roast 5 minutes more. Meanwhile, in saucepan, cook green onion in ½ cup butter over very low heat until tender, stirring frequently. Add wine and garlic salt; heat through, stirring frequently. To serve, slice roast; spoon on wine sauce. Garnish platter with fluted whole mushrooms and watercress, if desired.

BEEF FILLET WELLINGTON

Preparing: 1 hour   *Do Ahead*   *Yield: 8 servings*
Baking: 10 to 20 minutes

8 (5-ounce) fillets of beef, well
   trimmed
Vegetable oil
½ teaspoon salt
Dash pepper
1 pound fresh mushrooms
½ cup chopped onion
2 tablespoons butter, melted

1 cup soft bread crumbs
1 clove garlic, crushed
1 tablespoon chopped parsley
½ teaspoon thyme
½ teaspoon turmeric (optional)
9 frozen puff pastry shells, thawed
1 egg white, slightly beaten

Put fillets in freezer for 20 minutes to chill. Remove from freezer and brush with oil; sprinkle with salt and pepper. Sear in skillet 5 minutes on each side; chill in refrigerator. Process mushrooms in blender or food processor until they become a paté-like consistency. Sauté onion in butter until soft; add mushrooms, bread crumbs, garlic, parsley, thyme and turmeric. Remove from heat; mix and divide into 8 portions. Preheat oven to 450°F. Roll out each pastry shell to 9x5-inch rectangle ⅛-inch thick. Place 1 portion of mushroom mixture on each rectangle; top with 1 fillet turning ends in. Place sealed side down in shallow baking pan. Decorate with cut-outs from an additional rolled-out puffed shell. Brush with egg white. Bake 10 minutes (rare), 12 minutes (medium rare), 15 minutes (medium), or 20 minutes (well done). Serve with Tarragon or Bernaise Sauce.

Note: This can be made in the morning, covered with foil and refrigerated until needed.

Quick Bernaise Sauce:
2 tablespoons white wine
1 tablespoon tarragon vinegar
2 teaspoons chopped tarragon
2 teaspoons chopped onion
¼ teaspoon fresh ground pepper

½ cup butter
3 egg yolks
2 tablespoons lemon juice
¼ teaspoon salt
Pinch of cayenne pepper

Combine wine, vinegar, tarragon, onion and pepper in a skillet. Bring to a boil; cook rapidly until almost all liquid disappears. In a small saucepan heat butter to bubbling, not brown. Place egg yolks, lemon juice, salt and cayenne in blender. Flick on and off at high speed; gradually add hot butter while on high speed. Add vinegar-herb mixture. Blend 4 seconds.

Tarragon Sauce:

3 egg yolks
½ cup melted butter
2 tablespoons lemon juice
2 tablespoons hot water

½ teaspoon salt
1 teaspoon snipped parsley
⅛ teaspoon dried tarragon

Beat yolks in top of double boiler with wire whisk until smooth but not fluffy. Add butter, lemon juice, hot water and salt. Place over hot water and beat until sauce begins to thicken (about 5 minutes). Add parsley and tarragon. If mixture begins to separate, add small amount cold water and beat.

Note: To keep sauces warm, fill thermos bottle with boiling water; let stand 20 minutes. Empty out water; fill immediately with sauce; seal with cap. Will keep sauces warm up to 5 hours.

BAVETTE FARCIE AU JUS
(Braised Stuffed Flank Steak)

Preparing: 30 minutes   *Do Ahead: Partially*   *Yield: 6 to 8 servings*
Cooking: 1¼ hours

2-2½ pounds flank steak
5 tablespoons margarine
¼ cup vegetable oil
2 cups bread cubes (crusts removed)
1 pound ground round
2 eggs, slightly beaten
1½ cups chopped onion
½ stalk celery, chopped
1 tablespoon chopped parsley

1 teaspoon salt
½ teaspoon freshly ground black pepper
1 teaspoon thyme
¾ cup finely chopped or grated carrots
1 bay leaf
1 (15-ounce) can tomato sauce
½ cup beef broth
½ cup dry red wine

With sharp knife make pocket in beef to hold stuffing. Heat 2 tablespoons margarine and ¼ cup oil, sauté bread cubes until golden. In large bowl, combine ground beef, eggs, ¾ cup onion, celery, parsley, salt, pepper and ½ teaspoon thyme. Toss with bread cubes, fill pocket with stuffing. Tie steak every few inches to hold together. Season with salt and pepper. *(Can be done ahead to this point.)* Heat remaining margarine and oil; brown steak on all sides. Add ½ teaspoon thyme, ¾ cup onions, carrots, bay leaf, tomato sauce, broth and wine. Bring to a boil; cover and simmer 1¼ hours. Remove strings to serve. Strain gravy and serve with meat.

Joanne Stanek Murphy

STEAK DIANE

Preparing: 15 minutes   *Yield: 4 servings*
Cooking: 6 to 8 minutes

½ cup fresh sliced mushrooms   ¼ cup butter
2 tablespoons minced onion   2 tablespoons snipped fresh
1 clove garlic, minced   parsley
⅛ teaspoon salt   2 tablespoons butter
1 teaspoon lemon juice   1 pound beef tenderloin or strip
1 teaspoon Worcestershire sauce   steak cut into 8 slices

Sauce:
Cook and stir mushrooms, onions and seasonings in ¼ cup butter until tender. Stir in parsley; keep sauce warm. Melt 2 tablespoons butter in skillet, cook meat over moderate heat to medium doneness (2-4 minutes on each side). Serve with mushroom sauce.

Grace Burdett Nellis

PEPPERCORN STEAK

Preparing: 10 minutes   *Do Ahead: Partially*   *Yield: 6 servings*
Marinating: 30 minutes
Cooking: 15 minutes

1 (2½-pound) boneless round steak   ¼ cup minced onion
   or flank steak   1 tablespoon vegetable oil
Instant meat tenderizer   2 teaspoons peppercorns
⅓ cup burgundy wine

About 50 minutes before serving, trim any excess fat from meat. Prepare steak with meat tenderizer as label directs. Place steak in large flat baking dish. In measuring cup combine wine, onion and oil. Pour over steak; refrigerate loosely covered 30 minutes, turning occasionally. Preheat broiler. Coarsely crush peppercorns in pepper mill or wrap peppercorns in cloth then crush coarsely with rolling pin; press well into both sides of steak. Place steak on broiling pan; pour remaining marinade over steak. Broil about 15 minutes or until desired doneness turning once. Serve steak cut across grain in very thin slices.

Note: If using flank steak, score by cutting thin diagonal slashes across grain on both sides before tenderizing.

Catherine More Keller

FILET OF BEEF WRAPPED IN PHYLLO PASTRY

Preparing: 40 minutes   *Yield: 8 servings*
Baking: 40 to 45 minutes

3 pound filet mignon, trimmed   2 shallots, minced
Salt   1 package phyllo pastry
2 tablespoons sweet butter   ½ cup melted butter
½ pound fresh mushrooms,
   thoroughly dried and minced

Preheat oven to 400°F. Rub filet with salt. In heavy skillet, sear meat in sweet butter over high heat on all sides to seal in juices; set aside. In same pan, sauté mushrooms and shallots 2-3 minutes until soft; set aside. Brush 12 pieces of phyllo dough with melted butter and layer. Spread half of mushroom mixture on pastry; and place seared beef in middle of pastry. Place remaining mushrooms on top of filet. Brush 6 pieces of phyllo dough with butter; place over top of filet. Fold phyllo dough around filet and seal edges by overlapping; brush completely with melted butter, being certain to coat edges. Place beef in buttered baking pan; bake 40-45 minutes or until pastry is browned and flaky *(it will puff)*. Remove to a heated serving dish. May be served with Madeira Sauce.

Madeira Sauce:
3 tablespoons butter   1 teaspoon Kitchen Bouquet or
1½ tablespoons flour   Bovril
¾ cup beef stock   ¼ cup Madeira wine

Over low heat, melt butter; gradually stir in flour and cook for 5 minutes. Add beef stock, Kitchen Bouquet and Madeira wine. Cook until thickened.

Susan Johnson Mader

TOURNEDOS MADAGASCAR

Preparing: 5 minutes   *Yield: 8 servings*
Cooking: 15 minutes

4 tablespoons butter
2 tablespoons vegetable oil
8 tournedos (filet mignon)
   1½-2 inches thick
Salt to taste
4 shallots, finely chopped

1 cup beef broth
¾ cup dry red wine
1 teaspoon bovril (meat extract)
2 tablespoons green peppercorns
3 teaspoons cornstarch

Mix cornstarch with a little water. Heat butter and oil in heavy sauté pan; add beef which has been rubbed with salt. Brown well, about 5 minutes on each side. Remove from pan; set aside. Add shallots; sauté 3 minutes. Add beef broth, wine, bovril and peppercorns; simmer over high heat about 5 minutes. Continue simmering on low heat to desired doneness. Thicken sauce with cornstarch; serve.

ITALIAN ROUND STEAK

Preparing: 10 minutes   *Do Ahead*   *Yield: 6 servings*
Marinating: 8 hours or overnight
Cooking: 10 minutes

1½ pounds lean, boneless beef
   round steak
½ cup dry white wine
1 tablespoon vegetable oil
½ teaspoon salt
⅛ teaspoon pepper

1 (15-ounce) can tomato sauce
¼ cup chopped onion
1 clove garlic, minced
Parsley sprigs (optional)
1 pound pasta, cooked according
   to package directions

With sharp knife, score steak on both sides in diamond pattern. Combine wine, oil, salt and pepper; pour over meat. Cover and marinate in refrigerator for 8 hours or overnight, turning occasionally. *At serving time,* drain meat well, reserving marinade. Place meat on unheated rack of broiler pan and broil 3-inches from heat for 4-5 minutes. Turn and broil 4 minutes for medium rare. Meanwhile in saucepan, combine reserved marinade, tomato sauce, onion and garlic. Bring to boiling. Reduce heat, simmer uncovered 5 minutes. Thinly slice meat across grain. Arrange slices on platter with pasta and spoon marinade over all. Garnish with parsley.

Grace Burdett Nellis

ROAST FILET OF BEEF WITH WINE SAUCE

Preparing: 30 minutes   *Do Ahead: Partially*   *Yield: 8 servings*
Cooking: 40 minutes   *Freeze*

4-4½ pound filet of beef   **Salt**
Suet

Preheat oven to 425°F. Salt meat lightly. Place a piece of suet under filet and a narrow ribbon of fat on top. Roast about 40 minutes (9-10 minutes per pound for rare) approximately 120°F. on meat thermometer. Serve with Wine Sauce.

Wine Sauce:
2 carrots, coarsely chopped   **¼ teaspoon pepper**
2 stalks celery, chopped   **2 cups red wine**
¼ cup chopped shallots   **1 cup beef broth**
½ teaspoon thyme   **2 tablespoons butter**
½ teaspoon salt   **1 tablespoon flour**

Combine carrots, celery, shallots, thyme, salt, pepper and red wine in saucepan. Bring to a boil. Cook, uncovered over low heat 10 minutes. Add broth and cook 10 minutes longer; strain. Knead one tablespoon of butter and the flour together to make *beurre manié*. Stir into sauce a little at a time. At the last minute, stir in the other tablespoon of butter and taste for seasoning.

Note: Good served with any beef roast.

FIVE-HOUR STEW

Preparing: 30 minutes   *Do Ahead*   *Yield: 6 servings*
Baking: 5 hours   *Freeze*

2 pounds stewing beef   **1 teaspoon salt**
1 (15-ounce) can stewed tomatoes   **Dash of pepper**
1 (16-ounce) can tiny peas,   **1 bay leaf**
  drained   **1 (10¾-ounce) can mushroom,**
1 large raw potato, sliced   **celery or tomato soup, thinned**
1 cup sliced carrots (if using   **with ½ can water**
  canned, drain)   **1 cup red wine or sherry**
2 medium onions, chopped

Preheat oven to 275°F. Mix all ingredients in a casserole that has a tight lid, such as a Dutch oven. Bake 5 hours.

Gail White Dillon

BRAISED SWISS STEAK

Preparing: 30 minutes   *Yield: 6 servings*
Cooking: 2 hours

2 pounds round steak, 1-inch thick
2 tablespoons dried bread crumbs
1-2 teaspoons salt, to taste
¼ teaspoon pepper
1 tablespoon butter or margarine,
   melted

1 (8-ounce) can stewed tomatoes
2 medium onions, thinly sliced
1 tablespoon Worcestershire sauce
¼ cup chopped celery
1 clove garlic, crushed

Pat steak with damp paper towel to remove excess liquid. Combine bread crumbs, salt and pepper. Place steak on wooden board; sprinkle with half bread crumb mixture and pound with wooden mallet. Repeat on other side; cut into 6 pieces. Melt butter in Dutch oven. Brown meat over medium heat. Add tomatoes, onions, Worcestershire, celery and garlic; bring to boil. Reduce heat and simmer 2 hours.

Grace Burdett Nellis

OVEN BEEF BURGUNDY

Preparing: 20 minutes   *Yield: 6 to 8 servings*
Baking: 2½ hours

2 pounds beef chuck
1 tablespoon Kitchen Bouquet
¼ cup cream of rice (or flour)
4 carrots
2 cups thinly sliced onions
1 cup thinly sliced celery
1 clove garlic, minced

2 teaspoons salt
⅛ teaspoon pepper
⅛ teaspoon marjoram, crushed
⅛ teaspoon thyme, crushed
1 cup burgundy (or dry red wine)
1 (6-ounce) can mushrooms with
   broth

Preheat oven to 325°F. Trim meat and cut into 1½-inch cubes. Place in 2½-quart casserole; toss with Kitchen Bouquet to coat. Mix in cream of rice. Cut carrots in quarters lengthwise and in half crosswise; add with remaining ingredients. Mix gently. Cover and bake 2½ hours. Stir every 30 minutes. Serve with noodles, rice or potatoes.

Patricia Lawler Wiedinmyer

TORONADOES OF BEEF

Preparing: 25 minutes
Cooking: 15 minutes

Yield: 2 servings

2 (6-ounce) filets of beef
Butter
⅓ cup Marsala wine
⅓ cup mushroom stock (liquid
produced by sautéing ⅛ pound
mushrooms)

⅓ cup beef bouillon
1 teaspoon water
4 broccoli spears, cooked
Hollandaise sauce

Sauté filets in butter on both sides; pour off butter. Remove; set aside. Combine wine, mushroom stock, bouillon and water; simmer 15 minutes; thicken sauce to desired consistency. For each serving, place cooked filet on warm serving plate; top with wine sauce. Place warm broccoli spears on top of each filet; cover with hollandaise sauce. Serve immediately.

The Mile Post Inn
Wayne, Pennsylvania

PAUL LYNDE BEEF STEW

Preparing: 15 minutes
Baking: 8 to 10 hours

Do Ahead
Freeze

Yield: 4 to 6 servings

2 pounds stewing beef cubes
1 (16-ounce) can sliced carrots,
drained
1 (16-ounce) can potatoes, drained
1 (10¾-ounce) can beef consommé
½ cup sherry wine

1 tablespoon brown sugar
3 onions, quartered
3 teaspoons tapioca
Salt and pepper
½ cup bread crumbs

Preheat oven to 200°F. Combine all ingredients except bread crumbs. Place in deep 3-quart casserole. Stir once before baking. Top with bread crumbs. Bake covered 8-10 hours. *Can be made day before.*

Note: Fresh potatoes and carrots may be substituted.

Judilee Cronrath Traynor

BEEF STROGANOFF I

Preparing: 25 to 30 minutes   *Yield: 4 servings*
Cooking: 1 hour

2 pounds lean beef cubes
1 cup butter
1 onion, diced
1 cup sliced mushrooms
Dash of Tabasco
1 tablespoon Worcestershire
  sauce

½ green pepper, diced
1 clove garlic, minced
1 tablespoon garlic salt
1 cup sour cream
1 cup heavy cream
3 tablespoons wine vinegar
2 tablespoons flour

Sauté beef cubes in butter until brown. After meat begins to brown, add onions, mushrooms, Tabasco, Worcestershire, green pepper, garlic and garlic salt. When vegetables begin to soften, add sour cream, heavy cream and wine vinegar. Add flour. Let mixture continue to simmer 1 hour or until meat cubes are completely tender. Serve over rice or noodles.

Gwen Fields Gilmore

BEF STROGANOV
(Sautéed Beef with Mushrooms and Onions
in Sour-Cream Sauce)
(Classic Russian version)

Preparing: 30 minutes   *Do Ahead: Partially*   *Yield: 8 to 10 servings*
Cooking: 25 minutes

2 tablespoons dry mustard
3½ teaspoons sugar
4 teaspoons salt
8-9 tablespoons vegetable oil
8 cups thinly sliced onions,
  separated into rings
2 pounds fresh mushrooms, thinly
  sliced lengthwise

4 pounds fillet of beef, trimmed of
  all fat
2 teaspoons freshly ground black
  pepper
2 pints sour cream

In small mixing bowl, combine mustard, sugar, pinch of salt and enough hot water (about 2 tablespoons) to form a thick paste. Set mustard mixture aside at room temperature 15 minutes. Heat 4 tablespoons of oil in a heavy 12-inch skillet over high heat until light haze forms above it. Drop in onions and mushrooms, cover pan; reduce heat to low. Stirring occasionally, simmer 20-30 minutes, or until vegetables are soft. Drain, discard liquid; return mixture to skillet. With large, sharp knife cut fillet across grain into ¼-inch thick rounds. Lay each round on a board; slice it with the grains into ¼-inch wide strips. Heat 4 tablespoons oil in another heavy 12-inch skillet over high heat until very hot but not smoking. Drop in half of meat, tossing strips constantly with large spoon; fry 2 minutes or until meat is lightly brown. With slotted spoon, transfer meat to vegetables in other skillet; fry remaining meat similarly, adding additional oil if needed. When all meat has been combined with vegetables, stir in remaining salt, pepper and mustard sauce. Stir in sour cream, a tablespoon at a time. Add remaining ½ teaspoon sugar. Reduce heat to low; cover and simmer 2-3 minutes, until sauce is heated thoroughly. Taste for seasoning.

BEEF STROGANOFF II

Preparing: 30 minutes   *Do Ahead: Partially*   *Yield: 6 to 8 servings*

2 pounds beef sirloin, cut in
   bite-sized pieces
2 tablespoons flour
1 teaspoon salt
4 tablespoons butter or margarine
1 cup chopped onion
4 tablespoons butter or margarine

6 tablespoons flour
2 tablespoons tomato paste
2 (10-ounce) cans condensed beef
   broth
2 cups sour cream
4 tablespoons white wine
8 ounces wide egg noodles

Combine 2 tablespoons flour and salt; coat meat. Heat skillet; add butter or margarine. Add sirloin pieces to melted butter and brown quickly, turning pieces. Add onion; cook until transparent. Remove from pan. Add butter or margarine to pan drippings. Blend in 6 tablespoons flour; add tomato paste. Stir in beef broth. Cook and stir over medium-high heat until thickened and bubbly. *(Can be done ahead to this point.)* Return browned meat to skillet. Stir in sour cream and white wine. Cook slowly until heated through; do not boil. Serve over wide egg noodles, cooked according to package directions.

Note: To bake if done ahead; heat meat sauce mixture in 13x9x2-inch casserole in preheated 300°F. oven 30-45 minutes. Add sour cream and wine; heat 15-20 minutes more.

Susan Childs Carr

CHEESY MEAT LOAF

Preparing: 15 minutes   *Do Ahead*   *Yield: 8 servings*
Baking: 1½ hours

½ cup chopped onion
¼ cup chopped green pepper
1 (8-ounce) can or 1 cup tomato
 sauce
2 eggs, beaten
4 ounces (1 cup) diced, processed
 American cheese

1 cup soft bread crumbs (1¼ slices
 bread)
1 teaspoon salt
Dash pepper
¼ teaspoon dried thyme, crushed
1½ pounds ground beef
½ pound ground pork

Preheat oven to 350°F. Cook onion and green pepper in boiling water until tender; drain. Stir in all ingredients except beef and pork. Add meats; mix well and shape into loaf. Bake 1½ hours.

Ginny Moffitt Gehring

GOURMET MEAT LOAF

Preparing: 20 minutes   *Yield: 6 servings*
Baking: 50 to 60 minutes

4 slices fresh bread, shredded,
 crusts removed
1 hard-cooked egg, grated
¼ cup Italian-style bread crumbs
Salt and pepper to taste
⅛ teaspoon paprika
⅛ teaspoon onion powder
⅛ teaspoon celery salt
3 tablespoons catsup
1 teaspoon Worcestershire sauce

½ teaspoon oregano
1 teaspoon parsley
1 teaspoon dry mustard
2 tablespoons A-1 sauce
¾ cup milk
1½ pounds ground chuck
2-3 onions
6-8 stalks celery
1 green pepper
1 (8-ounce) can tomato sauce

Preheat oven to 350°F. In large bowl mix bread, egg, crumbs, seasonings, and milk. (Mixture should be quite moist.) Add ground chuck and blend well. Shape into loaf and place in roasting pan; surround with large chunks of onions, celery and green pepper. Cover with tomato sauce. Bake 30 minutes covered with foil; remove foil and bake 20-30 minutes.

Nancy Lynch Rivenburgh

EASY GROUND BEEF CASSEROLE

Preparing 30 minutes   *Do Ahead*   *Yield: 6 to 8 servings*
Baking: 45 minutes   *Freeze*

1 pound ground round or chuck
1 package sloppy joe mix
1 (6-ounce) can tomato paste
1¼ cups water

2 cups shell macaroni
1 (1-pound) can corn (optional)
2 cups shredded sharp Cheddar
  cheese

Preheat oven to 350°F. Cook ground beef over moderate heat; drain off fat. Stir in sloppy joe mix, tomato paste, and water; bring to a boil and simmer 10 minutes. Cook macaroni according to package directions; drain. Stir in meat, corn, 1 cup cheese. Pour into buttered 2-quart casserole; sprinkle with remaining cheese. Bake uncovered 45 minutes.

Variation:
1 (7½-ounce) package macaroni
  and cheese
1½ pounds ground beef
1 (16-ounce) can Manwich
  sandwich sauce

1 (10½-ounce) can golden
  mushroom soup

Preheat oven to 350°F. Prepare macaroni and cheese as directed on package. Brown ground meat and drain. Combine macaroni, sauce, and soup; add meat and mix together. Pour mixture into a buttered 2-quart casserole. Bake 45 minutes.

Frances Marincola Blair

TEXAS HASH

Preparing: 30 minutes   *Yield: 4 to 6 servings*
Baking: 1 hour

1 large onion, chopped
1 pound ground round
⅓ cup chopped green pepper
½ cup uncooked rice

1 (28-ounce) can tomatoes
1 teaspoon salt
½ teaspoon chili powder

Preheat oven to 350°F. Sauté onion and green pepper in oil; add meat and brown. Add remaining ingredients; mix well and turn into casserole dish. Cover; bake 1 hour.

Judy Lane Davies

DELROSSI MEATBALLS AND TOMATO GRAVY

Preparing: 45 minutes   *Do Ahead*   *Yield: 3 dozen meatballs*
Cooking: 3 hours   *Freeze*   *2 quarts tomato gravy*

Meatballs:

4 slices bread
1 pound ground beef
½ pound ground veal
½ pound ground pork
1 clove garlic, mashed
Dash black pepper

1-2 teaspoons salt, to taste
2 teaspoons fresh parsley
4 tablespoons fresh Italian cheese
    (Locatella, Parmesan, Romano)
2 tablespoons oil

Soak bread in water; squeeze dry. Mix remaining ingredients except oil. Add bread to meat mixture and mix well. Shape into balls. Brown on all sides in oil. Remove and set aside.

Tomato Gravy:

½ onion, chopped
1 green pepper, chopped
2 (28-ounce) cans whole tomatoes

1 (6-ounce) can tomato paste
2¼ cups water

In same skillet used for meatballs, cook onion and green pepper in oil until limp. In large pot, combine tomatoes, paste and water. Pour in vegetable mixture. Cook over medium heat for 3 hours, stirring occasionally. Add meatballs 1 hour before sauce is done.

Rosalie Basile DelRossi

TEXAS HOT SAUCE

Preparing: 5 minutes   *Do Ahead*   *Yield: 3½ cups*
Cooking: 20 minutes

2 cups catsup
⅔ cup Worcestershire sauce
½ cup cider vinegar
1 teaspoon salt

2 tablespoons vegetable oil
Dash cayenne pepper
2 cloves garlic, minced

In saucepan mix all ingredients and bring to boil. Simmer 20 minutes.

Note: Meat can be marinated in sauce. Also excellent on London Broil.

Grace Burdett Nellis

MEXICAN MEAT CUPS

Preparing: 25 minutes
Baking: 8 minutes

Yield: 4 to 6 servings

1 (10 each) package refrigerated
  biscuits
1 pound ground beef
1 (15½-ounce) can chili beans
1 (15¼-ounce) can Mexican-style
  sandwich sauce or Manwich

¼ cup water
1 cup shredded Cheddar
  cheese
Shredded lettuce
Chopped tomato

Preheat oven to 400°F. Roll or pat each biscuit to a 3½ to 4-inch circle; fit over backs of well-greased muffin pans. Bake 8-9 minutes. Brown meat; drain off fat. Stir in beans, sandwich sauce and water; heat to boiling. With metal spatula, remove biscuits from pans. Fill with meat sauce. Top with cheese, lettuce and tomato.

Peggy Biglin Owen

ITALIAN CASSEROLE

Preparing: 20 minutes
Baking: 1 hour

Do Ahead
Freeze

Yield: 8 to 10 servings

1½ pounds ground beef
Salt and pepper
1 tablespoon parsley
¼ cup chopped onion
1 (10¾-ounce) can cream of
  mushroom soup
1 (10¾-ounce) can cream of
  chicken soup

1 package long grain and wild rice
1 cup diced celery
½ cup water
¼ cup milk
Mushrooms (optional)

Preheat oven to 350°F. Brown meat and onions; drain off fat. Sprinkle with salt and pepper to taste. Combine remaining ingredients; add meat. Spread in 9x12 inch baking dish. Bake uncovered, 1 hour or until bubbly and slightly brown.

Sandra Perski Berg

BEEF CASSEROLE

Preparing: 30 minutes   *Do Ahead*   *Yield: 8 servings*
Cooking: 1½ hours   *Freeze*
Baking: 30 minutes

¼ cup vegetable oil
⅓ cup finely chopped onion
3 cloves garlic, crushed
1 cup diced carrots
1½ cups diced celery
1½ pounds ground chuck
1 (4-ounce) can sliced mushrooms
½ cup sherry
1 (6-ounce) can tomato paste
1 (16-ounce) can tomatoes,
    broken up

1 teaspoon salt
½ teaspoon pepper
½ teaspoon oregano
½ teaspoon basil
1 (8-ounce) package small shell
    macaroni
½ cup buttered fresh bread
    crumbs
1 cup shredded sharp Cheddar
    cheese
Grated Parmesan cheese

In hot oil in large skillet, sauté onion, garlic, carrots and celery until onion is golden, about 5 minutes. Add beef; cook, stirring until browned. Drain off fat. Add mushrooms, sherry, tomato paste, tomatoes, salt, pepper, oregano and basil. Simmer uncoverd 1½ hours. *(If desired, cool, cover and refrigerate until needed.)* About 45 minutes before serving, preheat oven to 350°F. Cook macaroni; drain. Reheat meat sauce; add well-drained macaroni. Turn into 3-quart casserole. Top with bread crumbs and cheese. Baked uncovered 30 minutes until bubbly and browned. Serve sprinkled with Parmesan cheese.

Grace Burdett Nellis

CHEESEBURGER PIE

Preparing: 20 to 30 minutes   *Do Ahead*   *Yield: 6 to 8 servings*
Baking: 30 minutes

Pastry for one crust 9-inch pie
1 pound ground beef
½ teaspoon oregano
1 teaspoon salt
¼ teaspoon pepper

¼ cup chopped onion
¼ cup chopped green pepper
    (optional)
½ cup fine dry bread crumbs
½ (8-ounce) can tomato sauce

Heat oven to 425°F. Brown beef in small amount of fat. Add remaining ingredients; mix well. Put in prepared pie crust. Spread cheese topping evenly over filling. Bake pie for 30 minutes. Serve with tomato sauce.

Cheese Topping:
6-8 ounce wedge sharp cheese,
   shredded
1 egg

¼ cup milk
½ teaspoon dry mustard
½ teaspoon Worcestershire sauce

Beat egg, milk; add seasonings, mix well with cheese.

Tomato Sauce:
½ (8-ounce) can tomato sauce   ½ cup chili sauce

Combine tomato sauce and chili sauce; heat through.

Mary Isabel Meade Laroque

BEEF BARBECUE

Preparing: 15 minutes   *Do Ahead*   *Yield: 6 to 100 servings*
Cooking: 1 to 2 hours   *Freeze*

Yield: 6 to 8 servings
Hamburger buns or sandwich rolls
1½ pounds ground beef
1 medium onion, chopped
¼ medium green pepper, chopped
1 tablespoon brown sugar

1 tablespoon vinegar
1 tablespoon prepared mustard
½ teaspoon salt
¼ teaspoon pepper
14-ounce bottle catsup

Brown ground beef; add onion and green pepper and continue cooking until all beef is well browned. Drain off fat. Add remaining ingredients; simmer 1 hour. Serve on rolls.

Yield: 100 servings
8½ dozen hamburger buns or
   sandwich rolls
20 pounds ground beef
13 medium onions, chopped
3-4 green peppers, chopped
¾ cup brown sugar

¾ cup vinegar
¾ cup prepared mustard
1 tablespoon salt
2 teaspoons pepper
14 (14-ounce) bottles catsup

Follow above directions; simmer 2 hours.

Ginny Moffitt Gehring

BILL'S LOAF

Preparing: 20 minutes   *Yield: 6 servings*
Baking: 1 hour

1½ pounds ground beef
¾ cup soft bread crumbs
1 egg, beaten
½ cup chopped onion
½ cup chopped green pepper
1 teaspoon salt
½ teaspoon pepper

⅛ teaspoon oregano
2 tablespoons catsup
1 teaspoon Worcestershire sauce
1 (10¾-ounce) can cream of
  mushroom soup
Additional slices of onion and
  green pepper

Preheat oven to 350°F. In a large bowl, mix all ingredients except soup. Form into a loaf and place in roasting pan. Pour soup over meat and alternate additional slices of green pepper and onion. Bake 1 hour.

Carol McKechnie Hansen

MEAT LOAF TERIYAKI

Preparing: 15 minutes   *Yield: 6 servings*
Cooking: 1 hour

2 pounds ground beef
2 eggs, slightly beaten
½ cup chopped green pepper
1 medium onion, finely chopped
2 slices bread, soaked in water and
  squeezed dry
2 tablespoons soy sauce

1 medium clove garlic, crushed
2 tablespoons brown sugar
2 tablespoons fresh lemon juice
1 tablespoon chopped fresh
  parsley
¾ teaspoon ground ginger

Preheat oven to 350°F. Combine all ingredients in medium bowl and blend well. Spoon into a 6-cup ring mold. *(Do not pack too tightly.)* Bake 1 hour. Remove from oven; let stand 5 minutes. Pour off juices. Invert onto heated platter.

Topping:
1 tablespoon brown sugar   Parsley (garnish)
1 tablespoon soy sauce

Mix brown sugar with soy sauce. Spoon topping on meat loaf and sprinkle with parsley.

Grace Burdett Nellis

BUSY DAY BUDGET BEEF

Preparing: 15 minutes
Baking: 3 to 4½ hours

Yield: 8 to 10 servings

4-6 pounds arm chuck roast
2 (10¾-ounce) cans cream of
  mushroom soup
½ cup plus 2 tablespoons
  A-1 sauce

2 single serving packages Lipton's
  Onion Cup-a-Soup
2 tablespoons apple butter

Preheat oven to 350°F. Place meat on large piece heavy duty foil. (If you wish, meat may be browned first.) Mix remaining ingredients; pour over meat. Bring foil up around sides and over top; gather together like a funnel with a small opening. Place in pan and bake 45 minutes per pound in 350°F. oven or 60 minutes per pound at 300°F. Add one hour to the total cooking time if roast is frozen.

Note: This budget cut of beef, such as chuck, cooks deliciously tender and will make its own spicy gravy to serve spooned over a baked potato, noodles or rice. (In summer use 250°F. oven for longer period, so kitchen will not be so hot.)

Helen Shaughnessy Duffy

HAMBURGER STROGANOFF

Preparing: 20 minutes
Cooking: 20 minutes

Yield: 4 servings

1 pound ground beef
½ cup chopped onion
¼ cup margarine
2 tablespoons flour
1 teaspoon salt
1 clove garlic, minced

¼ teaspoon pepper
1 (4-ounce) can mushrooms,
  drained
1 (10¾-ounce) can cream of
  chicken soup
1 cup sour cream

In large skillet, cook and stir meat and onion in margarine until meat is brown and onion tender. Drain off fat; add 2 tablespoons of fat to skillet. Stir in flour, salt, garlic, pepper, mushrooms and soup. Cook 5 minutes, stirring constantly. Reduce heat, simmer uncovered 10 minutes. Stir in sour cream; heat through. Do not allow to boil. Serve over noodles.

Grace Burdett Nellis

EYE OF ROUND ROAST

Preparing: 1½ hours   *Do Ahead*   *Yield: 6 to 8 servings*
Cooking: 2¼ hours

3-5½ pound eye of round roast   **2 cloves garlic**

Cut 4 pockets in bottom of roast and stuff each pocket with ½ clove garlic. Set at room temperature for 1½ hours. Remove garlic and preheat oven to 500°F. Place roast in shallow pan and roast for 4 minutes per pound. Turn oven off and leave door closed. Keep roast in the oven for 2 hours without opening door. Remove and sprinkle with garlic salt. Slice thin diagonally.

Note: Perfect medium rare meat every time.

Pam Bartels Morris

BAKED LASAGNE

Preparing: 35 minutes   *Do Ahead*   *Yield: 8 servings*
Cooking: 50 minutes   *Freeze*
Baking: 20 minutes

2 green peppers, chopped   **½ pound ground beef**
2 large onions, chopped   **2 quarts Tomato Gravy**
4 stalks celery, chopped (optional) **1 package #14 lasagne, cooked**
4 cloves garlic, chopped   **1 tablespoon chopped parsley**
3 tablespoons oil   **1½ pounds ricotta cheese**
Slice mushrooms (optional)   **2 eggs**
Salt and pepper   **Locatella or mozzarella cheese**

Prepare Tomato Gravy (see index). Sauté vegetables and garlic in oil for 20 minutes until tender. Add mushrooms, salt, pepper and ground beef. Cook another 30 minutes adding 1 cup Tomato Gravy. Cook lasagne noodles according to package directions. Preheat oven to 350°F. Spread about ½ cup gravy in bottom of 8x12-inch baking pan. Lay lasagne in pan overlapping. Top with meat sauce. Beat eggs slightly; add to ricotta with parsley. Spread cheese layer on top of meat; sprinkle small amount of locatella or mozzarella on top. Add another layer of lasagne; spread on ½ cup Tomato Gravy. Add mozzarella; another layer of lasagne. Spread another ½ cup Tomato Gravy. Top with mozzarella. Bake 20 minutes or until cheese melts. Let sit 20 minutes before serving. Pass remaining Tomato Gravy.

Rosalie Basile DelRossi

RARE ROAST RIBS OF BEEF
WITH YORKSHIRE PUDDING

Preparing: 5 minutes   *Do Ahead*   *Yield: 2 ribs—4 to 6 servings*
Baking: 1 hour 35 minutes   *3 ribs—8 servings*
Standing: 5 hours   *4 ribs—10 to 12 servings*

2, 3 or 4 standing ribs   **¼-¾ cup red wine (optional)**
   of beef   **and/or water (depending on**
Salt and pepper   **size of roast)**

Preheat oven to 375°F. Place roast, fat side up, on rack in shallow roasting pan. Sprinkle with salt and pepper. Put into preheated oven for exactly 1 hour; turn off oven. *This must be done 6 hours before serving.* Do not open oven door until ready to serve. Before serving, set oven to 300°F. Heat 2-rib roast for 22 minutes, 3-rib roast for 25-30 minutes and 4-rib roast for 35 minutes. Remove to heated platter. Let stand few minutes before slicing. Meat will be rare with juice all the way through. Drain excess fat from pan and reserve for Yorkshire Pudding; add red wine or water or combination of both (depending on size of roast) to pan. Stir to loosen meat drippings. Cook on top of stove until liquid boils; simmer 2 minutes. Add salt and pepper to taste. Serve beef with Yorkshire Pudding.

Yorkshire Pudding:
1 cup flour   **1 cup milk**
¼ teaspoon salt   **¼ cup hot fat from drippings**
3 eggs   **of roast**

Sift flour and salt together in bowl. Beat eggs until light; add sifted ingredients, mixing well. Add milk gradually; beat 2 minutes with rotary beater. Prepare pudding approximately 40 minutes before serving time. Allow batter to stand a few minutes while preparing roasting pan. Place hot fat in 11x17-inch jelly-roll pan or 13x9x2-inch baking pan and return to 400°F. oven to get hot. Beat batter to blend and pour in pan. Bake at 400°F. for approximately 30 minutes. Mixture should turn golden brown, rise on sides and sink slightly in middle.

Note: If preferred, use muffin pan with just a scant teaspoon of hot fat in each cup. Makes 18 individual puddings. Serve immediately with rib roast.

Ann Wheeler Sinatra

BEEF ROUND IN SOUR CREAM GRAVY

Preparing: 45 minutes   *Yield: 8 servings*
Cooking: 2½ hours

4 thin slices salt pork or bacon	1 teaspoon pepper
1 large onion, sliced	½ teaspoon salt
1 green onion, chopped	¾ cup red wine
1 large carrot, peeled and sliced	¾ cup sour cream
1 clove garlic, minced	3 tablespoons flour
4 pounds beef bottom round or	3 tablespoons water
rump roast	1 tablespoon lemon juice

Lay 2 slices salt pork in bottom of kettle. Add onions, carrot and garlic; sauté lightly. Remove vegetables from pan; set aside. Rub meat well with pepper and salt; brown on all sides. Reduce heat; stir in wine and sour cream, blending until smooth. Add sautéed vegetables; cover with remaining salt pork. Cover kettle; cook slowly 2½ hours. Transfer meat and vegetables to hot platter; discard salt pork. Blend flour and water to form a paste; add to juices. Cook and stir until thickened and smooth. Stir in lemon juice. Slice meat; pour gravy over meat to serve.

Jeanne Kronmiller Honish

MARINADE FOR EYE OF ROUND ROAST

Preparing: 10 minutes   *Do Ahead*   *Yield: 1½ cups*
Cooking: 35 minutes
Marinating: 24 hours

1½ cup vegetable oil	2 tablespoons sugar (optional)
¼ cup vinegar	Salt and pepper
½ cup sherry	¼ teaspoon garlic salt
3 tablespoons soy sauce	

Combine all ingredients with wire whisk. Marinate eye of round roast in mixture for at least 24 hours, turning occasionally. Roast on covered grill, using indirect heat, until meat thermometer registers rare. Baste occasionally with marinade. A 2½ pound roast will take about 35 minutes.

Lois Rising Pogyor

BARBECUE SAUCE

Preparing: 15 minutes   *Do Ahead*   *Yield: 2 cups*
                                 Freeze

¼ cup chopped onions   2 tablespoons brown sugar
3 tablespoons vinegar   1 (12-ounce) bottle chili sauce
¼ cup lemon juice   ½ teaspoon salt
1½ tablespoons Worcestershire ¼ teaspoon paprika
  sauce

Heat ingredients in saucepan. Use on spareribs, chicken, etc.

Alice Marks Preston

BRISKET BEEF BARBECUE

Preparing: 10 minutes   *Do Ahead*   *Yield: 8 to 10 servings*
Baking: 3 hours; 30 minutes
Chilling: 3 hours
Baking: 30 minutes

4 pounds brisket of beef   1 teaspoon salt
¼ bottle liquid smoke

Day before serving, rub brisket of beef with liquid smoke and salt. Preheat oven to 325°F.; bake covered 3 hours. Cool and refrigerate several hours until firm. Slice meat very thinly and cover with sauce.

Sauce:
1 cup catsup   1 cup water
¼ cup Worcestershire sauce   1 teaspoon celery seed
1 teaspoon chili powder   1 cup brown sugar

Combine all ingredients in saucepan; simmer 5 minutes. Place meat in baking dish; cover with sauce. Preheat oven to 325°F. Bake until heated thoroughly, about 30 minutes.

Judy Grenamyer Donohue

OLD EUROPE VEAL

Preparing: 25 minutes   *Do Ahead*   *Yield: 8 servings*
Baking: 35 minutes

16 veal tenders
½ cup flour
1½ teaspoons garlic salt
½ teaspoon pepper
¼ teaspoon oregano
2 eggs, beaten
½ cup light cream

⅔ cup fine bread crumbs
⅔ cup grated Parmesan cheese
2 tablespoons fine chopped parsley
4 tablespoons olive oil
2 tablespoons butter
1½ cups chablis wine

Dip each veal tender into a mixture of flour, garlic salt, pepper and oregano; then into mixture of eggs beaten with cream. Combine bread crumbs, cheese and parsley; dip coated veal into mixture. Preheat oven to 400°F. Brown meat slowly in olive oil mixed with butter (add a little more butter if needed at end of browning). Remove meat to a baking pan. Add wine to pan drippings; stir and bring to a boil. Pour over meat. Cover and bake 35 minutes.

Frances Marincola Blair

VEAL MARSALA

Preparing: 20 minutes   *Do Ahead: Partially*   *Yield: 4 to 6 servings*
Baking: 3 minutes

12 (2 ounces each) veal scallops
2 eggs, beaten
½ cup flour, seasoned with salt
  and pepper, optional
½ cup vegetable oil
¼ cup butter

Juice of 2 lemons (6 tablespoons)
¼ cup dry Marsala wine
6 large fresh mushrooms, halved
  or sliced
Parmesan cheese, freshly grated
Lemon wedges (garnish)

Dip veal in eggs until well coated; dust lightly with seasoned flour. In large skillet, heat oil and butter until hot. Brown veal quickly on both sides; transfer to oven-proof dish. *(Can be done ahead to this point.)* Preheat oven to 350°F. Add lemon juice and wine. Top each scallop with sliced mushrooms. Bake 3 minutes (longer if veal has been browned and refrigerated). Remove from oven and sprinkle with Parmesan cheese, if desired. Place under broiler quickly to melt cheese. Remove to warm platter. Garnish with lemon wedges.

Pam Bartels Morris

VEAL BERTRAND

Preparing: 1 hour   *Do Ahead: Partially*   *Yield: 6 servings*
Marinating: 30 minutes
Cooking: 15 minutes

2 pounds veal tenders (about   ¼ cup snipped parsley
  6 portions)   Dash garlic powder
1 pound whole small mushrooms,   6 tablespoons butter
  sautéed   3 slices Swiss cheese or Provolone,
⅔ cup dry sherry   cut in half

Slash edges of veal with knife to prevent curling. Combine mushrooms, sherry, parsley and garlic; pour over meat and marinate for 30 minutes, turning several times. Melt butter in large pan. Drain meat, reserving marinade. Quickly brown half the meat in butter, about 3 minutes on each side. Remove to warm platter. Cook remaining meat. Return all meat to pan; add marinade and bring to a boil. Reduce heat. Place cheese on top of meat; cover, cook about 2 minutes until cheese melts. Transfer to warm platter and spoon sauce over meat.

Nancy Lipson Swoyer

ESCALOPES DE VEAU DAUPHINAISE
(Veal Scallops with Ham and Mushrooms)

Preparing: 20 minutes   *Do Ahead: Partially*   *Yield: 8 servings*
Cooking: 20 minutes

16 small thin veal scallops   1 cup heavy cream
Salt and freshly ground pepper   2 cups julienne cut cooked ham
  to taste   6 tablespoons shredded Gruyere
4 tablespoons butter   cheese
2½ cups sliced mushrooms   2 egg yolks, lightly beaten
½ cup dry white wine

Season veal with salt and pepper. Sauté each side 3 or 4 minutes in butter until lightly browned. Remove to a round oven-proof serving dish, arranging them in the form of a crown. Keep warm. Preheat oven to 400°F. Using the same pan, quickly cook sliced mushrooms with white wine and cream. Reduce sauce to desired consistency. Add ham and cheese. Remove from heat and add egg yolks. Stir well. Check seasoning and pour sauce over veal. Glaze in a hot oven.

VEAL CORDON BLEU

Preparing: 15 minutes   *Yield: 2 servings*
Cooking: 10 minutes

½ pound veal round steak or   2 tablespoons flour
  cutlets, cut ¼-inch thick   1 slightly beaten egg
2 thin boiled ham slices, cut in half   ½ cup fine dry bread crumbs
2 slices processed Swiss cheese,   2 tablespoons butter
  cut in half   2 tablespoons dry white wine

Cut veal into 2 pieces for each serving; pound each with edge of plate until very thin (about ⅛ inch). If necessary, trim ham and cheese slices to make slightly smaller than veal pieces. On each of 2 veal pieces, layer ham and cheese. Top with remaining veal pieces; press edges together to seal tightly. Dip in flour, then egg, then bread crumbs. Melt butter in large skillet; brown meat over medium heat until golden brown, about 5 minutes on each side. Remove to warmed platter. Swish out skillet with wine and spoon over meat.

Pam Bartels Morris

ESCALOPES DE VEAU AUX POMMES

Preparing: 30 minutes   *Do Ahead: Partially*   *Yield: 12 servings*

2 medium golden or red delicious   ½ cup flour
  apples   2 tablespoons clarified butter
Juice of 2 lemons   2 tablespoons oil
12 veal cutlets   1 cup apple jack brandy
Salt and pepper   2 cups heavy cream

Peel, core and slice apples. Place in a bowl, adding lemon juice to prevent discoloring. Sprinkle veal cutlets with salt and pepper; dredge in flour. Add butter and oil to a heavy skillet; brown veal. When cooked, set aside in warm dish. In same pan add apples, lemon juice and brandy. Cook for 3 minutes stirring frequently. Add cream and cook until reduced by half. Season with salt, pepper and lemon juice. Return veal to pan and heat 1 minute. Arrange veal on a warm platter and spoon sauce over it.

Pam Bartels Morris

ITALIAN VEAL WITH MADEIRA MUSHROOM SAUCE

Preparing: 1 hour
Baking: 15 minutes
Marinating: 1 hour

Yield: 4 servings

2 eggs, lightly beaten
⅔ cup dry vermouth
⅓ cup lemon juice
1 teaspoon dried tarragon
¾ teaspoon salt
¼ teaspoon ground pepper
1½ pounds veal scaloppine

1 cup fine dry bread crumbs
¼ cup butter
¼ cup vegetable oil
¼ pound prosciutto, thinly sliced
¼ pound Swiss or Gruyere cheese,
  thinly sliced
1 cup heavy cream

Pound veal very thin; cut into serving pieces. Place eggs, vermouth, lemon juice, tarragon, salt and pepper in a bowl; beat together lightly. Add veal; set aside at room temperature for 30 minutes. Preheat oven to 400°F. Remove veal from mixture and dredge in bread crumbs. Heat butter and oil in skillet; brown veal on one side. Place browned side down, in a single layer in a large shallow baking dish. Top veal pieces with prosciutto and cheese. Stir cream into remaining egg mixture; pour around veal. Cover with foil (greased lightly on underside); bake 15 minutes. Remove foil, place casserole under broiler until cheese bubbles and is very lightly browned. Serve with Madeira Mushroom Sauce.

Madeira Mushroom Sauce:
2 shallots, finely chopped
1 tablespoon butter
1 (10¾-ounce) can condensed
  chicken broth
½ cup Madeira wine
2 tablespoons lemon juice
1 tablespoon chopped parsley

⅛ teaspoon dried tarragon
Pinch of ground cloves
1 tablespoon cornstarch
2 tablespoons water
2 tablespoons cognac
¼ pound mushrooms
Salt and ground pepper

Sauté shallots in butter until tender. Add chicken broth, Madeira, lemon juice, parsley, tarragon and cloves. Bring to boil; cook until reduced by ⅓. Mix cornstarch with water; add to sauce. Stir until mixture thickens. Sauté sliced mushrooms in 2 tablespoons of butter. Add cognac, sautéed mushrooms and salt and pepper to taste. Reheat and serve.

Note: Sauce can be made ahead.

Ann Bateman Capers

VEAL AND SHRIMP A LA WATERWORKS

Preparing: 30 minutes   *Yield: 6 servings*

24 jumbo shrimp
2 cups chablis wine
2 tablespoons pickling spices
5 tablespoons unsalted butter

1½ pounds veal medallions (24)
Sauce
Fresh parsley, chopped (garnish)

Place shrimp in large skillet; add chablis and pickling spices. Cover skillet; cook on high 2 minutes until poaching liquid begins to bubble. Immediately reduce heat to low and cook another 3 minutes. Remove shrimp from poaching liquid and set aside. In another large skillet, heat enough unsalted butter to sauté veal medallions. When butter is hot in skillet, sauté medallions; no more than a minute on each side. *(Veal cooks fast and continues to cook on platter.)* Do not crowd meat in skillet. Allow enough time to sauté all veal while sauce is cooking on the stove.

Sauce:
Poaching liquid from shrimp
3 tablespoons unsalted butter
2 cups heavy cream

1 tablespoon curry
Salt and pepper to taste

Immediately after shrimp is taken out of poaching liquid, turn burner on high and reduce liquid for 3 minutes; add unsalted butter. When butter is melted into wine reduction, pour in heavy cream; flavor sauce with curry, salt and pepper to taste. Sauce must reduce until a creamy consistency is achieved.

To serve: On individual plates, place 4 veal medallions topped with 4 shrimp. Pour sauce over each plate; garnish with a little fresh parsley.

Dennis F. Natoli
Waterworks Café, Philadelphia, Pennsylvania

ESCALOPE DE VEAU A LA NORMANDE

Preparing: 10 minutes   *Yield: 4 servings*
Cooking: 1 hour

4 veal cutlets
6-8 tablespoons butter
1 tablespoon flour
Salt to taste
3 tablespoons shallots, finely
  chopped

6-8 small mushrooms
1 cup light cream
Few drops of wine
Parsley or watercress
  (garnish)

Melt butter in skillet. Sprinkle veal with flour and salt; brown veal and shallots in butter. When slightly brown, add mushrooms. Add cream at intervals. Cover and simmer for 45-60 minutes; add few drops of wine. Immediately place each cutlet, topped with sauce, on a hot serving platter. Garnish with parsley or watercress.

Gwen Fields Gilmore

REUBEN CASSEROLE

Preparing: 15 minutes   *Do Ahead*   *Yield: 4 to 6 servings*
Baking: 30 minutes

2 cups cooked rice
1 (8-ounce) can sauerkraut, rinsed
  and drained
1 (12-ounce) can corned beef,
  diced or ¾ pound fresh corned
  beef, diced
1 cup Swiss cheese, shredded
½ cup mayonnaise

3 tablespoons sweet pickle relish
1 teaspoon prepared mustard
Black pepper
1 medium tomato, peeled and
  sliced
Salt and pepper
½ cup (1 slice) rye bread crumbs

Preheat oven to 350°F. Combine rice, sauerkraut, corned beef, and ½ cup Swiss cheese (reserve other ½ cup for topping). Blend mayonnaise, relish, mustard and pepper; stir into rice mixture. Turn into shallow 2-quart casserole, arrange tomato slices on top, season with salt and pepper. Sprinkle with remaining cheese; top with bread crumbs. Bake 30 minutes until hot and bubbly.

Frances Marincola Blair

SHOULDER LAMB CHOPS
WITH ZUCCHINI EN PAPILLOTE

Preparing: 30 minutes   *Yield: 4 servings*
Baking: 1 hour

4 shoulder lamb chops,   4 small potatoes
  ½-inch thick   1 teaspoon celery salt
2 small onions   ⅛ teaspoon pepper
4 small zucchini   1 teaspoon minced fresh parsley
4 small carrots

Trim excess fat from chops. Peel and thinly slice onions. Quarter zucchini lengthwise. Peel carrots; cut into 2-inch long and ½-inch wide strips. Peel and slice potatoes ¼-inch thick. Preheat oven to 350°F. Cut four 16-inch squares of heavy-duty aluminum foil. Place chop on each; sprinkle both sides with celery salt, pepper and parsley. Top with vegetables and sprinkle evenly with salt or seasoned salt. Wrap tightly; place in jelly-roll pan. Bake 60 minutes until chops are tender. Serve in foil packets.

Lucetta Bahn Ebbert

BARBECUED LEG OF LAMB

Preparing: 10 minutes   *Do Ahead*   *Yield: 8 to 10 servings*
Marinating: 3 hours
Cooking: 45 to 60 minutes

5-6 pound leg of lamb, boned and
  butterflied

Marinate lamb at room temperature 3 hours or more. Roast over medium coals 1 hour (45 minutes for rare), basting frequently with marinade. Cut cross grain into thin slices.

Marinade:
1-2 cloves garlic, minced   ½ teaspoon thyme
1 teaspoon salt   ¼ cup grated onion
1 teaspoon fine herbs (rosemary, ½ cup salad oil
  thyme, parsley)   ½ cup lemon juice
½ teaspoon black pepper

Combine ingredients in blender; mix well.

Judy Lane Davies

CORNISH PASTIES

Preparing: 45 minutes
Baking: 30 minutes

Yield: 4 to 6 servings

Paste:

4 cups flour
1 cup shortening

1 teaspoon salt
6 ounces milk

Mix flour and shortening; when of appearance of fine bread crumbs, add milk and salt (do not over-mix). Set aside.

Filling:

1 pound lamb, diced (any meat
   may be used)
1 cup diced potatoes
½ cup diced carrots

½ cup diced Swede or turnips
¼ cup diced onions
1 egg
2 tablespoons cream

Sear diced meat; blanch diced vegetables. Mix meat and vegetables together. Preheat oven to 400°F. Roll paste out to ¼-inch thickness. Cut into 6-inch circles. Dampen edge of each circle. Fill with approximately ½ cup filling; seal edges. Mix egg and cream and brush pastry; bake 30 minutes.

Dickens Inn
Philadelphia, Pennsylvania

GIGOT A LA MOUTARD

Preparing: 15 minutes
Marinating: 2 to 3 hours
Baking: 1 to 1½ hours

Do Ahead

Yield: 8 servings

1 (6½-pound) whole leg of lamb,
   trimmed and boned
½ cup Dijon mustard
2 tablespoons soy sauce
1 clove garlic, mashed

1 teaspoon ground rosemary
   or thyme
¼ teaspoon powdered ginger
2 tablespoons olive oil

Lamb should yield about 4 pounds after boning. Blend mustard, soy sauce, garlic, herbs and ginger together in bowl. Beat in olive oil by droplets to make a mayonnaise-like cream. Paint lamb with mixture and set it on rack of roasting pan. (Meat will pick up more flavor if it is coated several hours before roasting.) Preheat oven to 350°F. Roast 1 to 1¼ hours for medium rare, or 1¼ to 1½ hours for well done.

MOUSSAKA OF LAMB AND EGGPLANT A LA GRECQUE

Preparing: 1½ hours   *Do Ahead: Partially*   *Yield: 4 servings*
Chilling: 2 hours   *Freeze*
Baking: 20 minutes + 10 minutes

8 large eggplants	½ bunch parsley, finely chopped
Vegetable oil	4 tablespoons fresh mint, finely
1½ pounds ground lamb	chopped
1 tablespoon butter	½ teaspoon salt (to taste)
1 tablespoon vegetable oil	¼ teaspoon pepper (to taste)
1 large onion, chopped	Tomato sauce (preferably fresh)
4 cloves garlic, chopped	Fresh mint (garnish)

Preheat oven to 350°F. Cut 6 eggplants in half lengthwise; score pulp and salt. Place pulp side down on baking sheet; generously oil skins; bake until soft to touch. Remove and allow to cool several hours. Peel remaining 2 eggplants; cut into ⅓-inch rounds. Place on baking sheet; lightly oil; bake 10-12 minutes at 350°F. Remove from sheet and allow to cool. Sauté ground lamb, draining fat frequently; place in large bowl. Combine butter and oil in saucepan; add onion, garlic, parsley and mint. Sauté, stirring constantly until onion is translucent and parsley and mint are bright green, about 30-60 seconds. (Do not let onions brown.) Add to lamb. Remove pulp from cooled eggplant halves carefully, using hand and a scraping motion (very important not to damage skins). Purée pulp; measure 3 cups. Add to meat mixture; blend with salt and pepper. Mixture should be well seasoned with heavy flavoring of garlic and fresh mint. Line individual oven-proof casserole bowls (about 2-inch deep x 4-inch across) with eggplant skins. Taking care not to break or cut skin (overlapping is fine), cover bottom of bowl. To cover side of bowl, cut strips of skin and work in horizontally. Fill lined bowls with meat mixture, packing in well to within ¼-inch of top space. Cover with eggplant rounds, to enclose. Place casseroles in deep roasting pan; fill pan with water bath ⅔ up sides of crocks. Bake at 350°F. for 20 minutes. Remove from roasting pan. *(May be done ahead to this point and refrigerated. If done ahead, allow casserole to come to room temperature before proceeding.)* Place directly into oven. Increase oven to 500°F.; bake until bubbly. Remove from oven and run knife around crock to loosen sides. Place plate atop casserole and invert. Allow to sit a minute or two; remove crock. Garnish remainder of plate with tomato sauce and a sprig of fresh mint. Serve with additional sauce.

Note: In this dish, *fresh* parsley, onion and mint must be used.

Chef's Notes: Le Train Bleu Moussaka is my own variation of Escoffier's classical version. Presentation is the same and is very beautiful.

Le Train Bleu, Barbara C. Moglia, Executive Chef,
Bloomingdale's at The Court of King of Prussia, Pennsylvania

PORK CHOP CASSEROLE

Preparing: 15 minutes   *Do Ahead*   *Yield: 4 servings*
Baking: 45 minutes

4-5 center cut pork chops
¾ cup rice, uncooked
½ teaspoon salt
1 medium onion, sliced and
   separated

1 green pepper, cut in strips
1 (10¾-ounce) can beef bouillon

Preheat oven to 375°F. Brown pork chops slightly. Place rice and salt in casserole; top rice with browned pork chops. Place onion and green pepper on top. Pour bouillon over casserole; cover. Bake 45 minutes. *Do not allow to dry out.*

Shirley Richert Walsh

BAKED PORK CHOPS WITH DRESSING

Preparing: 30 minutes   *Do Ahead*   *Yield: 4 to 6 servings*
Baking: 1 hour

6 loin pork chops, 1-inch thick
2 tablespoons flour
1 teaspoon salt
1¼ teaspoons pepper

2 tablespoons drippings or
   vegetable oil
Dressing

Preheat oven to 350°F. Mix flour, salt and pepper; dredge chops in seasoned flour. Brown in oil. Stand chops in 9x5x3-inch loaf pan; distribute dressing evenly between chops. Insert 2 metal skewers, one on each end, to keep loaf together; handles may extend beyond sides of pan. Cover with foil; bake 45 minutes. Uncover; bake 15 minutes longer. Let stand in pan 5 minutes. Remove from pan, lifting carefully, using skewers. Let stand several minutes and remove skewers gently so chops do not separate.

Dressing:
4 cups bread cubes, cut in
   1½-inch cubes
1 tablespoon grated onion
½ cup minced celery

¼ cup melted butter
¾ teaspoon salt
1 teaspoon sage

Combine all ingredients; mix lightly.

Ginny Moffitt Gehring

POLYNESIAN PORK ROAST

Preparing: 5 minutes   *Yield: 6 to 8 servings*
Cooking: 1 hour and 45 minutes

4-5 pounds boneless pork loin   3 cloves garlic, minced
Salt and pepper   2 tablespoons chopped parsley
2½ cups Chianti wine

Preheat oven to 400°F. Salt and pepper pork; place in Dutch oven. Roast for
30 minutes or until browned. Add Chianti, garlic and parsley to pan. Cover;
reduce oven to 350°F. Roast for 1½ hours, basting occasionally. Remove cover
last 15 minutes. Serve wine as a sauce over rice, if desired.

Note: Roast seems to improve with cooking, so extra time in oven before
dinner is served is no problem.

UNCLE VIC'S PIZZA

Preparing: 15 minutes   *Yield: One 14-inch pie*
Rising: 1 hour
Baking: 20 minutes

1½ packages dry yeast   2 cups flour
1½ tablespoons sugar   Corn meal
⅔ cup warm water

Put flour in food processor. Mix water, sugar and yeast together; let bubble up.
Add yeast mixture to flour and process until a ball of dough forms. Let spin for
30 seconds to knead dough. (If food processor is not available, mix as directed
with electric mixer; knead dough about 2 minutes.) Lightly oil pizza pan
and sprinkle with corn meal. Spread dough onto pan. Cover and let rise
45-60 minutes.

Topping:
Tomato sauce or spaghetti sauce   Hamburger or Italian sausage,
Parmesan cheese   cooked and drained
Mozzarella cheese   Green pepper and/or onions
Oregano

Preheat oven to 425°F. Add sauce, cheeses, oregano and toppings of your
choice. Bake 20 minutes or until bottom is brown.

Nancy Bowen Rainey

STUFFED CROWN ROAST OF PORK FLAMBÉ

Preparing: 30 minutes   *Yield: 8 servings*
Cooking: 3 hours

8-10 pounds crown pork rib roast
Vegetable oil
Salt and pepper
¼ cup butter
3 green onions and tops, chopped
4 large mushrooms, sliced
2 tart apples, diced

3 cups packaged stuffing mix
½ cup applesauce
3 tablespoons brandy
1 (10-ounce) jar apricot preserves
½ cup brandy
Preserved kumquats

Preheat oven to 325°F. Brush meat with oil; rub salt and pepper into meat. Place meat on triple thickness of aluminum foil. Insert meat thermometer in thickest part of meat so tip does not touch bone or rest in fat. Roast for 1½ hours. Heat butter in large skillet until it bubbles. Cook and stir onions in butter until tender. Add mushrooms; cook and stir until just tender. Add apples; cook and stir 1 minute. Stir in stuffing mix, applesauce and 3 tablespoons brandy (add more applesauce if stuffing seems dry). Pack in center of roast, mounding high. Cover stuffing with foil cap. Roast 1 hour. Remove foil from stuffing. Heat apricot preserves and ¼ cup of brandy in small saucepan (reserve ¼ cup preserves mixture for flambé). Brush remaining preserves mixture on meat every 10 minutes. Roast until meat thermometer registers 170°F., about ½ hour. Remove roast from oven. Let stand 15 minutes. Cut ends off kumquats; scoop out centers with melon baller. Garnish bone tips with kumquats. Heat reserved ¼ cup preserves mixture; float remaining ¼ cup brandy on top. Ignite and pour over roast.

Note: If center of roast is too small for all the stuffing, bake remaining stuffing in a covered casserole about 20 minutes.

Barbara Wall Fensterle

CROWN ROAST OF PORK
WITH SAUSAGE AND RAISIN STUFFING

Preparing: 40 minutes   *Yield: 8 to 12 servings*
Cooking: 2½ hours

Crown pork roast, 16-18 chops   1 carrot, sliced
  with frenched ends and 2½-inch   ½ stalk celery, sliced
  cavity   2 tablespoons butter
Salt, pepper, thyme   Sausage and raisin stuffing
1 onion, sliced

Preheat oven to 400°F. Sprinkle pork well with salt, pepper, and thyme. Fit an empty tin can, top and bottom lids removed, into the hollow center. *(It will help the inner part of the roast to brown.)* Cover the ends of the chops with foil. Sauté onion, carrot and celery in butter. Put sautéed vegetables in roasting pan; place roast on top. Roast pork 20 minutes. Reduce heat to 325°F. and roast 40 minutes; *remove from oven, take out tin can.* Mound sausage and raisin stuffing in cavity of roast. Return to oven, and roast 1½ hours, or until meat thermometer inserted in thickest part of chop registers 170°F. Remove foil from ends of chops; replace with paper frills. Keep warm until ready to serve.

Sausage, Raisin Filling:
2 cups fresh French bread crumbs   ¼ cup cranberries (optional)
⅓ cup milk   ⅛ cup raisins
½ pound pork sausage (remove   2 medium tart apples, peeled
  casings)   and diced
½ cup chopped onion   Salt, pepper, thyme, sage to taste
¼ cup chopped celery

Moisten bread crumbs with milk; squeeze dry. In skillet, sauté sausage, breaking up the meat. Drain and set aside. Sauté onion in a little of the sausage fat. Add celery, and sauté another minute. Add cranberries, raisins and apples; cook 5 minutes. Add bread crumbs and combine well. Season stuffing with salt and pepper, sage, and thyme to taste. Makes 4 cups.

The Cooking School Waterloo Gardens
"Holiday Party" by Susan Norcini and Linda LeBoutillier

PORK TENDERLOIN A L' ASPARAGUS

Preparing: 30 minutes   *Yield: 4 servings*
Cooking: 45 minutes

1 (2-pound) pork tenderloin, cut
   into 8 slices
2 tablespoons butter
1 (10½-ounce) can cream of
   asparagus soup, undiluted
¼ cup milk

½ cup chopped onion
1 (3-ounce) can sliced mushrooms,
   drained
½ teaspoon curry powder
Dash pepper

Pound pork slices to flatten. In large skillet, melt butter and brown meat well. Remove meat. In same skillet, heat soup and milk together; stir in remaining ingredients. Return meat to skillet; cover and simmer slowly 45 minutes or until fork tender. Serve meat with sauce.

Pam Bartels Morris

MARINARA SAUCE A LA RICCARDO

Preparing: 10 minutes   *Do Ahead*   *Yield: 4 servings*
Cooking: 45 minutes   *Freeze*

2-4 tablespoons olive oil
2-3 cloves garlic, minced
1 (28-ounce) can tomatoes,
   crushed loosely by hand
¼ teaspoon salt

⅛ teaspoon pepper
1 tablespoon chopped fresh
   parsley
2-3 teaspoons oregano
1 teaspoon sugar (optional)

Heat oil in shallow fry pan; add garlic. When garlic is golden, add tomatoes, salt, pepper, parsley and oregano. Simmer uncovered 45 minutes. Serve over spaghetti or with meatballs and/or sausage.

Mary Ann Favale Corbisiero

CRANBERRY GLAZED HAM

Preparing: 5 minutes   *Yield: Varies with ham size*
Baking: 3 hours

1 boneless ham (or half)

Score fat side of ham and stud with cloves (12-18 per ham). Bake at 325°F.
3 hours (adjust time for size of ham).

Glaze:
1 (16-ounce) can whole cranberry   **½ cup burgundy**
   sauce   **2 teaspoons dry mustard**
1 cup brown sugar

Combine all ingredients in a saucepan; simmer 5 minutes. Baste ham with
glaze several times during last 30 minutes of baking. Serve remaining warm
sauce with ham.

Patricia Lawler Wiedinmyer

ALLAN'S FAVORITE HAM ROLL-UPS

Preparing: 30 minutes   *Do Ahead*   *Yield: 6 servings*
Baking: 30 minutes

12 slices baked ham, cut slightly   **12 ounces cream cheese, softened**
   thicker than for sandwiches   **12 ounces Cheddar cheese,**
24 canned asparagus spears   **shredded**

Preheat oven to 325°F. Roll 2 spears of asparagus in 1 slice of ham. Put seam-
side down in rectangular casserole. In large bowl, mix cheeses (use hands if
necessary). Form cheese mixture into thin "pancakes", placing one over each
ham roll. Bake 30 minutes.

Bonnie Kennedy Beverly

APPLE HAM CASSEROLE

Preparing: 25 minutes 　　　*Do Ahead* 　　　*Yield: 4 servings*
Baking: 45 minutes

3 cups diced, cooked ham
2 tablespoons prepared mustard
2 apples, sliced
2 tablespoons lemon juice

¼ cup brown sugar
1 teaspoon orange rind
2 tablespoons flour

Preheat oven to 350°F. Place ham in casserole; spread with mustard. Place apples over ham; sprinkle with lemon juice. Combine remaining ingredients; sprinkle over top. Bake 45 minutes.

Charity Power Folk

SPECIAL FRITTATA

Preparing: 30 minutes 　　　　　　　　　　*Yield: 4 servings*
Cooking: 30 minutes

½ pound sweet Italian sausage
　links
2 tablespoons olive oil
2 tablespoons butter
1 red onion, chopped
3 cloves garlic, thinly sliced
2 green peppers, chopped
2 potatoes, boiled and diced
2 tomatoes, peeled and diced

1½ teaspoons basil
1½ teaspoons oregano
2 tablespoons chopped parsley
Salt and pepper to taste
8 eggs
3 tablespoons water
Butter
½ cup Parmesan cheese

Boil sausage links 5-10 minutes until water has nearly evaporated. Drain and slice. Heat oil and butter; sauté onion, garlic, and peppers until soft. Add sausage, potatoes, tomatoes, herbs and salt and pepper. Mix and sauté. Beat eggs with water and pour into pan with other ingredients. Cook over medium heat until partially set. Sprinkle with cheese and place pan under broiler until puffed and cheese is melted. Serve with French bread, salad and white wine.

Variation: Great for using leftover ham or beef in place of sausage.

Cynthia Harris Helsel

MUSHROOM SAUSAGE STRUDEL

Preparing: 3 hours   *Do Ahead*   *Yield: 6 to 8 servings*
Baking: 20 minutes   *Freeze*

2 pounds mild sausage (or ½ hot)   Salt and pepper to taste
2 pounds fresh mushrooms,   ¾ cup butter, melted
  minced   2 (8-ounce) packages cream
¼ cup minced shallots or green   cheese
  onions   1 cup seasoned bread crumbs
6 tablespoons butter   Phyllo pastry
2 tablespoons oil

Preheat oven to 400°F. Remove sausage from casing and sauté meat, crumbling into small pieces. Drain and set aside. Sauté mushrooms with shallots in butter and oil. Stir frequently; cook until pieces separate and liquid has evaporated. Add salt and pepper; combine mushroom mixture, sausage and cream cheese blending well. Spread sheet of phyllo pastry on a lightly dampened towel. Quickly brush with melted butter and sprinkle with crumbs. Top with second sheet, butter and crumbs; repeat. Top with fourth sheet but omit crumbs. Spoon half of sausage mushroom mixture along narrow edge of phyllo sheet, leaving two-inch border at sides. Fold in sides and roll up pastry sheet. Put strudel on a buttered baking sheet and brush with melted butter. Repeat using four sheets of pastry and sausage mixture. Bake until browned (about 20 minutes). Cut and serve.

Lori Adams DelRossi

MUSTARD SAUCE

Preparing: 15 minutes   *Do Ahead*   *Yield: 1½ cups*
Chilling: ½ hour

2 teaspoons prepared mustard   ½ cup vinegar
1 teaspoon cornstarch   1 egg, beaten
½ teaspoon salt   1 tablespoon heavy cream
½ cup sugar   ½ cup heavy cream, whipped stiff

Combine all ingredients except whipped cream. Cook over medium high heat, stirring constantly, until thick. Cool; fold in whipped cream.

Note: Serves well with cold meat.

TORTA DI PASQUA
(Italian Easter Pie)

Preparing: 15 minutes   *Do Ahead*   *Yield: 8 to 10 servings*
Baking: 40 minutes

3 eggs
1½ pounds ricotta cheese
½ pound mild Italian sausage
8-10 slices prosciutto ham,
   coarsely chopped
½ pound mozzarella cheese, diced

1 cup grated Parmesan cheese
2 tablespoons minced parsley
Freshly ground pepper
Salt to taste

Drain ricotta in a strainer overnight. Slice sausage thinly; fry lightly in oil. Preheat oven to 350°F. Beat eggs into ricotta cheese; add remaining ingredients and season to taste. Butter 9x11-inch pan and pour in mixture. Bake 40-45 minutes or until top is lightly browned. Cut into squares and serve. Can be cut in small squares and served as an hors d'oeuvre.

WILD RICE CASSEROLE

Preparing: 40 minutes   *Yield: 8 servings*
Baking: 30 minutes

2 cups wild rice or 1 cup white rice
   and 1 cup wild rice
1 pound bulk sausage
1 pound mushrooms, sliced
2 onions, chopped
¼ cup flour
½ cup cream
2½ cups chicken broth
1 teaspoon monosodium
   glutamate (optional)

Pinch oregano
Pinch thyme
Pinch marjoram
1 tablespoon salt
⅛ teaspoon pepper
⅛ teaspoon hot pepper sauce
   (optional)
½ cup toasted slivered almonds

Sauté sausage; drain and break into small pieces. Sauté mushrooms and onions in drippings; add sausage. Wash rice thoroughly; cook in boiling water 15 minutes; drain. Preheat oven to 350°F. Mix flour with cream until very smooth. Add chicken broth; cook until thickened. Add seasonings. Combine with rice, sausage and vegetables. Toss lightly. Add hot pepper sauce, if desired. Pour into casserole and bake 25-30 minutes. Sprinkle with almonds.

Gretchen Dome Hagy

MEXICALI SAUSAGE CASSEROLE

Preparing: 20 minutes　　　*Do Ahead: Partially*　　　*Yield: 4 to 6 servings*
Baking: 25 to 30 minutes

1½ pounds sweet Italian sausage
2 tablespoons vegetable oil
　(optional)
3 cups zucchini, sliced
1 cup onion, sliced
2 cups cooked rice

1 (28-ounce) can tomatoes,
　undrained and slightly broken
½ teaspoon cumin
¼ teaspoon hot red pepper sauce
⅓ cup Parmesan cheese

Remove casing from sausages. In large skillet brown sausage, breaking up with spoon as it cooks. Drain sausage and set aside. In same skillet, sauté zucchini and onion until crisp-tender. Preheat oven to 350°F. In a 2-quart casserole, arrange half cooked sausage, 1 cup rice and half the zucchini and onion. Repeat with remaining sausage, rice and vegetables. Combine tomatoes, cumin, and red pepper sauce; pour over casserole. Sprinkle with Parmesan cheese. Bake 25-30 minutes or until hot and bubbly. Serve with additional pepper sauce, if desired.

Frances Marincola Blair

EGG BOWS LEONARDO

Preparing: 20 minutes　　　*Do Ahead: Partially*　　　*Yield: 6 servings*
Cooking: 55 minutes

2 pounds Italian sweet sausage
1 teaspoon salt
1 (6-ounce) can tomato paste
3½ cups (1-pound 13-ounce)
　canned plum tomatoes
¼ teaspoon instant minced garlic

1 tablespoon instant minced onion
1 teaspoon oregano leaves
½ teaspoon basil leaves
⅛ teaspoon ground black pepper
1 (8-ounce) package egg noodle
　bows (farfallette)

Cut sausage into slices ¼-inch thick and brown. Drain off fat. Add salt, tomato paste, tomatoes, garlic and onion; bring to boil and simmer uncovered, 45 minutes. Stir in oregano, basil and pepper. Cook 10 minutes. Cook noodles according to package directions. Drain and place in serving dish. Pour sauce over the top. Serve hot.

Jeanne Kronmiller Honish

SPICY SAUSAGE POTATO CASSEROLE

Preparing: 15 minutes   *Yield: 4 to 6 servings*
Baking: 1 hour and 20 minutes

4-5 tablespoons vegetable oil   ¾ teaspoon baking soda
1½ cups thinly sliced potatoes   ¼ cup Parmesan cheese
¾ pound sweet Italian sausage   Salt and pepper to taste
½ cup chopped green pepper   ½ cup tomato sauce
⅓ cup chopped onion   4 ounces mozzarella cheese,
6 eggs   shredded
½ cup milk

Preheat oven to 350°F. Coat 2-quart shallow casserole with oil. Cut sausage into small pieces. Arrange potatoes, sausage, green pepper and onion in casserole; bake 35-40 minutes. Beat together eggs, milk, baking soda and cheese; salt and pepper to taste. Pour over casserole; reduce heat to 325°F.; bake 30 minutes. Drizzle with tomato sauce; top with cheese. Bake 10 minutes more.

Regina Shehadi Guza

SAUSAGE-FILLED CREPES

Preparing: 40 minutes   *Do Ahead*   *Yield: 7 servings*
Baking: 45 minutes

12-14 crepes, using favorite recipe

Filling:
1 pound bulk sausage   ½ cup Cheddar cheese, shredded
¼ cup chopped onion   3-ounce package cream cheese

Cook sausage and onion; drain. Add Cheddar cheese, cream cheese; blend. Fill crepes with sausage filling. Roll up and place in baking dish. Cover and chill. Preheat oven to 350°F.; bake, covered 40 minutes.

Topping:
1½ cups sour cream   ¼ cup butter or margarine

Mix topping; spoon over crepes and bake, uncovered 5 minutes.

Variation: Add ¼ teaspoon marjoram and ¼ teaspoon celery salt to filling.

Robin Truitt Hayman

APPLE SAUSAGE RING

Preparing: 30 minutes   *Yield: 8 servings*
Baking: 1 hour

2 pounds bulk sausage   ¼ cup minced onion
2 eggs, slightly beaten   1 cup apples, pared and finely
½ cup milk   chopped
1½ cups cracker crumbs or
   herb stuffing

Preheat oven to 350°F. Combine sausage, eggs, milk, cracker crumbs, onion and apples. Mix thoroughly, press lightly into greased 6-cup mold. Bake 1 hour. Drain. *This can be made the day before and partially baked for 30 minutes.* Finish baking before serving.

Jeanne Kronmiller Honish

MARINADE FOR GRILLED BEEF SHISH-KA-BOBS

Preparing: 10 minutes   *Do Ahead*   *Yield: 2½ cups*
Marinating: 5 hours

½ cup vegetable oil   ½ cup red wine vinegar
¾ cup soy sauce   1½ teaspoons parsley flakes
3 tablespoons dry mustard   3 cloves garlic, crushed
¼ cup Worcestershire sauce   ½ cup lemon juice
1½ teaspoons salt

Mix all ingredients well. Marinate beef cubes (sirloin or round) for at least 5 hours. Make shish-ka-bobs using marinated beef cubes, cherry tomatoes, mushrooms and green pepper wedges.

Anne Rising Ott

Vegetables

Strafford

The Strafford train station has been described as one of the most interesting stations in North America. It is a unique example of highly ornate Victorian architecture with its ornamental cornices and gables.

The history of the building is part fact and part popular myth. According to local tradition, it was built by Japanese craftsmen as part of the Japanese Pavillion in the Centennial Exhibition in Philadelphia's Fairmount Park. It was used first as Wayne's station. A year later, it was moved to Eagle; later renamed Strafford at the request of a resident railroad executive whose ancestor was the Earl of Strafford. It is presently being considered for recognition by the National Register of Historic Places.

A Pool Party

hors d'oeuvre
Pineapple Cheese Ball

soup
Gazpacho

entrée
Chicken and Lobster Salad

salad
Cucumber Ring Mold

dessert
Fresh Fruit Flan

beverage
Mint Juleps

LEMON ARTICHOKES

Preparing: 40 minutes   *Do Ahead: Partially*   *Yield: 6 servings*
Cooking: 55 minutes

6 large artichokes   **⅓ cup olive oil**
½ cup white vinegar   **1½ cups chicken broth**
1 medium-large onion, finely   **¼ cup fresh lemon juice**
** diced**   **Salt and freshly ground pepper**
½ cup chopped fresh dill   **Lemon Sauce**

Trim base from artichokes; remove hard outer leaves and cut off top third. In large pan, boil enough water with vinegar to cover artichokes. Add artichokes and boil 15-20 minutes; drain. When cool, remove artichokes. Line bottom of casserole with onion and dill. Arrange artichokes on top; sprinkle with oil. Cook uncovered over medium heat about 10 minutes. Combine broth, lemon juice, salt, pepper and pour over artichokes. Cover and cook until artichokes are tender and juice is reduced, about 45 minutes. Transfer to serving platter and fill centers with warm Lemon Sauce.

Lemon Sauce:
2 egg yolks   **Salt and freshly ground pepper**
3 tablespoons fresh lemon juice   **1 cup chicken broth**
1 teaspoon cornstarch

Whisk egg yolks in non-aluminum saucepan until frothy. Add lemon juice, cornstarch, salt and pepper. Slowly whisk in broth. Cook over medium heat, stirring constantly until sauce thickens; *do not boil.* Keep warm.

CURRIED FRUIT

Preparing: 5 minutes   *Do Ahead*   *Yield: 6 servings*
Baking: 30 minutes   *Freeze*

1 (16-ounce) can pineapple chunks   **4 tablespoons butter**
1 (16-ounce) can pears   **⅓ cup brown sugar**
1 (16-ounce) can peaches   **2 teaspoons curry powder**
1 (16-ounce) can pitted light sweet
** cherries**

Preheat oven to 325°F. Drain fruit and put in 2-quart casserole. Melt butter; stir in sugar and curry powder. Pour over fruit. Bake 30 minutes.

Pat Sunner Horning

ARTICHOKE-STUFFED TOMATOES

Preparing: 10 minutes   *Do Ahead: Partially*   *Yield: 6 to 8 servings*
Baking: 30 minutes

6-8 small firm tomatoes
1 cup chopped onion
½ cup butter
2 jars marinated artichokes,
  drained

2 cups seasoned croutons
Salt and pepper

Preheat oven to 350°F. Remove tops and insides of tomatoes; drain upside down. Sauté onions in butter. Dice artichokes and add to onions; add croutons. Stir 5 minutes over medium heat; season. Stuff tomatoes with artichoke mixture; bake in shallow dish 30 minutes.

Note: Marinade from artichokes may be saved for salad dressing.

Denise Horton Jackson

ASPARAGUS WITH ORANGE BUTTER SAUCE

Preparing: 15 minutes   *Yield: 6 to 8 servings*
Cooking: 15 minutes

2 pounds fresh asparagus
½ teaspoon salt
½ teaspoon pepper (to taste)
4 medium oranges

⅔ cup butter, melted and clarified
½ cup orange juice
4 tablespoons grated orange rind

Wash asparagus well, cut off 3 inches of rough stalk ends. Peel lower parts of stalks. Lay asparagus in a 12 or 14-inch skillet; pour in 2 quarts boiling water, making sure water completely covers stalks. Add salt; cook uncovered over moderate heat 8 minutes. While asparagus is cooking, prepare sauce. Peel 2 oranges; remove seeds. Slice into 24 very thin round slices. Set aside for garnish. Extract juice from other oranges, strain through a fine sieve. Measure out ½ cup juice. In a small saucepan combine clarified butter, orange juice, and grated rind. Cook over moderate heat reducing mixture until slightly thickened, about 6 minutes. When just tender, remove stalks carefully with tongs and place on heated serving platter. Cover with hot orange sauce, garnish, and serve at once.

ITALIAN BAKED ASPARAGUS

Preparing: 10 minutes   *Do Ahead*   *Yield: 4 servings*
Baking: 45 minutes

1 pound fresh asparagus	**2 tablespoons fresh bread crumbs**
¼ cup butter, melted	**4 whole canned Italian tomatoes,**
3 tablespoons minced onion	**drained and diced**
3 tablespoons finely chopped	**Pinch of thyme and oregano**
celery	**Salt**
2 tablespoons grated Parmesan	**Freshly ground pepper**
cheese	

Preheat oven to 375°F. Break off tough ends of asparagus spears and clean. Pour butter in bottom of a 9x13-inch baking dish. Line bottom with asparagus; sprinkle with onion, celery, cheese, bread crumbs and tomatoes, in that order. Season with oregano, thyme, salt and pepper to taste. Cover and bake 45 minutes.

Christine Miller Lytton

ASPARAGUS VINAIGRETTE

Preparing: 10 minutes   *Do Ahead: Partially*   *Yield: 4 servings*
Cooking: 20 minutes

24 asparagus spears	**Freshly ground pepper to taste**
½ teaspoon salt	**¼ cup peanut or vegetable oil**
1½ teaspoons wine vinegar	**1½ teaspoons finely chopped**
1½ teaspoons Dijon or	**shallots or green onions**
Dusseldorf mustard	**1½ teaspoons finely chopped**
Salt to taste	**parsley**

Using potato peeler, scrape asparagus spears to within 2 inches of top. Cut off and discard tough bottoms of spears to make length uniform. Place spears in a skillet; add cold water to cover and salt. Bring to a boil and simmer until tender yet firm. Place vinegar, mustard, salt and pepper in mixing bowl; stir rapidly with wire whisk. Gradually add oil, stirring constantly. Stir in shallots. Drain asparagus spears while still hot. Arrange 6 spears on each of 4 serving dishes. Spoon dressing over spears and serve lukewarm or at room temperature. Sprinkle with parsley.

Ann Bateman Capers

MARINATED GREEN BEANS

Preparing: 15 minutes   *Do Ahead*   *Yield: 8 to 10 servings*
Chilling: 1 to 2 hours

2 (10-ounce) packages frozen
   green beans, cooked crisp and
   cooled

2 or 3 medium tomatoes, chopped
½ pound fresh mushrooms, sliced

Dressing:
½ cup vegetable oil
½ cup wine vinegar
1 tablespoon Dijon mustard
½ teaspoon basil
½ teaspoon garlic powder

½ teaspoon onion powder
1 teaspoon chives
1 teaspoon Italian seasoning
¼ teaspoon sugar
Salt and pepper to taste

Combine dressing ingredients and whisk. Marinate vegetables in dressing until chilled; serve.

HERBED GREEN BEANS

Preparing: 30 minutes   *Do Ahead*   *Yield: 8 servings*
Cooking: 10 to 12 minutes

2 pounds fresh green beans
½ cup butter
¾ cup minced onion
1 small clove garlic, minced
½ cup minced celery
¾ cup minced parsley

2 teaspoons fresh rosemary or
   ½ teaspoon dried
2 teaspoons fresh basil or
   ½ teaspoon dried
1 teaspoon salt

Snip ends from beans; cut diagonally into 2-inch pieces and set aside. Melt butter in small pan; add onion, garlic and celery. Cook 5 minutes. Add parsley, rosemary, basil and salt; cover and simmer over low heat 10 minutes. Set aside. *(Can be done ahead to this point.)* Boil 2-3 cups water plus 1 teaspoon salt in large saucepan. Drop beans, handful at a time, into rapidly boiling water. Bring water back to boil; cook beans slowly, uncovered 10-12 minutes; test frequently after 8 minutes. (Do not overcook; beans should be cooked until slightly firm.) Drain. While beans are cooking, reheat butter mixture over low heat. Toss beans with butter mixture.

FRESH GREEN BEANS IN WINE SAUCE

Preparing: 10 minutes   *Yield: 8 servings*
Cooking: 10 minutes

3 slices bacon, diced   3 tablespoons tarragon vinegar
1 medium onion, sliced   ½ cup sherry
3 tablespoons sugar   4 cups cooked fresh whole green
2 teaspoons cornstarch   beans

Sauté bacon and onion; add sugar, cornstarch, vinegar and sherry. Cook until thickened, stirring constantly. Pour over hot beans; serve.

ORIENTAL GREEN BEANS

Preparing: 15 minutes   *Yield: 8 to 10 servings*
Cooking: 15 minutes

3 cups fresh green beans, cut into   3 tablespoons vegetable oil
  1-inch pieces   1 tablespoon cornstarch
1 teaspoon salt   1 beef bouillon cube
1½ cups diced celery   1 tablespoon soy sauce
4-5 fresh large mushrooms   ½ cup slivered almonds

In medium saucepan, combine beans, salt and enough water to cover. Bring to boil; cook until tender. Drain, reserving 1 cup liquid. In large skillet, cook celery and mushrooms until celery is crisp tender. Combine reserved liquid with cornstarch, bouillon and soy sauce. Stir into celery mixture. Add beans. Cook and stir until mixture thickens and boils. Stir in almonds.

Grace Burdett Nellis

"PHILLY" CREAM SAUCE

Preparing: 15 minutes   *Do Ahead*   *Yield: 1½ cups*

1 (8-ounce) package cream   ¼ cup grated Parmesan cheese
  cheese, cubed   ½ teaspoon onion salt
½ cup milk

Combine cream cheese and milk over low heat; stir until smooth. Blend in Parmesan cheese and onion salt. Serve over broccoli, asparagus, or a slice of ham on toasted English muffin.

Pamela Petrella Winning

BROCCOLI AND RICE CASSEROLE

Preparing: 25 minutes   *Do Ahead: Partially*   *Yield: 8 servings*
Baking: 30 minutes

2 cups cooked rice
1½ (10-ounce) packages frozen
  chopped broccoli
2 tablespoons butter
¼ cup chopped onion
¼ cup chopped celery
½ (10¾-ounce) can cream of
  chicken soup, undiluted

½ (10¾-ounce) can Cheddar
  cheese soup, undiluted
½ (6½-ounce) can sliced water
  chestnuts
¼ teaspoon seasoned salt

Cook broccoli until not quite done; drain. Sauté onion and celery in butter until soft. Preheat oven to 350°F. Mix all ingredients; bake 30 minutes. *Can be made day ahead, refrigerated and brought to room temperature before baking.* If covered when baking, check for wateriness.

Velta Tompkins Dillon

BROCCOLI CASSEROLE

Preparing: 30 minutes   *Do Ahead*   *Yield: 8 servings*
Baking: 25 minutes

2 packages broccoli, cooked
  and drained
1 cup celery
½ cup chopped green onions
1 (10¾-ounce) can cream of
  mushroom soup

¼ cup sour cream
½ teaspoon pepper
½ teaspoon salt
¼ cup diced sharp Cheddar
  cheese

Preheat oven to 350°F. Put broccoli on bottom of casserole. Mix remaining ingredients except cheese; pour over broccoli. Place cheese over mixture; bake 25 minutes.

Sandra Schild Fletcher

BROCCOLI BAKE

Preparing: 20 minutes   *Do Ahead*   *Yield: 6 to 8 servings*
Baking: 30 minutes

2 (10-ounce) packages frozen
  cut broccoli
2 beaten eggs
1 (10¾-ounce) can condensed
  Cheddar cheese soup

½ teaspoon oregano
1 (8-ounce) can stewed tomatoes,
  cut up
3 tablespoons grated Parmesan
  cheese

Cook broccoli in unsalted water 5-10 minutes until tender; drain. Preheat oven to 350°F. Combine eggs, soup, oregano. Stir in tomatoes and cooked broccoli. Turn into 10x6x2-inch baking dish. Sprinkle with Parmesan. Bake uncovered 30 minutes.

Mary Jane Palmieri Durkin

BROCCOLI RING

Preparing: 20 minutes   *Do Ahead*   *Yield: 8 servings*
Chilling: 4 hours or overnight

1 (10-ounce) package frozen
  chopped broccoli
1 envelope unflavored gelatin
½ cup water
1 (10¾-ounce) can condensed
  chicken broth
⅔ cup mayonnaise or salad
  dressing

⅓ cup sour cream
1 tablespoon lemon juice
1 tablespoon minced onion
3 hard-cooked eggs
1 small jar pimento, drained and
  chopped (optional)

Cook broccoli according to package directions, drain well and chop very fine. In medium saucepan, soften gelatin in water; add chicken broth. Heat and stir until gelatin is dissolved. Add mayonnaise, sour cream, lemon juice and onion; beat smooth with rotary beater. Chill until partially set. (Mixture resembles consistency of unbeaten egg whites.) Chop eggs, fold into gelatin with broccoli and pimento. Turn into 4-cup mold; chill until firm (4 hours or overnight).

Barbara Trimble Blake

BROCCOLI WITH DEVILED CREAM SAUCE

Preparing: 5 minutes   *Yield: 10 servings*
Cooking: 10 minutes

3 pounds fresh broccoli or 3   1 teaspoon brown sugar
  (10-ounce) packages, frozen   ½ teaspoon Worcestershire sauce
2 tablespoons margarine or butter   ¼ teaspoon salt
2 tablespoons flour   1 cup milk
1½ teaspoons dry mustard   ½ cup sour cream

Wash broccoli, trim and cut into spears. Steam until tender. Arrange in a shallow serving dish; top with sauce.

Sauce:
Melt butter in saucepan. Blend in flour, dry mustard, sugar, Worcestershire sauce, salt and dash pepper. Add milk all at once. Cook and stir until bubbly. Stir small amount of hot mixture into sour cream. Add sour cream to rest of hot mixture. Heat through but *do not boil.*

Grace Burdett Nellis

MANDARIN CAULIFLOWER AND BROCCOLI

Preparing: 10 minutes   *Yield: 4 servings*
Cooking: 20 minutes

2 tablespoons oil   1½ cups fresh cauliflower
½ teaspoon salt   flowerets
10 small mushrooms, sliced   1½ cups fresh broccoli flowerets
  lengthwise through stems   ½ cup water
1 small onion, peeled, minced   2 teaspoons sugar
1 cup water   2 teaspoons cornstarch

Dissolve cornstarch in 1 tablespoon water. Heat oil with salt in wok. Add mushrooms and onion; stir-fry 2 minutes, until tender. Pour in water and bring to boil. Stir in cauliflower. Cover; steam 5 minutes. Add broccoli and mix well. Cover; steam 10 minutes, stirring occasionally. Add remaining water and sugar; simmer. Stir in dissolved cornstarch. Stir until sauce thickens and vegetables are coated.

John Goodchild

SAUCY CAULIFLOWER

Preparing: 20 minutes *Do Ahead: Partially* *Yield: 6 to 8 servings*
Cooking: 15 minutes

4 cups fresh cauliflower flowerets **1 cup milk**
  or 2 (10-ounce) packages frozen **½ teaspoon onion salt**
2 tablespoons butter **¼-½ teaspoon pepper**
2 tablespoons flour **½ teaspoon salt**
2 eggs

Cook cauliflower and keep warm. Separate eggs. Combine yolks with milk, onion salt, pepper and salt. Melt butter; blend in flour. Gradually add milk mixture to butter-flour mixture; cook over low heat, stirring constantly until thick. Remove from heat and cool slightly. Beat egg whites until stiff but not dry. Fold into sauce and pour over cauliflower.

Meredith Herting Swift

BAKED CABBAGE

Preparing: 15 minutes *Yield: 6 servings*
Cooking: 45 minutes

1 medium cabbage **Salt and pepper to taste**
2 tablespoons sugar **2-3 strips bacon**
2 tablespoons flour
1 cup heavy cream or
  evaporated milk

Preheat oven to 350°F. Shred cabbage and place in greased 1½-quart casserole. Mix thoroughly sugar, flour and cream; add salt and pepper. Pour over cabbage. Cut bacon in small pieces and place on top of cabbage. Cover and bake 45 minutes. Uncover the last 5-10 minutes of cooking time to crisp bacon.

Pam Bartels Morris

CARROT BLINI

Preparing: 20 minutes   *Do Ahead*   *Yield: 24 (5-inch) blinis*
Cooking: 30 minutes

1 pound whole, young, tender   1 teaspoon Red Salmon Caviar
  carrots   (per blini)
6 whole eggs   2 teaspoons sour cream
1⅔ cups flour   Limes and parsley (garnish)
½ cup half and half

Grate carrots on coarse side of a four-way grater. Beat eggs in a medium size bowl; add grated carrots. Work flour into carrot mixture; add half and half. Heat a heavy gauge skillet (cast iron) until hot. Place 1 heaping tablespoon of blini mixture in center of pan (spread with spoon). Cook until set. Turn with a large surfaced spatula. Press lightly. When brown turn again, this time pressing the blini until thin. Turn again. Remove to heated serving plate. Top with caviar and sour cream. Garnish with thin slice of lime, sprig of parsley.

Note: If mixture sets for a long period of time, the carrots will seep, making the blini watery. Add a small amount of flour to bind the mixture.

Charles and Helen Wilson's L'Auberge
Strafford, Pennsylvania

OFF-BEAT CARROTS

Preparing: 25 minutes   *Do Ahead*   *Yield: 8 to 10 servings*
Baking: 15 minutes

12 carrots, pared and sliced   1 teaspoon salt
1 cup mayonnaise   ½ teaspoon pepper
2 tablespoons horseradish   1 cup fresh, buttered bread
3 tablespoons grated onion   crumbs

Cook carrots until tender; drain. Put in 1-quart baking dish. Preheat oven to 300°F. Combine mayonnaise and horseradish. (Taste to make sure it is not too strong; add more mayonnaise if it is.) Add onion, salt and pepper. Mix well and stir into carrots. Sauté breadcrumbs in enough butter to coat and put on top of carrot mixture in baking dish. Bake 15 minutes.

SABZÏ PIEZ
(Braised Onions and Carrots)

Preparing: 25 minutes   *Yield: 8 servings*
Cooking: 30 minutes

4½ tablespoons butter
1½ cups thinly sliced onion
2 tomatoes
12 small carrots (3 cups)
¾ teaspoon salt

¼ teaspoon cayenne pepper
⅓ cup finely chopped scallions,
    including 2 inches green stem
3 tablespoons finely chopped fresh
    parsley or coriander

Separate onion into rings. Peel, seed and finely chop tomatoes. Scrape carrots; slice lengthwise into ⅛-inch strips. Melt butter in heavy 10 or 12-inch skillet over high heat. Cook onion rings over moderate heat 8-10 minutes, stirring frequently or until onions are golden brown. Add tomatoes, raise heat and boil briskly, uncovered, until most of liquid in pan has evaporated. Stir in carrots, salt and cayenne pepper. Pour in just enough water (about 1 cup) to barely cover carrots, bring to a boil and cover skillet tightly. Reduce heat to low and simmer about 10 minutes, or until carrots are just tender. Transfer carrots and sauce into serving bowl; sprinkle with scallions and parsley.

CARROT RING

Preparing: 30 minutes   *Do Ahead*   *Yield: 6 to 8 servings*
Baking: 1 hour

1½ cups butter (room
    temperature)
1 cup firmly packed brown sugar
4 eggs, separated
3 cups finely grated raw carrots
    (about 1 pound)
2 tablespoons cold water

2 tablespoons lemon juice
2 cups flour
1 teaspoon baking soda
2 teaspoons baking powder
1 teaspoon salt
¼ cup bread crumbs

Preheat oven to 350°F. Cream butter and brown sugar. Add egg yolks and beat until thick. Add carrots, water, lemon juice, flour, baking soda, baking powder and salt. Mix thoroughly. Beat egg whites until stiff, fold into carrot mixture. Generously oil 3-quart mold, dust with bread crumbs. Turn mixture into mold; bake 1 hour. Remove from oven and cool 3 minutes before loosening edges with dull-edged knife. Turn onto heated round platter.

Note: Ring may be prepared the day before. Bake just before serving.

Ann Keenan Seidel

MARINATED CARROTS

Preparing: 45 minutes   *Do Ahead*   *Yield: 8 to 10 servings*
Marinating: 24 hours

2 pounds carrots, sliced
1 green pepper, cut into rings
3 small onions, sliced and
    separated into rings
1 (10¾-ounce) can tomato soup
½ cup vegetable oil

¾ cup sugar (or ⅜ cup honey)
1 teaspoon dry mustard
1 teaspoon Worcestershire sauce
¼ cup vinegar
⅛ teaspoon dill (optional)
¼ teaspoon oregano (optional)

Cook carrots in 2 cups water until *just* tender, slightly underdone. Drain, reserving liquid. Mix liquid with rest of ingredients and pour over hot carrots. *Cover for 24 hours.* Dill and oregano make carrots especially tasty.

Gretchen Dome Hagy

MUSTARD VINAIGRETTE OVER CARROTS

Preparing: 15 minutes   *Do Ahead*   *Yield: 8 to 10 servings*

½ cup vegetable oil
2 tablespoons Dijon mustard
1 clove garlic, minced
1 tablespoon white wine vinegar

1 teaspoon sugar
Salt and freshly ground pepper
8-10 carrots, sliced and crisply
    steamed

Combine all ingredients except carrots in a small bowl. Whisk until well-blended. Pour over crisply steamed carrots. Serve hot or cold.

Grace Burdett Nellis

CELERY CASSEROLE

Preparing: 30 minutes   Do Ahead   Yield: 6 servings
Baking: 30 minutes

3 cups diced celery
¼ cup slivered almonds
½ cup sliced water chestnuts
5 tablespoons butter
3 tablespoons flour

1 cup chicken broth
¾ cup light cream
½ cup sliced canned mushrooms
½ cup Parmesan cheese
½ cup dry bread crumbs

Preheat oven to 350°F. Parboil celery 5 minutes. Drain and put in buttered casserole with almonds and water chestnuts. Melt 3 tablespoons butter; add flour and stir until bubbly. Slowly stir in broth and cream. Simmer 5 minutes. Add mushrooms to sauce and pour over celery. Sprinkle with cheese, remaining 2 tablespoons butter and bread crumbs. Bake 30 minutes or until bubbly.

Elizabeth Taylor Young

HOT APPLES AND CRANBERRIES

Preparing: 10 minutes   Do Ahead   Yield: 6 to 8 servings
Baking: 20 to 30 minutes

1 jar apple pie filling

1 (16-ounce) can whole cranberry sauce

Preheat oven to 350°F. Grease a 2-quart casserole. Put in half a jar of apple pie filling then half of whole cranberry, then rest of apple pie filling. Then top with the rest of whole cranberries. Bake to boiling hot (about 20-30 minutes). Serve with ham, pork, chicken or turkey.

Variation: Substitute 1½ pounds Granny Smith apples in place of pie filling. Peel, core and slice apples. Sauté apples in 2-3 tablespoons butter (add more butter if necessary) until tender. Toss apples with 1 teaspoon cinnamon. Then follow directions above.

Gretchen Dome Hagy

BAKED APPLE AND ONION

Preparing: 15 minutes   *Do Ahead*   *Yield: 4 to 6 servings*
Baking: 3 hours

4 apples, peeled and sliced   **1 teaspoon salt**
1 large onion, sliced   **¼ cup butter**
1 cup brown sugar   **½ cup bread or cracker crumbs**

Preheat oven to 300°F. Butter casserole dish. Cover a layer of apple slices with a layer of onions, separated into rings. Sprinkle generous amount of brown sugar and spare amount of salt on onions. Repeat layers until dish is *heaping*. (It will shrink, do not be afraid to heap.) Top with crumbs and generous dabs of butter; cover and bake about 3 hours. Uncover last ½ hour to brown and reduce juice.

Note: Great accompaniment for pork.

Carol Sutcliffe Kramer

CORN SOUFFLÉ

Preparing: 10 minutes   *Yield: 4 servings*
Baking: 1 hour

1 (16-ounce) can crushed or   **1 tablespoon sugar**
**   creamed corn**   **3-4 eggs**
½-¾ cup milk   **Salt and pepper**
2 tablespoons cornstarch,
**   dissolved in milk**

Preheat oven to 350°F. Mix all ingredients and place in soufflé dish. Bake uncovered 1 hour.

Judilee Cronrath Traynor

STUFFED EGGPLANT CREOLE

Preparing: 45 minutes   *Do Ahead*   *Yield: 2 to 4 servings*
Baking: 20 minutes

1 medium eggplant
2 strips bacon, minced
¼ cup minced onion
¼ cup minced green peppers
2 cups drained canned tomatoes
¼ cup diced celery

⅓ cup bread crumbs
Salt and freshly ground pepper
½ cup sautéed mushrooms or
   canned mushrooms, drained
Grated Parmesan cheese or
   shredded Cheddar cheese

Preheat oven to 350°F. Cut eggplant in half horizontally. Scoop out pulp and chop it; leaving a shell ¼-inch thick. Heat bacon in a skillet; add onion and green pepper. Sauté until bacon is cooked. Add eggplant pulp, tomatoes and celery. Simmer until eggplant is tender. Blend all ingredients well; thicken with bread crumbs. Season with salt and pepper; add mushrooms. Fill eggplant shells with mixture; cover top with cheese. Place eggplants in baking pan with very little water and bake 15-20 minutes or until heated through.

Bonnie Kennedy Beverly

SESAME EGGPLANT PARMESAN

Preparing: 30 minutes   *Do Ahead*   *Yield: 4 servings*
Baking: 15 minutes

⅓ cup olive oil
1 medium eggplant, sliced
   ½-inch thick
1 (16-ounce) jar spaghetti sauce
¼ teaspoon oregano
¼ teaspoon thyme
¼ teaspoon rosemary

½ onion, grated
½ green pepper, grated
1 carrot, grated
¼ cup Parmesan cheese
½ cup toasted ground sesame
   seeds
½ pound sliced mozzarella cheese

Sauté eggplant in oil over high heat until brown and soft. Remove from skillet. In same skillet, combine and simmer remaining ingredients except mozzarella cheese for 15 minutes. Preheat oven to 350°F. Place eggplant in large baking dish. Cover with sauce and place mozzarella cheese over top. Bake 15 minutes.

Christine Miller Lytton

DELMONICO POTATOES

Preparing: 25 minutes   *Do Ahead*   *Yield: 10 to 12 servings*
Chilling: Overnight
Baking: 1 hour

8-9 red potatoes	1 teaspoon salt
1 cup milk	1 teaspoon dry mustard
½ cup heavy cream	Dash pepper
½ pound sharp Cheddar cheese	Dash nutmeg

Cook potatoes in boiling salted water until tender. Cool, peel and slice. Place in buttered casserole. Combine remaining ingredients in saucepan. Heat and stir until cheese is melted and sauce is smooth; pour over potatoes. *Cover; refrigerate overnight.* Preheat oven to 325°F.; bake 1 hour.

Ginny Moffitt Gehring

SCALLOPED POTATOES IN GARLIC AND CREAM

Preparing: 20 minutes   *Yield: 8 servings*
Baking: 1 hour

2 pounds boiling potatoes, peeled (about 5-6 cups)	½ teaspoon freshly ground white pepper
2 cups milk	1 tablespoon butter
1½ cups heavy cream	½ cup shredded Swiss cheese (about 2 ounces)
1 large or 2 small cloves garlic	
¾ teaspoon salt	

Preheat oven to 400°F. Peel and crush garlic; mince to purée. Wash potatoes well; dry thoroughly. Slice potatoes ⅛-inch thick. In large saucepan combine potatoes, milk, cream, garlic, salt and pepper; bring liquid to a boil over moderate heat stirring to prevent scorching. Remove from heat. Pour potato mixture into well-buttered au gratin or shallow baking dish. Sprinkle shredded cheese over mixture; place on baking sheet. Bake 1 hour. Potatoes are done when nicely browned and tip of a knife pierces a potato easily. Let stand 15-20 minutes before serving.

Catherine More Keller

HASSELBACK POTATOES

Preparing: 20 minutes   *Yield: 8 servings*
Baking: 1 hour

8 small baking potatoes, unpeeled   ½ teaspoon paprika (or to taste)
½ cup butter   ¼ cup shredded Cheddar or
½ teaspoon salt   grated Parmesan cheese
¼ teaspoon onion salt or   2 tablespoons fine bread crumbs
   1 teaspoon onion flakes

Preheat oven to 350°F. Slice potatoes at ⅛-inch intervals, ¾ of the way through so they spread like a fan. Melt butter. Place each potato in a square of foil. Drizzle with the butter. Sprinkle each potato with the salt, onion flakes and paprika. Seal foil around each potato and bake at 350°F. for 45 minutes. Combine cheese and bread crumbs; sprinkle over potatoes leaving foil open like a cup and bake 15 minutes longer. Serve immediately.

Note: Can be done on the grill.

Pam Bartels Morris

WHIPPED POTATO CASSEROLE

Preparing: 25 minutes   *Do Ahead*   *Yield: 8 servings*
Baking: 20 minutes
Cooking: 20 minutes

8 medium potatoes, unpared   Salt and pepper to taste
10 tablespoons butter   4 eggs, separated
½ cup cream   Grated Parmesan cheese
2 large onions, chopped

Cook potatoes in boiling, salted water until tender. Drain and remove skins. Mash potatoes with electric mixer or potato masher. Gradually beat in 6 tablespoons butter and cream to make potatoes light and fluffy. Melt remaining butter in skillet. Add onion; sauté until tender. Add to potatoes. Season with salt and pepper; cool. Beat egg yolks into potatoes. Beat egg whites until stiff but not dry; fold into potatoes. Preheat oven to 350°F. Generously grease casserole; spoon in potato mixture. Sprinkle with cheese. Bake uncovered 15-20 minutes. Place under broiler for a few minutes to crisp top.

POTATO APPLE SKILLET

Preparing: 15 minutes   *Yield: 4 to 6 servings*
Cooking: 20 minutes

2 tablespoons cooking oil   ½ cup chopped onion
3 medium potatoes, pared and cut   ¼ cup diagonally sliced celery
   into ¼ inch julienne strips   1 cup (4 ounces) shredded
2 medium apples, cored and thinly   Cheddar cheese
   sliced

Heat oil in skillet. Sprinkle potatoes generously with salt and pepper; add to skillet with apple, onion and celery. Stir until coated; cover and cook over low heat stirring occasionally, until tender, about 20 minutes. Sprinkle with cheese. Serve immediately.

Bonnie Kennedy Beverly

TWICE BAKED POTATOES

Preparing: 1 hour   *Do Ahead: Partially*   *Yield: 8 servings*
Baking: 1 hour 15 minutes

8 extra large baking potatoes   1 teaspoon salt
¾ cup butter   Dash pepper
1½ cups sour cream   10 slices bacon, cooked crisp
¾ cup shredded Cheddar cheese   and crumbled
¾ cup milk

Preheat oven to 400°F. Clean and bake potatoes 1 hour or until done. Turn oven down to 350°F. Cool slightly. Cut a thin slice horizontally from top of each potato. Scoop out potatoes and mash. Blend in butter, sour cream, milk, cheese, salt and pepper. Beat until fluffy with electric mixer. Spoon mixture back into potato shells. Sprinkle with bacon. Put on baking sheet; bake 15 minutes.

Ginny Moffitt Gehring

SCOTTISH FRIED LYONNAISE POTATOES

Preparing: 15 minutes   *Yield: 6 servings*
Baking: 30 minutes

5-6 potatoes   1 onion, finely chopped
Salt and pepper   2-3 tablespoons butter

Preheat oven to 450°F. Thinly slice raw potatoes; mix in salt, pepper and onion.
In iron skillet melt butter; add potatoes and onions. Cook over high heat 3-4
minutes until underside is brown. Put lid on skillet; bake ½ hour. Remove from
oven and invert on platter.

Catherine More Keller

CHEESE POTATOES

Preparing: 35 minutes   *Do Ahead*   *Yield: 6 servings*
Baking: 30 minutes

6 large potatoes   3 ounces Parmesan cheese
8 ounces shredded Cheddar   1 pint half-and-half cream
   cheese   ½ cup butter
Salt and pepper to taste

Cook potatoes with skins. Leave in skins and refrigerate overnight. Peel and
grate potatoes. Alternately layer potatoes and Cheddar cheese, seasoning
each layer with salt and pepper. Sprinkle Parmesan cheese over top. Preheat
oven to 350°F. In saucepan, melt butter in cream. Pour over potatoes and bake
30 minutes.

Note: Can be frozen and cooked at later date.

Linda Stilwell Teets

STUFFED BAKED POTATOES

Preparing: 15 minutes   *Do Ahead*   *Yield: 6 servings*
Baking: 1 hour and 20 minutes

6 medium or large baking potatoes   **Milk**
1 (8-ounce) package cream cheese   **Parmesan cheese**
10 tablespoons butter

Preheat oven to 450°F. Bake potatoes 1 hour; test for doneness. Cool; slice off thin oval from top of potatoes and scrape potatoes out of skin. Combine potatoes, cream cheese and butter. Add milk to desired consistency. Fill scraped out skins and sprinkle Parmesan cheese on top. Bake 15-20 minutes.

Note: Chopped chives may be added to potato filling for added flavor and color.

Jean McCarron McGinley

POTATOES ROMANOFF

Preparing: 15 minutes   *Do Ahead: Partially*   *Yield: 8 servings*
Chilling: 6 hours or overnight
Cooling: 1 hour
Baking: 30 to 45 minutes

6 large potatoes, cooked, peeled   **1½ teaspoons salt**
**   and grated**   **¼ teaspoon pepper**
1½ cups shredded sharp cheese   **1 bunch green onions, cut finely**
1 pint sour cream   **Paprika (garnish)**

Boil potatoes in skins. Cool, peel and grate them. Mix all ingredients except ½ cup cheese. Put in greased 2-quart casserole; sprinkle with reserved cheese and paprika. Refrigerate at least 6 hours or overnight. *Allow casserole to reach room temperature before baking (about 1 hour).* Preheat oven to 350°F. Bake 30-45 minutes.

Dolly Eastburn Somers

POTATO PIE

Preparing: 30 minutes
Baking: 50 minutes

Yield: 8 to 10 servings

1 10-inch unbaked pastry shell
16 ounces cottage cheese
2 cups mashed potatoes (fresh
   or instant)
½ cup sour cream
2 eggs

2 teaspoons salt
⅛ teaspoon cayenne
½ cup sliced scallions
3 tablespoons grated Parmesan
   cheese

Preheat oven to 425°F. Put cottage cheese through a food mill to make it smooth. Beat mashed potatoes into cottage cheese. Beat in sour cream, eggs, salt and cayenne. Stir in scallions. Spoon into pastry shell. Sprinkle with grated cheese. Bake 50 minutes until golden brown.

POTATOES AU GRATIN

Preparing: 20 minutes
Baking : 1 hour and 10 minutes

Yield: 4 servings

4 potatoes
4 tablespoons butter
Salt and freshly ground pepper
½ cup grated Parmesan cheese

½ cup shredded Gruyere or
   Swiss cheese
¼-½ cup heavy cream

Preheat oven to 375°F. Peel potatoes; cut into thin slices. Wash thoroughly with cold water to remove excess starch; pat dry. Butter a heatproof baking dish and put a layer of sliced potatoes on the bottom. Cut butter into small pieces and place some on potatoes; season with salt and pepper and sprinkle some of cheese over it, continue layering until all the potatoes are used, finishing with cheese. Pour heavy cream over casserole; cover with foil. Bake 1 hour or until potatoes are soft. (Time depends on what type of dish you use.) Remove foil 10 minutes before serving to brown top. Serve immediately.

Susan Johnson Mader

POTATO PANCAKES ANNA

Preparing: 1 hour   *Do Ahead*   *Yield: 10 to 12 pancakes*

6 uncooked potatoes, peeled
  and grated
1 teaspoon baking powder
1 egg
¼ teaspoon salt

⅛-¼ teaspoon pepper to taste
1 teaspoon grated onion
¼ cup flour
1 cup corn oil

Drain off excess liquid from potatoes; squeeze dry. Add other ingredients except oil; mix well. Heat corn oil in large skillet; fry potato mixture in amounts to form 4-inch pancakes. Cook until crisp and quite brown. Drain on paper towels; sprinkle with salt. Leftovers are good refrigerated and eaten the next day with a salad. *Reheats well in microwave oven.*

Joanne Stanek Murphy

SAUERKRAUT FOR PICNICS

Preparing: 45 minutes   *Do Ahead*   *Yield: 6 to 8 servings*
Baking: 2 to 3 hours

1 (1 pound, 11-ounce) can
  sauerkraut
1 (16-ounce) can tomatoes
½ pound bacon, chopped

1 large onion, minced
¼ cup brown sugar or honey
  to taste

Drain sauerkraut and place in saucepan; add tomatoes with juice. Bring to a boil and simmer uncovered 30 minutes. Fry bacon; drain, reserving 3 tablespoons of fat. Fry minced onion in bacon fat; return chopped bacon to onions. Add brown sugar or honey. Preheat oven to 250°F. Combine sauerkraut and bacon mixtures; place in shallow casserole with lid. Bake 2-3 hours.

Note: For a main course, line bottom of dish with pork chops or hot dogs.

Laurie Rarick Ruhl

SPINACH TIMBALE

Preparing: 30 minutes   *Yield: 8 servings*
Cooking: 35 minutes

3 (10-ounce) packages frozen   ¼ teaspoon pepper
  chopped spinach   ⅛ teaspoon ground nutmeg
½ cup butter or margarine   1 cup milk
¾ cup sliced green onions   4 eggs
1 teaspoon salt   1 cup soft bread crumbs (2 slices)
½ teaspoon leaf tarragon,
  crumbled

Butter 6-cup ring mold generously. Roll large piece of foil jelly-roll fashion; form into 7-inch circle and "crunch" tightly. (To be used as a rack under mold.) Cook spinach following label directions; drain thoroughly into strainer, pressing out excess liquid. Sauté onions in butter in large skillet; add spinach, salt, tarragon, pepper and nutmeg. Stir in milk; heat thoroughly. Beat eggs lightly in a large bowl; add bread crumbs and spinach mixture, blending thoroughly. Spoon mixture evenly into mold. Cover with 12-inch square of foil; punch hole in center. Tighten foil around mold. Set foil circle in bottom of kettle of Dutch oven; carefully place ring mold on top. Pour boiling water in hole in center of mold to depth of 2 inches. Bring to boiling. Lower heat; cover. Simmer gently 35 minutes, or until knife inserted near center comes out clean. Carefully remove mold from hot water; place on wire rack; remove foil. Let stand at least 10 minutes. Run small knife or spatula around side and center of mold. Place serving plate on top of mold; invert and turn out. Fill center with HONEYED CARROTS AND ONIONS.

HONEYED CARROTS AND ONIONS

¼ cup honey   2 (16-ounce) cans small onions,
¼ cup butter or margarine   drained thoroughly
2 (16-ounce) cans whole carrots, 3 thin slices lemon
  drained thoroughly   1 teaspoon salt

Cook honey and butter in a large skillet over low heat until bubbly and caramel-like in consistency. Add carrots, onions, lemon slices and salt. Cook over high heat, tossing gently, until vegetables are glazed and liquid is absorbed. Spoon into center of SPINACH TIMBALE.

HERBED SPINACH AND RICE

Preparing: 20 minutes   *Do Ahead*   *Yield: 6 servings*
Baking: 20 to 25 minutes   *Freeze*

1 (10-ounce) package chopped
  spinach, thawed and
  squeezed dry
1 cup *cooked* rice
2 eggs, slightly beaten
⅓ cup milk

1 teaspoon salt
2 tablespoons chopped onion
½ teaspoon Worcestershire sauce
¼ teaspoon rosemary
1 cup shredded Cheddar cheese
2 tablespoons melted butter

Preheat oven to 350°F. Combine all ingredients. Pour into *buttered* 9x9-inch baking dish; bake 20-25 minutes or until knife inserted comes out clean. Cut into squares.

Dolly Eastburn Somers

INDIVIDUAL SPINACH CUSTARDS

Preparing: 25 minutes   *Yield: 4 servings*
Baking: 20 to 25 minutes

½ pound spinach, washed, stems
  removed
Salt and freshly ground pepper
  to taste
Freshly grated nutmeg to taste

1 tablespoon butter
1 cup heavy cream
1 egg
1 egg yolk

Butter four ½-cup ramekins; set aside. Bring large kettle of salted water to boiling; add spinach. Return to boiling. Remove spinach; place in bowl of ice water. Drain and squeeze spinach into a ball between hands to wring out; remove as much water as possible. Coarsely chop spinach; season with salt, pepper and nutmeg. In saucepan, heat butter until it foams. When foam subsides, pour into a bowl; allow to cool slightly. Add cream, egg and egg yolk; whisk together. Stir in spinach. Add more seasoning at this point to your taste. Preheat oven to 350°F. Fill ramekins with mixture; set in pan containing 1½ inches boiling water. Bake on shelf in middle of oven 20-25 minutes or until thin knife plunged into center comes out clean. Remove ramekins from water bath; run knife around edge of each and unmold. Can be served hot or cold.

Susan Johnson Mader

SPINACH-STUFFED TOMATOES

Preparing: 30 minutes   *Do Ahead*   *Yield: 8 servings*
Baking: 15 minutes

8 large tomatoes

**2 (10-ounce) packages frozen
chopped spinach, thawed and
squeezed dry**

Topping:
1 cup butter   **½ teaspoon salt**
2 tablespoons chopped shallots   **Pepper to taste**
2 cloves garlic, crushed   **1 cup grated Parmesan cheese**
2 tablespoons chopped parsley   **½ cup bread crumbs**

Preheat oven to 350°F. Cut thin slice from top of tomato; scoop out pulp. Fill
tomatoes with squeezed spinach. Mix topping ingredients together and spread
on each tomato. Top each tomato with Parmesan cheese and bread crumbs.
Bake 15 minutes.

Jeanne Kronmiller Honish

CHEESY SPINACH CASSEROLE

Preparing: 40 minutes   *Do Ahead*   *Yield: 6 servings*
Baking: 30 minutes

**1(10-ounce) package frozen
chopped spinach**
1 egg, slightly beaten
1-2 tablespoons grated onion
**1 (10½-ounce) can cream of
mushroom soup, undiluted**

¼ cup butter
¾ cup shredded sharp cheese
1¾ cups prepared stuffing cubes
Salt and pepper to taste

Preheat oven to 350°F. Grease 1-quart casserole. Cook spinach as directed on
package; drain well. Add egg, onion, soup, butter and cheese; mix well. Add 1
cup stuffing to mixture, reserving ¾ cup for topping. Add salt and pepper to
taste. Place in casserole and top with remaining stuffing. Dot with butter and
bake 30 minutes.

Note: Broccoli may be substituted for spinach. Recipe may be doubled. If
preparing in advance, do not add stuffing cubes to mixture until just prior to
baking.

Jeanie McCarron McGinley

SPINACH SOUFFLÉ PIE

Preparing: 15 minutes   *Do Ahead*   *Yield: 4 to 6 servings*
Baking: 30 to 40 minutes

1 package frozen spinach soufflé
  (thawed)
2 eggs (slightly beaten)
2 teaspoons chopped onion
½ cup sliced mushrooms

¾ cup chopped ham
¾ cup shredded Swiss cheese
3 tablespoons milk
1 9-inch unbaked pastry shell

Mix all ingredients together. Pour into pie shell. Bake at 400°F. for 30-40 minutes or until center is set.

Regina Shehadi Guza

SPINACH SOUFFLÉ

Preparing: 30 minutes   *Do Ahead: Partially*   *Yield: 6 servings as main dish*
Baking: 45 minutes   *10 servings as side dish*

¼ cup butter or margarine
¼ cup flour
1 teaspoon salt
Dash cayenne pepper
1½ cups milk
8 ounces shredded Swiss cheese

6 eggs, separated
2 (10-ounce) packages frozen
  chopped spinach, cooked and
  drained well
⅓ cup chopped onion
½ teaspoon thyme

Preheat oven to 350°F. Grease a 2-quart soufflé dish. Melt butter; stir flour, salt and pepper into butter until smooth. Slowly stir in milk and cook until thickened, stirring constantly. Add cheese; heat until cheese melts. (Mixture will be very thick.) Beat egg yolks slightly. Into egg yolks beat small amount of hot sauce. Slowly pour back into hot mixture, cooking and stirring 1 minute. Add spinach, onion and thyme. Stir to mix. *(You can do this recipe ahead of time to this point.)* Beat egg whites until stiff. Fold cheese-spinach mixture into egg whites. Pour into soufflé dish. Bake 45 minutes. Serve immediately.

Lori Adams DelRossi

SPINACH IN TARRAGON SAUCE

Preparing: 10 minutes   *Do Ahead: Partially*   *Yield: 8 servings*
Cooking: 5 minutes

2 pounds spinach, washed
  and drained
¾ cup sour cream
4 tablespoons butter

3-4 tablespoons horseradish
1 teaspoon tarragon
1 teaspoon salt
Fresh ground pepper

Place spinach in large covered pot; cook with water that clings to leaves until well wilted (approximately 2 minutes). Place spinach in cold water immediately. Drain well (press out water). Slice and place in covered bowl. *(This may be done earlier in day).* Place other ingredients in pan large enough to hold cooked spinach and sauce. Heat sauce until hot, then add spinach and heat through. Serve immediately.

SPINACH CASSEROLE

Preparing: 15 minutes   *Do Ahead*   *Yield: 8 servings*
Baking: 30 minutes

2 (10-ounce) packages frozen
  chopped spinach
3 (3-ounce) packages cream
  cheese with chives

Juice of 1 lemon
½ pound fresh mushrooms, sliced
Salt and pepper to taste
Buttered bread crumbs

Preheat oven to 350°F. Cook spinach until just tender; drain. Blend in other ingredients except bread crumbs. Place in 1-quart casserole and bake for ½ hour. Remove from oven. Sprinkle with bread crumbs and return to oven to brown.

Lois Rising Pogyor

ACORN SQUASH WITH APPLESAUCE

Preparing: 15 minutes   *Do Ahead*   *Yield: 8 servings*
Baking: 1 hour

4 acorn squash   ½ cup brown sugar
4 teaspoons lemon juice   6 tablespoons chopped walnuts
½ cup raisins   4 tablespoons butter
3 cups applesauce

Scrub, halve lengthwise, and remove seeds from squash. Mix remaining ingredients except butter. Put mixture into squash halves; dot with butter. *(The preceding can be done one day ahead.)* Preheat oven to 400°.F. Place in baking dish with ½-inch hot water in bottom. Cover and bake squash 1 hour. Remove cover after 30 minutes. *Can be baked ahead and reheated.*

SQUASH CASSEROLE

Preparing: 30 minutes   *Do Ahead*   *Yield: 6 servings*
Baking: 30 minutes   *Freeze*

1½ pounds yellow squash, sliced   1 cup sour cream
1 large onion, sliced   ½ cup butter, melted
1 (10¾-ounce) can mushroom   1(8-ounce) package corn bread
   soup   stuffing mix

Preheat oven to 350°F. Cook squash and onion in small amount of water until soft; drain well. Mix soup and sour cream; stir into squash and onion. Add butter to stuffing mix; stir. Put half of stuffing in bottom of 2-quart baking dish, add squash mixture; top with remaining stuffing. Bake 30 minutes or until bubbly.

Note: Can be frozen before cooking.

Gail White Dillon

SUMMER VEGETABLE STEW

Preparing: 20 minutes   *Do Ahead*   *Yield: 8 to 10 servings*
Baking: 1½ hours

1 large eggplant	1 cup chili sauce
2 zucchini	Juice of 1 lemon
1 green pepper	1½ teaspoons salt
2 yellow summer squash	½ teaspoon pepper
1 large onion	Garlic powder and oregano to taste
¼ cup olive oil, heated	

Preheat oven to 300°F. Cut vegetables into 1-inch cubes; place in 3-quart casserole dish. Stir in hot oil until all vegetables are coated; add remaining ingredients. Cover and bake 1½ hours. Serve hot as a vegetable or cold as an appetizer.

Margaret Quayle Bellew

FRESH VEGETABLE MARINADE

Preparing: 30 minutes   *Do Ahead*   *Yield: 10 to 12 servings*
Chilling: 3 hours

6 stalks fresh broccoli	2 teaspoons dry mustard
8-10 large fresh mushrooms, sliced	1 teaspoon salt
1 medium green pepper, chopped	½ cup cider vinegar
1 small head cauliflower, broken into flowerets	1½ cups vegetable oil
1 cup sugar	1 small onion, grated
	2 tablespoons poppy seeds

Remove flowerets from broccoli; reserve stalks for later use. Combine all vegetables; toss lightly. Combine remaining ingredients; mix well and pour over vegetables. Chill at least 3 hours, preferably overnight.

Elizabeth Taylor Young

SAUTÉ CHERRY TOMATOES

Preparing: 10 minutes   *Yield: 8 servings*
Baking: 5 minutes

32 cherry tomatoes (2 pints)   **2 teaspoons dried basil**
1 tablespoon vegetable oil   **1 clove garlic, crushed**
3 tablespoons butter

Preheat oven to 350°F. Wash tomatoes and remove stems. Heat oil, butter, and basil in oven; add tomatoes. Spoon mixture over tomatoes. Heat 4-5 minutes. *Do not allow skins to crack.* Stir tomatoes once or twice to coat.

MUSHROOM STUFFED TOMATOES

Preparing: 15 minutes   *Do Ahead: Partially*   *Yield: 6 servings*
Baking: 25 minutes

6 fresh medium sized tomatoes   **2 beaten egg yolks**
1 pint fresh mushrooms, finely   **½ cup bread crumbs**
  chopped (1½ cups)   **1 teaspoon salt**
2 tablespoons butter   **⅛ teaspoon thyme**
½ cup sour cream   **⅛ teaspoon pepper**

Preheat oven to 375°F. Cut top off tomatoes and scoop out pulp. Invert tomatoes to drain. Chop pulp fine to measure 1 cup. Sauté mushrooms in butter until tender. Mix sour cream and yolks; add to mushrooms. Add tomato pulp to mixture. Stir in crumbs, salt, pepper and thyme; cook until thickened. Spoon mixture into shells, place in flat pan; bake 25 minutes.

Ruth Henderson Campbell

BAKED CHEESE-STUFFED TOMATOES

Preparing: 20 minutes   *Do Ahead*   *Yield: 6 servings*
Baking: 20 to 25 minutes

6 medium tomatoes	1 teaspoon dried marjoram
4 cups shredded Swiss cheese	2 teaspoons dry mustard
1 cup light cream	2 teaspoons salt
4 egg yolks, slightly beaten	⅔ cup seasoned bread crumbs
4 tablespoons grated onion	4 tablespoons melted butter

Peel tomatoes; carefully core and scoop out pulp, leaving shells intact. Chop pulp coarsely, discarding seeds. Combine pulp with all other ingredients except bread crumbs and butter. Spoon cheese mixture into tomato shells. Toss bread crumbs with butter; sprinkle over cheese mixture. Preheat oven to 350°F. Arrange in greased 12x8-inch shallow baking dish. Bake 20-25 minutes. Serve at once.

Note: Tomatoes may be prepared early in the day and held in the refrigerator up to 6 hours before baking.

CHILLED HERBED TOMATOES

Preparing: 15 minutes   *Do Ahead*   *Yield: 8 to 10 servings*
Chilling: 3 hours or overnight

6 tomatoes or 1 pint cherry tomatoes	¼ cup sliced green onions
⅔ cup vegetable oil	2 teaspoons marjoram
¼ cup vinegar	1 teaspoon salt
¼ cup fresh or dried parsley	¼ teaspoon pepper
	Lettuce

Wash tomatoes and slice large ones ¼-inch thick. (Keep cherry tomatoes whole or slice in half.) Place tomatoes in bowl. In a screw-top jar, combine other ingredients except lettuce; shake. Pour over tomatoes. *Cover and chill several hours or overnight.* Spoon dressing over tomatoes occasionally. Arrange tomatoes on bed of lettuce.

Carol Sutcliffe Kramer

SCALLOPED PINEAPPLE

Preparing: 15 minutes   *Yield: 8 servings*
Baking: 45 minutes

½ cup butter   1 (20-ounce) can crushed
1 cup sugar   pineapple, drained
4 eggs   5 slices fresh bread, cubed

Preheat oven to 350°F. Cream butter and sugar. Add eggs, two at a time; mix well. Add pineapple; blend. Fold bread into mixture. Pour into greased 2-quart casserole. Bake 45 minutes. *Great with ham!*

Variation: Can be made using 2 eggs. In this version, melt butter and combine with bread; combine sugar, eggs and *undrained* pineapple. Fold in bread and bake as above.

Denise Horton Jackson

THANKSGIVING YAMS

Preparing: 10 minutes   *Yield: 6 to 8 servings*
Baking: 45 minutes

2 apples, sliced   2 (17-ounce) cans yams, drained
⅓ cup chopped pecans   ¼ cup margarine
½ cup brown sugar, packed   2 cups miniature marshmallows
½ teaspoon cinnamon

Preheat oven to 350°F. Toss apples and nuts with combined brown sugar and cinnamon. Alternate layers of apple-cinnamon mixture and yams in a 1½-quart casserole. Dot with margarine. Cover and bake 40-45 minutes or until heated through. Sprinkle marshmallows over yams and apples. Broil a few seconds to lightly brown top.

Pam Bartels Morris

VEGETABLE JULIENNE

Preparing: 20 minutes   *Yield: 6 servings*

2 small zucchini
2 carrots
2 medium white turnips
3 tablespoons butter

2 tablespoons finely minced
   shallots
Salt and freshly ground pepper
   to taste

Cut ends off zucchini; cut lengthwise into ¼-inch strips. Cut strips in fourths. Scrape carrots and turnips, trim ends; cut into ¼-inch sticks. Put carrots in saucepan, cover with water. Bring to boil for 2 minutes. Add turnips; cook 1 minute more. Drain and refresh under cold water. Melt butter in wok or frypan until foam subsides. Add vegetables, salt, pepper and shallots. Cook, tossing, until heated through.

Jeffrey Preston

ZUCCHINI CASSEROLE

Preparing: 30 minutes   *Do Ahead: Partially*   *Yield: 6 servings*
Baking: 10 to 15 minutes

1 large zucchini, chopped into
   ¼-inch slices
2 tablespoons butter or margarine
1 medium onion, chopped
½-1 pound mushrooms, chopped
1 green pepper, chopped (optional)

Croutons
1 tomato, sliced
4-5 slices American cheese
   or sharp Cheddar cheese
Salt and pepper to taste

Preheat oven to 350°F. Cook zucchini 10 minutes or until tender; drain well. Sauté onions, mushrooms and green pepper in butter. Add zucchini to sautéed mixture; season with salt and pepper. Put mixture into buttered 2-quart shallow baking dish. Top with croutons, then sliced tomatoes. Arrange cheese slices on top. Bake 10-15 minutes until cheese melts.

Note: Vegetable mixture may be prepared ahead of time. If so, heat casserole longer to warm through.

Betsy Gillespie Miller

ZUCCHINI FRITTATA

Preparing: 25 minutes   *Yield: 6 to 8 servings*
Cooking: 20 minutes

6-8 small zucchini   ½ teaspoon freshly grated pepper
3 tablespoons olive oil   1 teaspoon salt
2 tablespoons margarine or butter   ½ cup grated Parmesan cheese
8 eggs

Wash unpeeled zucchini. Slice into ¼-inch slices and cook slowly in butter and oil until just tender. Beat eggs. Add salt and pepper; pour gently over zucchini. Cook until just set. Sprinkle cheese on top and place under broiler to brown lightly. Let fritatta stand for a minute or two, cut into wedges and serve.

Grace Burdett Nellis

ZUCCHINI STUFFED TOMATOES

Preparing: 1 hour   *Yield: 8 servings*
Baking: 25 minutes

8 medium tomatoes   1 clove garlic, minced
¼ cup butter or margarine   1 teaspoon salt
1 pound unpeeled zucchini,   1 teaspoon dried basil, crushed
   chopped (about 4 cups)   ½ teaspoon sugar
2 cups sliced fresh mushrooms   Dash pepper
1 medium onion, chopped (½ cup)   1 cup plain croutons

Preheat oven to 350°F. Cut ½-inch slice off tops of tomatoes; scoop out and reserve pulp. Sprinkle shells with salt. Chop pulp; discard seeds. In a 12-inch skillet, melt butter; add tomato pulp with other ingredients except croutons. Cook uncovered over medium high heat 20 minutes or until liquid evaporates. Stir in croutons; spoon mixture into tomato shells. Place shells in 12x7x2-inch baking dish. Bake, covered 15 minutes; uncover and bake 10 minutes.

Barbara Sue Massengale Brodie

Desserts

Devon Station

Devon

Possessing unspoiled "woodland glades" and "salubrious air," the Devon countryside was inviting to city residents. The Devon Inn, built by the Pennsylvania Railroad to take advantage of the area's hot springs, became a fashionable resort where hotel patrons soon discovered the locally famous horse and carriage trails. Area leaders, supported by the railroad, first created the Devon Horse Show to encourage farmers to breed "more and superior" horses for increasing public demand.

After the
Devon Horse Show

entrée
Shrimp with Dill Sauce

vegetable
Rice Pilaf   Individual Spinach Custards

salad
Hearts of Palm with Regency Dressing

bread
Zucchini Bread

dessert
Ice Cream Frappé

beverage
Spiced Coffee

CHOCOLATE INTEMPERANCE

Preparing: 1 hour   *Do Ahead*   *Yield: 8 to 10 servings*
Baking: 10 minutes
Chilling: 4 hours

Filling:

1½ pounds semi-sweet chocolate   ½ cup Tia Maria
½ cup strong coffee   2 tablespoons sugar
3 eggs, separated   ½ cup heavy cream

Melt chocolate with coffee in top of a double boiler. When chocolate is completely melted, remove pan from heat. Beat egg yolks until pale yellow and stir
into chocolate. Gradually stir in Tia Maria; cool. In separate bowl, beat egg
whites, gradually adding sugar, until stiff. Whip cream; gently fold into cooled
chocolate mixture; then fold in egg whites.

Cake:

1 (23-ounce) package brownie mix   3 eggs
2 tablespoons water

Preheat oven to 350°F. Beat ingredients together at medium speed of electric
mixer until batter is smooth. Grease 11x15-inch jelly-roll pan; line with waxed
paper. Grease and lightly flour paper, shaking off excess flour. Spread batter
evenly in pan. Bake 10-12 minutes or until cake tests done. Turn cake onto a
rack and peel off paper. Lightly oil a 2-quart charlotte mold and line with cooled
cake. Cut cake rounds to fit both top and bottom of mold, and a strip for sides.
Place smaller round in bottom of mold. Wrap strip around inside of mold. (You
will probably have to piece one section of side to cover completely—glaze
will hide patchwork.) Spoon chilled filling mixture into lined mold. Fit larger
round of cake on top of mold. Chill 3-4 hours or until firm. Unmold and cover
with glaze.

Chocolate Glaze:

½ pound semi-sweet chocolate   ⅓ cup water

Melt chocolate in water and stir until smooth. Spread over top of mousse-cake
and drizzle down sides. Chill again. Serve in slender slices.

BAKED APPLES WITH CURRANTS

Preparing: 30 minutes　　　*Do Ahead: Partially*　　　*Yield: 6 servings*
Baking: 30 minutes

6 large apples

Filling:
¼ pound brown sugar　　　　**¼ cup currants**
¼ cup sweet butter, melted　　**6 cinnamon sticks**
¼ cup chopped pecans

Slice a piece from bottom of each apple so it will sit firmly in baking dish. Core each apple being careful not to pierce through bottom. Make a well in center of each apple large enough to hold generous amount of filling. Mix filling ingredients, except cinnamon. Place apples in buttered baking dish; stuff with filling. Place cinnamon stick in center of each. Preheat oven to 300°F. Bake apples 30-35 minutes, until soft, yet retaining shapes.

Carol Sutcliffe Kramer

APPLE CRANBERRY CRISP

Preparing: 30 minutes　　　*Do Ahead*　　　*Yield: 8 servings*
Baking: 40 minutes

4 medium-sized cooking apples　　**1 cup uncooked quick rolled oats**
　　(about 1⅓ pounds)　　　　**½ cup flour**
1 teaspoon cinnamon　　　　　**1 cup dark brown sugar, firmly**
1 (16-ounce) can whole cranberry　　　**packed**
　　sauce　　　　　　　　　　**½ cup butter**

Preheat oven to 350°F. Peel apples and thinly slice. Arrange in 10x6-inch baking dish; sprinkle with cinnamon. Spoon cranberry sauce over apples. In separate bowl combine oats, flour and brown sugar. Cut in butter until evenly mixed and crumbly. Sprinkle over cranberry layer. Bake until apples are cooked through and top is lightly browned, about 40 minutes. Serve warm either plain, with whipped cream or vanilla ice cream. *Very tasty served cold.*

Jeanne Kronmiller Honish

BRENNAN'S BANANA FOSTER

Preparing: 20 minutes   *Do Ahead: Partially*   *Yield: 8 servings*
Cooking: 10 minutes

4 tablespoons butter	**Dash ground cinnamon**
8 small bananas, cut into	**2 tablespoons banana liqueur**
halves lengthwise	**½ cup rum**
4 tablespoons brown sugar	**Vanilla ice cream**

Melt butter and sauté bananas until golden. Sprinkle with brown sugar and cinnamon. Remove to serving dish; pour pan juices over fruit. Heat banana liqueur and rum. Pour over fruit and set aflame. Serve blazing with ice cream.

BLAZING BERRY BINGE

Preparing: 15 minutes   *Do Ahead: Partially*   *Yield: 12 servings*

1 pint fresh strawberries	**1 tablespoon grain alcohol (or**
1 pint fresh blueberries	**lemon extract if alcohol is**
1 pint fresh raspberries	**unavailable)**
1 cup sugar	**Angel food cake or 12 meringue**
⅓ cup apricot brandy	**shells**
	Vanilla ice cream

Wash whole berries; remove stems. Mix ⅓ cup sugar with each pint of berries. Add ½ cup water to chafing dish; add berries. Heat almost to boiling. Mix brandy and alcohol and warm; pour over berries and blaze. Serve over angel food cake or meringue shells with vanilla ice cream.

Note: If any of the fresh fruits is unavailable, 1 package frozen berries may be substituted for each pint. If using frozen berries, thaw and place in chafing dish, omitting addition of sugar and water.

Shirley Richert Walsh

BANANAS ON THE HALF SHELL

Preparing: 20 minutes   *Yield: 12 servings*
Baking: 10 to 15 minutes

6 firm bananas   2 tablespoons lemon juice
6 tablespoons rum   1 teaspoon fresh ginger root,
1 (16-ounce) can crushed   minced
   pineapple, drained   Grated coconut for garnish

Preheat oven to 400°F. Carefully split bananas in half lengthwise; remove fruit
pulp and reserve skins. Mash bananas and combine with remaining ingredients
in blender. Place combined puree in pastry bag. Using #5 star tip, pipe banana
decoratively into halved skins. Bake until fruit is golden brown. Sprinkle with
grated coconut.

BLENDER CHOCOLATE MOUSSE

Preparing: 10 minutes   *Do Ahead*   *Yield: 6 servings*

6 ounces semi-sweet chocolate bits   2 tablespoons brandy
2 whole eggs   ¾ cup scalded milk
3 tablespoons very strong coffee

Mix all ingredients in blender at high speed for 2 minutes. Pour into 4-5 ounce
cups and chill.

Jeanne Kronmiller Honish

BISCUIT TORTONI

Preparing: 15 minutes   *Do Ahead*   *Yield: 14 to 16 servings*
Freezing: 4 hours   *Freeze*

2 cups heavy cream   1 cup plus 2 tablespoons ground
½ cup powdered sugar   toasted almonds or hard almond
2 egg whites, stiffly beaten   macaroons, crumbled
                                        2 tablespoons Marsala or cream
                                           sherry

Whip cream until it begins to stiffen. Beat in sugar a little at a time, beating until
stiff. Fold in beaten egg whites, wine, crumbs, reserving 2 tablespoons for
sprinkling on top. Fill 14-16 paper dessert cups, sprinkle with reserved crumbs.
Freeze until firm.

CHANTILLY FRUIT CREAM

Preparing: 10 minutes   *Do Ahead: Partially*   *Yield: 8 servings*

3 fresh peaches, quartered
1 pint fresh raspberries
1 pint fresh blueberries
2 cups fresh bing cherries, pitted
1 cup almonds, chopped

½ cup Kirsch (or Grand Marnier)
2½ dozen almond macaroons,
  crumbled
Vanilla ice cream

Place fruit and almonds into bowl. Pour Kirsch over top. Mix in macaroons. Put into frosted silver bowl; add spoonfuls of ice cream. Fold gently into fruit. Serve immediately.

Gwen Fields Gilmore

CHOCOLATE CREAM DESSERT

Preparing: 45 minutes   *Do Ahead*   *Yield: 8 servings*
Chilling: 8 hours

1 (6-ounce) package semi-sweet
  chocolate bits
6 eggs, separated
1½ teaspoons vanilla

1-2 packages lady fingers
  (depending on pan size)
1 cup heavy cream, chilled
3 tablespoons chocolate syrup

Melt chocolate bits in top of a double boiler, over hot water. Add egg yolks, one at a time, beating well after each addition. Add vanilla; stir well. Whip egg whites until stiff, but not dry. Fold into chocolate mixture. Line a 9x5-inch loaf pan with strips of waxed paper, allowing paper to extend over edges of pan. Split lady fingers and place a layer on bottom of the pan and around sides. Spoon in half the chocolate mixture. Top with another layer of split lady fingers; spoon in remaining chocolate mixture. Chill until firm. *Can be made day before up to this point or the morning you are serving it.* Several hours before serving, whip cream. Fold in chocolate syrup, one tablespoon at a time. Lift dessert from the pan; invert on a serving platter, removing the waxed paper strips. Frost dessert with the whipped cream mixture.

Dolly Eastburn Somers

CHOCOLATE MOUSSE

Preparing: 40 minutes   *Do Ahead*   *Yield: 8 to 12 servings*
Chilling: 12 hours   *Freeze*

16 ounces semi-sweet chocolate	**1 cup egg whites**
½ cup unsalted butter	**¼ teaspoon cream of tartar**
1 cup superfine sugar	**1 cup heavy cream**
6 tablespoons white corn syrup	**Whipped cream, grated chocolate**
¼ cup water	**or nuts (garnish)**
½ cup egg yolks	

Melt chocolate and butter in double boiler. Prepare a syrup with sugar, corn syrup and water in heavy-bottomed pot. Place over moderate heat approximately 15 minutes until an 8-inch thread forms (230°-234°F. on candy thermometer). While the syrup is boiling, whip egg yolks at high speed with mixer about 10-15 minutes until ribbons are formed. Beat yolks at low speed, adding syrup in a thin stream. Continue to beat, adding melted chocolate and butter in small amounts until all is incorporated. Transfer to large bowl; let cool to room temperature. Beat egg whites at high speed with cream of tartar until stiff, moist peaks are formed. Fold into chocolate base with rubber spatula. *Refrigerate at least 6 hours or overnight.* Beat cream until very stiff and fold into chilled mousse. Place in serving bowls and decorate with more whipped cream, grated sweet chocolate or nuts. *Refrigerate 6 hours before serving.*

Note: Keeps up to 2 weeks in the refrigerator.

Shirley Huckins Beckwith

GRAPES JUANITA

Preparing: 15 minutes   *Yield: 8 servings*
Chilling: 2 hours

2 pounds seedless grapes	**½ cup light brown sugar**
1 cup sour cream	**Grated orange rind**

Combine grapes and sour cream. Sprinkle with brown sugar. *Chill at least 2 hours.* Garnish with grated orange rind. Pineapple is an excellent substitute for the grapes.

Jeanne Kronmiller Honish

DOUBLE CHOCOLATE CREAM PUFFS

Preparing: 2 hours　　　　*Do Ahead: Partially*　　　　*Yield: 12 servings*
Chilling: 1 hour

Puffs:
1 cup water
½ cup butter or margarine
¼ teaspoon salt

1 cup unsifted flour
4 eggs

Preheat oven to 400°F. Heat water, butter and salt to a rolling boil in a sauce-pan. Add flour all at once; stir vigorously over low heat for about 1 minute or until mixture leaves sides of pan and forms a ball. Remove from heat; cool slightly. Add eggs, one at a time, beating until smooth after each addition. Drop dough by scant ¼ cupfuls about 2 inches apart onto ungreased baking sheet. Bake 35-40 minutes or until puffed and golden brown. Slice off a small horizontal portion of top; reserve. Remove any soft filaments of dough; cool.

Filling:
1¼ cups sugar
⅓ cup unsweetened cocoa
⅓ cup cornstarch
¼ teaspoon salt

3 cups milk
3 egg yolks, slightly beaten
2 tablespoons butter
1½ teaspoons vanilla extract

Combine dry ingredients in a heavy saucepan; stir in milk. Cook over medium heat, stirring constantly until mixture boils; boil and stir 1 minute. Remove from heat and gradually stir half of mixture into egg yolks; return to saucepan. Stir and heat just to boiling point. Remove from heat; blend in butter and vanilla. Pour into a bowl; press plastic wrap onto surface. Cool. Fill each puff, replace tops.

Chocolate Glaze:
2 tablespoons butter
2 tablespoons unsweetened cocoa
2 tablespoons water

1 cup powdered sugar
½ teaspoon vanilla extract

To prepare glaze, melt butter in a small saucepan over low heat. Add cocoa and water, stirring constantly until mixture thickens; do not boil. Remove from heat; cool slightly. Blend in sugar and vanilla extract. Spoon over puffs.

COLD LEMON SOUFFLÉ WITH WINE SAUCE

Preparing: 1 hour   *Do Ahead*   *Yield: 8 servings*
Chilling: 4½ hours

1 envelope unflavored gelatin	2 teaspoons grated lemon rind
¼ cup cold water	1½ cups sugar
5 eggs, separated	1 cup heavy cream
¾ cup fresh lemon juice	

Sprinkle gelatin over cold water to soften; set aside. Mix egg yolks with lemon juice, rind and ¾ cup of sugar. Place in double boiler over boiling water and cook, stirring constantly, until lemon mixture is slightly thickened (about 8 minutes). Remove from heat and stir in gelatin until dissolved. Chill 30-40 minutes or until mixture mounds slightly when dropped from spoon. Beat egg whites until they begin to hold their shape; gradually add remaining ¾ cup sugar until all has been added and whites are stiff. Beat cream until stiff. Fold whites and cream into yolk mixture until no white streaks remain. Pour into 2-quart soufflé dish and chill 4 hours or more. Serve with Wine Sauce.

Wine Sauce:

½ cup sugar	1 teaspoon grated lemon rind
3 teaspoons cornstarch	2 tablespoons butter
½ cup water	½ cup dry white wine
3 tablespoons fresh lemon juice	

In small saucepan, mix together sugar and cornstarch. Stir in water, lemon juice and rind until smooth. Add butter. Bring to a boil, lower heat and cook until thickened (about 2 minutes). Remove from heat and stir in wine. Chill, stirring occasionally.

COFFEE MOUSSE

Preparing: 5 minutes   *Do Ahead*   *Yield 8 servings*
Chilling: 6 to 10 hours
Cooking: 15 minutes

32 marshmallows   **2 teaspoons vanilla**
1 cup strong coffee   **Toasted slivered almonds**
2 cups heavy cream   **(garnish)**

Place marshmallows and coffee in top of double boiler. Heat until marshmallows have melted. Remove from heat and cool until mixture just begins to thicken. Whip cream with vanilla; fold into coffee mixture. Pour into sherbet glasses and refrigerate 6-10 hours. Serve with bits of toasted slivered almonds.

Susie Curtiss Linvill

CUSTARD FLAN

Preparing: 30 minutes   *Do Ahead*   *Yield: 8 to 10 servings*
Chilling: 3 to 4 hours
Baking: 1½ hours

¼ cup sugar

Melt sugar in saucepan until smooth and golden brown. Do not rush melting sugar; low heat works well, taking 10-15 minutes to melt completely. Stir with wooden spoon (rubber or plastic may melt). Pour melted sugar into mold or tube pan.

Custard:
1 dozen eggs   **½ cup plus 1 tablespoon sugar**
4 cups milk   **2 teaspoons vanilla**

Preheat oven to 350°F. Blend all ingredients well. Pour mixture into mold over sugar. Bake in pan of water 1½ hours until knife inserted comes out clean. Chill; unmold.

Garnish:
2 large oranges, cut in half and   **¼ cup dry sherry**
   sectioned

Let oranges stand in sherry in refrigerator. At serving time, garnish flan with orange segments.

CHERRIES JUBILEE

Preparing: 20 minutes   *Do Ahead: Partially*   *Yield: 6 to 8 servings*
Chilling: 1 hour

½ gallon vanilla ice cream
2 (16-ounce) cans *pitted* sour red
   cherries
Grated rind of 2 lemons

½ cup sugar
⅛ teaspoon cinnamon
3-4 tablespoons Kirsch or Cognac

Drain cherries, reserving juice; toss in bowl with lemon rind, sugar, cinnamon and liqueur. Let steep until needed.

1½ tablespoons cornstarch
3 tablespoons sugar

½ cup Cognac
Chafing dish

Blend cornstarch in bowl with cherry juices; beat in a few tablespoons of canned cherry juice. In medium size saucepan, stir over heat until thickened, adding *more* cherry juice if needed. Stir in cherries and heat thoroughly; transfer to chafing dish. At the table, sprinkle with sugar and add Cognac. Set afire with a lighted match. Spoon flaming mixture until blaze dies down; serve over ice cream. (Serving will go more smoothly if ice cream is dished and served before the jubilee is brought in the dining room.)

MELON IN RUM-LIME SAUCE

Preparing: 30 minutes   *Do Ahead*   *Yield: 8 servings*
Chilling: 3 to 4 hours

1 cantaloupe
1 small honeydew melon
1 cup fresh blueberries
¼ small watermelon
⅔ cup sugar

½ cup water
1 teaspoon grated lime rind
6 tablespoons lime juice
½ cup light rum
Fresh mint (garnish)

Cut cantaloupe and honeydew melons in half; remove seeds. With melon scoop, form fruit into small balls. Do same with watermelon, working around seeds. Pile melon balls and blueberries into serving bowl and chill. In small saucepan, mix sugar with water; bring to boil. Reduce heat and simmer 5 minutes. Add lime rind; let cool to room temperature. Stir in lime juice and rum. Pour sauce over balls and berries and chill, covered, for several hours. Decorate with sprigs of mint and add additional rum, if desired.

Jeanne Kronmiller Honish

CRANBERRY PUDDING

Preparing: 20 minutes   *Do Ahead*   *Yield: 12 servings*
Cooking: 1¼ hours   *Freeze*

3 cups raw cranberries   **3 teaspoons baking soda**
¾ cup light raisins   **¾ cup light molasses**
¾ cup chopped nuts (optional)   **½ cup hot water**
2¼ cups sifted flour

Rinse cranberries and raisins; drain. Place in bowl along with nuts; sift flour and soda over fruit. Add molasses and water; stir until batter is smooth. Turn into two 1-pound greased and sugared coffee cans; cover with foil and secure with rubber bands. Place on trivet in deep kettle. Add enough boiling water to come halfway up sides of cans. Steam, covered 1¼ hours. Serve with Butter Cream Sauce.

Butter Cream Sauce:
1 cup sugar   **½ cup light cream**
½ cup butter   **1 teaspoon vanilla extract**

Combine all ingredients in a saucepan. Heat to boiling. Serve on hot pudding.

DANISH BAKED CUSTARD

Preparing: 10 minutes   *Yield: 6 to 8 servings*
Baking: 35 to 45 minutes

3 eggs   **Nutmeg to taste**
¼ teaspoon salt   **3 cups scalded milk**
⅓ cup sugar   **Day old good Danish**
½ teaspoon vanilla   **½ cup whipped cream**

Preheat oven to 375°F. Mix eggs, salt, sugar, nutmeg and vanilla; add milk; pour over Danish. Bake in water bath 35-45 minutes or until knife inserted in the middle comes out clean. Remove from oven; allow to cool 10 minutes. Serve with whipped cream.

Note: Be sure when scalding milk, that it does not burn, as this will most definitely affect the flavor of product. A dash of cinnamon may be added to whipped cream.

Mrs. Doe Goff, Top of the Plaza
Girard Bank, Philadelphia, Pennsylvania

ORANGE CREAM

Preparing: 15 minutes   *Do Ahead*   *Yield: 4 to 6 servings*
Chilling: 3 to 4 hours

1 (3-ounce) package orange   1 (11-ounce) can mandarin
  gelatin   oranges
1 cup boiling water   ½ cup chopped nuts
1 pint vanilla ice cream   1 cup miniature marshmallows

Dissolve gelatin in boiling water; add ice cream and stir until completely melted.
Add oranges, nuts, marshmallows and mix well. Pour into dish or 5-cup mold.
Chill until firm.

Nancy Kuper Crowell

HOT SPICED FRUIT SALAD

Preparing: 20 minutes   *Do Ahead: Partially*   *Yield: 12 servings*
Baking: 25 minutes

1 (16-ounce) can peach halves   ½ teaspoon cinnamon
1 (16-ounce) can pear halves   ¼ teaspoon ground cloves
1 (16-ounce) can apricot halves   ⅓ cup brown sugar
1 (16-ounce) can pineapple chunks   ¼ cup butter
1 (16-ounce) can pitted light sweet   2 cups fresh seedless grapes
  cherries   3 bananas
2 tart apples, peeled, cored, cubed   Sour cream or whipped cream
Juice of 1 lemon   (optional)
½ teaspoon nutmeg

Preheat oven to 350°F. Drain syrup from all canned fruits; measure and reserve
1½ cups combined fruit syrup. Turn fruits and apple cubes into 2½-quart covered baking dish or casserole. Sprinkle lemon juice over fruit. To reserved
syrup, add nutmeg, cinnamon, cloves and brown sugar; pour over fruit. Dot
top of fruit with pieces of butter; cover and bake 20 minutes. Remove dish from
oven; lightly stir in grapes and bananas. Cover and bake 5 minutes. Serve hot,
plain or with whipped cream.

Variation: Leave out apples, grapes, bananas and spices; substitute 2 teaspoons curry powder.

Jeanne Kronmiller Honish

MARINATED FRUIT

Preparing: 20 minutes   *Do Ahead*   *Yield: 6 servings*
Chilling: 1 hour

1 (20-ounce) can unsweetened
    pineapple chunks
2 green apples, peeled and sliced
1 banana, sliced
1 large orange, peeled and
    sectioned

Several strawberries
5-6 fresh mint leaves, diced
2 tablespoons honey
4 ounces orange juice

Drain pineapple; reserve juice. Mix with orange juice, honey and mint. Pour over fruit and chill. Serve in glass bowls and garnish with whole fresh mint leaves.

Variation: Fresh fruit in season (melon, peaches, kiwi, blueberries, etc.) may be added or substituted.

Grace Burdett Nellis

PINEAPPLE ROMANOFF

Preparing: 30 minutes   *Do Ahead*   *Yield: 6 to 8 servings*
Chilling: 1 hour

1 large pineapple
½ cup powdered sugar
3 tablespoons Cointreau
3 tablespoons rum

1¼ cups heavy cream
3 tablespoons Kirsch
Grated rind of 1 orange

Slice pineapple, cut off outer shell and hard central core, and cut into segments. Toss segments with ¼ cup powdered sugar. Arrange segments in a bowl suitable for serving at the table, and pour over them a mixture of Cointreau and rum; chill. *One hour before serving:* whip cream; add remaining powdered sugar and flavor with Kirsch. Spoon whipped cream into marinated pineapple pieces, tossing until every piece is coated with creamy liqueur mixture. Top with finely grated orange rind, and keep cold until time to serve.

RASPBERRY GINGER

Preparing: 10 minutes   *Do Ahead*   *Yield: 6 to 8 servings*
Chilling: 1 hour

3 (10-ounce) packages frozen   1 cup sifted brown sugar
  raspberries   ½ teaspoon ground ginger
1½ pints heavy cream

Thaw, drain and separate berries. Whip cream until stiff. Mix brown sugar with ginger and fold into cream. Fold in berries lightly so as not to crush them. *Chill for at least 1 hour or until ready to serve.* Before serving, stir gently to blend in any berry juice.

Dorothy O'Hara Eke

STRAWBERRIES ELEGANTE

Preparing: 10 minutes   *Do Ahead*   *Yield: 8 servings*
Chilling: 1 hour

1 (8-ounce) package cream   ⅓ cup powdered sugar
  cheese, softened   2 teaspoons orange liqueur
1 cup sour cream   1 quart fresh strawberries

Beat all ingredients except strawberries together until smooth; *chill 1 hour.* Wash and hull strawberries. Fill 8 cordial or tiny cups with cream dip. Place on dessert plate and surround with berries. To eat, dip strawberries in cream.

Karen Klabau Meyers

STRAWBERRY MOLD

Preparing: 15 minutes   *Do Ahead*   *Yield: 8 servings*

2 (3-ounce) packages strawberry   1 (16-ounce) package frozen
  gelatin   strawberries
½ pint sour cream

Dissolve gelatin in 2 cups boiling water; cool. Add sour cream and beat until smooth. Add strawberries with juice. Pour into a 5-cup mold and chill.

Dolly Eastburn Somers

FRESH FRUIT FLAN

Preparing: 1 hour   *Do Ahead*   *Yield: 8 servings*
Chilling: 1 hour + 1 hour
Baking: 45 minutes

Flan Shell:
¼ cup soft butter   ½ teaspoon grated lemon peel
2 tablespoons sugar   1 egg white
3 tablespoons almond paste   ¾ cup sifted flour

Grease and lightly flour an 8x1½ inch round layer cake pan or tart pan. In small bowl, using electric mixer at medium speed, cream butter, sugar, almond paste and lemon peel until well combined. Add egg white, beat at high speed until smooth. Gradually beat in flour. With fingers, press evenly onto bottom and sides of pan. Refrigerate 1 hour. Preheat oven to 300°F. Bake shell 45-55 minutes or until golden. Cool 15 minutes. Gently turn out onto rack. Cool.

Pastry Cream:
1 (3⅛-ounce) package vanilla   1 teaspoon vanilla extract
  pudding and pie filling (not   1½ cups milk
  instant)

In small pan, combine pudding mix with milk. Cook according to package directions. Remove from heat. Pour into bowl; stir in vanilla. Cover with waxed paper. Refrigerate until chilled.

Apricot Glaze:
½ cup apricot preserves   2 tablespoons water

In small saucepan, heat preserves with water, stirring until melted.

Assemble at least 1 hour before serving:
4 lady fingers, split   8-10 strawberries, halved
2 tablespoons Kirsch or creme de   ⅓ cup fresh raspberries, halved
  cassis, to taste   ¼ cup fresh blackberries or
13 banana slices, cut diagonally   blueberries
⅓ cup green grapes, halved
  vertically

Spread half pastry cream over bottom of shell. Arrange ladyfingers over cream; sprinkle with Kirsch. Cover with remaining pastry cream, arrange fruit by placing single row of bananas overlapping from top to bottom down center of shell. On either side of bananas, place 1 row grapes overlapping each other. Next to grapes, place a row of strawberries, then a row of raspberries, ending with a row of blackberries or blueberries. Brush with glaze and refrigerate.

Grace Burdett Nellis

STRAWBERRY CASSIS PARFAIT

Preparing: 15 minutes   *Do Ahead*   *Yield: 4 servings*
                               Freeze

1 cup fresh strawberries
10 ounces (1½ cups) frozen
  unsweetened raspberries
2 tablespoons creme de cassis

1 tablespoon sugar
1 pint vanilla ice cream,
  slightly soft

Wash, hull and slice strawberries. Combine raspberries, cassis and sugar in blender or food processor. Transfer to a bowl; gently stir in strawberries. Layer berries with ice cream in parfait or large wine glass. Freeze until serving.

Grace Burdett Nellis

STRAWBERRIES ROMANOFF

Preparing: 20 minutes   *Do Ahead*   *Yield: 8 to 10 servings*
Chilling: 4 hours or overnight

1 pint strawberries
¼ cup sugar
2 (3-ounce) packages strawberry
  gelatin
2 cups boiling water
2 tablespoons brandy (or use
  ½ teaspoon brandy extract and
  3 tablespoons orange juice)

1 tablespoon Cointreau or
  Curacao liqueur
2 cups Cool Whip or 1 envelope
  whipped topping mix, prepared

Wash and stem strawberries. Set aside few whole berries for garnish; slice remaining berries. Add sugar; let stand 15 minutes. Reserving syrup, drain and measure adding water to make 1 cup. Dissolve gelatin in boiling water. Measure ¾ cup of gelatin; add brandy liqueur and ½ cup of measured syrup. Chill until slightly thickened. Fold in whipped topping. Pour into 5-6 cup mold. Chill until set but not firm. Add remaining ½ cup measured syrup to remaining gelatin. Chill until thickened. Stir in strawberries. Spoon over first layer in mold. Chill until firm (4 hours) or overnight.

Note: Recipe may be doubled but do not mold. Serve in salad bowl.

Lori Adams DelRossi

STRAWBERRY CREPES

Preparing: 25 minutes   *Do Ahead: Partially*   *Yield: 8 servings*
Cooking: 5 minutes

16 dessert crepes (Use favorite
  dessert crepe recipe and
  substitute ¼ cup Grand Marnier
  for ¼ cup of liquid in recipe)

Filling:
3 ounces cream cheese, softened   **½ cup sour cream**

Mix cream cheese and sour cream. Place tablespoon of mixture down center of each crepe and roll up. *These may be done ahead and refrigerated.* At serving time, arrange 2 crepes on individual dessert plates. Serve with sauce.

Sauce:
2 cups strawberries, partially   **¼ cup strawberry liqueur or**
  crushed   **2 tablespoons Kirsch or**
½ cup sugar   **Grand Marnier**
2-3 tablespoons unsalted butter

In saucepan, combine strawberries, sugar and butter. Heat and transfer to chafing dish. Pour liqueur over berry mixture and ignite. Spoon sauce over crepes.

STRAWBERRY ICE

Preparing: 30 minutes   *Do Ahead*   *Yield: 1 to 1½ quarts*
Freezing: 4 hours   *Freeze*

4 cups fresh strawberries   **1 cup superfine sugar**
2 cups water   **4 tablespoons fresh lemon juice**

Purée strawberries in a blender and set aside. In 2-quart saucepan, bring water and sugar to a boil over medium heat, stirring until sugar dissolves. Let mixture cook exactly 5 minutes, timing from moment sugar and water begin to boil. Remove pan from heat and allow syrup to cool. Stir berries into cooled syrup; add lemon juice. Pour mixture into freezer trays. *Freeze 4 hours, removing from freezer 5 or 6 times to stir well, scraping sides and edges of trays.* Stirring will give ice a smoother texture.

CRANBERRY-RASPBERRY SHERBET

Preparing: 30 minutes   *Do Ahead*   *Yield: 8 to 10 servings*
Freezing: 2 hours; 6 hours   *Freeze*

3 cups fresh cranberries
3 cups water
1 envelope unflavored gelatin
1 (10-ounce) package frozen
    raspberries, thawed

1½ cups sugar
3 tablespoons fresh lemon
    juice
2 egg whites

Cook cranberries in 2½ cups water, over high heat, about 5 minutes until skins pop. Meanwhile, sprinkle gelatin in remaining ½ cup water to soften. Force cranberry mixture through a sieve or food mill to extract all juices. Discard skins. Force raspberries through a strainer to remove seeds. Combine both purées in medium-sized saucepan and heat. Add sugar; stir until dissolved. Remove from heat; stir in lemon juice. Pour into 2 freezer trays; freeze until firm. Transfer to a large mixing bowl; break up lumps. Beat with mixer until smooth and softened, but not melted. Beat egg whites until stiff peaks form; fold into sherbet. Return sherbet to freezer trays, cover with foil and freeze several hours until firm.

FRUIT MOLD

Preparing: 20 minutes   *Do Ahead*   *Yield: 8 servings*
Freezing: 4 to 6 hours   *Freeze*

1 (8-ounce) package cream cheese
¼ cup powdered sugar
¼ cup mayonnaise
2 tablespoons lemon juice
½ teaspoon vanilla extract
1 (10-ounce) package frozen
    blueberries, drained

1 (10-ounce) package frozen
    peaches, drained
1 (8¾-ounce) can pineapple tidbits,
    drained
1 cup miniature marshmallows
1 cup heavy cream, whipped

Mix cream cheese, sugar, mayonnaise, lemon juice and vanilla. Add blueberries, peaches and pineapple. Fold in marshmallows and whipped cream. Pour into 9-cup mold; freeze. When ready to serve, let stand at room temperature at least 20 minutes; unmold.

Note: 10 ounces fresh blueberries and peaches may be substituted for frozen.

Dede Dubois Shimrak

ORANGE ICE

Preparing: 15 minutes   *Do Ahead: Partially*   *Yield: 4 to 6 servings*
Freezing: 4 to 6 hours   *Freeze*

1 (2-inch) square orange peel
4 cups freshly squeezed orange
   juice

1 cup sugar
⅓ cup Grand Marnier

Combine orange peel, 1 cup orange juice, sugar and Grand Marnier. Process until blended. (Food processor preferred but blender will work.) Add processed ingredients to remaining 3 cups orange juice and mix well. Pour into 2 ice cube trays and freeze. Just before serving, add frozen cubes, one tray at a time, and process until a fine ice forms (about 2-3 minutes in processor). Serve immediately.

Robert Somers

RED, WHITE AND BLUE PRALINE PARFAIT

Preparing: 10 minutes   *Do Ahead*   *Yield: 8 servings*
Chilling: 1 hour   *Freeze*

2 tablespoons cornstarch
¼ cup water
⅔ cup firmly packed light brown
   sugar
⅓ cup dark corn syrup
1 cup Planters Tavern Nuts

1 tablespoon margarine
½ gallon vanilla ice cream
1 pint strawberries, cleaned and
   sliced
1 pint blueberries, cleaned

In medium saucepan combine cornstarch and water. Stir in brown sugar and corn syrup; bring to a boil. Remove from heat; mix in nuts and margarine. Chill. In large glass bowl or individual parfait glasses, alternate layers of vanilla ice cream with sliced strawberries and blueberries. Top with praline sauce.

Note: Other fresh fruits may be substituted for berries. Recipe may be halved.

Carol Myers Anderson

FROZEN GRAND MARNIER SOUFFLÉ

Preparing: 30 minutes   *Do Ahead*   *Yield: 8 to 12 servings*
                                 Freeze

6 egg yolks   **3 ounces Grand Marnier (or**
¾ cup sugar   **Kahlua, Créme de Menthe, Tia**
2¾ cups heavy cream, whipped **Maria, etc.)**

Combine egg yolks and sugar, beat until thickened and lemon colored. Fold 2 cups whipped cream into egg mixture; fold in Grand Marnier. Fill soufflé ramekins and freeze. *(Cover if to be in freezer for a while.)* Defrost 20 minutes before serving and top with remaining ¾ cup whipped cream. Garnish on top with strawberry, orange slice or powdered hot cocoa mix. A fantastically easy and delicious dessert!

Judy Lane Davies

FROZEN CREAM CHEESE
AND BRANDIED STRAWBERRY SAUCE

Preparing: 1 hour   *Do Ahead*   *Yield: 8 servings*
Freezing: 6 to 8 hours   *Freeze*

½ cup sugar   **1 cup heavy cream**
2 tablespoons water   **½ teaspoon vanilla**
12 ounces cream cheese, beaten

Dissolve sugar in water over moderate heat. Remove from heat. Add cream cheese; gradually beat in cream, sugar-syrup, and vanilla; beat until fluffy. Pour into ice tray or serving dish and freeze. To serve, cut into squares and serve with strawberry sauce.

Sauce:
1 cup sliced strawberries   **Pinch salt**
¼ cup sugar   **1 tablespoon brandy**
1 tablespoon quick cooking   **1 teaspoon lemon juice**
tapioca

Sprinkle sugar on berries; let stand 30 minutes. Drain juice and add enough water to equal ¾ cup. Combine juice with tapioca and pinch salt. Let stand 5 minutes. Cook until mixture boils; remove from heat. Add brandy, lemon juice and berries. Let stand 20 minutes.

Ann Adams Ledger

ICE CREAM FRAPPÉ

Preparing: 10 minutes   *Do Ahead*   *Yield: 4 servings*
Freezing: 1 hour   *Freeze*

½ pint chocolate ice cream   ¼ cup brandy
1 pint coffee ice cream   1 cup whipped cream

In a small bowl, blend chocolate ice cream until smooth. In a separate bowl, blend coffee ice cream and brandy. Layer in parfait glasses; freeze. Top with whipped cream at serving time.

Carol Sutcliffe Kramer

WORLD'S EASIEST EVER STRAWBERRY ICE CREAM

Preparing: 15 minutes   *Do Ahead*   *Yield: 1 quart*
Freezing: 12 hours   *Freeze*

2 cups buttermilk   1½ cups strawberry jam

Stir buttermilk into jam. Pour into refrigerator tray; freeze until firm, about 6 hours. Cut up frozen mixture and place in chilled mixer bowl. Whip with mixer until fluffy. Return to tray; cover and freeze until firm. Spoon into sherbet dishes. Garnish with fresh strawberries and mint leaves, if desired.

Frances Marincola Blair

TORTONI

Preparing: 20 minutes   *Do Ahead*   *Yield: 4 servings*
Freezing: 3 to 4 hours

1 egg white   ⅛ teaspoon almond extract
1 tablespoon instant coffee   (or more to taste)
  (or less to taste)   ¼ cup sugar
½ teaspoon salt   1 cup heavy cream
1 teaspoon vanilla   ¼ cup slivered almonds, toasted

Combine egg white, coffee and salt; beat until stiff. Add vanilla, almond extract and sugar to cream; beat until stiff. Fold in nuts and egg white mixture. Put into ramekins or paper cups. Sprinkle with a few more nuts and freeze.

Judy Lane Davies

TORTA DI SUPREMA

Preparing: 30 minutes   *Do Ahead*   *Yield: 8 to 10 servings*
Freezing: 12 hours   *Freeze*

¾ cup sugar   2 teaspoons vanilla
3 egg yolks   ½ teaspoon almond flavoring
Dash of salt   1½ cups chilled heavy cream,
1 cup crumbled pound cake   whipped
2 tablespoons Grand Marnier   4-6 thin slices pound cake

Mix all ingredients except whipped cream and pound cake slices. With spatula fold in whipped cream very carefully. Place half of mixture in 9x5 inch loaf pan; cover with thin slices of pound cake and cover with remaining mixture. *Freeze overnight.* Remove from mold and serve with warm sauce.

Sauce:
1 (10-ounce) package frozen   2 tablespoons cornstarch
   raspberries   1 tablespoon Grand Marnier
1 (10-ounce) package frozen
   strawberries

Thaw berries; put in blender and crush. In saucepan, combine crushed berries and cornstarch, stir to remove all lumps. Bring to a boil, stirring constantly; cook until clear. Remove from heat; add Grand Marnier. Serve hot over mold.

FROZEN ROCKY ROAD

Preparing: 1 hour   *Do Ahead*   *Yield: 6 to 8 servings*
Freezing: 3 to 4 hours   *Freeze*

¼ cup sugar   1 tablespoon cold water
¾ cup milk   ¾ cup miniature marshmallows
1(1-ounce) square unsweetened   ½ cup chopped nuts
   chocolate   3 tablespoons Kahlua
1 teaspoon unflavored gelatin   1 small container Cool Whip

Combine sugar, milk and chocolate in saucepan; bring to boil, stirring constantly. Soften gelatin in water; stir into milk mixture. Remove from heat and cool slightly; stir in remaining ingredients. Pour into a 9x9 inch pan and freeze; will be about 1-inch thick.

Elizabeth Taylor Young

CHOCOLATE SIN

Preparing: 45 minutes   **Do Ahead**   *Yield: Two 9x5 inch tortes*
Baking: 25 minutes   *(about 16 servings)*
Chilling: 12 hours

Cake:

3 (1-ounce) squares unsweetened   2 teaspoons baking soda
   chocolate   ½ teaspoon salt
½ cup butter   2¼ cups sifted cake flour
2¼ cups brown sugar   1 cup sour cream
3 eggs   1 cup hot milk
1½ teaspoons vanilla

Preheat oven to 350°F. Grease and flour one 11x16-inch jelly-roll pan and one 9x9-inch square cake pan. Melt chocolate in saucepan over low heat. Beat butter until smooth; add brown sugar and eggs. Beat on high speed until light and fluffy, about 5 minutes. Beat in vanilla and chocolate with mixer on low speed; beat in baking soda and salt. Add flour alternately with sour cream; pour in hot milk. Stir with spoon until well-blended; pour into prepared pans. Bake 25-30 minutes. Cool in pans on wire racks. When cool, invert pans. Cut turned out cake into 6 rectangles approximately 9x5 inches (4 cross-wise; 2 lengthwise). Use remaining 9x9-inch cake as you wish. *(Cake alone may be frozen.)*

Coffee Mixture:

1 cup strong black coffee   ¼ cup sugar
¼ cup Grand Marnier

Combine ingredients. Sprinkle cut 11x16-inch cake with coffee mixture. In two 9x5-inch loaf pans which have been lined with waxed paper, alternate layers of chocolate filling and cake (cut to fit pan), beginning and ending with chocolate. (There will be 4 layers of chocolate and 3 layers of cake.) *Must refrigerate overnight.* After refrigeration, remove cake from pan. Ice with remaining chocolate filling.

Chocolate Filling:

¾ pound sweet butter   3 medium eggs
18 ounces semi-sweet chocolate

Melt chocolate and butter in top of double boiler; cool slightly. Beat eggs; beat in slightly cooled chocolate mixture. Continue to beat until of spreading consistency. Depending on room temperature it may be necessary to chill mixture for a short time.

Fish Market
Philadelphia, Pennsylvania

RUM CAKE

Preparing: 30 minutes   *Do Ahead*   *Yield: 10 to 12 servings*
Baking: 1 hour

1 (18½-ounce) box yellow cake mix   ½ cup dark rum
1 (3-ounce) box instant vanilla   ½ cup oil
   pudding mix   1 cup chopped nuts
4 eggs

Preheat oven to 325°F. Combine all ingredients, except nuts and beat 3 minutes. Grease bottom of bundt pan; sprinkle bottom with chopped nuts, then pour in batter. Bake 1 hour; cool. Prick cake full of holes with a fork. Drizzle cake with topping.

Topping:
½ cup butter or margarine   1 cup sugar
½ cup water   ½ cup rum

Place butter, water and sugar in a saucepan and bring to a boil. Remove from heat and add rum. Drizzle over cake.

Carol Nelson DeVol

EGG NOG CAKE

Preparing: 1 hour   *Do Ahead*   *Yield: 6 to 8 servings*
Chilling: 24 hours   *Freeze*

1 angel food cake, split in 3 layers   1 cup toasted slivered almonds
¾ cup butter (room temperature)   1 cup heavy cream
2½ cups sifted powdered sugar   1 ounce semi-sweet chocolate,
4 egg yolks   shaved into curls
¼ cup brandy or rum

Cream butter; stir in sugar until well-blended. Mix in egg yolks one at a time, blending well after each addition. Gradually stir in brandy or rum (do not beat). Chop and fold in ¾ cup almonds. Spread between layers of angel food cake. Cover and chill 24 hours (or put in foil and freeze). Before serving, whip heavy cream and frost top and sides of cake. Decorate with chocolate curls and remaining almonds.

Bonnie Kennedy Beverly

VIENNA TORTE

Preparing: 50 minutes   *Do Ahead*   *Yield: 10 to 12 servings*
Baking: 30 minutes

1 cup sugar   ½ pound pecans, finely chopped
7 eggs, separated   ¼ teaspoon salt
1 tablespoon instant coffee

Preheat oven to 350°F. Cover bottom of two 9-inch layer pans with greased waxed paper. Add sugar to egg yolks; beat until thick. Combine coffee and nuts. Add salt to egg whites; beat until stiff. Fold ½ of the coffee-nut mixture into egg yolk mixture. Fold in egg whites. Fold in remaining coffee-nut mixture. Pour into prepared pans; bake 30 minutes. Cool cakes on wire racks 5 minutes before removing from pans. Spread chocolate filling and frosting between layers and on top and sides of torte. Sprinkle with carmelized almonds.

Chocolate Filling and Frosting:
¼ cup flour   1 cup sifted powdered sugar
¼ cup granulated sugar   ½ teaspoon vanilla
1 cup milk   ½ ounce sweet chocolate,
½ cup butter   melted

Combine flour and granulated sugar in saucepan over medium heat. Add milk gradually, stirring constantly, cooking until thick. Chill. Cream butter. Add powdered sugar gradually; cream until fluffy. Add vanilla and chocolate. Combine mixtures and mix well.

Carmelized Almonds:
3 tablespoons sugar   ¼ cup chopped blanched almonds

Melt sugar slowly in a small heavy skillet stirring constantly, until it becomes a rich brown syrup. Pour over almonds in a buttered shallow pan. Cool and put through a nut grater.

Ardyth Beidleman Sobyak

CHOCOLATE CHIP CAKE

Preparing: 10 minutes   Do Ahead   Yield: 1 tube cake
Baking: 45 minutes   Freeze

½ cup butter, softened   1 teaspoon baking powder
1 cup sugar   1 cup sour cream
2 cups flour   ¼ teaspoon salt
2 eggs   1 cup chocolate chips
1 teaspoon vanilla   1 cup chopped walnuts
1 teaspoon baking soda

Preheat oven to 350°F. Cream butter and sugar. Add all ingredients except chips and nuts. Beat at medium speed for two minutes until creamy; add ¾ of chips and ¾ of nuts to batter and blend. Place in greased tube pan and sprinkle remaining chips and nuts on top, plus 1-2 tablespoons of sugar. Bake 45 minutes. *Cool 1 hour before removing from pan.*

Kathy Mohn Wilmot

BUTTERSCOTCH POUND CAKE

Preparing: ½ hour   Do Ahead   Yield: 16 servings
Baking: 45 to 50 minutes   Freeze

1 (6-ounce) package butterscotch   3 cups flour
   bits   ½ teaspoon baking soda
2 tablespoons instant coffee (dry)   ¼ teaspoon salt
¼ cup water   ¾ cup buttermilk
1 cup butter   4 eggs
1½ cups sugar

Preheat oven to 350°F. Grease and flour bundt pan. Melt butterscotch bits, instant coffee and water together in top of double boiler, cool slightly. Cream butter and sugar; add butterscotch mixture. Mix flour, soda, and salt together. Add dry ingredients and buttermilk alternately to creamed mixture, beginning and ending with dry. Beat in eggs one at a time at medium speed. Pour into bundt pan and bake 45-50 minutes. Cool 10 minutes before removing from pan. When cool, dust with powdered sugar *or* serve with ice cream or whipped cream.

Joan Stievater Lindstrom

BLACK FOREST TORTE

Preparing: 1 hour   *Do Ahead*   *Yield: 12 to 16 servings*
Baking: 15 minutes   *Freeze*

Cake:
1¾ cups flour
1¾ cups sugar
1¼ teaspoons baking soda
1 teaspoon salt
¼ teaspoon baking powder
⅔ cup tub-style margarine

4 (1-ounce) squares unsweetened
  chocolate, melted
1¼ cups water
1 teaspoon vanilla
3 eggs

Preheat oven to 350°F. Grease and flour four 9-inch cake pans. Beat all ingredients except eggs for 1 minute on low speed. Scrape bowl and beat 2 minutes at medium speed. Add eggs and beat 2 minutes. Pour batter into each of the 4 greased pans, (about 1 cup per pan). Layers will be thin. Bake 15-18 minutes. Cool slightly. Remove from pan; cool.

Chocolate Filling:
6 ounces German sweet chocolate   ¾ cup tub-style margarine
½ cup chopped toasted almonds

Melt chocolate over hot water. Cool. Blend in margarine. Stir in almonds.

Cream Filling:
2 cups heavy cream   1 teaspoon vanilla
1 tablespoon sugar

Beat cream with sugar and vanilla until stiff.

To Assemble Torte:
Place one layer of cake on serving plate. Spread with ½ of chocolate filling. Add another layer of cake. Spread with ½ of whipped cream filling. Add third layer of cake and spread with remaining half of chocolate filling. Add fourth layer and spread top with remaining cream filling. Pipe edges with whipped cream and grate some of remaining chocolate bar on top of cake. (Do not frost sides completely.) Refrigerate until ready to serve.

Note: Cake may be made ahead and frozen.

Lois Rising Pogyor

CHOCOLATE BUTTERNUT SAUCE

Preparing: 5 minutes   *Do Ahead*   *Yield: 6 to 8 servings*
Cooking: 15 to 30 minutes

1 (12-ounce) package chocolate   **1 cup butter**
morsels   **½ cup chopped walnuts or pecans**

Heat chocolate morsels and butter over very low heat in a heavy saucepan or in double boiler over simmering water until melted and hot. Just before serving, add nuts and mix. Serve warm over vanilla ice cream. This sauce will harden over ice cream. *Keeps in refrigerator for one month.*

Joanne Stanek Murphy

RICOTTA TORTE

Preparing: 30 minutes   *Do Ahead*   *Yield: One 9x5-inch torte*
Chilling: 15 minutes   *Freeze*

1½ pounds ricotta cheese   **1 Pound cake (from scratch or**
½ pound powdered sugar   **store bought)**
6 tablespoons rum   **1 cup whipped cream**
1 tablespoon Crème de Noyeaux   **1-2 tablespoons Grand Marnier**
1 (12-ounce) package semi-sweet   **or Cointreau**
chocolate bits

Drain cheese well, until dry (wring out in cheesecloth if necessary, should be of dry consistency); add sugar and liquors. Add 4 ounces of chocolate bits; fold lightly; adjust for sweetness and liquor flavor. Slice pound cake horizontally into 5 layers; spread mixture evenly between layers, being careful not to get it on sides. Melt remaining chocolate over double boiler. When cake is assembled, chill in freezer 15 minutes to set. Pull from freezer; slowly pour chocolate over top of cake; spread carefully on sides. Entire cake should be coated evenly with chocolate. When chocolate has set, carefully heat a knife in hot water and outline servings (about ¼ inch of cake per guest is fine). Decorate with scrolls of fresh whipped cream flavored lightly with Grand Marnier or Cointreau. *Can be frozen up to 5 days in advance; thaw slightly.* During summer months, it can be served frozen as an ice cream cake roll.

T. C. Ambrosia, Executive Chef, CEC
The Marriott Corporation, Philadelphia, Pennsylvania

SACHER TORTE

Preparing: 45 minutes   *Do Ahead*   *Yield: 12 to 16 servings*
Baking: 1 hour 15 minutes

1 cup plus 2 tablespoons unsalted
   butter, softened
¾ teaspoon salt
2 teaspoons vanilla extract
1 cup sugar
⅓ cup flour

9 ounces finely ground walnuts
9 eggs, separated
9 ounces sweet chocolate, melted
½ cup heated and sieved apricot
   jam

Preheat oven to 350°F. Cream together butter, salt, vanilla and sugar. In separate bowl toss together flour and walnuts; set aside. To creamed mixture add egg yolks one at a time, beating well after each addition. Stir in chocolate and nuts. Beat egg whites until stiff; fold into chocolate mixture. Spread batter in buttered and floured 9-inch springform pan. Bake 1 hour and 15 minutes. Remove from oven. Let cool 20 minutes; remove from pan and invert. Set cake on rack over waxed paper. When cake has cooled completely, spread with apricot jam. Pour warm icing over cake, rotating it to distribute icing evenly; work spatula around sides of cake to cover with icing letting excess drip onto waxed paper. Put clean waxed paper under rack; chill cake on rack until icing is completely set, about 1 hour. With 2 wooden spatulas, transfer cake to a serving plate. Decorate top as desired and serve with sweetened whipped cream.

Icing:

½ cup heavy cream
2 teaspoons instant coffee

6 ounces chopped sweet chocolate

Scald cream; whisk in coffee. Add chocolate; stir for 1 minute over heat; remove from heat and continue stirring until smooth.

The Commissary
Philadelphia, Pennsylvania

WINE CAKE

Preparing: 20 minutes　　　*Do Ahead*　　　*Yield: 10 servings*
Baking: 1 hour

1 (18½-ounce) package yellow　　　3 tablespoons butter
　cake mix　　　　　　　　　　　½ cup vegetable oil
1 (3⅛-ounce) package instant　　　¼ cup hot water
　vanilla pudding　　　　　　　　1 cup white port wine
4 eggs　　　　　　　　　　　　　1 teaspoon nutmeg

Preheat oven to 350°F. Blend and mix all ingredients for 6 minutes. Place in buttered bundt pan; bake for 1 hour.

Sauce:
¼ cup butter　　　　　　　　　　¾ cup sherry
1 cup sugar　　　　　　　　　　　¼ teaspoon nutmeg
1 egg

Heat ingredients over low heat until well mixed. Puncture top of cake with several toothpick holes. Pour wine sauce over cake, making sure some sauce seeps into holes.

Optional: Save some sauce and heat before serving. Spoon sauce over each cake slice.

Note: Better if made 2 days ahead.

Mary Leslie DiSanto

A-1 CHOCOLATE SAUCE

Preparing: 10 minutes　　　*Do Ahead*　　　*Yield: 1 cup*
Cooking: 5 minutes

2 (1-ounce) squares unsweetened　　½ cup evaporated milk, undiluted
　chocolate　　　　　　　　　　　1 teaspoon vanilla
2 tablespoons butter　　　　　　　¼ cup sherry (optional)
⅔ cup sugar

Melt chocolate over low heat with butter; stir in sugar and milk. Cook gently until sugar dissolves and sauce thickens. Add vanilla and sherry.

Liz Nelson Mayer

FESTIVE CAKE

Preparing: 20 minutes   *Yield: 12 to 16 servings*
Baking: 1 hour 25 minutes

3 cups flour	3 eggs
2 cups sugar	1½ cups vegetable oil
1 teaspoon baking soda	1 teaspoon almond extract
1 teaspoon salt	2 cups chopped, firm, ripe bananas
1 teaspoon cinnamon	1 (8-ounce) can crushed pineapple
1 cup chopped almonds	French icing

Mix and sift flour, sugar, baking soda, salt and cinnamon; stir in almonds. Beat eggs slightly; combine with oil, almond extract, bananas and undrained pineapple. Add to dry ingredients; mix thoroughly, but do not beat. Spoon into well-oiled 10-inch tube pan. Bake at 325°F. for 1 hour and 20-25 minutes. Remove from oven; let stand 10-15 minutes; invert on wire cake rack; remove pan. Cool thoroughly before frosting.

French Icing:

1 cup milk	1 cup sugar
5 tablespoons flour	1 teaspoon vanilla
½ pound margarine or butter, softened	

In top of double boiler, stir flour and milk over boiling water until thick (custard consistency). Set aside to cool. In medium mixing bowl, whip margarine with sugar; add cooled milk and flour mixture and vanilla; mix to blend.

Eve Pantellas Walker

SOUR CREAM-CHOCOLATE FROSTING

Preparing: 20 minutes   *Yield: Frosts a 9x13x2-inch cake*

1 (6-ounce) package semi-sweet chocolate pieces	1 teaspoon vanilla
4 tablespoons butter or margarine	¼ teaspoon salt
½ cup sour cream	2½-2¾ cup powdered sugar

Melt semi-sweet chocolate pieces and butter or margarine over low heat. Remove from heat; blend in sour cream, vanilla and salt. Gradually add sifted powdered sugar to make spreading consistency; beat well.

Ann Marie Remillard

GERMAN APPLECAKE

Preparing: 40 minutes   *Do Ahead*   *Yield: One 9-inch cake*
Baking: 1 to 1½ hours

Crust:
1 cup sugar   2 cups butter or margarine
3 cups flour   1 egg

Combine ingredients quickly to a pastry consistency (do not overwork dough). *Let rest in refrigerator for a while.* Grease and flour 9-inch springform pan. Press dough into pan, covering bottom and reaching about halfway up the sides. (Recipe makes enough dough for 2 cakes or excess can be used for cookies or as a crust for fruit tarts.)

Filling:
4-5 large baking apples   1 cup sour cream
Bread crumbs   ½ cup sugar (or less, depends
½ cup heavy cream   on apples)
Juice of 1 lemon   Few drops vanilla
2 eggs   Apricot glaze (garnish)
1 tablespoon cornstarch

Preheat oven to 375°F. Peel apples, core and cut in half. Cut small strips crosswise on top of the apples to score them. Sprinkle bottom of crust with bread crumbs to form a thin even layer. Place apples in pan, rounded side up. Fill in spaces with pieces of apples. Mix remaining ingredients together and pour over apples. Bake 1½ hours, or until apples are tender and filling set. Cool slightly; paint top of cake with melted apricot glaze.

Chef Tell Erhardt

OATMEAL CAKE

Preparing: 30 minutes   *Do Ahead*   *Yield: 8 servings*
Baking: 50 minutes   *Freeze*

1½ cups boiling water   1 teaspoon baking soda
1 cup minute oatmeal   1 teaspoon salt
½ cup butter   1 teaspoon cinnamon
1 cup brown sugar   2 eggs
1 cup sugar   ½ cup chopped walnuts or
1½ cups sifted flour   pecans (optional)
1 teaspoon vanilla

Preheat oven to 350°F. Combine boiling water, oatmeal, butter and brown sugar; mix together and set aside to cool for 20 minutes. Add all other ingredients except nuts; blend with electric mixer. Fold in nuts. Bake in greased tube or bundt pan 50 minutes. Cool partially; remove from pan. When completely cool, sprinkle with powdered sugar.

Judy Grenamyer Donohue

KID-SIZE CARROT CUPCAKES

Preparing: 15 to 20 minutes   Do Ahead   Yield: 12 large or
Baking: 15 minutes for small cupcakes   24 small cupcakes
or 20 to 25 minutes for larger cupcakes

¾ cup safflower oil   ½ teaspoon salt
¾ cup brown sugar   1 teaspoon cinnamon
2 eggs   ¼ teaspoon grated orange peel
¾ cup whole wheat flour   (optional)
¼ cup unbleached white flour   1½ cups grated carrots
½ teaspoon baking powder   6 tablespoons raisins and/or
¼ teaspoon baking soda   chopped nuts

Preheat oven to 350°F. Grease cupcake tins or line with papers. Cream oil and brown sugar together until well-mixed. Add eggs, one at a time, beating well after each addition. Mix flours, baking powder, soda, salt and cinnamon. Add flour mixture to egg mixture; beat well. Add orange peel and carrots; mix well. Add raisins and/or nuts and spoon batter into tins. Bake 15 minutes for miniature cupcakes, 20-25 minutes for large cupcakes. Test for doneness by inserting toothpick. If desired, tops may be sprinkled lightly with powdered sugar. Refrigerate any leftover cupcakes; they are even better the second day.

Gail Agerton Ebert

"IT'LL KILL YOU" CHOCOLATE ICE CREAM CAKE

Preparing: 30 minutes   *Do Ahead*   *Yield: 12 servings*
Freezing: 6 hours   *Freeze*

35-40 chocolate icebox wafer   ½ pound English toffee bits
  cookies, crushed   (or crushed Heath bars)
1 quart dark chocolate ice cream   Fudge sauce
1 quart mocha ice cream   Strawberries (optional garnish)

Lightly grease sides and bottom of springform pan. Put ½ of crushed cookies
on bottom; spread 1 quart softened ice cream over crumbs. Drizzle some fudge
sauce over ice cream; top with remaining crumbs. Add second quart of softened ice cream; drizzle sauce again. Sprinkle crushed toffee on top; freeze. Five
minutes before serving, remove from pan and serve with warm fudge sauce.
May decorate with strawberries.

Fudge Sauce:
8 ounces chocolate chips   1 tablespoon dark rum (or cognac
1 cup heavy cream   or brandy)
½ teaspoon instant coffee

Melt chocolate chips with heavy cream, instant coffee, and dark rum in a heavy
saucepan. Whisk until blended.

Note: Try experimenting with different ice cream flavors. *May be made and
frozen one week ahead.* If rushed, one jar of prepared fudge sauce can be
substituted in place of fudge sauce in recipe.

Bonnie Kennedy Beverly

BLACK BOTTOM CAKES

Preparing: 30 minutes   *Do Ahead*   *Yield: 20 muffin size;*
Baking: 20 to 30 minutes   *Freeze*   *48 mini size*

Cheese Batter:
1 (8-ounce) package cream   ⅛ teaspoon salt
  cheese, softened and whipped   1 (6-ounce) package chocolate
1 egg   chips
⅓ cup sugar

Mix cream cheese, egg, sugar and salt together. Add chocolate chips; set aside.

Chocolate Batter:

1½ cups flour
1 cup sugar
¼ cup unsweetened cocoa
1 teaspoon baking soda
½ teaspoon salt

1 cup water
⅓ cup oil
1 teaspoon vinegar
1 teaspoon vanilla

In separate bowl, sift flour, sugar, cocoa, soda and salt. Add water, oil, vinegar and vanilla; mix until well-blended. Preheat oven to 350°F. Grease and lightly flour muffin tins or mini tart pans. Fill tins ⅓ full with chocolate batter. Top each with 1 tablespoon cream cheese batter. Bake 20-30 minutes; do not overbake. Cool slightly and remove from pan.

Joyce Kenny Cassetta

CARROT CAKE

Preparing: 25 minutes   *Do Ahead*   *Yield: One 9-inch layer cake*
Baking: 35 to 45 minutes   *Freeze*

2 cups sugar
1½ cups corn oil
4 eggs, beaten
2 cups flour
1 teaspoon salt

2 teaspoons baking soda
2 teaspoons cinnamon
½ cup chopped nuts, optional
3 cups grated carrots

Preheat oven to 350°F. Grease and flour tube pan or two 9-inch round cake pans. Mix sugar, oil and beaten eggs well. Sift flour, salt, soda and cinnamon together. Add flour mixture to creamed mixture in four portions; fold in nuts and carrots. Bake in tube pan 45-60 minutes or in 9-inch pans 35 minutes. Cool partially; remove from pan and cool completely. Frost with cream cheese icing.

Icing:

1 (1-pound) box powdered sugar
½ cup margarine, room
  temperature
2 teaspoons vanilla

1 (8-ounce) package cream
  cheese, room temperature
½ cup chopped pecans

Cream together margarine and cream cheese. Add sugar and vanilla and pecans. Beat well.

Dolly Eastburn Somers

COMMISSARY CARROT CAKE

Preparing: 55 minutes   *Do Ahead*   *Yield: 12 to 16 servings*
Baking: 1 hour 10 minutes

Cake:

1¼ cups vegetable oil
2 cups sugar
2 cups minus 2 tablespoons flour
2 teaspoons cinnamon
2 teaspoons baking powder
1 teaspoon baking soda

1 teaspoon salt
4 eggs
4 cups peeled and grated carrots
1 cup raisins
1 cup chopped pecans

In large bowl, whisk oil and sugar. Sift flour, cinnamon, baking powder, baking soda and salt. Sift half the dry ingredients into sugar mixture and mix. Sift in remaining dry ingredients alternately with eggs, mixing well after each addition. Stir in *by hand* carrots, raisins and pecans. Preheat oven to 350°F. Pour batter into greased and floured 10-inch tube pan. Bake 1 hour and 10 minutes, or until cake tests done. Cool upright in pan. Invert onto serving plate; split into 3 layers.

Pecan Filling:

2 cups sugar
6 tablespoons flour
1 teaspoon salt
2 cups heavy cream

1 cup unsalted butter
1½ cups chopped pecans
1 tablespoon vanilla

In heavy saucepan, combine sugar, flour and salt. Gradually stir in cream; work in butter. Cook over lowest heat, stirring constantly, until mixture simmers. Let simmer 20-30 minutes, stirring occasionally, until golden brown. Remove from heat. When lukewarm, add pecans and vanilla; cool completely, preferably overnight.

Cream Cheese Frosting:

1 cup unsalted butter, softened
8 ounces cream cheese, softened

1 pound box powdered sugar
1 teaspoon vanilla

With mixer, cream butter; add cream cheese. Sift in powdered sugar; add vanilla and beat. Chill a bit if too soft to spread.

Toasted Coconut:
4 ounces shredded coconut

Preheat oven to 300°F. Toast coconut on baking sheet 10-15 minutes or until lightly colored. Toss with fork to help brown evenly; cool.

To Assemble:
Spread pecan filling between 3 layers of cake. Spread frosting on top and sides. Pat toasted coconut onto sides.

Optional: Decorate top with colored icing in carrot shapes.

The Commissary
Philadelphia, Pennsylvania

FRESH APPLE CAKE

Preparing: 30 minutes   Do Ahead   Yield: One 9-inch three layer cake
Baking: 30 to 40 minutes

3 cups sifted flour
1½ teaspoons baking soda
½ teaspoon salt
3 cups finely chopped apples
½ cup chopped walnuts or pecans

1 teaspoon grated lemon peel
2 cups sugar
1½ cups vegetable oil
2 eggs

Preheat oven to 350°F. Grease and flour three 9-inch round cake pans. Sift flour with baking soda and salt. In small bowl combine apple, nuts and lemon peel. In large bowl combine sugar, oil and eggs; beat well with wooden spoon. Add sifted dry ingredients, mixing until smooth. Add apple mixture; stir until well combined. Spread evenly into prepared pans. Bake 30-40 minutes or until surface springs back. Cool in pans 10 minutes. Remove from pans and cool. Prepare frosting. Fill and frost cake. Press nuts on sides of cake.

Frosting:
1 (8-ounce) package cream cheese
1 tablespoon butter
1 teaspoon vanilla

1 (1-pound) box powdered sugar
1 cup chopped walnuts or pecans
  (garnish)

Cream butter and cream cheese; add vanilla. Mix in powdered sugar; beat well.

Carol Sutcliffe Kramer

BEST EVER CHOCOLATE CAKE

Preparing: 15 minutes	*Do Ahead*	*Yield: One 9-inch cake*
Baking: 30 to 40 minutes	*Freeze*	

2 cups flour (cake flour is best)	¾ cup buttermilk
2 cups sugar	½ cup shortening
1 teaspoon baking soda	2 eggs
1 teaspoon salt	1 teaspoon vanilla
½ teaspoon baking powder	4 (1-ounce) squares unsweetened
¾ cup water	chocolate

Melt and cool chocolate squares. Preheat oven to 350°F. Grease and flour two 9-inch round cake pans. Measure all ingredients into large mixer bowl. Blend ½ minute on low speed, scraping bowl constantly; beat 3 minutes high speed, scraping bowl occasionally. Pour evenly into 2 pans. Bake 30-35 minutes or until done; remove from oven. Cool 10 minutes; remove from pans to finish cooling. Frost with Chocolate Icing.

Chocolate Icing:

2 (4-ounce) bars German sweet chocolate	2 tablespoons evaporated milk or cream
2 (3-ounce) packages cream cheese	2-2½ cups powdered sugar
	1 teaspoon vanilla

Melt chocolate over hot water in double boiler; cool slightly. In mixing bowl, combine chocolate and cream cheese; add milk and beat well. Beat in sugar gradually (adjust amount to produce good spreading consistency). Mix in vanilla.

Robert L. Pogyor

MAGIC CHOCOLATE SAUCE

Preparing: 10 minutes	*Do Ahead*	*Yield: 1½ cups*
Cooking: 10 minutes		

1 can sweetened condensed milk	⅛ teaspoon salt
2 (1-ounce) squares unsweetened chocolate	¼-½ cup hot water
	½ teaspoon vanilla extract

In top of double boiler, add milk, chocolate and salt. Cook over rapidly boiling water, stirring often, until thickened. Remove from heat. Slowly stir in hot water until sauce is of desired consistency. Stir in vanilla extract. Serve hot or chilled.

Pamela Petrella Winning

GINGERBREAD

Preparing: 15 minutes   *Do Ahead*   *Yield: 9 servings*
Baking: 45 to 55 minutes   *Freeze*

2 cups cake flour   **⅔ cup oil**
1½ teaspoons baking soda   **⅔ cup hot water**
½ teaspoon salt   **⅔ cup dark molasses**
1½ teaspoons cinnamon   **2 eggs**
2 teaspoons ginger   **⅔ cup sugar**

Preheat oven to 350°F. Sift flour, soda, salt, ginger and cinnamon. Add oil, water and molasses. Beat until a very smooth batter forms. In a separate bowl, beat eggs until thick and foamy. Gradually add sugar; continue beating until very well-blended. Fold egg and sugar mixture thoroughly into batter. Pour into greased, waxed paper lined 9-inch square pan. Bake 45-55 minutes or until it tests done; cool. Cut in squares and serve with whipped cream or lemon sauce.

Janet Stewart Watson

WHOLE WHEAT CARROT CAKE

Preparing: 20 minutes   *Do Ahead*   *Yield: One 9-inch layer cake*
Baking: 45 minutes   *Freeze*

2 cups sifted whole wheat flour   **2 cups sugar**
1 teaspoon baking powder   **1½ cups corn oil**
2 teaspoons baking soda   **2 cups finely grated carrots**
2 teaspoons cinnamon   **4 eggs**
1 teaspoon salt

Preheat oven to 300°F. Mix dry ingredients together. Add oil, carrots; beat in eggs, one at a time. Spread into 2 well-greased and floured 9-inch cake pans; bake 45 minutes. Cool 10 minutes; remove from pan and finish cooling. Frost if desired.

Note: May also be made in cupcake paper-lined muffin tins. Bake 15-20 minutes in preheated 325°F. oven.

Ann Keenan Seidel

FUNNEL CAKE

Preparing: 10 minutes   *Yield: Varies with size of cakes*

Vegetable oil
1 egg
⅔ cup milk
¼ teaspoon salt

2 tablespoons sugar
1⅓ cups sifted flour
¾ tablespoon baking powder
Powdered sugar

Pour fat or vegetable oil to measure 1½ inches deep in skillet or electric fry pan. Preheat to 375°F. Beat egg and add milk. Sift salt, sugar, flour and baking powder together. Add egg and milk mixture; beat until smooth. If batter is too thick, thin with milk. Pour batter into a funnel allowing batter to run out into fat making swirls from center out. Fry until golden brown on both sides; drain on paper. Sprinkle with powdered sugar and serve hot.

Ann Keenan Seidel

TEXAS SHEET CAKE

Preparing: 30 minutes   *Freeze*   *Yield: 10 to 12 servings*
Baking: 20 to 25 minutes

½ cup margarine
4 tablespoons cocoa
½ cup shortening
1 cup water
2 cups sugar

2 cups flour
1 teaspoon baking soda
2 eggs, beaten
½ cup buttermilk
1 teaspoon vanilla

Preheat oven to 350°F. Put margarine, cocoa, shortening and water in saucepan; bring to a boil. Remove from heat and pour into mixing bowl. Add sugar and flour; mix well. Add soda, eggs, buttermilk and vanilla; mix well. Pour into greased jelly-roll pan (15½x18½x1-inch or 9x13-inch cake pan) and bake 20-25 minutes. *Prepare icing in same saucepan while cake is baking.*

Icing.
½ cup margarine
4 tablespoons cocoa
⅓ cup milk
1 teaspoon vanilla
1 pound box powdered sugar,
   sifted

1 cup nuts, finely chopped (½ cup
   coconut or ½ cup
   marshmallows, optional)

Put margarine, cocoa and milk in saucepan. Bring to a boil, stirring constantly. Remove from heat immediately. Add vanilla, sugar and nuts. Stir all ingredients and spread over hot cake.

Gwen Fields Gilmore

JEWISH APPLE CAKE

Preparing: 30 minutes   Do Ahead   Yield: 12 to 16 servings
Baking: 1½ hours   Freeze

4 cups peeled, cored apples
2 tablespoons sugar
1 teaspoon cinnamon
2½ teaspoons vanilla
4 eggs

1 cup oil
½ cup orange juice
3 cups flour
2 cups sugar
3 teaspoons baking powder

Thinly slice apples; set aside. Mix 2 tablespoons sugar and cinnamon; set aside. Preheat oven to 350°F. Beat remaining ingredients (except apples and cinnamon-sugar) 10 minutes. Pour ½ batter in greased tube pan; add 2 cups apples. Sprinkle ½ cinnamon-sugar mixture. Pour in remaining batter; repeat apples and sugar. Bake 1½ hours.

Lucetta Bahn Ebbert

EVI'S POUND CAKE

Preparing: 20 minutes   Do Ahead   Yield: One 9x5-inch loaf cake
Baking: 1 hour 20 minutes   Freeze

1½ cups sugar
1 (8-ounce) package cream
   cheese, softened
¾ cup margarine, softened

1½ teaspoons vanilla
4 eggs
2 cups sifted cake flour
1½ teaspoons baking powder

Preheat oven to 325°F. Combine sugar, cream cheese, margarine and vanilla. Add eggs; mix at low speed until well-blended. Gradually add flour sifted with baking powder; blend well. Grease and flour 9x5 inch loaf pan (no smaller). Bake 1 hour and 20 minutes. Cool 5 minutes; remove from pan to finish cooling.

Edie and Ginger's
Wayne, Pennsylvania

SOUR CREAM FUDGE CHOCOLATE CHIP CAKE

Preparing: 10 minutes   *Do Ahead*   *Yield: 8 to 12 servings*
Baking: 50 to 60 minutes   *Freeze*

1 (18-ounce) package fudge cake   ½ cup warm water
   mix   4 eggs
1 package instant fudge pudding   1 teaspoon vanilla
   mix   1 (6-ounce) package chocolate
1 cup sour cream   chips
½ cup oil

Preheat oven to 350°F. Blend all ingredients, except chips, 5 minutes in mixer. Fold in chips; pour into greased bundt or angel food pan. Bake 50-60 minutes or until cake pulls away from sides of pan. *Do not underbake.* Cool in pan 15 minutes. Remove from pan and cool on rack. This may be served with whipped cream.

Dede Dubois Shimrak

CHOCOLATE ICE BOX CAKE

Preparing: 30 minutes   *Do Ahead*   *Yield: 12 servings*
Freezing: 6 hours or overnight   *Freeze*

6 eggs   1 teaspoon vanilla
10 ounces semi-sweet chocolate   5 dozen lady fingers
2 tablespoons powdered sugar   1 pint heavy cream, whipped
2 tablespoons boiling hot water   Chocolate Jimmies
1 tablespoon chocolate liqueur

Separate eggs and set aside. Melt chocolate over low heat; cool slightly. Add powdered sugar slowly, stirring to eliminate lumps. Add water, liqueur and vanilla. Cool; add egg yolks one at a time. Beat egg whites stiff; gradually fold into chocolate mixture until smooth and no white shows. Place lady fingers upright around side of springform pan; one layer on bottom of pan with flat sides down. Add half of chocolate mixture, another layer of lady fingers and remaining chocolate; top with lady fingers. Cover to make airtight with plastic or foil; freeze overnight or at least six hours. Several hours before serving, take from freezer and remove sides of springform pan; place in refrigerator at least several hours ahead. Close to serving time, whip cream; add ½ teaspoon powdered sugar. Place whipped cream in center of cake and spread until it touches edges of lady fingers. Sprinkle with Jimmies. Keep refrigerated until ready to serve.

Susan Johnson Mader

BITTERSWEET CHOCOLATE TWEED CAKE

Preparing: 1 hour   *Do Ahead*   *Yield: 12 to 16 servings*
Baking: 20 to 25 minutes

½ cup butter   1 cup milk
½ cup sugar   1 teaspoon vanilla
2 cups cake flour   3 squares baking chocolate
3 teaspoons baking powder   2 egg whites
Pinch salt   ½ cup sugar

Cream butter and ½ cup sugar thoroughly. Sift flour; measure and sift with baking powder and salt. Add dry ingredients to cream mixture alternately with milk combined with vanilla—beginning and ending with dry ingredients. After each addition, beat until smooth. Finely grate chocolate. Blend into batter. Beat egg whites until foamy; add ½ cup sugar, tablespoons at a time; beat until stiff. Carefully fold into batter. Pour into three 8-inch pans, or two 9-inch pans, greased and floured. Bake at 350°F. for 20-25 minutes or until toothpick inserted in center comes out clean. Cool slightly. Turn layers out of pans. Cool thoroughly on wire racks. Frost between layers and on top and sides with frosting.

Frosting:
¾ cup soft butter   2¼ cups sifted powdered sugar
3 egg yolks

Beat together butter and yolks. Blend powdered sugar into butter and egg mixture until smooth. Refrigerate cake to set frosting for a few minutes before drizzling topping.

Chocolate Topping:
3 ounces semi-sweet chocolate   2 tablespoons water
   chips

Melt chips in top of double boiler. Add water and stir until smooth. Cool slightly. Pour over top of cake, allowing small amount to drip down sides of cake.

Jeanne Kronmiller Honish

CHOCOLATE CHIP CHEESECAKE

Preparing: 30 minutes   *Do Ahead*   *Yield: 12 to 14 servings*
Baking: 1 hour 45 minutes
Chilling: 3 to 4 hours

3 pounds cream cheese, softened   ¾ cup sour cream
2¾ cups sugar   ¼ teaspoon vanilla
3 tablespoons cornstarch   ¾ cup grated semi-sweet
½ teaspoon salt   chocolate
6 eggs   1 lemon rind, grated
6 egg yolks   Juice of 1 lemon

Preheat oven to 425°F. Cream cheese until smooth. Add sugar, cornstarch and salt; mix until smooth. Gradually add eggs and yolks, scraping sides while mixing. Stir in remaining ingredients; blend to a smooth batter. Pour into greased 10-inch springform pan with sides 3 inches deep, which has been lined with graham cracker crust. Place cake pan into larger pan and fill with 1-inch of warm water. Bake at 425°F. 15 minutes. Remove from oven, reduce heat to 325°F. Return pan with cold water to oven. Continue baking 1½ hours or until knife inserted in center comes out clean. Cool in pan thoroughly, remove sides; chill.

Graham Cracker Crust:
1½ cups graham cracker crumbs   2 tablespoons sugar
2 tablespoons melted butter

Blend all ingredients; press firmly into bottom and sides of greased pan.

Gwen Fields Gilmore

CHOCOLATE CHEESECAKE

Preparing: 30 minutes   *Do Ahead*   *Yield: 16 servings*
Baking: 1 hour

Start with all ingredients at room temperature. Preheat oven to 350°F.

Crust:
1 (8½-ounce) package chocolate   ½ cup margarine
  ice box cookies, crushed   2 tablespoons sugar

Combine crumbs, margarine and sugar. Press over bottom and 2½ inches up sides of a 10-inch springform pan. Set aside—do not refrigerate.

Filling:

3 large eggs	1 teaspoon vanilla
1 cup sugar	1 cup sour cream
3 (8-ounce) packages cream	Dash salt
cheese	½ cup sour cream (garnish)
1½ cups chocolate chips, melted	

In a large bowl beat eggs and sugar at high speed until light and foamy (about one minute). Add cream cheese and beat at high speed until very smooth (4 minutes). Add melted chocolate chips, vanilla, sour cream and salt; beat at high speed until blended. Pour mixture into crust. Bake 1 hour or until cake is just firm when pan is shaken gently. Remove from oven and cool. Remove sides of springform pan when partly cool. Spread top with sour cream when completely cool.

Note: Do not worry if top of cake cracks while cooling.

Lois Rising Pogyor

WILSON CHEESECAKE

Preparing: 40 minutes	*Do Ahead*	*Yield: 12 to 16 servings*
Chilling: 1 hour	*Freeze*	
Baking: 1 hour 10 minutes		

Pastry:

1 cup flour	½ teaspoon vanilla
¼ cup sugar	1 egg yolk
1 teaspoon lemon juice	¼ cup butter

Mix all ingredients; refrigerate 1 hour. Preheat oven to 400°F. Grease bottom of springform pan; cover with ½ of pastry. Bake 8-10 minutes. Grease sides of pan; put remaining pastry ¾ up sides.

Cake:

5 (8-ounce) packages cream	1½ teaspoons lemon peel
cheese	¼ teaspoon vanilla
1¾ cups sugar	5 whole eggs and 2 extra yolks
3 tablespoons flour	¼ cup heavy cream

Preheat oven to 500°F. Blend cream cheese, sugar, flour, lemon peel and vanilla. Add eggs one at a time; beat well. Add cream. Bake 10 minutes; reduce oven to 250°F; bake 1 hour. Turn off oven; let cake stand 1 hour with door partly open. *Chill before serving.*

Patti Lord Frederick

OLD ORIGINAL BOOKBINDER'S
FABULOUS CHEESECAKE

Preparing: 20 minutes   *Do Ahead*   *Yield: 16 servings*
Baking: 1½ hours
Chilling: Overnight

Butter   **1 teaspoon vanilla**
Graham cracker crumbs   **¼ fresh lemon (juice and grated**
4 pounds cream cheese (room   **rind)**
temperature)   **Pinch of salt**
1 pound sugar   **Fresh strawberries (garnish)**
7 large eggs

Preheat oven to 325°F. Generously butter a 10-12 inch springform pan and sprinkle with graham cracker crumbs. Blend cream cheese and sugar together in large mixing bowl, beating until well combined. Add eggs and continue beating until smooth and creamy. Add lemon juice, rind, vanilla and salt; beat until well combined. Pour mixture into springform pan and place in a pan of hot water in oven. Bake 1½ hours or longer if necessary. Cake should be firm around the edges and soft in the center. Remove from oven, cool in pan. Let cake stand in refrigerator overnight before removing. Garnish cheesecake with large fresh strawberries.

The Old Original Bookbinder's Restaurant
Philadelphia, Pennsylvania

MINUTEMAN MACAROONS

Preparing: 5 minutes   *Do Ahead*   *Yield: 30*
Baking: 8 to 10 minutes

2⅔ cups flaked coconut   **1 teaspoon vanilla**
⅔ cup sweetened condensed milk

Preheat oven to 350°F. Combine ingredients and mix well. Drop from teaspoon 1-inch apart onto well-greased baking sheet or brown paper covered baking sheets. Bake 8-10 minutes or until lightly browned. Remove from oven and baking sheet *at once*.

Diane DelRossi Bakley

NO BAKE NAVINO BARS

Preparing: 40 minutes   Do Ahead   *Yield: 8 dozen*
Chilling: 20 to 30 minutes

Crust:
½ cup margarine, softened
¼ cup sugar
5 tablespoons cocoa
1 egg, beaten

1 teaspoon vanilla
2 cups graham cracker crumbs
1 cup shredded coconut
½ cup nuts, chopped

Place margarine, sugar, cocoa, vanilla and egg in top of double boile.. Set over *warm, not boiling water;* cook and stir until mixture resembles custard. Cook 5 minutes longer. Combine crumbs, coconut and nuts. Add cooked mixture; mix thoroughly. Pat into 9x13-inch cake pan tightly and evenly; refrigerate.

Filling:
2 tablespoons instant vanilla
   pudding
¼ cup margarine or butter

3 tablespoons milk
2 cups powdered sugar

Mix pudding, margarine and milk. Blend in sugar; beat well. Spread over chocolate mixture; return to refrigerator.

Topping:
1 (6-ounce) package chocolate
   bits

4 tablespoons butter or margarine

Melt chips with butter in top of double boiler; blend well. When like custard, spread over bars carefully. Return to refrigerator about 30 minutes. Cut into 1½-inch squares when topping is set but not hard.

Lois Rising Pogyor

CREAM CHEESE BROWNIES

Preparing: 30 minutes   *Do Ahead*   *Yield: 16 to 24*
Baking: 35 to 40 minutes

1 (4-ounce) package German sweet chocolate
5 tablespoons butter
1 (3-ounce) package cream cheese
1 cup sugar
3 eggs
½ cup + 1 tablespoon unsifted flour
1½ teaspoons vanilla
½ teaspoon baking powder
¼ teaspoon salt
½ cup chopped nuts
¼ teaspoon almond extract

Preheat oven to 350°F. Melt chocolate and 3 tablespoons butter over very low heat; cool. Cream 2 tablespoons butter with cream cheese. Gradually add ¼ cup sugar, beating until fluffy. Blend in 1 egg, 1 tablespoon flour and ½ teaspoon vanilla; set aside. In another bowl, beat 2 eggs until light colored. Slowly beat remaining ¾ cup sugar until mixture thickens. Add baking powder, salt and ½ cup flour. Blend in chocolate mixture, 1 teaspoon vanilla, nuts and almond extract. Spread half the chocolate mixture in greased 8 or 9-inch square pan. Top with cheese mixture. Carefully spoon on remaining chocolate batter. Zig-zag knife back and forth to marbelize. Bake 35-40 minutes.

Jeanne Kronmiller Honish

CHOCOLATE VANILLA WAFER BARS

Preparing: 15 to 20 minutes   *Do Ahead*   *Yield: 30 bars*
Chilling: 60 to 90 minutes   *Freeze*

2 cups crushed vanilla wafers
2 cups coarsely chopped pecans
1 can sweetened condensed milk
4 (1-ounce) semi-sweet chocolate squares
Powdered sugar

Heat chocolate until melted; add milk. Mix and heat until blended. Combine nuts and wafers; pour chocolate over wafers and nuts. Mix completely. Grease 8x10-inch cookie sheet. Pat mixture out with fingers; *refrigerate until hard.* Cut into thin strips and roll in powdered sugar.

Peggy Biglin Owen

CONGO BARS

Preparing: 20 minutes   *Do Ahead*   *Yield: 5 dozen*
Baking: 30 minutes

⅔ cup margarine, melted   ½ to 1 cup chocolate bits
1 (16-ounce) package brown sugar   2¾ cups flour
3 eggs   2½ teaspoons baking powder
½ to 1 cup nuts   ¼ teaspoon salt

Preheat oven to 350°F. Sift flour with baking powder and salt. Melt shortening
in large saucepan; stir in brown sugar. Cool slightly. Add eggs, one at a time,
beating well after each addition. Add flour mixture, nuts and chocolate bits;
blend well. Turn into greased 9x13-inch pan and bake 25-30 minutes; cool
and cut in squares.

Judy Lane Davies

GINGERBREAD COOKIES

Preparing: 30 minutes   *Do Ahead*   *Yield: 4 dozen*
Chilling: 1½ hours   *Freeze*
Baking: 15 minutes

⅔ cup packed light brown sugar   ½ teaspoon salt
⅔ cup dark corn syrup   1½ teaspoons baking soda
1 teaspoon ginger   ⅔ cup butter
1 teaspoon cinnamon   1 egg
½ teaspoon ground cloves   4 cups flour

Bring to boil sugar, corn syrup, spices and salt in large saucepan. Add soda
and butter; stir until butter melts. Quickly stir in egg; add flour and mix well.
Chill until firm enough to roll (about 1½ hours). Preheat oven to 325°F. Lightly
flour board; roll dough to ¼-inch thickness; cut with cookie cutter. Bake on
ungreased cookie sheet for 15 minutes.

Frosting:
1 egg white   1 cup plus 3 tablespoons
                                        powdered sugar

In small bowl beat egg white with powdered sugar until smooth. You may add
food coloring and a touch of cream of tartar to thicken for better decorating.

Harlene Galloway DeMarco

MARGUARITES

Preparing: 15 minutes   *Do Ahead*   *Yield: 30 petite muffins or*
Baking: 12 minutes   *Freeze*   *15 regular muffins*

2 eggs
1 cup brown sugar
½ cup flour
½ teaspoon salt

1 cup pecans, chopped (save
   some for decoration)
¼ teaspoon baking powder

Preheat oven to 350°F. Slightly beat eggs. Add ingredients in the order listed. Mix well and fill small buttered muffin tins ½-⅔ full. Place half a pecan on each. Bake until mixture begins to leave sides, about 8-12 minutes.

Sandra Schild Fletcher

NUT ROLLS

Preparing: 1 hour   *Do Ahead*   *Yield: 4 rolls*
Chilling: 5 hours   *Freeze*
Rising: 1 hour
Baking: 25 minutes

Pastry:
3 cups flour
½ teaspoon salt
1 cup margarine
½ cup warm milk

1 package dry yeast
2 tablespoons sugar
4 egg yolks, slightly beaten

Combine flour and salt; cut in margarine. In separate bowl, combine milk, yeast and sugar; let stand 5 minutes. Add yeast mixture to flour mixture; blend well. Add egg yolks to dough; mix well. *Refrigerate at least 5 hours or overnight.*

Filling:
4 egg whites
1 cup sugar

½ pound nuts, finely ground
Powdered sugar for rolling pastry

Beat egg whites and sugar until looks like marshmallow. Add nuts and stir gently. Divide dough into 4 parts. Roll out one at a time on powdered sugar. Spread nut mixture on rolled out dough; roll up jelly-roll fashion. Place seam-side down on baking sheets. *Stand 1 hour.* Preheat oven to 350°F. Bake 25 minutes. Remove from baking sheets; cool. To serve, cut into crosswise slices.

Linda Zajicek Moore

MACAROONS

Preparing: 15 minutes   Do Ahead   Yield 16 to 24
Baking: 30 minutes

½ pound almond paste   ½ teaspoon vanilla
¾ cup sugar   Scant ¼ teaspoon almond extract
2 ounces egg whites   Sugar
⅛ teaspoon salt

Preheat oven to 300°F. Blend all ingredients until smooth, using a food processor or electric mixer. Put into a decorating bag fit with an open or closed extra large star tip. Grease and flour a baking sheet or line it with parchment paper. Pipe out the cookies or if decorating bag unavailable, drop by teaspoonful. Sprinkle with sugar and bake 25-30 minutes. Allow to cool completely. *Store tightly covered, otherwise cookies will dry out quickly.*

Variation: Top each cookie with an almond or a piece of candied fruit before baking. Or add 2 ounces of finely grated bitter chocolate and the grated rind of one orange to the food processor before blending dough.

The Commissary
Philadelphia, Pennsylvania

CAPE COD OATMEAL COOKIES

Preparing: 20 minutes   Do Ahead   Yield: 5 dozen
Baking: 12 minutes   Freeze

1½ cups flour   ½ cup chopped nuts
1 teaspoon cinnamon   ½ cup shortening, melted
½ teaspoon baking soda   ½ cup margarine, melted
½ teaspoon salt   1 egg, slightly beaten
1¾ cups uncooked oatmeal   ¼ cup milk
1 cup sugar   1 tablespoon molasses
½ cup raisins

Preheat oven to 350°F. In large bowl, stir together flour, cinnamon, baking soda and salt. Stir in remaining ingredients. Drop by teaspoonsful 1½ inches apart on an ungreased cookie sheet. Bake 12 minutes or until edges are brown. Remove and cool.

Sandra Johnson McConnell

BUTTER PECAN TURTLE COOKIES

Preparing: 25 minutes   *Do Ahead*   *Yield: 3 to 4 dozen*
Baking: 20 minutes

Crust:
2 cups flour
1 cup packed brown sugar
½ cup softened butter

1¼ cups whole pecan halves
  or large pecan pieces
1 cup chocolate chips

Preheat oven to 350°F. In 3-quart bowl, combine flour, sugar and butter. Mix at medium speed until blended, about 2-3 minutes. Pat firmly into ungreased 13x9x2-inch pan. Sprinkle pecans evenly over unbaked crust. Prepare caramel layer; pour over pecans and crust. Bake 18-22 minutes or until caramel layer is bubbly and crust is light brown. Remove from oven. Immediately sprinkle with chips; allow chips to melt 2-3 minutes. Slightly swirl chips; *do not* spread chips. Cool completely; cut into 3-4 dozen bars.

Caramel Layer:
⅔ cup butter

½ cup brown sugar

In heavy 1-quart saucepan, combine brown sugar and butter. Cook over medium heat, stirring constantly, until entire surface of mixture begins to boil. Boil 1 minute, stirring constantly.

Dorothy O'Hara Eke

OATMEAL BARS

Preparing: 30 minutes   *Do Ahead*   *Yield: 24 bars*
Baking: 12 minutes

1 cup melted butter or margarine
2 cups oatmeal
½ cup brown sugar
¼ cup dark corn syrup
½ teaspoon salt

1½ teaspoons vanilla
6 ounces semi-sweet chocolate
  chips
¼ cup chopped nuts

Preheat oven to 450°F. Grease a 7x11-inch pan. Pour melted butter over oats in mixing bowl; add brown sugar, corn syrup, salt and vanilla. Mix well; pack firmly into pan. Bake 12 minutes or until a rich brown color. Partially cool in pan; turn out. Melt chocolate and spread over cake; sprinkle with chopped nuts. Let stand until chocolate is set. Cut into 24 bars.

Sandra Johnson McConnell

OATMEAL CAROB CHEWIES

Preparing: 10 minutes *Do Ahead* *Yield: 3 dozen*
Baking: 15 minutes

½ cup soft butter or margarine
3 tablespoons brown sugar
2 tablespoons beaten egg
½ cup whole wheat flour
½ cup rolled oats

¼ teaspoon baking soda
½ teaspoon cinnamon
1 tablespoon milk
¼ cup carob dots

Preheat oven to 350°F. Grease cookie sheets. In large bowl, combine butter and brown sugar; blend well. Add beaten egg and mix. Add flour, rolled oats, baking soda and cinnamon; mix well. Add milk and mix; add carob dots and mix again. Drop by spoonfuls onto cookie sheet, spacing about 1-inch apart. Bake 15 minutes.

Note: Store leftovers in airtight tin; do *not* refrigerate.

Gail Agerton Ebert

MOLASSES SUGAR COOKIES

Preparing: 1 hour *Do Ahead* *Yield: 3 dozen*
Chilling: 15 minutes
Baking: 10 minutes

¾ cup shortening
1 cup sugar
¼ cup molasses or dark corn
  syrup
1 egg
2 teaspoons baking soda

2 cups flour
½ teaspoon cloves
½ teaspoon ginger
1 teaspoon cinnamon
½ teaspoon salt

Melt shortening; cool. Add sugar, molasses and egg; beat well. Sift and add all dry ingredients. Mix well. Cover and chill 15 minutes. Preheat oven to 375°F. Roll into 1-inch balls and roll each one in granulated sugar. Place on greased cookie sheet about 1 inch apart. Bake 8-10 minutes. *Do not overcook!* These should be moist and chewy.

Elizabeth Taylor Young

COWBOY COOKIES

Preparing: 20 minutes   *Do Ahead*   *Yield: 5 to 6 dozen*
Baking: 10 minutes   *Freeze*

1 cup sugar
1 cup light brown sugar
1 cup shortening
2 eggs
1 teaspoon vanilla
2 cups flour

1 teaspoon baking soda
½ teaspoon salt
½ teaspoon baking powder
2 cups quick-cooking oatmeal
1 (12-ounce) package chocolate
  bits

Preheat oven to 350°F. Cream sugars and shortening together; add remaining ingredients and mix well. Drop by teaspoonsful onto ungreased cookie sheet. Bake 8-10 minutes. Remove from cookie sheet and cool.

Sandra Johnson McConnell

CHOCOLATE PEANUT BUTTER BARS

Preparing: 30 minutes   *Do Ahead*   *Yield: 4 dozen*
Baking: 20 to 25 minutes   *Freeze*

1 (18-ounce) package yellow
  cake mix
1 cup peanut butter
½ cup melted butter
2 eggs

1 cup chocolate chips
2 tablespoons butter
1 can sweetened condensed milk
1 package coconut pecan frosting
  mix

Preheat oven to 350°F. Stir cake mix, peanut butter, ½ cup melted butter and eggs together. Press ⅔ of mixture in a 9x13-inch pan. In a saucepan combine chips, 2 tablespoons butter and condensed milk over low heat until melted; add frosting mix. If mix is unavailable, substitute 1 cup coconut and ½ cup chopped pecans. Spread frosting over dough. Crumble remaining dough on top. Bake 20-25 minutes. Cool; cut into squares.

Margaret Quayle Bellew

PEPPERMINT PINWHEELS

Preparing: 45 minutes   Do Ahead   Yield: 5 dozen
Baking: 10 minutes   Freeze

2 cups sifted flour   1 egg yolk
½ teaspoon baking powder   1 teaspoon vanilla
½ teaspoon salt   ½ teaspoon peppermint extract
¾ cup butter   Few drops red food coloring
¾ cup sugar

Sift flour, baking powder and salt together. In large bowl, beat butter with sugar until fluffy; beat in egg yolk and vanilla. Stir in flour mixture, a third at a time, blending well after each addition, to make a soft dough. Divide dough in half; to half add peppermint extract and enough red food coloring to tint deep pink. *Chill briefly.* Roll out each color into a 16x10-inch rectangle, between sheets of waxed paper. Remove top sheet of waxed paper from pink dough. Place dough top-side down on plain dough; peel off paper. Roll up tightly, jelly-roll fashion. Wrap in waxed paper or foil; chill several hours until very firm. *(May freeze and take out of freezer half hour before cutting and baking.)* When ready to bake, preheat oven to 350°F. Unwrap and cut into ¼-inch slices with sharp knife; place on ungreased cookie sheets. Bake 10 minutes, or until cookies are firm, but not browned. Remove to wire racks; cool completely.

Lucetta Bahn Ebbert

COCONUT-GRANOLA BARS

Preparing: 15 minutes   Do Ahead   Yield: 2 dozen bars
Baking: 35 to 40 minutes

1 (17-ounce) package date   ½ teaspoon ground cinnamon
   quick-bread mix   1 egg
½ cup quick-cooking rolled oats   1 cup orange juice
½ cup flaked coconut

Preheat oven to 350°F. In a bowl, stir together bread mix, oatmeal, coconut and cinnamon. Beat egg and orange juice together. Stir into dry ingredients just until moistened. Spoon into greased and floured 11x7x1½-inch baking pan. Bake 35-40 minutes. Cool on wire rack. Cut into bars.

Catherine More Keller

CHOCOLATE CHIP COOKIES

Preparing: 15 minutes 　　*Do Ahead* 　　*Yield: 6 dozen*
Baking: 10 minutes 　　*Freeze*

1 cup butter
¾ cup sugar
1 cup light brown sugar
2 eggs
1½ teaspoons vanilla

2¼ cups flour
1 teaspoon baking soda
1 teaspoon salt
1 (12-ounce) package chocolate
　chips

Preheat oven to 350°F. Beat butter and 2 kinds of sugar; add eggs and vanilla. Beat well. Gradually add flour, baking soda and salt; mix well. Dough should be sticky. Add chocolate chips and mix. Drop dough from a teaspoon onto a greased cookie sheet. Bake 8-10 minutes.

Nancy DiSabatino D'Angelo

S'MORE COOKIES

Preparing: 20 minutes 　　*Do Ahead* 　　*Yield: 3 dozen*
Baking: 30 minutes

¾ cup sugar
1 large egg
½ cup soft butter
1½ teaspoons vanilla
1½ cups flour
1 teaspoon baking powder

1 teaspoon salt
1 (6-ounce) package chocolate
　chips
1 package miniature
　marshmallows

Preheat oven to 350°F. Beat butter, sugar, vanilla until fluffy; beat in egg. Sift flour, baking powder, salt and add to butter mixture. Spread half of dough in greased 9x9-inch pan. Press in chocolate chips, then marshmallows. Spread remaining half of dough mixture by teaspoonsful as evenly as possible. Bake 30 minutes. Cool and cut in squares.

Note: This recipe is easily doubled and baked in a 9x13 inch pan.

Gretchen Dome Hagy

LEMON SQUARES

Preparing: 30 minutes   *Do Ahead*   *Yield: 2½ dozen*
Baking: 1 hour

1 cup butter, softened   6 tablespoons lemon juice
½ cup powdered sugar   1 tablespoon flour
2 cups flour   ½ teaspoon baking powder
4 eggs   1 cup coarsely chopped pecans
2 cups sugar

Preheat oven to 325°F. Mix butter, powdered sugar and 2 cups flour; press into a 10x14-inch pan. Bake 15 minutes. Beat eggs slightly; add sugar, lemon juice, baking powder, pecans and 1 tablespoon flour. Pour over pastry. Bake 40-50 minutes. Dust with additional powdered sugar. Cut into squares.

Mary Murtagh Krull

WHOLE WHEAT SUGAR COOKIES

Preparing: 15 minutes   *Do Ahead*   *Yield: 2 dozen*
Baking: 8 to 10 minutes   *Freeze*

1 cup sugar   1 egg
1 teaspoon baking powder   1 tablespoon grated lemon
½ teaspoon salt   or orange rind
½ teaspoon baking soda   2 cups whole wheat flour
½ teaspoon nutmeg   1 cup chopped nuts
½ cup melted butter   2 tablespoons sugar
2 tablespoons milk   ½ teaspoon cinnamon
1 teaspoon vanilla

Preheat oven to 375°F. Combine all but last 4 ingredients. Stir in flour and nuts. Mix cinnamon and sugar in shallow dish. Shape dough into 1-inch balls and dip in cinnamon and sugar mixture. Place on ungreased cookie sheets; bake 8-10 minutes or until center is soft. Better to underbake if in doubt.

Elise Rice Payne

POTATO CHIP COOKIES

Preparing: 45 minutes   *Do Ahead*   *Yield: 4 dozen*
Baking: 12 to 15 minutes   *Freeze*

2 cups shortening or margarine   3 cups flour
  (or ½ margarine and ½ butter)   2 cups potato chips (crumbled
1 tablespoon vanilla   by hand)
1 cup sugar   1 cup pecan bits (optional)

Preheat oven to 350°F. Cream shortening, vanilla and sugar. Add flour, potato chips and pecans; mix. Drop by teaspoonful onto ungreased baking pan. Press down with fingers and bake 12-15 minutes. Carefully remove from pan and sprinkle with powdered sugar. *Freezes well.* Delicious short-bread type cookies with its own unique taste!

Carol Houston Robinson

PIZZELLE COOKIES

Preparing: 15 minutes   *Do Ahead*   *Yield: 5 dozen*
Cooking: At least 1 hour

6 eggs   2 tablespoons anise
1¾ cups sugar   3½ cups flour
1 cup butter, melted and cooled   1 teaspoon vanilla

Pizzelle iron must be used. Beat eggs; add sugar gradually. Beat until smooth. Add butter and anise. Add flour and vanilla. Dough will be sticky enough to be dropped from a spoon. Drop 1 teaspoon of batter onto iron and press closed 30 seconds. Remove cookie and allow to dry on flat surface. Pizzelles are best when thin and light. (They should not be golden brown.) Cookies taken off iron are very soft. Place on rack to cool and harden.

Variation: Spread favorite frosting on soft pizzelle and roll up.

Nancy DiSabatino D'Angelo

OATMEAL-RAISIN COOKIES

Preparing: 30 minutes   *Do Ahead*   *Yield: 3 dozen*
Soaking: 1 hour
Baking: 10 minutes

¾ cup margarine   ¼ teaspoon salt
1 cup sugar   1 teaspoon ginger
1 egg, beaten   1 teaspoon cinnamon
¼ cup molasses   1 cup quick-cook oatmeal
1½ cups flour   ⅔ cup raisins, soaked and drained
1 teaspoon baking soda

Earlier in day, cover raisins with water and soak 1 hour; drain thoroughly. Preheat oven to 325°F. Grease cookie sheets. Cream together margarine and sugar. Add molasses and beaten egg; blend in sifted dry ingredients, except oats. Add oatmeal and raisins; mix briefly. Drop by teaspoonsful onto greased cookie sheets. Bake 8-10 minutes.

Liz Nelson Mayer

SNICKERDOODLES

Preparing: 15 minutes   *Do Ahead*   *Yield: 5 dozen*
Chilling: 15 minutes   *Freeze*
Baking: 8 to 10 minutes

1 cup soft shortening   1 teaspoon soda
1½ cups sugar   ½ teaspoon salt
2 eggs   2 tablespoons sugar
2¾ cups flour   2-4 teaspoons cinnamon
2 teaspoons cream of tartar

Preheat oven to 400°F. Mix shortening, sugar, and eggs thoroughly. In separate bowl mix flour, cream of tartar, soda and salt. Stir into creamed mixture. Chill dough 15 minutes. Roll dough into small balls (walnut sized). Roll each ball in mixture of sugar and cinnamon. Place 2-inches apart on ungreased cookie sheet and bake for 8-10 minutes.

Susan Childs Carr

MINT BROWNIES

Preparing: 45 minutes   Do Ahead   Yield: 5 dozen
Baking: 15 minutes   Freeze

1 package Duncan Hines brownie
   mix
½ cup plus 6 tablespoons
   margarine

2 cups powdered sugar
2 tablespoons crème de menthe
   (green)
6 ounces chocolate chips

Preheat oven to 350°F. Follow instructions on box for brownies and bake *only 15 minutes* in a 11x16-inch jelly-roll pan. Refrigerate. Combine ½ cup softened margarine with powdered sugar and crème de menthe. Ice brownies and refrigerate. Melt 6 tablespoons margarine and chocolate chips together; mix thoroughly. Dribble or spread over iced brownies. Refrigerate; cut into small squares.

Margaret Quayle Bellew

SPRITZ COOKIES

Preparing: 15 minutes   Do Ahead   Yield: 3 dozen
Baking: 8 to 10 minutes   Freeze

1 cup butter
¾ cup sugar
1 teaspoon almond extract
1 egg

2½ cups sifted flour
½ teaspoon baking powder
¾ teaspoon salt

Cream butter and sugar until fluffy. Add almond extract and egg; beat well. Sift dry ingredients; add gradually to creamed mixture and mix well. Preheat oven to 400°F. Force through cookie press or place teaspoonful amounts on cookie sheet and press flat. Bake 8-10 minutes.

Note: Cookies can be decorated or served plain.

Mary Hofstetter Armstrong

STRAWBERRY CREAM CHEESE PIE

Preparing: 1 hour   *Do Ahead*   *Yield: 8 servings*
Chilling: 3 to 4 hours

1 envelope whipped topping mix   Strawberry Filling (see below)
1 (8-ounce) package cream cheese   9-inch graham cracker crust,
½ cup sugar   cooled

Prepare topping mix as directed on package. Beat cream cheese until soft; beat in sugar. Blend whipped topping into cream cheese mixture. Pour into crust, lining crust with mixture and mounding high at edges. Pour cooked strawberry filling into center of shell, leaving a rim of cream filling around edge of pie. Chill until set (at least 3 hours).

Strawberry Filling:
1 quart fresh strawberries, cleaned   1½ tablespoons cornstarch
½ cup sugar   1 tablespoon lemon juice

Wash and hull berries. Put aside 1½ cups whole berries. Mash remaining 1½ cups berries with ¼ cup plus 2 tablespoons sugar; let stand 30 minutes. Mix remaining 2 tablespoons sugar with cornstarch; add to mashed berries. Cook over moderate heat stirring constantly until mixture boils. Continue cooking until thick and clear (5-10 minutes). Stir in lemon juice. Allow to cool. Stir in reserved whole berries and pour into pastry shell as directed.

Note: This filling recipe can be doubled to make a fresh strawberry pie in a 9-inch pastry shell without the cream cheese filling.

Lois Rising Pogyor

COCONUT BUTTER CRUST

Preparing: 10 minutes   *Do Ahead*   *Yield: One 9-inch crust*
Baking: 15 to 20 minutes

2-3 tablespoons butter, melted   1½ cups shredded coconut

Preheat oven to 300°F. Combine butter and coconut in 9-inch pie pan. Spread and pat evenly over sides and bottom of pan, pressing firmly. Bake 15-20 minutes until just golden. *Use for chiffon pies or any light chocolate pie filling.*

Lois Rising Pogyor

PECAN PIE

Preparing: 20 minutes   *Do Ahead*   *Yield: One 9-inch pie*
Baking: 40 minutes

1 unbaked 9-inch pastry shell   ½ cup butter or margarine
1 cup granulated sugar   1½ teaspoons vanilla
½ teaspoon salt   2 cups coarsely chopped pecans
1 cup dark corn syrup   1 cup heavy cream, whipped or
3 eggs   vanilla ice cream

Preheat oven to 325°F. In saucepan combine sugar, salt and corn syrup. Simmer until sugar dissolves. Meanwhile, beat eggs foamy. Stir butter, vanilla and pecans into syrup. Add eggs; turn into pie shell. Bake 40 minutes; cool; refrigerate. Serve with whipped cream or vanilla ice cream (which we prefer).

Ginny Thornburgh
Wife of the Govenor of Pennsylvania

NO CRUST PECAN PIE

Preparing: 10 minutes   *Do Ahead*   *Yield: 6 servings*
Baking: 35 minutes   *Freeze*

3 egg whites   20 Ritz crackers, crushed
1 cup sugar   ½ cup chopped pecans
1 teaspoon vanilla

Preheat oven to 350°F. Beat egg whites until stiff. Add sugar and vanilla. Gently fold in pecans and crackers. Turn into greased 8-inch pie pan. Bake 35 minutes; chill. Before serving, prepare topping.

Topping:
½ pint heavy cream   1½ teaspoons instant coffee
3 teaspoons powdered sugar   ½ teaspoon vanilla

Whip cream; add sugar. Dissolve coffee in vanilla; add to cream. Spread on pie.

Gwen Fields Gilmore

PINEAPPLE CHEESE PIE

Preparing: 40 minutes   *Do Ahead*   *Yield: One 10-inch pie*
Baking: 1 hour

Crust:
6 tablespoons butter or margarine   1½ cups flour
4½ tablespoons sugar   1½ teaspoons baking powder
1 large egg

Cream butter and sugar; add egg and mix well. Add flour sifted with baking powder. Dough will be soft. Pat into deep 10-inch greased pie pan. Set aside.

Pineapple Filling:
1 (20-ounce) can crushed   2 tablespoons cornstarch
   pineapple

Drain some syrup from pineapple and mix with cornstarch, making sure all lumps are dissolved. Return to pineapple in saucepan blending well. Cook over medium heat until mixture boils, stirring constantly; continue cooking 1 minute. Remove from heat and spread over crust.

Cheese Filling:
1 (8-ounce) package cream cheese   Juice of ½ lemon
6 tablespoons sugar   1 teaspoon vanilla
2 tablespoons flour   1½ cups milk
2 eggs   Cinnamon

Preheat oven to 325°F. Mix cream cheese with sugar, adding 1 tablespoon at a time. Add eggs, one at a time, beating well after each addition. Add flour and milk, alternately, stirring well. Add vanilla and lemon juice; beat until very smooth. Pour into crust over pineapple filling. Sprinkle cinnamon on top. Bake 1 hour. Serve warm or cold.

RAISIN PIE

Preparing: 10 minutes *Do Ahead* *Yield: One 9-inch pie*
Chilling: 3 hours

1 cup raisins	1 cup Cool Whip, thawed
1 (6-ounce) package instant vanilla	1 teaspoon lemon juice
pudding	1/8 teaspoon cinnamon
2 cups milk	One 9-inch pastry shell, baked

Cover raisins with boiling water, set aside for 5 minutes; drain. Combine pudding mix and milk; blend well. Beat 1 minute. Fold in raisins, Cool Whip, lemon juice and cinnamon. Spoon mixture into pastry shell. Chill 3 hours.

Gretchen Dome Hagy

MILE HIGH STRAWBERRY PIE

Preparing: 30 minutes *Do Ahead* *Yield: 8 servings*
Freezing: 3 to 4 hours *Freeze*

9-Inch Pie Crust:

1½ cups graham cracker crumbs	½ teaspoon cinnamon
1/3 cup brown sugar	1/3 cup melted butter or margarine

Measure crumbs into medium bowl; toss with remaining ingredients until well mixed. With back of spoon, press mixture to bottom and side of 9-inch pie plate. *Do not bake.*

Filling:

1 (16-ounce) package frozen	½ cup sugar
strawberries	3 egg whites, room temperature
½ pint heavy cream	1 tablespoon lemon juice
1 teaspoon vanilla	Fresh strawberries (garnish)

Partially thaw strawberries. Whip cream, add vanilla; place in refrigerator. Place strawberries, sugar, egg whites and lemon juice in large mixing bowl. Beat 10-15 minutes at medium speed or until mixture is thick; fold in whipped cream with wooden spoon. Pile lightly into pie shell and place in freezer immediately. *Thaw in bottom of refrigerator 15 minutes before serving.* Garnish with fresh berries.

Lucetta Bahn Ebbert

MARBLED CHOCOLATE RUM PIE

Preparing: 1 hour   *Do Ahead*   *Yield: One 9-inch pie*
Chilling: 3 to 4 hours

1 envelope unflavored gelatin	¼ cup rum
1 cup sugar	12 ounces semi-sweet chocolate
⅛ teaspoon salt	chips
2 eggs, separated	1 cup heavy cream
1 cup milk	1 teaspoon vanilla extract
	1 9-inch pastry shell, baked

In top of double boiler mix gelatin, ¼ cup sugar and salt. Beat in egg yolks, milk and rum. Cook over boiling water, stirring constantly, until slightly thickened. Remove from heat; stir in chocolate until thoroughly blended. Chill until thickened but not set. Beat egg whites until foamy soft peaks form; gradually add ½ cup sugar beating until very stiff. Fold into chilled chocolate mixture. Whip cream with remaining ¼ cup sugar and vanilla until stiff. Alternate 2 mixtures in pie shell; swirl with spoon to achieve attractive swirled effect on top of pie. Chill until firm.

Pam Bartels Morris

FRENCH SILK PIE

Preparing: 30 minutes   *Do Ahead*   *Yield: 6 to 8 servings*
Chilling: 2 to 3 hours

½ cup butter	2 eggs
¾ cup sugar	1 8-inch baked pastry shell
1½ squares unsweetened	or graham cracker shell
chocolate, melted	1 cup heavy cream, whipped
1 teaspoon vanilla	

Cream butter and sugar, beating until light. Add melted chocolate and vanilla. Add 1 egg and beat 5 minutes (by the clock) at high speed. Add other egg and beat 5 minutes more. Pour into baked pastry shell or graham cracker crust and chill. Before serving, cover with whipped cream.

Note: Triple recipe yields two 9-inch pies.

Elizabeth Taylor Young

FISHERMAN'S APPLE PIE

Preparing: 45 minutes   *Do Ahead*   *Yield: One 10-inch pie*
Baking: 1 hour

Pastry for 10-inch pie

Filling:

1½ cups sour cream
1 large egg
1 cup sugar
¼ cup flour
2 teaspoons vanilla extract

½ teaspoon salt
2½ pounds McIntosh or similar
    apples, pared, cored and sliced
    (6 large or 9 small apples)

Preheat oven to 450°F. Line a 10-inch pie plate with pastry. Allow enough around edge to make a thick fluted rim. Combine sour cream, egg, sugar, flour, vanilla and salt in large bowl. Add sliced apples to mixture, stirring to coat. (Slice apples into the mixture as it retards the browning of the apples.) Turn filling mixture into pie shell just before placing in pre-heated oven. Bake for 10 minutes, then reduce heat to 350°F. for 35-40 minutes.

Topping:

6 tablespoons butter
1 tablespoon flour
⅓ cup white sugar
⅓ cup brown sugar

1 tablespoon cinnamon
¼ teaspoon salt
1 cup chopped walnuts

Meanwhile prepare topping by mixing all dry ingredients together. Melt butter and reserve. After the pie is baked, remove from oven and with a wooden spoon carefully stir the filling in the crust. Mix thoroughly but gently. Pour melted butter into dry ingredients of topping mixture and combine thoroughly. With your fingers, sprinkle mixture over top of pie so that it is covered evenly. Return pie to 350°F. oven and bake 15 minutes. Allow to cool before serving.

Columbia Hotel
Phoenixville, Pennsylvania

RICOTTA PIE

Preparing: 15 minutes   *Do Ahead*   *Yield: 6 servings*
Chilling: 4 hours

9-inch baked pastry shell
1 (3¾-ounce) package instant
  lemon pudding
1 (3¾-ounce) package instant
  vanilla pudding
1 cup heavy cream

2 cups sour cream
1 tablespoon lemon rind
3-5 tablespoons rum
1 pound ricotta cheese
1 small can mandarin oranges,
  drained (garnish)

Combine all ingredients except ricotta cheese and oranges until well blended. Fold in cheese. Put in cool pie shell; chill. Decorate with mandarin oranges before serving. *Best if made a day ahead.*

Regina Shehadi Guza

BLUEBERRY SOUR CREAM STREUSEL PIE

Preparing: 20 minutes   *Do Ahead*   *Yield: 8 servings*
Baking: 40 to 45 minutes

1 9-inch unbaked pastry shell
¾ cup sugar
2 tablespoons flour
1 egg
1¾ cup sour cream
1 teaspoon cinnamon

1 teaspoon vanilla
¼ teaspoon grated lemon rind
¼ teaspoon nutmeg
¼ teaspoon salt
3 cups fresh blueberries

Preheat oven to 350°F. Combine filling ingredients in order given. Fill pastry shell; bake 20 minutes. Remove pie from oven and stir up, bringing sides into center. Return to oven for 10 minutes; remove.

Streusel Topping:
⅓ cup white sugar
¼ cup brown sugar
½ cup flour

2 teaspoons cinnamon
½ cup very cold butter
½ cup coarsely chopped walnuts

Combine white and brown sugars, flour and cinnamon. Cut in butter. Toss with walnuts. Sprinkle streusel over pie and bake 10-15 minutes.

The Commissary
Philadelphia, Pennsylvania

MY FAVORITE DESSERT

Preparing: 30 minutes   *Do Ahead*   *Yield: 6 to 8 servings*
Chilling: 1 hour

Crust:
1 cup flour   1 cup chopped pecans
½ cup margarine

Preheat oven to 350°F. Combine ingredients. Press mixture into a 9-inch pie pan. Bake 15 minutes; cool completely.

Filling:
1 (8-ounce) package cream cheese   2 (3-ounce) packages *instant*
1 cup powdered sugar   French vanilla pudding mix
1 teaspoon vanilla   2 cups milk
1 (16-ounce) container Cool Whip   1 cup fresh strawberries

Mix cream cheese, powdered sugar, and vanilla. Fold 1 cup Cool Whip into cream cheese mixture; spread over cooled baked crust. Combine pudding mix with milk; beat 2 minutes. Pour over cream cheese layer. Top with remaining 2 cups Cool Whip. Place halved strawberries on top. *Refrigerate 1 hour or until ready to serve.*

Variation: Chocolate pudding may be substituted for vanilla; eliminate strawberries.

Nancy Lynch Rivenburgh

APPLE PIZZA PIE

Preparing: 30 minutes   *Do Ahead*   *Yield: 12 servings*
Baking: 30 minutes

1¼ cups flour, unsifted   ⅓ cup sifted flour
1 teaspoon salt   ¼ teaspoon salt
½ cup shortening   1 teaspoon cinnamon
1 cup shredded Cheddar cheese   ½ teaspoon nutmeg
¼ cup ice water   ¼ cup butter
½ cup powdered non-dairy   6 cups cored apples, cut into
   creamer   ½-inch wedges (skin on)
½ cup brown sugar   2 tablespoons lemon juice
½ cup sugar

Mix flour and salt; cut in shortening until crumbly. Add cheese; sprinkle ice water over mixture gradually. (May not need all the water.) Shape dough into a ball. Roll into a 15-inch circle on a floured surface. Place on baking sheet and turn up the edges. Preheat oven to 450°F. Combine dry ingredients. Sprinkle half this mixture over crust. Cut butter into remaining half until crumbly. Arrange apple slices, overlapping them, on crust. Sprinkle with lemon juice and remaining crumbs. Bake for 30 minutes or until apples are tender. Serve warm.

Ann Keenan Seidel

AMISH VANILLA PIE

Preparing: 30 minutes   *Do Ahead*   *Yield: One 9-inch pie*
Baking: 40 to 45 minutes

One 9-inch pastry shell, unbaked

Filling:
½ cup dark brown sugar   **1 beaten egg**
½ cup light corn syrup or light   **1 cup water**
** molasses**   **1 teaspoon vanilla**
1 tablespoon flour

In a saucepan combine ingredients; cook until thickened, stirring constantly (about 15 minutes).

Crumb Topping:
1 cup flour   **½ teaspoon baking soda**
½ teaspoon baking powder   **¼ cup shortening**
½ cup light brown sugar

Preheat oven to 375°F. Combine all ingredients; mix with pastry blender until crumb consistency. Put filling into pie shell and top with crumbs. Bake 40-45 minutes.

Dru Huber Hammond

SOUTHERN STRAWBERRY PIE

Preparing: 30 minutes   *Do Ahead*   *Yield: One 9-inch pie*
Chilling: 3 hours

¾ cup sugar
2 tablespoons cornstarch
2 tablespoons light corn syrup
1 cup water

3 tablespoons strawberry gelatin
1 quart fresh cleaned whole
 strawberries
One 9-inch baked pastry shell

Combine sugar, water, corn syrup and cornstarch in saucepan; bring to boil. Cook, stirring constantly, until clear and thickened. Add gelatin, stirring until dissolved; cool until partially thickened. Place strawberries in pastry shell flat end down; pour in gelatin mixture. Chill until firm.

Variation: ¼ cup sugar may be substituted for 2 tablespoons corn syrup. Pie may be garnished with whipped cream. (Use 1 cup heavy cream and 1 tablespoon powdered sugar.) A piped lattice pattern and fluted edge make a particularly nice garnish.

Barbara Sue Massengale Brodie

PAT NIXON'S PUMPKIN PIE

Preparing: 20 minutes   *Do Ahead*   *Yield: 8 servings*
Baking: 55 minutes

1 unbaked 10-inch pastry shell
1¼ cups sugar
5 tablespoons plus 1 teaspoon
 flour
Pinch salt
½ teaspoon allspice
⅓ teaspoon ginger

1 (16-ounce) can pumpkin
4 eggs
3 cups milk
1¼ teaspoons vanilla
1 teaspoon molasses
2 tablespoons plus 2 teaspoons
 melted butter

Preheat oven to 375°F. Line unbaked pie crust with brown paper to come up sides. Fill center with uncooked rice or beans (to weight down); bake 15 minutes. Meanwhile, blend sugar, flour, salt, allspice and ginger. Stir in pumpkin; beat in eggs. Blend milk and vanilla thoroughly into mixture; stir in molasses and melted butter. Remove paper and rice from pie shell; pour in pumpkin filling. Bake 40 minutes, until custard is set.

SHOO-FLY PIE

Preparing: 15 minutes　　　*Do Ahead*　　　*Yield: Two 8-inch pies*
Baking: 40 minutes

4 cups flour	**2 cups hot water**
2 cups sugar	**1 teaspoon baking soda**
1 cup shortening	**1 cup dark baking molasses**
1 teaspoon salt	

Preheat oven to 350°F; grease pie pans. Mix flour, sugar, shortening and salt together to make crumbs. In large bowl blend hot water, soda and molasses. (It will foam.) Starting with crumb mixture, alternate layers of mixed ingredients; top layer should be crumbs. Bake 40 minutes until toothpick comes out fairly clean.

Meredith Herting Swift

ANGEL PIE

Preparing: 30 minutes　　　*Do Ahead*　　　*Yield: 6 to 8 servings*
Baking: 40 minutes
Chilling: 3 hours

4 egg whites	**Pinch salt**
½ teaspoon cream of tartar	**1 cup sugar**

Preheat oven to 300°F. Beat whites until frothy; sprinkle in cream of tartar and salt and beat until stiff. Beat in sugar, 2 tablespoons at a time until glossy and stands in stiff peaks. With back of tablespoon spread meringue in well-greased 9-inch pie pan pushing it high on sides so that it resembles pie shell. Bake 40 minutes. Cook on rack. Fill shell with filling and chill several hours.

Filling:
4 egg yolks	**3 tablespoons lemon juice**
½ cup sugar	**½ pint heavy cream**
Grated peel of 2 lemons	

Beat egg yolks and sugar in top of double boiler until lemon colored. Stir in lemon peel and juice; cook over hot water until thick, stirring constantly (about 8-10 minutes). Chill. Whip cream and fold into chilled mixture.

Jeanne Kronmiller Honish

DAISYFIELD'S COFFEE PIE

Preparing: 1 hour   *Do Ahead*   *Yield: 6 servings*
Chilling: 1 to 2 hours

½ cup water   Pinch of salt
2 tablespoons instant coffee   ¼ teaspoon nutmeg
  powder   1 cup finely chopped nuts
½ pound marshmallows   1 cup heavy cream
2 egg yolks, slightly beaten   9-inch baked crumb crust
1 teaspoon vanilla

Combine water, instant coffee and marshmallows in top of double boiler. Heat over hot water, stirring occasionally, until marshmallows melt; add to egg yolks slowly. Return to double boiler; cook and stir 1 or 2 minutes. Stir in vanilla, salt and nutmeg. *Chill until mixture begins to set.* Beat smooth; fold in nuts. Whip cream; fold in marshmallow mixture. Pour into cooled pie shell; chill. If desired, garnish with additional whipped cream.

Frances Marincola Blair

FROZEN LIME PIE

Preparing: 30 minutes   *Do Ahead*   *Yield: 6 servings*
Freezing: 4 to 6 hours   *Freeze*

8 or 9-inch graham cracker crust   1 cup whipped cream (Cool Whip
  (or crust of your choice)   works well, too)
3 eggs, separated   2 teaspoons grated lime rind
½ cup sugar   ¼ cup lime juice

Beat egg whites until frothy; gradually add sugar. Beat until stiff and glossy. Beat egg yolks until thick and lemon colored. Fold into egg white mixture. Fold rind and juice into egg mixture along with whipped cream. Pour into crust and freeze. Decorate with slices of citrus. Lemon rind and lemon juice may be substituted for lime rind and lime juice to make a Frozen Lemon Pie.

Pam White Brotschul

COFFEE SUNDAE PIE

Preparing: 20 minutes   *Do Ahead*   *Yield: 8 to 10 servings*
Freezing: 1 hour   *Freeze*

22-25 chocolate wafer cookies   1 (6-ounce) package semi-sweet
  (1½ cups crushed)   chocolate chips
6 tablespoons melted butter   1 (6-ounce) can evaporated milk
1 quart coffee ice cream

Crush cookies. Mix with melted butter; press into bottom and sides of *greased* 10-inch pie pan. Refrigerate until firm. Soften ice cream slightly. Turn into pie shell and freeze until firm. Melt chocolate chips over hot water. Slowly add milk, stirring constantly. Simmer a few minutes; let cool. When ice cream is firm, remove from freezer, spread chocolate over ice cream and return to freezer.

Pam Bartels Morris

PECAN TARTS

Preparing: 20 to 25 minutes   *Do Ahead*   *Yield: 24 to 36 miniature tarts;*
Cooking: 5 minutes   *12 medium tarts*
Baking: 15 minutes

Tarts:
½ cup margarine   1 teaspoon almond extract
½ cup sugar   2 cups sifted flour
2 egg yolks

Preheat oven to 450°F. Mix ½ cup margarine and ½ cup sugar well. Add egg yolks, almond extract and sifted flour. Press firmly into tiny fluted tart pans or miniature muffin tins about 1-inch in diameter. Bake 8-10 minutes.

Filling:
½ cup margarine   1 cup chopped pecans
⅓ cup dark corn syrup   Pecan halves to top each tart
1 cup powdered sugar   (optional)

Turn oven down to 350°F. In medium saucepan melt margarine; mix in syrup and powdered sugar and bring to a boil. Stir in chopped pecans. Spoon mixture into shells; top with pecan halves. Bake 5 minutes.

Liz Nelson Mayer

CRANBERRY TARTS

Preparing: 30 minutes   Do Ahead   Yield: 24
Baking: 20 minutes   Freeze

Pastry:
½ cup margarine, softened   1 cup flour
1 (3-ounce) package cream
  cheese, softened

Mix margarine and cream cheese; add flour and blend. Divide pastry into 24 pieces and push into greased mini-tart pans.

Filling:
72 cranberries, washed and   1 teaspoon vanilla
  drained   2 tablespoons soft butter
1 egg   ½ cup chopped nuts
¾ cup sugar

Preheat oven to 325°F. Place 3 cranberries in each cup. Mix remaining ingredients. Spoon 1 teaspoonful in each cup. Bake 20-25 minutes; cool 10-15 minutes in pan. Remove tarts from pan, using knife to help release.

Alice Marks Preston

FROZEN BRANDY ALEXANDER PIE

Preparing: 10 minutes   Do Ahead   Yield: 6 to 8 servings
Freezing: 4 to 6 hours

1 (9-inch) graham cracker crumb   2 tablespoons crème de cacao
  crust   2 tablespoons brandy
1 (14-ounce) can sweetened   Shaved chocolate (garnish)
  condensed milk
1 cup heavy cream, whipped

In large bowl, combine sweetened condensed milk, whipped cream, crème de cacao and brandy. Pour into prepared crust; freeze 4-6 hours until firm. Garnish with shaved chocolate. *Return unused pie to freezer after serving.*

Regina Shehadi Guza

CREAM CHEESE TARTS

Preparing: 25 minutes *Do Ahead* *Yield: 48 mini tarts*
Baking: 15 minutes *Freeze* *or 18 muffin size tarts*

Crust:
2¼ cups graham cracker crumbs   1½ tablespoons cinnamon
3 tablespoons sugar   ¾ cup butter, melted

Line tart pans with paper cups. Toss crumbs, sugar and cinnamon together. Blend in melted butter. Line base of paper liner with crust mixture, pressing firmly; set aside. For a quick and easy base, a vanilla wafer may be used in place of crumb mixture.

Filling:
2 (8-ounce) packages cream   2 teaspoons vanilla
   cheese   Sour cream topping (optional)
2 eggs   1 jar or can cherry pie filling
1 cup sugar   or Nectarine Glaze

Preheat oven to 350°F. Beat together cream cheese, eggs, sugar and vanilla. Fill tins full with cheese mixture. Bake 10-12 minutes. Remove from oven; top with sour cream topping. Bake 5 minutes more; cool. Top each tart with about 1 teaspoon cherry pie filling or nectarine glaze; refrigerate. Tarts can be frozen before adding topping.

Sour Cream Topping:
1 cup sour cream   2 tablespoons sugar
½ tablespoon vanilla

Blend ingredients and top tarts as directed.

Nectarine Glaze:
½ cup sugar   ½ cup boiling water
1 rounded tablespoon cornstarch   1½ tablespoons peach gelatin
Pinch salt   Sliced nectarines

Mix sugar, cornstarch and salt together; add water and mix. Bring to a boil and cook, stirring constantly, until clear. Remove from heat; add peach gelatin. Let cool; add sliced nectarines or peaches. Top cheesecake tarts; chill until firm.

Gail White Dillon

BLUM'S COFFEE TOFFEE PIE

Preparing: 45 minutes   *Do Ahead*   *Yield: One 10-inch pie*
Baking: 10 minutes
Chilling: 12 hours

Pie Crust:
½ (10-ounce) package pie crust
  mix
¼ cup brown sugar
¾ cup finely chopped walnuts

1 square unsweetened chocolate,
  grated
1 teaspoon vanilla
1 tablespoon water

Preheat oven to 400°F. Combine all ingredients. Push into pie pan with fingers to make smooth. Bake 10 minutes; cool.

Filling:
½ cup soft butter
¾ cup sugar
1 (1-ounce) square unsweetened
  chocolate, melted

2 teaspoons instant coffee
2 eggs

Beat butter until creamy; gradually add sugar. Blend in cooled chocolate and coffee. Add 1 egg, beat 5 minutes. Add remaining egg, beat another 5 minutes. Put in cooled crust. *Refrigerate overnight.*

Coffee Topping:
2 cups heavy cream
2 teaspoons instant coffee

¼ cup powdered sugar

Whip cream, adding coffee and sugar, until just stiff. Cover pie and garnish with chocolate curls. Chill until serving time.

PÂTE BRISÉE

Preparing: 15 minutes   *Do Ahead*   *Yield: One 9-inch crust*
Chilling: 1 to 2 hours
Baking: 15 minutes

1 cup flour, sifted
4 tablespoons butter
1½ tablespoons vegetable
   shortening

2-3 tablespoons cold water
¼ teaspoon salt
Pinch sugar or 1 tablespoon sugar
   for sweeter crust

Place flour, butter, shortening, salt and sugar in bowl. Rub flour and fat together rapidly between fingers until mixture resembles meal, or cut in with pastry blender. Add water; blend quickly until dough just holds together and is pliable. Place on floured board; press pastry down and away to blend fat and flour. Gather into a ball; wrap in waxed paper and refrigerate 1-2 hours. Roll out dough quickly on floured board. Lift into 9-inch flan or cake pan; trim. Prick bottom and sides with fork. Line with foil and fill with rice or dried beans. Preheat oven to 400°F. Bake 8-9 minutes; remove foil and beans; bake 5 minutes longer until crust just starts to color. This is a nice crust for fruit tarts and cold fruit pies.

Ann Adams Ledger

LEMON CHESS PIE

Preparing: 30 minutes   *Do Ahead*   *Yield: 6 servings*
Baking: 45 minutes

3 eggs
1 cup sugar
¼ cup butter or margarine,
   softened

Juice of 2 lemons
8-inch unbaked pastry shell
½ pint heavy cream, whipped

Preheat oven to 325°F. Beat eggs until frothy. Add sugar, butter and lemon juice; pour into unbaked pastry shell. Bake 45 minutes; cool. Before serving, top with whipped cream.

Mary Jo Quinerly Jefferson

BASIC PASTRY

Preparing: 15 minutes   *Do Ahead*   *Yield: One 9-inch crust*
Baking: 10 to 15 minutes *Freeze*

1⅓ cups flour   **½ cup shortening**
½ teaspoon salt   **3 tablespoons cold water**

Preheat oven to 425°F. Combine flour and salt in mixing bowl. With pastry blender (or 2 knives), cut shortening into flour until uniform coarse meal is formed. Sprinkle with water; a little at a time, tossing gently with a fork. Work dough into a firm ball with hands. Press dough into flat circle. Roll between 2 sheets of floured waxed paper or on a lightly floured surface until a circle 1½ inches larger than inverted pie pan is formed. Gently ease pastry into pie pan, being careful not to stretch it. Trim to ½ inch beyond edge of pie plate; fold under to make a double thickness and flute edges. If baking without filling, prick bottom and sides with fork. Bake 10-15 minutes.

Variation: For double crust pie, use 2 cups flour, ¾ cup shortening, 1 teaspoon salt and ¼ cup water.

Note: To keep bottom crust from getting soggy, center pie on cookie sheet and bake in preheated oven.

Lois Rising Pogyor

BASIC CRUMB CRUST

Preparing: 10 minutes   *Do Ahead*   *Yield: One 9-inch crust*
Baking: 8 minutes

1⅔ cups graham cracker crumbs   **⅓ cup margarine or butter,**
   or chocolate wafer crumbs   **melted**
¼ cup sugar

Preheat oven to 375°F. Combine crumbs and sugar; add margarine; blend well. Pour into 9-inch pie pan; press crumbs evenly over sides and bottom of pan. Bake 8 minutes; cool before filling.

Optional: Chill in refrigerator 30 minutes instead of baking for a softer crust.

Lois Rising Pogyor

CHOCOLATE RUM TART

Preparing: 45 minutes   *Do Ahead*   *Yield: One 10-inch tart*
Baking: 35 minutes
Chilling: 1 to 2 hours

6 whole eggs	**¼ cup plus 3 tablespoons**
¾ cup plus 2 tablespoons sugar	**cornstarch**
1 cup cake flour	**2 tablespoons melted butter**
¼ cup cocoa powder	**1 teaspoon vanilla extract**

Preheat oven to 350°F. Whip eggs and sugar until mixture is light and fluffy. Concentrate on one side of bowl and you will notice the constant rise of mixture as it absorbs air. When mixture has absorbed all the air it can take, it begins to fall below the previous mark it has made. Mixture is now ready for flour. Sift flour, cocoa and cornstarch; fold into creamed mixture. Fold butter and vanilla into batter. Pour into greased and floured deep 10-inch cake pan. Bake until cake center springs back to the touch (about 35-40 minutes). Allow cake to cool. Cut into 3 layers. Spread filling between layers and over top.

Filling:

1 pint heavy cream	**2 ounces dark rum**
½ cup butter	
16 ounces semi-sweet chocolate	
bits	

Bring cream and butter to boil; remove from heat. Add chocolate and stir until dissolved. Pour into pan; refrigerate until firm. When firm, place in top of double boiler; heat slightly over warm water. Mix on low speed to desired spreading consistency. Slowly add dark rum. If mixture begins to break or is too hard to work, heat a little more. If you overheat it, and it is too soft to work with, rechill it and begin again.

Dickens Inn
Philadelphia, Pennsylvania

ALMOND TOFFEE

Preparing: 15 minutes   Do Ahead   Yield: 6 to 7 dozen pieces
Cooking: 15 minutes
Cooling: 1 hour

1 cup butter
1 cup sugar
1 cup unblanched almonds

3-4 ounces semi-sweet chocolate
  chips

In frying pan over medium heat, blend butter, sugar and almonds. Stirring constantly, cook until skins start to loosen and candy becomes light brown. (If candy is light brown, do not wait for almonds.) Pour into 9x13-inch pan or jelly-roll pan. Cool a minute or so until candy begins to firm. Top with chocolate chips; with rubber spatula spread to melt and form a thin layer of chocolate. Chill until set; break into pieces.

Vickie Spatola Letulle

ROCKY ROAD CANDY

Preparing: 30 minutes   Do Ahead   Yield: 9 dozen pieces
Chilling: 8 hours or overnight

1 pound milk chocolate
1 tablespoon vegetable oil
  (or cocoa butter)
½ pound large marshmallows

1 cup lightly toasted walnuts,
  broken
Marshmallows and walnuts
  (garnish), optional

Combine chocolate and oil in top of double boiler. Heat over hot water until chocolate melts (microwave on high for 3 minutes). Cut marshmallows in half. Butter 9x13-inch baking pan; spread half of chocolate in bottom of pan. Sprinkle with marshmallows and nuts; spread remaining chocolate over marshmallows. Place reserved garnish on top. Cool overnight or at least 8 hours. Cut into inch squares with oiled knife.

Mary Lou Kerigan Batchelder

PEANUT BUTTER FUDGE

Preparing: 25 minutes   *Do Ahead*   *Yield: 6 dozen*

4½ cups sugar
¼ cup butter
1 (13-ounce) can evaporated milk
1 (7-ounce) jar marshmallow fluff

2 (12-ounce) packages chocolate
chips
1 (12-ounce) jar peanut butter

In saucepan combine sugar, butter and milk; boil 7 minutes, stirring constantly. Remove from heat; add marshmallow fluff, chocolate chips and peanut butter. Beat until thick and creamy. Pour into two greased 8-inch square pans until set. Cut into squares.

Madeline Dilkus Henne

RADNOR MIDDLE SCHOOL BUCKEYES

Preparing: 1 hour   *Do Ahead*   *Yield: 8 to 10 dozen*
Chilling: 1 hour   *Freeze*

2 cups peanut butter (plain
or chunky)
1 pound powdered sugar
1 cup margarine, melted
and cooled

1 (12-ounce) package chocolate
bits
½ sheet paraffin wax, grated

Sift sugar, add to peanut butter, ½ cup at a time. Using fork, mix by hand. Add margarine and knead until well-blended; chill. Shape into balls the size of buckeyes (large marbles). Chill. Over low heat, melt chocolate bits and paraffin in double boiler. Using a toothpick to hold balls, dip into melted chocolate. Leave one spot of peanut butter mixture showing. Place on plate or tray lined with waxed paper to dry.

Note: Do not let chocolate mixture get too hot while dipping. Keep water hot but not boiling. If you don't want to use paraffin, refrigerate candy.

Whit Beverly

CARAMELS

Preparing: 20 minutes   Do Ahead   Yield: 12 dozen
Chilling: 3 hours

½ cup butter or margarine   1 cup sweetened condensed milk
1½ cups light corn syrup   1 teaspoon vanilla
2 cups sugar   ½ cup chopped nuts (optional)

Melt butter in 2-quart saucepan. Add remaining ingredients and mix. Stir constantly over low heat until mixture comes to a full boil. Boil 12 minutes, stirring occasionally. Remove from heat; add 1 teaspoon vanilla. Pour into two greased 9-inch pie tins. (If you want half plain and half with nuts, pour half caramel mixture into one pie tin, stir nuts into remaining mixture in saucepan and pour into remaining pie tin.) Cool until firm. Cut into 1-inch squares and wrap with waxed paper.

Lois Rising Pogyor

MAMIE'S MILLION DOLLAR FUDGE

Preparing: 30 minutes   Do Ahead   Yield: 6 dozen

4½ cups sugar   3 (4-ounce) bars German sweet
2 tablespoons butter   chocolate
⅛ teaspoon salt   1(7-ounce) jar marshmallow
1 (13-ounce) can evaporated milk   cream
1 (12-ounce) package semi-sweet   2 cups chopped nuts
  chocolate bits

Bring sugar, salt, butter and evaporated milk slowly to a boil; boil 6 minutes. Put chocolate bits, German chocolate pieces, marshmallow cream and nuts in a bowl; pour over *boiling* syrup. Beat until chocolate is melted; pour in 13x9x2-inch lightly buttered pan. Let stand a few hours before cutting. Store in tin box or tightly covered container.

Note: Fudge is better the second day.

LELLY'S BELLY-BUTTONS

Preparing: 1½ hours   *Do Ahead*   *Yield: 6 to 8 dozen*
                              Freeze

⅓ (1-pound) box graham crackers, crushed
¾-1 (1-pound) box powdered sugar
1 cup chopped nuts
2 cups peanut butter (not all-natural)

1 teaspoon vanilla
1 cup margarine, melted
1 (6-ounce) package chocolate chips
½ sheet of paraffin wax

Mix graham cracker crumbs, sugar and nuts. Add peanut butter, vanilla and margarine. Stir by hand; refrigerate. When firm, roll into balls; refrigerate again. Melt chips and wax in top of double boiler over medium heat. Dip peanut butter balls half-way into chocolate by using toothpick. Keep in refrigerator or freeze.

Note: These can be made without the wax but are less stable and should be refrigerated.

Cathy Crowl Mentzer

FRENCH CHOCOLATES

Preparing: 10 minutes   *Do Ahead*   *Yield: 1½ pounds*

1 (12-ounce) package semi-sweet chocolate pieces
1 cup chopped walnuts
¾ cup sweetened condensed milk

1 teaspoon vanilla
Dash salt
Chopped coconut, chopped walnuts, or chocolate sprinkles

Melt chocolate pieces in double boiler over hot, not boiling, water. Stir in nuts, milk, vanilla and salt. Cool about 5 minutes, until easy to shape into 1-inch balls. Roll balls into chopped coconut, walnuts or chocolate sprinkles.

Judy Lane Davies

CHOCOLATE COVERED STRAWBERRIES

Preparing: 25 minutes   *Do Ahead*   *Yield: 8 servings*
Marinating: 3 hours

2 pints strawberries   12 ounces semi-sweet chocolate
¼ cup sugar   chips
½ cup rum, brandy or Cognac

Wash strawberries. Mix liqueur and sugar; add strawberries and marinate 3 hours. Drain fruit and pat dry. Melt semi-sweet chocolate chips and dip fruit into chocolate. Refrigerate.

Note: Pass as a side dish with a plain dessert such as pound cake.

Gail White Dillon

COCONUT EGGS

Preparing: 1 hour   *Do Ahead*   *Yield: 3 dozen*
Chilling: 1 to 2 hours

1 pound box powdered sugar   1 teaspoon vanilla
½ cup butter   1 (12-ounce) package chocolate
3 ounces cream cheese   chips
14 ounces coconut (or peanut   ½ bar grated paraffin wax
   butter)

Cream sugar, butter, cream cheese, coconut and vanilla. Form mixture into 1-inch balls, then press into egg shapes. Refrigerate on waxed paper 1-2 hours. Heat chocolate and wax over double boiler. Dip eggs one at a time in chocolate. (May use a toothpick.) Put on waxed paper to harden.

Variation: In place of butter and cream cheese, use 6 tablespoons melted butter, 1 egg, 3 tablespoons evaporated milk. Mix with sugar, coconut and vanilla as directed. Melt chocolate chips without paraffin and dip. Store in refrigerator.

Sarah Gist Jerrell

Microwave and Processor

Berwyn Station
Berwyn, Pa.

Joan Curtis
© 1978

Berwyn

Cockletown grew from a few isolated farms into a thriving community of log cabins as travel increased along the old Indian trail, known as Conestoga Road. With the completion of the Lancaster Turnpike, numerous taverns and businesses developed to meet the needs of wagon drivers carrying produce and merchandise between Lancaster and Philadelphia. Cockletown later became known as Reesville.

The arrival of the railroad lessened the importance of roads but increased community growth and pride. A local Welsh settler suggested the name change to Berwyn after the Berwyn Hills overlooking the River Dee in Wales. Local citizens also petitioned the Pennsylvania Railroad to build a "pretty and varied" new depot as commuter traffic increased.

After an Evening Paddle Tennis Game

hors d'oeuvre
Mini Cheese Quiches

entrée
Oven Beef Burgundy

salad
Green and White Salad Bowl

bread
Beer Bread

dessert
Cowboy Bars

beverage
Brandied Hot Chocolate

Time is a precious commodity in the life of today's busy woman and new kitchen appliances geared to saving it are appearing every day. As these new appliances appear, there is usually a cookbook of wonderful recipes enclosed in the box. We all enjoy trying new recipes and adding them to our repertoire. However, we don't want to give up using our family's favorites, our "classics," simply because we don't know how to utilize them using the new appliances. Hoping to bridge that gap, this chapter is dedicated to helping you adapt your favorite recipes to two of the most time-efficient appliances on the market today—the microwave oven and the food processor.

MICROWAVE OVENS

Microwave ovens vary greatly as to wattage, power settings and accessory features; therefore, it is difficult to give exact rules for adapting recipes. Use the following hints as a guide as you experiment to find out what works best for your particular oven.

First of all determine what is to be done to the food. (Defrost? Cook? Reheat?) Second, examine what the food is like and how much is being cooked. (How dense is it? How sensitive is the food to microwaves?)

To utilize the answers to these questions it will help to understand certain basic facts about microwave cooking:

1) Fat, sugar and liquid attract microwaves causing molecules to vibrate; these rapidly moving molecules in turn cause others to vibrate and thus produce heat. Because the cooking/heating takes place through this chain reaction of vibrating molecules, cooking continues to take place AFTER the food is removed from the microwave oven. This is important to understand to prevent overcooking.

2) Heat is produced by vibrating molecules, thus porous food like bread heats more quickly than dense food such as meat. Dense foods take longer to heat because penetration of microwaves is slower and some cooking toward center of food takes place by conduction of heat.

3) Foods absorb the microwave energy, thus the cooking time will increase only slightly as the volume of food increases (one egg will cook faster than two).

4) Covering food being microwaved traps steam and hastens cooking.

5) Some ingredients are particularly sensitive to microwaves and cause overcooking, curdling or "popping." These foods include cheese, eggs, cream, sour cream, mayonnaise, snails, scallops, kidney beans and mushrooms. They should be cooked at a lower setting or added part way through cooking period.

One of the most popular features of microwave ovens is the ability to reheat food quickly without overcooking. Food or beverage may be reheated in the serving dish itself (i.e., coffee in a cup, dinner on a plate). Leftovers may be frozen in serving size portions and later placed directly on a dinner plate and reheated. Remember the quantity and density of food will affect cooking time. Reheating should be done on medium setting or about 80% power.

CASSEROLES:

One of the easiest dishes to microwave.

1. Decreasing the amount of liquid by half is the general rule, although the amount will vary depending on other ingredients.

2. Seasonings (herbs and spices) should be reduced by half; there is less liquid to dilute them.

3. Cut all ingredients approximately the same size; casseroles will cook more evenly.

4. Cheese should be sprinkled over the top of dish toward the end of cooking period. Its high fat content attracts microwave energy faster than other foods.

5. Pasta is one of the foods that does not microwave well. It tends to cook unevenly, become hard in spots and takes as long to microwave as to cook conventionally. It is not a good choice for casseroles which are to be microwaved unless it is "pre-cooked" before being add to the casserole.

FISH:

1. When microwaved, it is very easy to overcook.
2. Cook on high power for minimum time; allow to stand about 2 minutes. Test for doneness by flaking with a fork. If it does not flake easily, microwave again briefly.
3. Thicker cuts of fish and fillets in a cream sauce require lower settings for even cooking.
4. To seal in juices, fish should be covered during cooking. Use clear plastic wrap if fish is in a delicate sauce. Waxed paper can be used for covering if fish is crumb-coated.

CHICKEN:

1. Use only a broiler-fryer weighing 2½-3 pounds. Use of a larger chicken or stewing hen will not only take longer to cook, but will also be less tender.
2. Do not turn crumb-coated chicken during cooking time in order to keep top coating crisp.
3. Since microwaved chicken does not brown nor become very crisp, a mixture of butter and a brown sauce (soy sauce, brown bouquet, etc.) should be brushed on before cooking for a browned appearance.
4. In order to minimize differences in density, arrange chicken on platter in a circle with the thickest part of the piece to the outside.

QUICHE:

Quiches are perhaps the easiest to adapt to microwave cooking since the conventional and microwave methods are almost identical. A few suggestions to help convert your favorite quiche recipe are:
1. Reduce the liquid by ¼ to ½ cup.
2. Reduce cooking time to about half.
3. Allow quiche to stand about 10 minutes after cooking.
4. Quiche is done when knife inserted *off-center* comes out clean. *Do not cook until center is set.*
5. Turn dish a half turn mid-way through cooking time.

QUICK 'N EASY LASAGNA

Preparing: 10 minutes　　　　　　　　　*Yield: 6 to 8 servings*
Cooking: 15 minutes

1 pound ground beef
½ cup sliced fresh mushrooms
½ cup chopped onion
¼ cup chopped green pepper
1 clove garlic, minced
1 (15½-ounce) jar spaghetti sauce
½ teaspoon dried whole oregano
¼ teaspoon dried basil leaves

¼ teaspoon salt
⅛ teaspoon pepper
4 ounces lasagna noodles, cooked
　and drained
1 cup cottage cheese
1 (8-ounce) package sliced
　mozzarella cheese

Crumble beef into 2-quart casserole; add mushrooms, onion, green pepper and garlic. Cover with waxed paper; microwave at HIGH for 5-6 minutes or until done, stirring twice. Drain off excess drippings. Add spaghetti sauce and seasonings to meat mixture, stirring well. Cover and microwave at HIGH for 2-3 minutes until thoroughly heated, stirring once. Layer half of noodles, cottage cheese, mozzarella cheese and meat mixture in a 12x8x2-inch baking dish; repeat layers. Cover and microwave at MEDIUM HIGH for 6-8 minutes until thoroughly heated, giving dish a half turn after 5 minutes. Let stand 10 minutes before serving.

LEMON COATED FILLETS

Preparing: 5 minutes　　　　　　　　　*Yield: 4 servings*
Cooking: 5 minutes

¼ cup butter or margarine
2 teaspoons lemon juice
1 (16-ounce) package frozen fish
　fillets, thawed
Salt and pepper to taste

¾ cup seasoned dry bread crumbs
Paprika
Lemon slices (optional)
Fresh parsley sprigs (optional)

Place butter in 1-cup glass measure. Microwave at HIGH for 30 seconds or until butter is melted. Stir in lemon juice. Sprinkle fillets with salt and pepper; brush both sides of each with butter mixture. Dredge fillets in breadcrumbs; sprinkle with paprika. Arrange fillets in a 12x8x2-inch baking dish with thicker portion to outside (thinner portion may overlap if necessary. Cover with waxed paper. Microwave at HIGH for 3-5 minutes or unti lfish flakes easily when tested with fork; give dish one-half turn during cooking. Garnish with lemon slices and parlsey if desired.

FOOD PROCESSOR

A food processor is *energy* and *time* saving. Not only will it chop, slice, and shred almost any food, but it will also stir, whip and purée like a blender. Adapting favorite recipes to take advantage of a food processor is simple since you do not have to make changes in the amount of any ingredient. Look at your recipe and think in terms of what can be done to make the preparation easier and faster. You may also have to change the order of preparation slightly.

Here are a few things to remember about your food processor:

1. Work from the dry ingredients to the wet; otherwise you have to wash the beaker after each ingredient.

2. Always use a dry bowl when chopping, starting with hard small ingredients like garlic or ginger root. Next add larger solid ingredients like onion or green pepper. Always add hardest ingredients first.

3. Cut ingredients to be chopped into 1-inch pieces before adding them to the beaker. Turn the machine on and off rapidly(pulse action) until the food is chopped as finely as desired.

4. When making pastry, cut butter or shortening into 1-inch pieces and freeze; the food processor will "cut" the butter into the flour much more rapidly and finely.

5. Add flour last when preparing quick breads, cakes and cookies. Process by pulse action only until the flour disappears. If using raisins or nuts, add just before the flour to avoid overchopping.

6. Food processors do not aerate; thus they will *not* whip egg whites or cream.

7. The food processor can be helpful in lowering your grocery bill. Some of the prepared and processed foods you buy at the supermarket can be prepared in your food processor at a considerable savings. The following ingredients require minimal preparation time and can be stored in the refrigerator or freezer in plastic bags or freezer containers; breadcrumbs, chopped onions, chopped green pepper, chopped nuts, chopped parsley, hors d'oeuvres spreads, mayonnaise, salad dressings, shredded cheeses and grated Parmesan or Romano. Take advantage of seasonal and sale opportunities. Purchase foods when they are at their lowest prices; process and freeze for later use. Leftover vegetables can be used to make frozen vegetable cubes. Purée vegetables in the processor and freeze in ice-cube trays. The vegetable cubes are excellent for thickening sauces, soups or stews.

8. Fresh baby food can be made easily in a food processor without additives or preservatives. Simmer or steam fresh vegetables in a small amount of water; drain well and purée with the metal blade. Fruits can be prepared in a similar

manner. Poach fresh or dried fruits in a small amount of water and purée. Cooked chicken and meats can be processed with the metal blade, then softened with broth or milk. For convenience, any of the above can be frozen in ice-cube trays and placed in plastic bags labeled and dated.

9. Do not process hot liquids.

10. Processor does not mash potatoes successfully; they become "gluey."

11. The following tasks are not done successfully in a food processor: slicing or shredding soft cheeses and candied or dried fruit; slicing hard cooked eggs or hard nuts; grinding spices with a high oil content, unless combined with other foods; chopping marshmallows.

12. Medium loads chop more evenly than large ones. Therefore if four whole vegetables are required, more even processing with less chance of over processing will take place by chopping two at a time. This requires just a few seconds more time.

13. Smaller pieces generally process more evenly than larger ones.

QUICK AND EASY ROLLS

Preparing: 10 minutes   *Do Ahead*   *Yield: 1 dozen*
Rising: 15 minutes + 15 minutes *Freeze*
Baking: 12 minutes

2 cups unsifted flour	**2 tablespoons butter or margarine**
1½ tablespoons sugar	**½ cup milk**
½ teaspoon salt	**¼ cup water**
1 package dry yeast	

With metal blade in place, add flour, sugar, salt and yeast to bowl of food processor. Process about 5 seconds. Add butter and process until combined, about 15 seconds. In a saucepan, combine milk and water. Heat to 120-130 degrees. Start food processor and gradually add milk mixture until a ball of dough forms on blades (you may not need all the liquid). Allow ball of dough to spin on blades about 50 times. Place dough in a greased bowl, turn to grease top and cover with plastic wrap. Place bowl in pan of warm water at about 98 degrees. Let rise 15 minutes. Turn dough out onto floured board and shape into clovers, by dividing dough into 12 equal pieces. Form each into a ball and place in greased muffin pans. With scissors, cut top of each ball first in half, then in quarters. Place shaped rolls in warm place and cover. Let rise another 15 minutes. Preheat oven to 425° F; bake 12 minutes or until golden brown. Remove immediately from muffin pans and cool on wire racks.

FRESH COCONUT-CARROT CAKE

Preparing: 40 minutes   *Do Ahead*   *Yield: One 9-inch layer cake*
Baking: 35 minutes   *Freeze*

1½ cups whole wheat flour
½ cup unbleached all-purpose
   flour
2 teaspoons baking powder
2 teaspoons baking soda
1 teaspoon salt
2 teaspoons ground cinnamon
2 teaspoons freshly grated nutmeg
3 tablespoons wheat germ

1¼ cups pecan pieces
5-6 medium carrots, peeled
1 medium coconut, shelled
2 cups firmly packed brown sugar
4 eggs
1½ cups vegetable oil
1 teaspoon vanilla extract
Cream Cheese Frosting

Position knife blade in processor bowl. Combine first 7 ingredients in processor bowl; add wheat germ, if desired. Process 10 seconds. Remove flour mixture to a large bowl. Add pecans to processor bowl; pulse 3 to 4 times or until pecans are chopped. Remove; set aside ¼ cup for garnishing.

Position shredding blade in processor bowl. Slice carrots into about 5-inch lengths. Fill food chute with carrot pieces, shred. Reload food chute; shred remaining carrots. Remove from bowl and set aside.

Peel brown husk from coconut; cut meat to fit chute. Shred, using firm pressure with pusher. Set aside ¼ cup coconut for garnishing. Add remaining coconut, 1 cup chopped pecans and carrots to flour mixture; stir well.

Position plastic blade in dry processor bowl; add sugar and eggs. Process 10 seconds or until mixture is smooth. With processor running, pour oil and vanilla through food chute; process 10 seconds or until well combined. Add sugar mixture to flour mixture, mixing well.

Spoon batter into 3 well-greased and floured 9-inch cake-pans. Bake at 350° F. for 35 minutes or until cake tests done. Let cool in pans 10 minutes; remove from pans and cool completely. Spread Cream Cheese Frosting between layers and on top and sides of cake. Garnish with ¼ cup chopped pecans, ¼ cup shredded coconut and carrot curls if desired. Chill.

Cream Cheese Frosting:
1 (8-ounce) package cream
   cheese, softened
½ cup unsalted butter, softened

1 (16-ounce) box powdered sugar,
   sifted
1 teaspoon vanilla extract

Cut cream cheese and butter into about 1 inch pieces. Position plastic blade in processor bowl; add cream cheese and butter. Process 8-10 seconds or until mixture is smooth. Add sugar and vanilla; cover and process 15-20 seconds or until combined well (scrape bowl once, if necessary).

RACK OF LAMB, QUO VADIS

Preparing: 10 minutes   *Yield 2 to 3 servings*
Baking: 40 minutes
Broiling: 5 minutes

1 rack of lamb, about 6 chops	**1 tablespoon butter**
Butter	**1 cup stock (lamb or chicken)**
Pepper	**¼ cup soft bread crumbs**
2 small carrots, minced	**¼ cup minced parsley**
1 medium onion, minced	**Watercress (garnish)**

Preheat oven to 500° F. Trim excess fat from lamb. Wrap ends of rib bones with foil. Rub meat with butter and sprinkle with pepper. Spread minced carrots and onion in bottom of a shallow roasting pan. Dot with butter. Place lamb, fat side down, on vegetables. Roast 20 minutes; reduce heat to 400° F. Turn lamb over and add ½ cup stock. Roast for 15-20 minutes. Sprinkle lamb with mixture of crumbs and parsley and slide under broiler for 4-5 minutes. Transfer to a hot platter. Add remaining ½ cup stock to pan, then purée the vegetable-stock mixture and correct for seasoning. Serve as a sauce with lamb. To serve, carve into chops or parallel to the bone in medium slices. Garnish platter with watercress.

Food Processor Adaptation:
The breadcrumbs and parsley are used together in the recipe and they should be chopped together. With the metal blade in place, combine 1 bread slice, torn into quarters, and 8-10 sprigs of parsley in the beaker of the processor. Process until evenly chopped. Empty the beaker and reserve the crumbs and parsley mixture, covered. With the metal blade in place again, combine the onion, cut into quarters, and the carrots, cut into pieces. Process, turning on and off rapidly a few times, or until coarsely minced. Just before carving the chops, add the stock and vegetables to the beaker of the processor which again has been fitted with the metal blade. Process, turning on and off for about 6 seconds, then let run continuously for another 10 seconds to form a smooth purée. Prepare lamb following above directions.

Index

Index

Main Line Classics

The following recipes are suggested for those who wish to reduce fats and cholesterol, sodium, and calories in their diets.

APPETIZERS AND SOUPS

*It is recommended to remove all skin from poultry prior to cooking.
**Whenever oil is called for, polyunsaturated vegetable oil or olive oil should be used.
***Whenever mayonnaise, salad dressings, and soy sauce are called for, "lite" or diet should be used.

Nutritional Advisors: Barbara Fowler
Sandra Mowry

Equivalent Measures

3 teaspoons = 1 tablespoon
4 tablespoons = ¼ cup
5 tablespoons plus 1 teaspoon = ⅓ cup
16 tablespoons = 1 cup
2 cups = 1 pint

Metric System

The metric system is based on units of 10. The multiples of 10 are always designated by the same prefix regardless of the base unit specified. Some commonly used prefixes include:

> Kilo—1000
> deci—0.1
> centi—0.01
> milli—0.001

To convert to metric the following general rules will help:

1 meter is about 3 inches longer than a yard

1 kilogram (1000 grams) is about 2.2 times as heavy as a pound (1 kilogram of meat would weight about 2.2 pounds.)

1 liter is equal to about 1.1 quarts

100 grams (of cheese for instance) is 3½ ounces

To determine ° Celsius, subtract 32 from ° Fahrenheit and then multiply by .555.

0 degrees Celsius is 32 degrees Fahrenheit

100 degrees Celsius is 212 degrees Fahrenheit

EMERGENCY SUBSTITIONS

Buttermilk, 1 cup . . . . use 1 or 2 tablespoons vinegar with sweet milk to fill cup (let stand 5 minutes)

Chocolate, 1 ounce or square . . . . . use 3 tablespoons cocoa plus 1 tablespoon butter

Cornstarch, 1 tablespoon . . . . use 2 tablespoons flour

Baking powder, 1¼ teaspoons . . . . . use ½ teaspoon baking soda plus 2 tablespoons vinegar (for 1 cup flour)

Milk, 1 cup . . . . ½ cup evaporated milk plus ½ cup water

"Low-Cal" Sour Cream . . . . 1 cup cottage cheese plus 1 tablespoon lemon juice blended until smooth

Sugar, 1¼ cups . . . . 1 cup honey; reduce liquid in recipe by one-fourth

Honey, 1 cup . . . . ¾ cup sugar plus ¼ cup liquid

Cake flour, 1 cup sifted . . . . 1 cup sifted all-purpose flour less 2 tablespoons

Philadelphia MAIN LINE CLASSICS
P.O. Box 521
Wayne, Pennsylvania, 19087

Please send _____ copies at . . . .$18.95 each _____
Plus postage and handling . . . .$ 3.50 each _____
Tax for Pennsylvania residents . . . .$ 1.14 each _____
Enclosed is a check or money order . . . . . .   Total _____
(Please make checks payable to Philadelphia MAIN LINE CLASSICS.)

NAME _____

ADDRESS_____

CITY _____ STATE _____ ZIP_____

Proceeds from the sale of this book benefit the philanthropies supported
by the SATURDAY CLUB.

Philadelphia MAIN LINE CLASSICS
P.O. Box 521
Wayne, Pennsylvania, 19087

Please send _____ copies at . . . .$18.95 each _____
Plus postage and handling . . . .$ 3.50 each _____
Tax for Pennsylvania residents . . . .$ 1.14 each _____
Enclosed is a check or money order . . . . . .   Total _____
(Please make checks payable to Philadelphia MAIN LINE CLASSICS.)

NAME _____

ADDRESS_____

CITY _____ STATE _____ ZIP_____

Proceeds from the sale of this book benefit the philanthropies supported
by the SATURDAY CLUB.

MAIN LINE CLASSICS II: *Cooking Up A Little History*
P.O. Box 521
Wayne, Pennsylvania, 19087

Please send _____ copies at . . . .$18.95 each _____
Plus postage and handling . . . .$ 3.50 each _____
Tax for Pennsylvania residents . . . .$ 1.14 each _____
Enclosed is a check or money order . . . . .   Total _____
(Please make checks payable to MAIN LINE CLASSICS II.)

NAME_____

ADDRESS _____

CITY _____ STATE _____ ZIP _____

Proceeds from the sale of this book benefit the philanthropies supported by
the SATURDAY CLUB.